Product Liability Casebook

Leading US and UK judgments

Commentaries by
Derrick Owles LL.M., Ph.D.

and

Anthea Worsdall, Solicitor

Compiled by
J. Stuart Ashworth LL.B.
Editor, *Product Liability International*

Colchester
Lloyd's of London Press Ltd
1984

Printed by Vineyard Press Ltd, Colchester, England

C

PREFACE

The decision to compile this book came about in several ways. Talks with insurers at conferences or phone calls from lawyers and businessmen asking about the background to a particular product liability case prompted me to investigate the concept of a book. Many admitted their knowledge was sketchy; even the familiar cases were known only by name and basic subject matter.

It soon became clear there was a need to bring together into one convenient volume all these significant cases, which are really the stepping stones to strict product liability. Now the user of 'Product Liability Casebook' will no longer have to check through various journals and law reports to find his material.

This collection of 29 cases is based on discussions with people who understand the subject and who gave me valuable advice, but in the end the final choice was mine, and I must stand by it.

You will soon realise that this book is more than a mere selection of important decisions. The expert commentary helps the reader to place each case in its context, and shows how the law is developing. I was fortunate to be able to call on two experienced commentators. Derrick Owles has written a column and provided US case notes for every issue of *Product Liability International*, since its first appearance in January 1979. He is also author of 'The Development of Product Liability in the USA'. Although he is British, his direct experience of the business and academic world in the States makes him uniquely qualified to interpret the US legal system to readers from other countries.

For the UK cases, the choice of Anthea Worsdall was equally appropriate. She can look at a case from both the manufacturer's and consumer's viewpoint. Her business career, particularly as legal adviser to a leading trade association, and her previous writing (she is author of 'Consumer Law for the Motor Trade') have helped to foster this ability.

I am also grateful for the assistance of Lesley Parkinson, formerly assistant editor of *Product Liability International* during the preparation of this work.

Readers will appreciate that, in a book of this length, I had to omit certain passages from some of the cases. I have made deletions where repetition of facts and references, or discussion of issues outside the product liability concept, might deter the reader from tackling the complete text of a particular case. Here again, the responsibility for selection or omission rests with me.

A few words of explanation on style and presentation are called for. In the US judgments, American spelling has been retained—perhaps this enhances the transatlantic flavour. I have not over-standardised from such a variety of language, references, publications and documents, but any minor inconsistencies should not detract from your understanding. An asterisk (*) in the judgment denotes the first mention in each case of one which is fully covered elsewhere in the book.

Perhaps those of you whose appetite is whetted after reading this compilation may be encouraged to look at our monthly journal, *Product Liability International*, which presents a compelling subject from many different angles. Its aim is to combine news items, feature articles and comment to give businessmen, lawyers and insurers a better understanding of what has become a complex issue.

Stuart Ashworth

Colchester
October 1984

CONTENTS

Page

Preface

The development of product liability law in the USA

THE DEVELOPMENT OF PRODUCT LIABILITY LAW IN THE USA

Anybody who reads through all the cases reported in this book will notice how often judges justify their decisions on the grounds of public policy. It is the judicial concept of what society needs that is the source and origin of product liability law in the USA, and since each judge can have his own idea about the needs of society, we must not be surprised when we find a complicated and uncertain system of law. Even so, reliance on public policy is not necessarily a bad thing, although references to it as an unruly horse that may run away with its rider are common enough. In America it has been used creatively, to develop a set of legal principles that in other systems would have had to wait for the attention of a legislature. Usually public policy is used negatively: 'it would be contrary to public policy to allow a remedy in this instance' is what the judges tend to say. American judges have been more inclined to think along the same lines as Lord Denning. 'With a good man in the saddle', he wrote,[1] 'the unruly horse can be kept in control. It can jump over obstacles'. Such obstacles as privity of contract, for example, have been overcome by the courts in their progress towards strict liability.

Public policy is not the only reason why product liability law is complicated and uncertain. Another reason is the independence of each state. It is rare to find a legal principle defined in terms acceptable in all the courts of all the states. This means that no product liability action can safely be started or defended without advice from a local lawyer. When the laws of more than one state are concerned, as often happens, more than one local lawyer is necessary.

A further reason for complication is the number of different theories under which compensation can be claimed. We speak of 'product liability law', and in the USA that is almost, but not quite, the same as 'strict liability', although traditional breach of warranty rules or negligence law may also be the basis for a claim. Many of the decisions reported under the general heading of product liability were in fact based on breach of warranty or on negligence, although the courts do not always state specifically the basis for a decision. The interaction of strict liability with negligence or breach of warranty has caused some of the difficulties in the development of the law, as, for example, in the attempts made to reconcile the defence of contributory negligence with the frequent statements that strict liability does not depend on any negligence by the defendant. When liability depends solely on a defect in a product, and there is no enquiry into the behaviour of the defendant that may have caused that defect, it is not logical to excuse the defect because the plaintiff was himself negligent. The concepts of 'misuse' and 'assumption of risk' have therefore been called in to overcome this logical difficulty when the plaintiff has in some way brought about his own harm.

[1] *The Discipline of Law*, 1979.

The first step towards strict liability was taken, at least for the purposes of our selection of cases, in *MacPherson v Buick*. That decision established the principle that a manufacturer has a duty to take care towards a person who is not the customer who bought the product from him. Then, in *Escola*, it was decided that *res ipsa loquitur* could be applied to prove a breach of duty. So far, the courts were thinking in terms of negligence, but in *Greenman*, Justice Traynor held that the defect in a product was itself sufficient grounds for compensation, and that negligence did not have to be proved.

In *Greenman*, the defect was the cause of the accident. In the next case, *Larsen v GM*, the defect was the cause of some of the injuries suffered, but not the cause of the accident itself, and the decision started the long line of 'second collision' cases. They were known as 'second collision' because in the early cases the injured person was damaged by being thrown against some part of an automobile after an accident brought about by some other cause. The principle applies as much to other products as to cars.

The decision in *Greenman* coincided with the preparation of the second edition of the Restatement of the Law of Torts, and the editors sowed the seed for much future controversy when they put the words 'unreasonably dangerous' into the definition of an actionable defect. It seems that the wording of section 402A was passed at the end of a long discussion when the editors were tired and ready to go home, but what they had in mind was the need to insist on a defect in the product. Some products are not at all defective, but can do harm if wrongly used (such as whisky) and manufacturers should not be held liable in such circumstances. Occasional and unsuccessful efforts have been made to impose liability on manufacturers of products capable of causing great harm even when not defective (cigarettes or firearms, for example). The argument has been that such products are not seen as benefitting society as a whole. The main controversy, however, is whether liability depends on the existence of a defect pure and simple, or of an unreasonably dangerous defect. In *Cronin v Olson*, the California court decided that it was not necessary to prove that the product was unreasonably dangerous, but the decision applies only to California, and not all of the other states have followed suit. It is interesting, but probably not significant, that three of the judges who decided *Cronin* were also among the members of the *Greenman* court.

A later case, *Owens v Allis-Chalmers*, was concerned with the nature of the defect, in this instance a design defect, and discussed the standards by which a design should be assessed. Then, in *Barker v Lull*, the California court came back to 'unreasonably dangerous', and following its own decision in *Cronin* decided that there was no need to prove that a design defect was unreasonably dangerous. There was much discussion in the opinions about jury instructions, and it will be seen that in many cases appeals have been based on

The development of product liability law in the USA

allegations that the wrong instructions were given to the jury.

The connection between negligence and strict liability was emphasised by *Smith v ER Squibb* in which the defect was failure to warn. A product is defective when it lacks a necessary warning, and a plaintiff could sue either in negligence or in strict liability. The claim in negligence, however, would require proof that the defendant had not behaved reasonably, whereas in strict liability what matters is whether or not there ought to be a warning. The difference is subtle, and it would be more straightforward if failure to warn cases were to be decided according to negligence and not under strict liability. That was one of the conclusions of the Interagency Task Force on Product Liability that led to the drafting of a federal model Act. Such an Act does not seem to be in the immediate future, but there is a Bill before Congress, and there is a strong movement towards a federal approach. The elimination of differences between the various state laws would be a move towards much-needed simplification.

The decision after *Smith v ER Squibb* illustrates how various issues have come up as the courts apply the basic principle of strict liability. One such issue is that of jurisdiction, and in *Piper v Reyno* the court was concerned with its power to refuse a case even when it had jurisdiction. So long as verdicts in the US courts continue to be higher than in the courts of other countries, plaintiffs will seek to bring their defendants before an American court, and the doctrine of *forum non conveniens* will continue to be important. On occasions American judges have tended to accept cases on the grounds that American courts were more likely to provide justice for injured plaintiffs than the courts of other systems. In general, there seems to be a tendency now for courts to look at their own overburdened calendars, and send cases to more convenient tribunals.

Another modern issue in product liability has been the long-term effects of defective drugs and chemicals, and *Sindell v Abbott* is an example of a court seeking an answer to the problem of the plaintiff who cannot identify the manufacturer. The conflict here is between the basic rule that a defendant cannot be held liable unless the plaintiff can show he was responsible for making or marketing the defective product, and the fact that an application of this rule will send some plaintiffs away without a remedy. The law has never said that every injured person must be awarded compensation, but on the grounds of public policy the courts are reluctant to deny compensation to a plaintiff injured by a clearly dangerous product that has been marketed in large quantities at some time in the past. Asbestos is another example of a product that causes injury after a long period of use, and although in asbestos cases the identity of the manufacturer is usually easier to prove, the problem of limitation periods arises.

All the states have statutes that fix various periods of limitation, and here again there is a basic principle, that

defendants should not be harassed by stale claims. There is therefore a conflict between this principle and the importance of finding a remedy for a person who could not know for a long time that he had been injured. The problem is one of deciding when to start the limitation period running, and courts have adopted various answers. Usually, it is discovery of the injury and its cause that triggers the limitation period, but occasionally a court holds that it is the date of the injury itself that is the beginning. That means that a plaintiff can lose a right to compensation before he even knows of his injury, and it is not an answer that appeals to the majority of courts. The practical result of the different approaches is that the success of a claim may depend on the choice of the state in which to sue.

Other issues that arise are illustrated by the remaining cases in the selection. They include the problem of punitive damages (*Wangen v Ford*); the state of the art controversy (*Beshada v Johns-Manville*; government immunity and its extension to contractors (*McKay v Rockwell*). The latest case included (*Green v Firestone*) illustrates the effect on product liability of takeovers and mergers. A successor corporation can be liable for defects in a product made by its predecessor.

The overall picture is of a development that starts with the statement of a basic principle, and then deals firstly with the elaboration and further definition of the principle, and subsequently with the issues that arise when the principle is applied in a variety of circumstances.

Product liability legislation

1 *Federal*
Product Liability Risk Retention Act 1981 which facilitates the formation of self-insurance groups (overrides state regulatory rules).

2 *State*
Two states have passed Product Liability Risk Retention Acts. One, Texas, has passed an Act to 'regulate the formation and operation of risk retention groups' in the state under the provisions of the federal Act. The other, Vermont, has defined a retention group for the purposes of the federal legislation.

Other states have passed statutes specifically addressing the problems of product liability. They tend to be pro-manufacturer rather than pro-consumer, usually enacting 'statutes of repose', banning a claim after a period of years has elapsed since the product was first sold to a user. In some cases, however, plaintiffs have been helped by a provision that periods of limitation should begin from the date of discovery of an injury and not from the date of the injury itself.

All states except Louisiana have adopted the Uniform Commercial Code, which controls claims based on breach of warranty and establishes limitation periods for contracts of sale. State product liability Acts have to be

The development of product liability law in the USA

considered in relation to any relevant provisions of the Uniform Commercial Code and other legislation. For example, many states have statutes, not restricted to product liability, dealing with contributory and comparative negligence, and there are other statutes establishing limitation periods, usually different for tort and contract actions.

State product liability statutes do not provide a code and many principles developed by the courts are left unaffected. The topics dealt with by legislation do, however, indicate either where court decisions have been thought unsatisfactory or where the courts have not found a solution to a particular problem. Legislation usually results from pressure by influential groups and, by the nature of things, it is manufacturers who are most likely to bring pressure to bear on state legislatures. Thus, many states have statutes of repose, to safeguard a manufacturer from a claim many years after a product was made and sold. The effect of a statute of repose is that an occasional victim will be deprived of a remedy according to a more or less arbitrarily chosen period of time, and courts have tended to find such statutes to be unconstitutional. The reasoning is that a person must not be denied access to the courts.

Another provision in some statutes is a clear statement that a manufacturer is not liable when he complied with the state of the art or with government standards. There is a general reluctance to allow compliance with industry standards as a defence, on the grounds that an entire industry can well be out of date. Other statutes merely provide that state of the art evidence is admissible.

The law has long been familiar with statutes of limitation, but one difficulty has been the choice of a starting date when the injury is latent. This is a difficulty that has not yet been completely solved in English law, and all that state legislation has done is to specify that limitation periods will start to run from the date of discovery in asbestosis cases. Not all states have such a provision, and only one state, Ohio, has gone beyond asbestosis to include Agent Orange.

Some states have been concerned over the liability of sellers as opposed to manufacturers, and have restricted by legislation the liability of sellers. Usually there is a proviso that the seller will be liable if for some reason the manufacturer cannot be reached or is insolvent.

Some lawyers believe that the amount of an award is influenced by the amount demanded by the plaintiff in the statement of claim. A few states therefore provide that an amount shall not be specified in the complaint, the demand being for reasonable damages.

Individual states have included uncommon provisions. Thus, Michigan provides for the award of costs against a party raising a frivolous claim or defence, and Maine requires an attorney to give notice of an intention to make a claim (which was a provision that appeared in the draft federal product liability law).

SECTION I   US landmark cases

1916 *MacPherson v Buick*

COMMENTARY

Since we can never point with any certainty to the absolute beginning of any development, our choice of this case as the first in our selection may be open to challenge. In fact, Judge Cardozo referred to the earlier decision in *Devlin v Smith,* and indicated that he was doing no more than following the principle laid down then. However, *MacPherson* is quoted much more often than *Devlin,* and it does mark a significant stage in the development of the modern law of tort. The expression 'strict liability' may not have been used, but Judge Cardozo went very near when he said 'If the nature of a thing is such that it is reasonably certain to place life and limb in peril when negligently made, it is then a thing of danger'.

The issue in the case was narrow. It was concerned with duty, and the question that the court set out to answer was whether the manufacturer's duty to take care extended to others than the actual purchaser. The answer was that the duty did extend to others, to those whose danger could be reasonably foreseeable. The doctrine of privity of contract was thus given its quietus. It will be apparent that any liability was based on negligence, and at this stage of development American law had not taken the divergent path that was to lead it away from English law into the intricacies of strict liability.

MacPherson did discourage another line of development, that of fraud or intentional misrepresentation. Fraud is never easy to prove, but on occasions, under the more acceptable title of 'intentional misrepresentation', plaintiffs have been able to recover on the allegation that the manufacturer had wrongly described the qualities of the product. There was an example in 1932 when the Supreme Court of Washington (the state, not the city) held that the Ford Motor Company had falsely claimed the windscreens on its cars to be 'shatter-proof'. The plaintiff recovered damages for a lost eye, but the basis for the award was breach of implied warranty, not fraud (*Baxter v Ford,* 12 P2d 409), although even today allegations of fraud are included in complaints almost as a matter of routine. The decision in *MacPherson* made this line of attack unnecessary.

References to the development of American law should not conceal the fact that there is really no such thing as 'American' law. *MacPherson* was a decision under the law of New York State, and although it has led to similar decisions in other states, common principles do not mean that state laws are identical. Each state has its own precedents, and it is quite possible for a case to be won in state A that would have been lost in state B. With these reservations in mind, we can say that the principles set out by Judge Cardozo have been generally accepted. These principles are:
1 the liability of manufacturers is not limited to dangerous articles;

2 the manufacturer is liable only if he knows or should know that persons other than the buyer would use the product or would be in danger;
3 as a matter of law, there is a duty on a manufacturer to inspect component parts even when purchased outside.
4 the danger to be foreseen must be probable and not merely possible.

Once it had been established that a manufacturer owed a duty to persons other than the purchaser, and that this duty was founded on negligence, it was open to plaintiffs to make use of the doctrine of *res ipsa loquitur.* The mere existence of a defect led to the conclusion that the manufacturer had been negligent, and the acceptance of such an argument opened the way to strict liability. It is, of course, the manufacturer who is deemed to have been negligent, not the retailer or distributor, and there has not yet been the suggestion that liability should be imposed on anyone who puts a product into the 'stream of commerce'. The basic question answered in *MacPherson v Buick* is: 'to whom does the manufacturer owe a duty?'

JUDGMENT

Court of Appeals of New York
March 14, 1916

MacPherson
versus
Buick Motor Company

Before Chief Judge Willard Bartlett and Judges Cardozo, Hiscock, Chase, Cuddeback, Hogan and Pound

Cardozo, *Judge.* The defendant is a manufacturer of automobiles. It sold an automobile to a retail dealer. The retail dealer resold to the plaintiff. While the plaintiff was in the car it suddenly collapsed. He was thrown out and injured. One of the wheels was made of defective wood, and its spokes crumbled into fragments. The wheel was not made by the defendant; it was bought from another manufacturer. There is evidence, however, that its defects could have been discovered by reasonable inspection, and that inspection was omitted. There is no claim that the defendant knew of the defect and willfully concealed it. The case, in other words, is not brought within the rule of *Kuelling v Lean Mfg Co.* The charge is one, not of fraud, but of negligence. The question to be determined is whether the defendant owed a duty of care and vigilance to any one but the immediate purchaser.

The foundations of this branch of the law, at least in this state, were laid in *Thomas v Winchester,* 6 NY 397. A poison was falsely labeled. The sale was made to a druggist, who in turn sold to a customer. The customer recovered damages from the seller who affixed the label.

MacPherson v Buick

'The defendant's negligence,' it was said, 'put human life in imminent danger.' A poison falsely labeled is likely to injure any one who gets it. Because the danger is to be foreseen, there is a duty to avoid the injury. Cases were cited by way of illustration in which manufacturers were not subject to any duty irrespective of contract. The distinction was said to be that their conduct, though negligent, was not likely to result in injury to any one except the purchaser. We are not required to say whether the chance of injury was always as remote as the distinction assumes. Some of the illustrations might be rejected to-day. The principle of the distinction is, for present purposes, the important thing. *Thomas v Winchester* became quickly a landmark of the law. In the application of its principle there may, at times, have been uncertainty or even error. There has never in this state been doubt or disavowal of the principle itself. The chief cases are well known, yet to recall some of them will be helpful. *Loop v Litchfield* is the earliest. It was the case of a defect in a small balance wheel used on a circular saw. The manufacturer pointed out the defect to the buyer, who wished a cheap article and was ready to assume the risk. The risk can hardly have been an imminent one, for the wheel lasted five years before it broke. In the meanwhile the buyer had made a lease of the machinery. It was held that the manufacturer was not answerable to the lessee. *Loop v Litchfield* was followed in *Losee v Clute,* the case of the explosion of a steam boiler. That decision has been criticized (*Thompson on Negligence,* 223; *Shearman & Redfield on Negligence* section 117); but it must be confined to its special facts. It was put upon the ground that the risk of injury was too remote. The buyer in that case had not only accepted the boiler, but had tested it. The manufacturer knew that his own test was not the final one. The finality of the test has a bearing on the measure of diligence owing to persons other than the purchaser. Bevan, *Negligence* (3d Ed.) pp50, 51, 54; Wharton, *Negligence* (2d Ed.) section 134.

These early cases suggest a narrow construction of the rule. Later cases, however, evince a more liberal spirit. First in importance is *Devlin v Smith,* 89 NY 470. The defendant, a contractor, built a scaffold for a painter. The painter's servants were injured. The contractor was held liable. He knew that the scaffold, if improperly constructed, was a most dangerous trap. He knew that it was to be used by the workmen. He was building it for that very purpose. Building it for their use, he owed them a duty, irrespective of his contract with their master, to build it with care.

From *Devlin v Smith* we pass over intermediate cases and turn to the latest case in this court in which *Thomas v Winchester* was followed. That case is *Statler v Ray Mfg Co,* 88 NE 1063. The defendant manufactured a large coffee urn. It was installed in a restaurant. When heated, the urn exploded and injured the plaintiff. We held that the manufacturer was liable. We said that the urn 'was of such a character inherently that, when applied to the purposes for which it was designed, it was liable to become a source of great danger to many people if not carefully and properly constructed.'

It may be that *Devlin v Smith* and *Statler v Ray Mfg Co* have extended the rule of *Thomas v Winchester.* If so, this court is committed to the extension. The defendant argues that things imminently dangerous to life are poisons, explosives, deadly weapons—things whose normal function it is to injure or destroy. But whatever the rule in *Thomas v Winchester* may once have been, it has no longer that restricted meaning. A scaffold (*Devlin v Smith supra*) is not inherently a destructive instrument. It becomes destructive only if imperfectly constructed. A large coffee urn (*Statler v Ray Mfg Co supra*) may have within itself, if negligently made, the potency of danger, yet no one thinks of it as an implement whose normal function is destruction. What is true of the coffee urn is equally true of bottles of aerated water. *Torgesen v Schultz,* 84 NE 956. We have mentioned only cases in this court. But the rule has received a like extension in our courts of intermediate appeal. In *Burke v Ireland,* in an opinion by Cullen J it was applied to a builder who constructed a defective building; in *Kahner v Otis Elevator Co,* to the manufacturer of an elevator; in *Davies v Pelham Hod Elevating Co,* affirmed in this court without opinion, to a contractor who furnished a defective rope with knowledge of the purpose for which the rope was to be used. We are not required at this time either to approve or to disapprove the application of the rule that was made in these cases. It is enough that they help to characterize the trend of judicial thought.

Devlin v Smith was decided in 1802. A year later a very similar case came before the Court of Appeal in England (*Heaven v Pender,* 11 QBD 503). We find in the opinion of Brett MR, afterwards Lord Esher, the same conception of a duty, irrespective of contract, imposed upon the manufacturer by the law itself:

'Whenever one person supplies goods or machinery, or the like, for the purpose of their being used by another person under such circumstances that every one of ordinary sense would, if he thought, recognize at once that unless he used ordinary care and skill with regard to the condition of the thing supplied, or the mode of supplying it, there will be danger of injury to the person or property of him for whose use the thing is supplied, and who is to use it, a duty arises to use ordinary care and skill as to the condition or manner of supplying such thing.'

He then points out that for a neglect of such ordinary care or skill whereby injury happens, the appropriate remedy is an action for negligence. The right to enforce this liability is not to be confined to the immediate buyer. The right, he says, extends to the persons or class of persons for whose use the thing is supplied. It is enough that the goods 'would in all probability be used at once ..

before a reasonable opportunity for discovering any defect which might exist,' and that the thing supplied is of such a nature 'that a neglect of ordinary care or skill as to its condition or the manner of supplying it would probably cause danger to the person or property of the

US landmark cases

person for whose use it was supplied, and who was about to use it.' On the other hand, he would exclude a case 'in which the goods are supplied under circumstances in which it would be a chance by whom they would be used or whether they would be used or not, or whether they would be used before there would probably be means of observing any defect,' or where the goods are of such a nature that 'a want of care or skill as to their condition or the manner of supplying them would not probably produce danger of injury to person or property.' What was said by Lord Esher in that case did not command the full assent of his associates. His opinion has been criticized 'as requiring every man to take affirmative precautions to protect his neighbors as well as to refrain from injuring them.' (Bohlen, 'Affirmative Obligations in the Law of Torts', 44 Am Law Reg (NS) 341.) It may not be an accurate exposition of the law of England. Perhaps it may need some qualification even in our own state. Like most attempts at comprehensive definition, it may involve errors of inclusion and of exclusion. But its tests and standards, at least in their underlying principles, with whatever qualification may be called for as they are applied to varying conditions, are the tests and standards of our law.

We hold, then, that the principle of *Thomas v Winchester* is not limited to poisons, explosives, and things of like nature, to things which in their normal operation are implements of destruction. If the nature of a thing is such that it is reasonably certain to place life and limb in peril when negligently made, it is then a thing of danger. Its nature gives warning of the consequences to be expected. If to the element of danger there is added knowledge that the thing will be used by persons other than the purchaser, and used without new tests, then, irrespective of contract, the manufacturer of this thing of danger is under a duty to make it carefully. That is as far as we are required to go for the decision of this case. There must be knowledge of a danger, not merely possible, but probable. It is possible to use almost anything in a way that will make it dangerous if defective. That is not enough to charge the manufacturer with a duty independent of his contract. Whether a given thing is dangerous may be sometimes a question for the court and sometimes a question for the jury. There must also be knowledge that in the usual course of events the danger will be shared by others than the buyer. Such knowledge may often be inferred from the nature of the transaction. But it is possible that even knowledge of the danger and of the use will not always be enough. The proximity or remoteness of the relation is a factor to be considered. We are dealing now with the liability of the manufacturer of the finished product, who puts it on the market to be used without inspection by his customers. If he is negligent, where danger is to be foreseen, a liability will follow.

We are not required, at this time, to say that it is legitimate to go back of the manufacturer of the finished product and hold the manufacturers of the component parts. To make their negligence a cause of imminent danger, an independent cause must often intervene; the manufacturer of the finished product must also fail in his duty of inspection. It may be that in those circumstances the negligence of the earlier members of the series is too remote to constitute, as to the ultimate user, an actionable wrong. We leave that question open. We shall have to deal with it when it arises. The difficulty which it suggests is not present in this case. There is here no break in the chain of cause and effect. In such circumstances, the presence of a known danger, attendant upon a known use, makes vigilance a duty. We have put aside the notion that the duty to safeguard life and limb, when the consequences of negligence may be foreseen, grows out of contract and nothing else. We have put the source of the obligation where it ought to be. We have put its source in the law.

From this survey of the decisions, there thus emerges a definition of the duty of a manufacturer which enables us to measure this defendant's liability. Beyond all question, the nature of an automobile gives warning of probable danger if its construction is defective. This automobile was designed to go 50 miles an hour. Unless its wheels were sound and strong, injury was almost certain. It was as much a thing of danger as a defective engine for a railroad. The defendant knew the danger. It knew also that the car would be used by persons other than the buyer. This was apparent from its size; there were seats for three persons. It was apparent also from the fact that the buyer was a dealer in cars, who bought to resell. The maker of this car supplied it for the use of purchasers from the dealer just as plainly as the contractor in *Devlin v Smith* supplied the scaffold for use by the servants of the owner. The dealer was indeed the one person of whom it might be said with some approach to certainty that by him the car would not be used. Yet the defendant would have us say that he was the one person whom it was under a legal duty to protect. The law does not lead us to so inconsequent a conclusion. Precedents drawn from the days of travel by stagecoach do not fit the conditions of travel to-day. The principle that the danger must be imminent does not change, but the things subject to the principle do change. They are whatever the needs of life in a developing civilization require them to be.

In reaching this conclusion, we do not ignore the decisions to the contrary in other jurisdictions. It was held in *Cadillac Co v Johnson*, 221 Fed 801, that an automobile is not within the rule of *Thomas v Winchester*. There was, however, a vigorous dissent. Opposed to that decision is one of the Court of Appeals of Kentucky. *Olds Motor Works v Shaffer*. The earlier cases are summarized by Judge Sanborn in *Huset v JI Case Threshing Machine Co*, 120 Fed 865. Some of them, at first sight inconsistent with our conclusion, may be reconciled upon the ground that the negligence was too remote, and that another cause had intervened. But even when they cannot be reconciled, the difference is rather in the application of the principle than in the principle itself. Judge Sanborn says, for example, that

MacPherson v Buick

the contractor who builds a bridge, or the manufacturer who builds a car, cannot ordinarily foresee injury to other persons than the owner as the probable result. We take a different view. We think that injury to others is to be foreseen not merely as a possible, but as an almost inevitable, result. See the trenchant criticism in Bohlen, *supra*. Indeed Judge Sanborn concedes that his view is not to be reconciled with our decision in *Devlin v Smith, supra*. The doctrine of that decision has now become the settled law of this state, and we have no desire to depart from it.

In England the limits of the rule are still unsettled. *Winterbottom v Wright* is often cited. The defendant undertook to provide a mail coach to carry the mail bags. The coach broke down from latent defects in its construction. The defendant, however, was not the manufacturer. The court held that he was not liable for injuries to a passenger. The case was decided on a demurrer to the declaration. Lord Esher points out in *Heaven v Pender, supra*, that the form of the declaration was subject to criticism. It did not fairly suggest the existence of a duty aside from the special contract which was the plaintiff's main reliance. See the criticism of *Winterbottom v Wright*, in Bohlen, *supra*, at pages 281, 283. At all events, in *Heaven v Pender, supra*, the defendant, a dock owner, who put up a staging outside a ship, was held liable to the servants of the shipowner. In *Elliot v Hall*, 15 QBD 315, the defendant sent out a defective truck laden with goods which he had sold. The buyer's servants unloaded it, and were injured because of the defects. It was held that the defendant was under a duty 'not to be guilty of negligence with regard to the state and condition of the truck.' There seems to have been a return to the doctrine of *Winterbottom v Wright* in *Earl v Lubbock*, (1905) 1 KB 253. In that case, however, as in the earlier one, the defendant was not the manufacturer. He had merely made a contract to keep the van in repair. A later case (*White v Steadman*, (1913) 3 KB 340, 348) emphasizes that element. A livery stable keeper who sent out a vicious horse was held liable, not merely to his customers, but also to another occupant of the carriage, and *Thomas v Winchester* was cited and followed, *White v Steadman, supra*, at pages 348, 349. It was again cited and followed in *Dominion Natural Gas Co v Collins*, (1909) AC 640, 646. From these cases a consistent principle is with difficulty extracted. The English courts, however, agree with ours in holding that one who invites another to make use of an appliance is bound to the exercise of reasonable care. *Caledonian Ry Co v Mulholland*, (1898) AC 216, 227; *Inderman v Dames*, LR (1 CP) 274. That at bottom is the underlying principle of *Devlin v Smith*. The contractor who builds the scaffold invites the owner's workmen to use it. The manufacturer who sells the automobile to the retail dealer invites the dealer's customers to use it. The invitation is addressed in the one case to determinate persons and in the other to an indeterminate class, but in each case it is equally plain, and in each its consequences must be the same.

There is nothing anomalous in a rule which imposes upon A, who has contracted with B, a duty to C and D and others according as he knows or does not know that the subject-matter of the contract is intended for their use. We may find an analogy in the law which measures the liability of landlords. If A leases to B a tumble-down house, he is not liable, in the absence of fraud, to B's guests who enter it and are injured. This is because B is then under the duty to repair it, the lessor has the right to suppose that he will fulfill that duty, and, if he omits to do so, his guests must look to him. Bohlen, *supra*, at page 276. But if A leases a building to be used by the lessee at once as a place of public entertainment, the rule is different. There injury to persons other than the lessee is to be foreseen, and foresight of the consequences involves the creation of a duty. *Junkermann v Tilyou R Co* and cases there cited.

In this view of the defendant's liability there is nothing inconsistent with the theory of liability on which the case was tried. It is true that the court told the jury that 'an automobile is not an inherently dangerous vehicle.' The meaning, however, is made plain by the context. The meaning is that danger is not to be expected when the vehicle is well constructed. The court left it to the jury to say whether the defendant ought to have foreseen that the car, if negligently constructed, would become 'imminently dangerous.' Subtle distinctions are drawn by the defendant between things inherently dangerous and things imminently dangerous, but the case does not turn upon these verbal niceties. If danger was to be expected as reasonably certain, there was a duty of vigilance, and this whether you call the danger inherent or imminent. In varying forms that thought was put before the jury. We do not say that the court would not have been justified in ruling as a matter of law that the car was a dangerous thing. If there was any error, it was none of which the defendant can complain.

We think the defendant was not absolved from a duty of inspection because it bought the wheels from a reputable manufacturer. It was not merely a dealer in automobiles. It was a manufacturer of automobiles. It was responsible for the finished product. It was not at liberty to put the finished product on the market without subjecting the component parts to ordinary and simple tests. Under the charge of the trial judge nothing more was required of it. The obligation to inspect must vary with the nature of the thing to be inspected. The more probable the danger the greater the need of caution.

There is little analogy between this case and *Carlson v Phoenix Bridge Co*, where the defendant bought a tool for a servant's use. The making of tools was not the business in which the master was engaged. Reliance on the skill of the manufacturer was proper and almost inevitable. But that is not the defendant's situation. Both by its relation to the work and by the nature of its business, it is charged with a stricter duty.

Other rulings complained of have been considered, but no error has been found in them.

US landmark cases

The judgment should be affirmed, with costs.

Willard Bartlett, *Chief Judge* (dissenting). The plaintiff was injured in consequence of the collapse of a wheel of an automobile manufactured by the defendant corporation which sold it to a firm of automobile dealers in Schenectady, who in turn sold the car to the plaintiff. The wheel was purchased by the Buick Motor Company, ready made, from the Imperial Wheel Company of Flint, Mich, a reputable manufacturer of automobile wheels which had furnished the defendant with 80,000 wheels, none of which had proved to be made of defective wood prior to the accident in the present case. The defendant relied upon the wheel manufacturer to make all necessary tests as to the strength of the material therein, and made no such test itself. The present suit is an action for negligence, brought by the subvendee of the motor car against the manufacturer as the original vendor. The evidence warranted a finding by the jury that the wheel which collapsed was defective when it left the hands of the defendant. The automobile was being prudently operated at the time of the accident, and was moving at a speed of only eight miles an hour. There was no allegation or proof of any actual knowledge of the defect on the part of the defendant, or any suggestion that any element of fraud or deceit or misrepresentation entered into the sale.

The theory upon which the case was submitted to the jury by the learned judge who presided at the trial was that, although an automobile is not an inherently dangerous vehicle, it may become such if equipped with a weak wheel; and that if the motor car in question, when it was put upon the market was in itself inherently dangerous by reason of its being equipped with a weak wheel, the defendant was chargeable with a knowledge of the defect so far as it might be discovered by a reasonable inspection and the application of reasonable tests. This liability, it was further held, was not limited to the original vendee, but extended to a subvendee like the plaintiff, who was not a party to the original contract of sale.

I think that these rulings, which have been approved by the Appellate Division, extend the liability of the vendor of a manufactured article further than any case which has yet received the sanction of this court. It has heretofore been held in this state that the liability of the vendor of a manufactured article for negligence arising out of the existence of defects therein does not extend to strangers injured in consequence of such defects, but is confined to the immediate vendee. The exceptions to this general rule which have thus far been recognized in New York are cases in which the article sold was of such a character that danger to life or limb was involved in the ordinary use thereof; in other words, where the article sold was inherently dangerous. As has already been pointed out, the learned trial judge instructed the jury that an automobile is not an inherently dangerous vehicle.

. . . . .

I do not see how we can uphold the judgment in the present case without overruling what has been so often said by this court and other courts of like authority in reference to the absence of any liability for negligence on the part of the original vendor of an ordinary carriage to any one except his immediate vendee. The absence of such liability was the very point actually decided in the English case of *Winterbottom v Wright,* and the illustration quoted from the opinion of Chief Judge Ruggles in *Thomas v Winchester, supra,* assumes that the law on the subject was so plain that the statement would be accepted almost as a matter of course. In the case at bar the defective wheel on an automobile, moving only eight miles an hour, was not any more dangerous to the occupants of the car than a similarly defective wheel would be to the occupants of a carriage drawn by a horse at the same speed, and yet, unless the courts have been all wrong on this question up to the present time, there would be no liability to strangers to the original sale in the case of the horse-drawn carriage.

The rule upon which, in my judgment, the determination of this case depends, and the recognized exceptions thereto, were discussed by Circuit Judge Sanborn, of the United States Circuit Court of Appeals in the Eighth Circuit, in *Huset v JI Case Threshing Machine Co,* 120 Fed 865, in an opinion which reviews all the leading American and English decisions on the subject up to the time when it was rendered (1903). I have already discussed the leading New York cases, but as to the rest I feel that I can add nothing to the learning of that opinion or the cogency of its reasoning. I have examined the cases to which Judge Sanborn refers, but if I were to discuss them at length, I should be forced merely to paraphrase his language, as a study of the authorities he cites has led me to the same conclusion; and the repetition of what has already been so well said would contribute nothing to the advantage of the bench, the bar, or the individual litigants whose case is before us.

A few cases decided since his opinion was written, however, may be noticed. In *Earl v Lubbock,* (1905) LR 1 KB Div 253, the Court of Appeal in 1904 considered and approved the propositions of law laid down by the Court of Exchequer in *Winterbottom v Wright, supra,* declaring that the decision in that case, since the year 1842, had stood the test of repeated discussion. The Master of the Rolls approved the principles laid down by Lord Abinger as based upon sound reasoning; and all the members of the court agreed that his decision was a controlling authority which must be followed. That the Federal Courts still adhere to the general rule, as I have stated it, appears by the decision of the Circuit Court of Appeal in the Second Circuit, in March, 1915, in the case of *Cadillac Motor Car Co v Johnson.* That case, like this, was an action by a subvendee against a manufacturer of automobiles for negligence in failing to discover that one of its wheels was defective, the court holding that such an action could not be maintained. It is true there was a dissenting opinion in that case, but it was based chiefly upon the proposition that rules applicable to stagecoaches are archaic when applied to automobiles, and that if the law did not afford a remedy to strangers to the contract, the law should be changed. If this be true, the change should be effected by the legislature and not by the courts. A perusal of the opinion in that case and in the *Huset* case will disclose how uniformly the courts throughout this country have adhered to the rule and how consistently they have refused to broaden the scope of the exceptions. I think we should adhere to it in the case at bar, and therefore I vote for a reversal of this judgment.

Judges Hiscock, Chase, Cuddeback and Hogan concur with Judge Cardozo. Chief Judge Willard Bartlett dissents. Judge Pound did not vote.

Judgment affirmed.

1944 *Escola v Coca Cola*

COMMENTARY

One of the points made about the *MacPherson* case was that plaintiffs could obtain some of the advantages of strict liability by making use of the concept of *res ipsa loquitur*. The *Escola* case, 28 years later, was decided on that basis.

Res ipsa loquitur shifts the burden of proof, but only when the defendant had exclusive control over the product that caused the harm and the accident could not have happened without negligence. There has been some discussion about the time at which the defendant's control must be effective, because an accident can happen after a product has left the hand of the defendant. That is what happened in *Escola;* the bottle exploded while it was under the immediate control of the plaintiff, and it was therefore necessary to show that it was not the plaintiff herself who negligently handled the bottle. The tort of negligence consists of two stages. First there is a careless act or omission, and then there is the infliction of harm. One without the other is not enough to justify a claim. The court said that the more logical view was that *res ipsa loquitur* required that the defendant had control at the time of the careless act or omission and not necessarily at the time of injury. The plaintiff must also be able to prove that the product had not been changed after it left the defendant's control.

What is perhaps more significant about *Escola* is not the successful pleading of *res ipsa loquitur,* but the separate opinion of Justice Traynor. He concurred in the court's decision, but said that it was time to abandon altogether the requirement of negligence. It was time to recognise that there is an absolute liability on a manufacturer when a defective product causes injury to human beings, when he knows that the product is to be used without further inspection. Another 19 years were to go by before he was able to apply that opinion in *Greenman v Yuba* (which is discussed later). Anybody who expects legal developments to happen at anything other than a snail's pace will be disappointed. The snail, however, does usually cover quite a distance, and so does legal history.

JUDGMENT

Supreme Court of California
July 5, 1944

Escola
versus
Coca Cola Bottling Company of Fresno

Before Chief Justice Gibson and Justices Shenk, Curtis, Carter, Schauer, Traynor and Edmonds

US landmark cases

Gibson, *Chief Justice.* Plaintiff, a waitress in a restaurant, was injured when a bottle of Coca Cola broke in her hand. She alleged that defendant company, which had bottled and delivered the alleged defective bottle to her employer, was negligent in selling 'bottles containing said beverage which on account of excessive pressure of gas or by reason of some defect in the bottle was dangerous . . . and likely to explode.' This appeal is from a judgment upon a jury verdict in favor of plaintiff.

Defendant's driver delivered several cases of Coca Cola to the restaurant, placing them on the floor, one on top of the other, under and behind the counter, where they remained at least 36 hours. Immediately before the accident, plaintiff picked up the top case and set it upon a near-by ice cream cabinet in front of and about three feet from the refrigerator. She then proceeded to take the bottles from the case with her right hand, one at a time, and put them into the refrigerator. Plaintiff testified that after she had placed three bottles in the refrigerator and had moved the fourth bottle about 18 inches from the case 'it exploded in my hand.' The bottle broke into two jagged pieces and inflicted a deep five-inch cut, severing blood vessels, nerves and muscles of the thumb and palm of the hand. Plaintiff further testified that when the bottle exploded, 'It made a sound similar to an electric light bulb that would have dropped. It made a loud pop.' Plaintiff's employer testified, 'I was about 20 feet from where it actually happened and I heard the explosion.' A fellow employee, on the opposite side of the counter, testified that plaintiff 'had the bottle, I should judge, waist high, and I know that it didn't bang either the case or the door or another bottle . . . when it popped. It sounded just like a fruit jar would blow up . . . .' The witness further testified that the contents of the bottle 'flew all over herself and myself and the walls and one thing and another'.

The top portion of the bottle, with the cap, remained in plaintiff's hand, and the lower portion fell to the floor but did not break. The broken bottle was not produced at the trial, the pieces having been thrown away by an employee of the restaurant shortly after the accident. Plaintiff, however, described the broken pieces, and a diagram of the bottle was made showing the location of the 'fracture line' where the bottle broke in two.

One of defendant's drivers, called as a witness by plaintiff, testified that he had seen other bottles of Coca Cola in the past explode and had found broken bottles in the warehouse when he took the cases out, but that he did not know what made them blow up.

Plaintiff then rested her case, having announced to the court that being unable to show any specific acts of negligence she relied completely on the doctrine of *res ipsa loquitur.*

Defendant contends that the doctrine of *res ipsa loquitur* does not apply in this case, and that the evidence is insufficient to support the judgment.

Many jurisdictions have applied the doctrine in cases involving exploding bottles of carbonated beverages. See *Payne v Rome Coca-Cola Bottling Co,* 73 SE 1087; *Stolle v Anheuser-Busch,* 271 SW 497; *Bradley v Conway Springs Bottling Co,* 118 P2d 601. Other courts for varying reasons have refused to apply the doctrine in such cases. See *Gerber v Faber,* 129 P2d 485; *Loebig's Guardian v Coca-Cola Bottling Co,* 81 SW2d 910; *Stewart v Crystal Coca-Cola Bottling Co,* 68 P2d 952. It would serve no useful purpose to discuss the reasoning of the foregoing cases in detail, since the problem is whether under the facts shown in the instant case the conditions warranting application of the doctrine have been satisfied.

Res ipsa loquitur does not apply unless (1) defendant had exclusive control of the thing causing the injury and (2) the accident is of such a nature that it ordinarily would not occur in the absence of negligence by the defendant. *Honea v City Dairy Inc,* 140 P2d 369, and authorities there cited; *Cf Hinds v Wheadon,* 121 P2d 724; *Prosser on Torts* (1941) 293-301.

Many authorities state that the happening of the accident does not speak for itself where it took place some time after defendant had relinquished control of the instrumentality causing the injury. Under the more logical view, however, the doctrine may be applied upon the theory that defendant had control at the time of the alleged negligent act, although not at the time of the accident, *provided* plaintiff first proves that the condition of the instrumentality had not been changed after it left the defendant's possession. See cases collected in *Honea v City Dairy Inc, supra.* As said in *Dunn v Hoffman Beverage Co,* 20 A2d 352, 'defendant is not charged with the duty of showing affirmatively that something happened to the bottle after it left its control or management; . . . to get to the jury the plaintiff must show that there was due care during that period.' Plaintiff must also prove that she handled the bottle carefully. The reason for this prerequisite is set forth in *Prosser on Torts, supra,* at page 300, where the author states: 'Allied to the condition of exclusive control in the defendant is that of absence of any action on the part of the plaintiff contributing to the accident. Its purpose, of course, is to eliminate the possibiity that it was the plaintiff who was responsible. If the boiler of a locomotive explodes while the plaintiff engineer is operating it, the inference of his own negligence is at least as great as that of the defendant, and *res ipsa loquitur* will not apply until he has accounted for his own conduct.' See also *Olson v Whitthorne & Swan,* 263 P 518. It is not necessary, of course, that plaintiff eliminate every remote possibility of injury to the bottle after defendant lost control, and the requirement is satisfied if there is evidence permitting a reasonable inference that it was not accessible to extraneous harmful forces and that it was carefully handled by plaintiff or any third person who may have moved or touched it. *Cf* Prosser, *supra,* p 300. If such evidence is presented, the question becomes one for the trier of fact

Escola v Coca Cola

(see *eg MacPherson v Canada Dry Ginger Ale Inc,* 29 A2d 868,) and, accordingly, the issue should be submitted to the jury under proper instructions.

In the present case no instructions were requested or given on this phase of the case, although general instructions upon *res ipsa loquitur* were given. Defendant, however, has made no claim of error with reference thereto on this appeal.

Upon an examination of the record, the evidence appears sufficient to support a reasonable inference that the bottle here involved was not damaged by any extraneous force after delivery to the restaurant by defendant. It follows, therefore, that the bottle was in some manner defective at the time defendant relinquished control, because sound and properly prepared bottles of carbonated liquids do not ordinarily explode when carefully handled.

The next question, then, is whether plaintiff may rely upon the doctrine of *res ipsa loquitur* to supply an inference that defendant's negligence was responsible for the defective condition of the bottle at the time it was delivered to the restaurant. Under the general rules pertaining to the doctrine, as set forth above, it must appear that bottles of carbonated liquid are not ordinarily defective without negligence by the bottling company. In *1 Shearman and Redfield on Negligence* (Rev Ed 1941), page 153, it is stated that: 'The doctrine . . . requires evidence which shows at least the probability that a particular accident could not have occurred without legal wrong by the defendant'.

An explosion such as took place here might have been caused by an excessive internal pressure in a sound bottle, by a defect in the glass of a bottle containing a safe pressure, or by a combination of these two possible causes. The question is whether under the evidence there was a probability that defendant was negligent in any of these respects. If so, the doctrine of *res ipsa loquitur* applies.

The bottle was admittedly charged with gas under pressure, and the charging of the bottle was within the exclusive control of defendant. As it is a matter of common knowledge that an overcharge would not ordinarily result without negligence, it follows under the doctrine of *res ipsa loquitur* that if the bottle was in fact excessively charged an inference of defendant's negligence would arise. If the explosion resulted from a defective bottle containing a safe pressure, the defendant would be liable if it negligently failed to discover such flaw. If the defect were visible, an inference of negligence would arise from the failure of defendant to discover it. Where defects are discoverable, it may be assumed that they will not ordinarily escape detection if a reasonable inspection is made, and if such a defect is overlooked an inference arises that a proper inspection was not made. A difficult problem is presented where the defect is unknown and consequently might have been one not discoverable by a reasonable, practicable

inspection. In the *Honea* case we refused to take judicial notice of the technical practices and information available to the bottling industry for finding defects which cannot be seen. In the present case, however, we are supplied with evidence of the standard methods used for testing bottles.

A chemical engineer for the Owens-Illinois Glass Company and its Pacific Coast subsidiary, maker of Coca Cola bottles, explained how glass is manufactured and the methods used in testing and inspecting bottles. He testified that his company is the largest manufacturer of glass containers in the United States, and that it uses the standard methods for testing bottles recommended by the Glass Containers Association. A pressure test is made by taking a sample from each mold every three hours—approximately one out of every 600 bottles— and subjecting the sample to an internal pressure of 450 pounds per square inch, which is sustained for one minute. (The normal pressure in Coca Cola bottles is less than 50 pounds per square inch.) The sample bottles are also subjected to the standard thermal shock test. The witness stated that these tests are 'pretty near' infallible.

It thus appears that there is available to the industry a commonly-used method of testing bottles for defects not apparent to the eye, which is almost infallible. Since Coca Cola bottles are subjected to these tests by the manufacturer, it is not likely that they contain defects when delivered to the bottler which are not discoverable by visual inspection. Both new and used bottles are filled and distributed by defendant. The used bottles are not again subjected to the tests referred to above, and it may be inferred that defects not discoverable by visual inspection do not develop in bottles after they are manufactured. Obviously, if such defects do occur in used bottles there is a duty upon the bottler to make appropriate tests before they are refilled, and if such tests are not commercially practicable the bottles should not be re-used. This would seem to be particularly true where a charged liquid is placed in the bottle. It follows that a defect which would make the bottle unsound could be discovered by reasonable and practicable tests.

Although it is not clear in this case whether the explosion was caused by an excessive charge or a defect in the glass there is a sufficient showing that neither cause would ordinarily have been present if due care had been used. Further, defendant had exclusive control over both the charging and inspection of the bottles. Accordingly, all the requirements necessary to entitle plaintiff to rely on the doctrine of *res ipsa loquitur* to supply an inference of negligence are present.

It is true that defendant presented evidence tending to show that it exercised considerable precaution by carefully regulating and checking the pressure in the bottles and by making visual inspections for defects in the glass at several stages during the bottling process. It is well settled, however, that when a defendant produces evidence to rebut the inference of negligence which arises upon application of the doctrine of *res ipsa loquitur,* it is ordinarily a question of fact for the jury to determine whether the inference has been dispelled. *Druzanich v Criley,* 122 P2d 53; *Michener v Hutton,* 265 P 238.

The judgment is affirmed.

Justices Shenk, Curtis, Carter and Schauer concurred.

Traynor, *Justice.* I concur in the judgment, but I believe the manufacturer's negligence should no longer be singled out as the basis of a plaintiff's right to recover in cases like the present one. In my opinion it should now be recognized that a manufacturer incurs an absolute liability when an article that he has placed on the market, knowing that it is to be used without inspection, prove to have a defect that causes injury to human beings. *MacPherson v Buick Motor Co,* 111 NE 1050 established the principle, recognized by this court, that irrespective of privity of contract, the manufacturer is responsible for an injury caused by such an article to any person who comes in lawful contact with it. *Sheward v Virtue,* 126 P2d 345; *Kalash v Los Angeles Ladder Co,* 34 P2d 481. In these cases the source of the manufacturer's liability was his negligence in the manufacturing process or in the inspection of component parts supplied by others. Even if there is no negligence, however, public policy demands that responsibility be fixed wherever it will most effectively reduce the hazards to life and health inherent in defective products that reach the market. It is evident that the manufacturer can anticipate some hazards and guard against the recurrence of others, as the public cannot. Those who suffer injury from defective products are unprepared to meet its consequences. The cost of an injury and the loss of time or health may be an overwhelming misfortune to the person injured, and a needless one, for the risk of injury can be insured by the manufacturer and distributed among the public as a cost of doing business. It is to the public interest to discourage the marketing of products having defects that are a menace to the public. If such products nevertheless find their way into the market it is to the public interest to place the responsibility for whatever injury they may cause upon the manufacturer, who, even if he is not negligent in the manufacture of the product, is responsible for its reaching the market. However intermittently such injuries may occur and however haphazardly they may strike, the risk of their occurrence is a constant risk and a general one. Against such a risk there should be general and constant protection and the manufacturer is best situated to afford such protection.

The injury from a defective product does not become a matter of indifference because the defect arises from causes other than the negligence of the manufacturer, such as negligence of a submanufacturer of a component part whose defects could not be revealed by inspection (see *Sheward v Virtue, supra; O'Rourke v Day & Night Water Heater Co Ltd,* 88 P2d 191; *Smith v Peerless Glass Co,* 181 NE 576), or unknown causes

that even by the device of *res ipsa loquitur* cannot be classified as negligence of the manufacturer. The inference of negligence may be dispelled by an affirmative showing of proper care. If the evidence against the fact inferred is 'clear, positive, uncontradicted, and of such a nature that it can not rationally be disbelieved, the court must instruct the jury that the nonexistence of the fact has been established as a matter of law.' *Blank v Coffin,* 126 P2d 868. An injured person, however, is not ordinarily in a position to refute such evidence or identify the cause of the defect, for he can hardly be familiar with the manufacturing process as the manufacturer himself is. In leaving it to the jury to decide whether the inference has been dispelled, regardless of the evidence against it, the negligence rule approaches the rule of strict liability. It is needlessly circuitous to make negligence the basis of recovery and impose what is in reality liability without negligence. If public policy demands that a manufacturer of goods be responsible for their quality regardless of negligence there is no reason not to fix that responsibility openly.

In the case of foodstuffs, the public policy of the state is formulated in a criminal statute. Section 26510 of the Health and Safety Code, St 1939 p 989, prohibits the manufacturing, preparing, compounding, packing, selling, offering for sale, or keeping for sale, or advertising within the state, of any adulterated food. Section 26470, St 1941, p 2857, declares that food is adulterated when 'it has been produced, prepared, packed or held under insanitary conditions whereby it may have become contaminated with filth, or whereby it may have been rendered diseased, unwholesome or injurious to health.' The statute imposes criminal liability not only if the food is adulterated, but if its container, which may be a bottle (section 26451, St 1939, p 983), has any deleterious substance (section 26470(6)), or renders the product injurious to health (section 26470(4)). The criminal liability under the statute attaches without proof of fault, so that the manufacturer is under the duty of ascertaining whether an article manufactured by him is safe. *People v Schwartz,* 70 P2d 1017. Statutes of this kind result in a strict liability of the manufacturer in tort to the member of the public injured. See cases cited in Prosser, *Torts,* p 693, note 69.

The statute may well be applicable to a bottle whose defects cause it to explode. In any event it is significant that the statute imposes criminal liability without fault, reflecting the public policy of protecting the public from dangerous products placed on the market, irrespective of negligence in their manufacture. While the Legislature imposes criminal liability only with regard to food products and their containers, there are many other sources of danger. It is to the public interest to prevent injury to the public from any defective goods by the imposition of civil liability generally.

The retailer, even though not equipped to test a product, is under an absolute liability to his customer, for the implied warranties of fitness for proposed use and merchantable quality include a warranty of safety of the

Escola v Coca Cola

product. *Goetten v Owl Drug Co,* 59 P2d 142; *Mix v Ingersoll Candy Co,* P2d 144; *Gindraux v Maurice Mercantile Co,* 47 P2d 708. This warranty is not necessarily a contractual one (*Chamberlain Co v Allis-Chalmers Co,* 125 P2d 113; See *1 Williston on Sales,* 2d ed, sections 197-201), for public policy requires that the buyer be insured at the seller's expense against injury. *Chapman v Roggenkamp,* 182 Ill App 117, 121; *Ward v Great Atlantic & Pacific Tea Co,* 120 NE 225; see Prosser, 'The Implied Warranty of Merchantable Quality,' 27 Minn L Rev 117, 124; Brown, 'The Liability of Retail Dealers For Defective Food Products,' 23 Minn L Rev 585. The courts recognize, however, that the retailer cannot bear the burden of this warranty, and allow him to recoup any losses by means of the warranty of safety attending the wholesaler's or manufacturer's sale to him. *Ward v Great Atlantic & Pacific Tea Co, supra;* see Waite, 'Retail Responsibility and Judicial Law Making', 34 Mich L Rev 494, 509. Such a procedure, however, is needlessly circuitous and engenders wasteful litigation. Much would be gained if the injured person could base his action directly on the manufacturer's warranty.

The liability of the manufacturer to an immediate buyer injured by a defective product follows without proof of negligence from the implied warranty of safety attending the sale. Ordinarily, however, the immediate buyer is a dealer who does not intend to use the product himself, and if the warranty of safety is to serve the purpose of protecting health and safety it must give rights to others than the dealer. In the words of Judge Cardozo in the *MacPherson* case *supra:* 'The dealer was indeed the one person of whom it might be said with some approach to certainty that by him the car would not be used. Yet the defendant would have us say that he was the one person whom it was under a legal duty to protect. The law does not lead us to so inconsequent a conclusion.' While the defendant's negligence in the *MacPherson* case made it unnecessary for the court to base liability on warranty, Judge Cardozo's reasoning recognized the injured person as the real party in interest and effectively disposed of the theory that the liability of the manufacturer incurred by his warranty should apply only to the immediate purchaser. It thus paves the way for a standard of liability that would make the manufacturer guarantee the safety of his product even when there is no negligence.

This court and many others have extended protection according to such a standard to consumers of food products, taking the view that the right of a consumer injured by unwholesome food does not depend 'upon the intricacies of the law of sales' and that the warranty of the manufacturer to the consumer in absence of privity of contract rests on public policy. *Klein v Duchess Sandwich Co Ltd,* 93 P2d 799; *Ketterer v Armour & Co,* 247 F 921; see Perkins, 'Unwholesome Food As a Source of Liability', 5 Iowa L Bull 6, 86. Dangers to life and health inhere in other consumers' goods that are defective and there is no reason to differentiate them

from the dangers of defective food products. See Bohlen, 'Studies in Torts, Basis of Affirmative Obligations, American Cases Upon The Liability of Manufacturers and Vendors of Personal Property,' 109, 135; Llewellyn, 'On Warranty of Quality and Society,' 36 Col L Rev 699, 704, note 14; Prosser, *Torts,* p 692.

In the food products cases the courts have resorted to various fictions to rationalize the extension of the manufacturer's warranty to the consumer: that a warranty runs with the chattel; that the cause of action of the dealer is assigned to the consumer; that the consumer is a third party beneficiary of the manufacturer's contract with the dealer. They have also held the manufacturer liable on a mere fiction of negligence: 'practically he must know if (the product) is fit, or take the consequences, if it proves destructive.' *Parks v CC Yost Pie Co,* 144 P 202; see Jeanblanc, 'Manufacturer's Liability to Persons Other Than Their Immediate Vendees', 24 Va L Rev 134.

. . . . .

As handicrafts have been replaced by mass production with its great markets and transportation facilities, the close relationship between the producer and consumer of a product has been altered. Manufacturing processes, frequently valuable secrets, are ordinarily either inaccessible to or beyond the ken of the general public. The consumer no longer has means or skill enough to investigate for himself the soundness of a product, even when it is not contained in a sealed package, and his erstwhile vigilance has been lulled by the steady efforts of manufacturers to build up confidence by advertising and marketing devices such as trade-marks. See *Thomas v Winchester; Baxter v Ford Motor Co,* 15 P2d 1118; see Handler, 'False and Misleading Advertising,' 39 Yale LJ 22; Rogers, *Good Will, Trade-Marks and Unfair Trading* (1914) ch. VI, 'A Study of The Consumer,' p 65 et seq; Williston, 'Liability For Honest Misrepresentations As Deceit, Negligence Or Warranty', 42 Harv L Rev 733; 18 Cornell LQ 445. Consumers no longer approach products warily but accept them on faith, relying on the reputation of the manufacturer or the trade mark. See *Max Factor & Co v Kunsman,* 55 P2d 177; *Old Dearborn Distributing Co v Seagram-Distillers Corp,* 299 US 183; Schechter, 'The Rational Basis of Trade Mark Protection,' 40 Harv L Rev 813. Manufacturers have sought to justify that faith by increasingly high standards of inspection and a readiness to make good on defective products by way of replacements and refunds. See Bogert and Fink, 'Business Practices Regarding Warranties in the Sale of Goods,' 25 Ill L Rev 400. The manufacturer's obligation to the consumer must keep pace with the changing relationship between them; it cannot be escaped because the marketing of a product has become so complicated as to require one or more intermediaries. Certainly there is greater reason to impose liability on the manufacturer than on the retailer who is but a conduit of a product that he is not himself able to test. See Soule, 'Consumer Protection,' 4 *Encyclopedia of The Social Sciences,* 282; Feezer,

'Manufacturer's Liability For Injuries Caused By His Products: Defective Automobiles', 37 Mich L Rev 1; Llewellyn, *Cases and Materials on Sales,* 340 et seq.

The manufacturer's liability should, of course, be defined in terms of the safety of the product in normal and proper use, and should not extend to injuries that cannot be traced to the product as it reached the market.

Rehearing denied; Justice Edmonds dissenting.

1960 *Henningsen v Bloomfield Motors*

COMMENTARY

The two cases so far discussed have shown the movement away from privity of contract and the indication of a movement away from negligence to strict liability. The next case in our selection will show that a claim for breach of implied warranty also does not depend on privity of contract. That will be a logical development because breach of warranty has long been regarded as a tort, even though it arises in a contract situation.

Once again there is a long gap between decisions. In 1916 the principle was established that a duty in negligence could exist without privity, and in 1944 that principle was extended by the use of *res ipsa loquitur.* Now, after 16 years, we come back to contract law, and find that a warranty protects persons who were not party to the sale. So privity of contract received yet another blow.

In 1960, however, the courts were well used to putting privity on one side when sufficient reason could be found. For example, ever since the early years of the century the courts had allowed claims by persons harmed by defective food products, whether or not they had actually bought the product. There was a social need for a remedy in these cases, and that need had been recognised very early in the history of the common law. In 1266 a statute of Henry III said 'It is ordained that none shall sell corrupt victuals', and by the time of the first Tudor monarch, Henry VII, an action on the case was allowed against the seller.

The American settlers carried with them the principles of the English common law, and a New York judge in 1815 repeated the sentiments of Henry III. He said 'In the case of provisions for domestic use, the vendor is bound to know that they are sound and wholesome at his peril'. The importance of *Henningsen* is that liability without the limitation of privity was extended beyond food, to defective products generally. It was not the first case to make the transition, but the courts had in the past been more concerned with products that were 'intimately connected with the person'. This meant drugs, cosmetics, and then cleaning products.

One reason for the willingness to abandon privity of contract was the theory that breach of warranty was based on tort, and not on contract. This theory is long-established, as is shown by the rule in the time of Henry VII, that a person injured by 'corrupt food' had an action on the case. That is the language of tort, not of contract. Even so, not every court was willing in 1960, or in later years for that matter, to forego the requirement of privity, although in most jurisdictions there was no argument. Even the Uniform Commercial Code was amended to allow a third party to sue, and states wishing to adopt the Code have the choice of three alternative wordings. Most states have adopted alternative A, which extends

Henningsen v Bloomfield Motors

the benefit of any express and implied warranty to 'any natural person who is in the family or household of the buyer or who is a guest in his home if it is reasonable to expect that such person may use, consume or be affected by the goods'.

Alternative B extends the warranty to any 'natural person who may be reasonably expected to use, consume or be affected by the goods'. Alternative C has the same wording but refers to a person 'injured by the breach of warranty', whereas Alternative B refers to 'injured in person'. This reference points to a problem that will come up in future cases, the problem of personal as opposed to property injury. Decisions up to *Henningsen* have been concerned mainly with personal injury.

The decision by the *Henningsen* court was based on public policy. Experience had shown that society needed more extensive remedies that would be available if the courts continued to insist on privity of contract. One comment to be noted in the opinion is: 'In that way the burden of losses consequent on use of defective articles is borne by those who are in a position either to control the danger or make an equitable distribution of losses when they do occur'. This statement of policy appears in many product liability cases. Thus, in May 1984 a US Court of Appeals held that a manufacturer was liable under strict liability in Admiralty law for financial loss caused by a defective engine, and justified the decision by saying that a manufacturer could predict the consequences of a failure of his product and could include in his costs the expense of adequate insurance (*Emerson GM Diesel Inc v Alaskan Enterprise,* US Court of Appeals, Ninth Circuit, May 11, 1984).

After *Henningsen* the law was in a stage of development that allowed a decisive step forward, if we assume that strict liability was a step forward. Our next landmark is *Greenman v Yuba Power Products.*

JUDGMENT

Supreme Court of New Jersey
May 9, 1960

Henningsen
versus
Bloomfield Motors Inc

Before Chief Justice Weintraub and Justices Burling, Jacobs, Francis, Proctor and Schettino

Francis, *Justice.* Plaintiff Claus H Henningsen purchased a Plymouth automobile, manufactured by defendant Chrysler Corporation, from defendant Bloomfield Motors Inc. His wife, plaintiff Helen Henningsen, was injured while driving it and instituted suit against both defendants to recover damages on account of her injuries. Her husband joined in the action seeking compensation for his consequential losses. The complaint was predicated upon breach of express and implied warranties and upon negligence. At the trial the negligence counts were dismissed by the court and the cause was submitted to the jury for determination solely on the issues of implied warranty of merchantability. Verdicts were returned against both defendants and in favor of the plaintiffs. Defendants appealed and plaintiffs cross-appealed from the dismissal of their negligence claim. The matter was certified by this court prior to consideration in the Appellate Division.

The facts are not complicated, but a general outline of them is necessary to an understanding of the case.

On May 7, 1955 Mr and Mrs Henningsen visited the place of business of Bloomfield Motors Inc, an authorized De Soto and Plymouth dealer, to look at a Plymouth. They wanted to buy a car and were considering a Ford or a Chevrolet as well as a Plymouth. They were shown a Plymouth which appealed to them and the purchase followed. The record indicates that Mr Henningsen intended the car as a Mother's Day gift to his wife. He said the intention was communicated to the dealer. When the purchase order or contract was prepared and presented, the husband executed it alone. His wife did not join as a party.

The purchase order was a printed form of one page. On the front it contained blanks to be filled in with a description of the automobile to be sold, the various accessories to be included, and the details of the financing. The particular car selected was described as a 1955 Plymouth, Plaza '6', Club Sedan. The type used in the printed parts of the form became smaller in size, different in style, and less readable toward the bottom where the line for the purchaser's signature was placed. The smallest type on the page appears in the two paragraphs, one of two and one-quarter lines and the second of one and one-half lines, on which great stress is laid by the defense in the case. These two paragraphs are the least legible and the most difficult to read in the instrument, but they are most important in the evaluation of the rights of the contesting parties. They do not attract attention and there is nothing about the format which would draw the reader's eye to them. In fact, a studied and concentrated effort would have to be made to read them. De-emphasis seems the motive rather than emphasis. More particularly, most of the printing in the body of the order appears to be 12 point block type, and easy to read. In the short paragraphs under discussion, however, the type appears to be six point script and the print is solid, that is, the lines are very close together.

The two paragraphs are: 'The front and back of this Order comprise the entire agreement affecting this purchase and no other agreement or understanding of any nature concerning same has been made or entered into, or will be recognized. I hereby certify that no credit has been extended to me for the purchase of this motor vehicle except as appears in writing on the face of this agreement.

'I have read the matter printed on the back hereof and agree to it as a part of this order the same as if it were printed above my signature. I certify that I am 21 years of age, or older, and hereby acknowledge receipt of a copy of this order.'

On the right side of the form, immediately below these clauses and immediately above the signature line, and in 12 point block type, the following appears: 'CASH OR CERTIFIED CHECK ONLY ON DELIVERY.'

On the left side, just opposite and in the same style type as the two quoted clauses, but in eight point size, this statement is set out: 'This agreement shall not become binding upon the dealer until approved by an officer of the company.'

The two latter statements are in the interest of the dealer and obviously an effort is made to draw attention to them.

The testimony of Claus Henningsen justifies the conclusion that he did not read the two fine print paragraphs referring to the back of the purchase contract. And it is uncontradicted that no one made any reference to them, or called them to his attention. With respect to the matter appearing on the back, it is likewise uncontradicted that he did not read it and that no one called it to his attention.

. . . . .

After the contract had been executed, plaintiffs were told the car had to be serviced and that it would be ready in two days. According to the dealer's president, a number of cars were on hand at the time; they had come in from the factory about three or four weeks earlier and at least some of them, including the one selected by the Henningsens, were kept in the back of the shop for display purposes. When sold, plaintiffs' vehicle was not 'a serviced car ready to go'. The testimony shows that Chrysler Corporation sends from the factory to the dealer a 'New Car Preparation Service Guide' with each new automobile. The guide contains detailed instructions as to what has to be done to prepare the car for delivery. The dealer is told to: 'Use this form as a guide to inspect and prepare this new Plymouth for delivery.' It specifies 66 separate items to be checked, tested, tightened or adjusted in the course of the servicing, but dismantling the vehicle or checking all of its internal parts is not prescribed. The guide also calls for delivery of the Owner Service Certificate with the car.

This Certificate, which at least by inference is authorized by Chrysler, was in the car when released to Claus Henningsen on May 9, 1955. It was not made part of the purchase contract, nor was it shown to him prior to the consummation of that agreement. The only reference to it therein is that the dealer 'agrees to promptly perform and fulfill all terms and conditions of the owner service policy'. The Certificate contains a

warranty entitled 'Automobile Manufacturers Association Uniform Warranty'. The provisions thereof are the same as those set forth on the reverse side of the purchase order, except that an additional paragraph is added by which the dealer extends that warranty to the purchaser in the same manner as if the word 'Dealer' appeared instead of the word 'Manufacturer'.

The new Plymouth was turned over to the Henningsens on May 9, 1955. No proof was adduced by the dealer to show precisely what was done in the way of mechanical or road testing beyond testimony that the manufacturer's instructions were probably followed. Mr Henningsen drove it from the dealer's place of business in Bloomfield to their home in Keansburg. On the trip nothing unusual appeared in the way in which it operated. Thereafter, it was used for short trips on paved streets about the town. It had no servicing and no mishaps of any kind before the event of May 19. That day, Mrs Henningsen drove to Asbury Park. On the way down and in returning the car performed in normal fashion until the accident occurred. She was proceeding north on Route 36 in Highlands, New Jersey, at 20-22 miles per hour. The highway was paved and smooth, and contained two lanes for northbound travel. She was riding in the right-hand lane. Suddenly she heard a loud noise 'from the bottom, by the hood'. It 'felt as if something cracked'. The steering wheel spun in her hands; the car veered sharply to the right and crashed into a highway sign and a brick wall. No other vehicle was in any way involved. A bus operator driving in the left-hand lane testified that he observed plaintiffs' car approaching in normal fashion in the opposite direction; 'all of a sudden it veered at 90 degrees right into this wall.' As a result of the impact, the front of the car was so badly damaged that it was impossible to determine if any of the parts of the steering wheel mechanism or workmanship or assembly were defective or improper prior to the accident. The condition was such that the collision insurance carrier, after inspection, declared the vehicle a total loss. It had 468 miles on the speedometer at the time.

The insurance carrier's inspector and appraiser of damaged cars, with 11 years of experience, advanced the opinion, based on the history and his examination, that something definitely went 'wrong from the steering wheel down to the front wheels' and that the untoward happening must have been due to mechanical defect or failure; 'something down there had to drop off or break loose to cause the car' to act in the manner described.

As has been indicated, the trial court felt that the proof was not sufficient to make out a *prima facie* case as to the negligence of either the manufacturer or the dealer. The case was given to the jury, therefore, solely on the warranty theory, with results favorable to the plaintiffs against both defendants.

. . . . .

Putting aside for the time being the problem of the efficacy of the disclaimer provisions contained in the express warranty, a question of first importance to be decided is whether an implied warranty of merchantability by Chrysler Corporation accompanied the sale of the automobile to Claus Henningsen.

Preliminarily, it may be said that the express warranty against defective parts and workmanship is not inconsistent with an implied warranty of merchantability. Such warranty cannot be excluded for that reason. *Knapp v Willys-Ardmore Inc,* 100 A2d 105 (1953).

Chrysler points out that an implied warranty of merchantability is an incident of a contract of sale. It concedes, of course, the making of the original sale to Bloomfield Motors Inc, but maintains that this transaction marked the terminal point of its contractual connection with the car. Then Chrysler urges that since it was not a party to the sale by the dealer to Henningsen, there is no privity of contract between it and the plaintiffs, and the absence of this privity eliminates any such implied warranty.

There is no doubt that under early common-law concepts of contractual liability only those persons who were parties to the bargain could sue for a breach of it. In more recent times a noticeable disposition has appeared in a number of jurisdictions to break through the narrow barrier of privity when dealing with sales of goods in order to give realistic recognition to a universally accepted fact. The fact is that the dealer and the ordinary buyer do not, and are not expected to, buy goods, whether they be foodstuffs or automobiles, exclusively for their own consumption or use. Makers and manufacturers know this and advertise and market their products on that assumption; witness, the 'family' car, the baby foods, etc. The limitations of privity in contracts for the sale of goods developed their place in the law when marketing conditions were simple, when maker and buyer frequently met face to face on an equal bargaining plane and when many of the products were relatively uncomplicated and conducive to inspection by a buyer competent to evaluate their quality. See Feezer, 'Manufacturer's Liability for Injuries Caused by His Products', 37 Mich L Rev 1 (1938)
. . . . .

Thus, where the commodities sold are such that if defectively manufactured they will be dangerous to life or limb, then society's interests can only be protected by eliminating the requirement of privity between the maker and his dealers and the reasonably expected ultimate consumer. In that way the burden of losses consequent upon use of defective articles is borne by those who are in a position to either control the danger or make an equitable distribution of the losses when they do occur. As Harper & James put it, 'The interest in consumer protection calls for warranties by the maker that *do* run with the goods, to reach all who are likely to be hurt by the use of the unfit commodity for a purpose ordinarily to be expected.' 2 Harper & James, *Torts* 1571; Prosser, *supra,* 506-511. As far back as 1932, in the well known case of *Baxter v Ford Motor Co,* 12 P2d

409 (Sup Ct 1932), the Supreme Court of Washington gave recognition to the impact of then existing commercial practices on the straitjacket of privity, saying: 'It would be unjust to recognize a rule that would permit manufacturers of goods to create a demand for their products by representing that they possess qualities which they, in fact, do not possess, and then, because there is no privity of contract existing between the consumer and the manufacturer, deny the consumer the right to recover if damages result from the absence of those qualities, when such absence is not readily noticeable.'

The concept was expressed in a practical way by the Supreme Court of Texas in *Jacob E Decker & Sons Inc v Capps,* 164 SW2d 828 (1942):
'In fact, the manufacturer's interest in the product is not terminated when he has sold it to the wholesaler. He must get it off the wholesaler's shelves before the wholesaler will buy a new supply. The same is not only true of the retailer, but of the house wife, for the house wife will not buy more until the family has consumed that which she has in her pantry.'
. . . . .

In *Patargias v Coca-Cola Bottling Co of Chicago,* 74 NE2d 162 (App Ct 1947), involving the sale of a bottle of Coca-Cola by a dealer, the court said:
'We are impelled to hold that, where an article of food or drink is sold in a sealed container for human consumption, public policy demands that an implied warranty be imposed upon the manufacturer thereof that such article is wholesome and fit for use, that said warranty *runs with the sale* of the article for the benefit of the consumer thereof . . . .'

And in *Worley v Proctor & Gamble Mfg Co,* 243 SW2d 532 (Ct App 1953) it was said that:
'In the case of food products sold in original packages, and other articles dangerous to life (here a box of soap powder), if defective, the manufacturer, who alone is in a position to inspect and control their preparation, should be held as a warrantor, whether he purveys his products by his own hand, or through a network of independent distributing agencies. In either case, the essence of the situation is the same—the placing of goods in the channels of trade, representations directed to the ultimate consumer, and damaging reliance by the latter on those representations. Such representations, being inducements to the buyers making the purchase, should be regarded as warranties imposed by law, independent of the vendors' contractual intentions. The liability thus imposed springs from representations directed to the ultimate consumer, and not from the breach of any contractual undertaking on the part of the vendor. This is in accord with the original theory of the action.'
. . . . .

We see no rational doctrinal basis for differentiating between a fly in a bottle of beverage and a defective automobile. The unwholesome beverage may bring illness

US landmark cases

to one person, the defective car, with its great potentiality for harm to the driver, occupants, and others, demands even less adherence to the narrow barrier of privity. 2 Harper & James, *supra,* 1572; 1 Williston, *Sales,* section 244a, p 648; Note, 46 Harv L Rev 161 (1932). In *Mannsz v Macwhyte Co,* 155 F2d 445 (1946) Chief Judge Biggs, speaking for the Third Circuit Court of Appeals said: 'We think it is clear that whether the approach to the problem be by way of warranty or under the doctrine of negligence, the requirement of privity between the injured party and the manufacturer of the article which has injured him has been obliterated from the Pennsylvania law. The abolition of the doctrine occurred first in the food cases, next in the beverage decisions and now it has been extended to those cases in which the article manufactured, not dangerous or even beneficial if properly made, injured a person because it was manufactured improperly.'

Under modern conditions the ordinary layman, on responding to the importuning of colorful advertising, has neither the opportunity nor the capacity to inspect or to determine the fitness of an automobile for use; he must rely on the manufacturer who has control of its construction, and to some degree on the dealer who, to the limited extent called for by the maufacturer's instructions, inspects and services it before delivery. In such a marketing milieu his remedies and those of persons who properly claim through him should not depend 'upon the intricacies of the law of sales. The obligation of the manufacturer should not be based alone on privity of contract. It should rest, as was once said, upon "the demands of social justice."' *Mazetti v Armour & Co,* 135 P 633 (Sup Ct 1913). 'If privity of contract is required' then, under the circumstances of modern merchandising, 'privity of contract exists in the consciousness and understanding of all right-thinking persons'. *Madouros v Kansas City Coca-Cola Bottling Co,* 90 SW2d 445.

Accordingly, we hold that under modern marketing conditions, when a manufacturer puts a new automobile in the stream of trade and promotes its purchase by the public, an implied warranty that it is reasonably suitable for use as such accompanies it into the hands of the ultimate purchaser. Absence of agency between the manufacturer and the dealer who makes the ultimate sale is immaterial.

The effect of the disclaimer and limitation of liability clauses on the implied warranty of merchantability

Judicial notice may be taken of the fact that automobile manufacturers, including Chrysler Corporation, undertake large scale advertising programs over television, radio, in newspapers, magazines and all media of communication in order to persuade the public to buy their products. As has been observed above, a number of jurisdictions, conscious of modern marketing practices, have declared that when a manufacturer engages in advertising in order to bring his goods and their quality

to the attention of the public and thus to create consumer demand, the representations made constitute an express warranty running directly to a buyer who purchases in reliance thereon. The fact that the sale is consummated with an independent dealer does not obviate that warranty. *Mannsz v Macwhyte Co, supra; Baxter v Ford Motor Co, supra;* 1 Williston, *Sales, supra,* section 244a.

In view of the cases in various jurisdictions suggesting the conclusion which we have now reached with respect to the implied warranty of merchantability, it becomes apparent that manufacturers who enter into promotional activities to stimulate consumer buying may incur warranty obligations of either or both the express or implied character. These developments in the law inevitably suggest the inference that the form of express warranty made part of the Henningsen purchase contract was devised for general use in the automobile industry as a possible means of avoiding the consequences of the growing judicial acceptance of the thesis that the described express or implied warranties run directly to the consumer.

. . . . .

In these times, an automobile is almost as much a servant of convenience for the ordinary person as a household utensil. For a multitude of other persons it is a necessity. Crowded highways and filled parking lots are a commonplace of our existence. There is no need to look any farther than the daily newspaper to be convinced that when an automobile is defective, it has great potentiality for harm.

No one spoke more graphically on this subject than Justice Cardozo in the landmark case of *MacPherson v Buick Motor Co,* 111 NE 1050 (Ct App 1916): 'Beyond all question, the nature of an automobile gives warning of probable danger if its construction is defective.'

In the 44 years that have intervened since that utterance, the average car has been constructed for almost double the speed mentioned; 60 miles per hour is permitted on our parkways. The number of automobiles in use has multiplied many times and the hazard to the user and the public has increased proportionately. The Legislature has intervened in the public interest, not only to regulate the manner of operation on the highway but also to require periodic inspection of motor vehicles and to impose a duty on manufacturers to adopt certain safety devices and methods in their construction. It is apparent that the public has an interest not only in the safe manufacture of automobiles, but also, as shown by the Sales Act, in protecting the rights and remedies of purchasers so far as it can be accomplished consistently with our system of free enterprise. In a society such as ours, where the automobile is a common and necessary adjunct of daily life, and where its use is so fraught with danger to the driver, passengers and the public, the manufacturer is under a special obligation in connection with the construction, promotion and sale of his cars. Consequently, the courts must examine purchase

Henningsen v Bloomfield Motors

agreements closely to see if consumer and public interests are treated fairly.

What influence should these circumstances have on the restrictive effect of Chrysler's express warranty in the framework of the purchase contract? As we have said, warranties originated in the law to safeguard the buyer and not to limit the liability of the seller or manufacturer. It seems obvious in this instance that the motive was to avoid the warranty obligations which are normally incidental to such sales. The language gave little and withdrew much. In return for the delusive remedy of replacement of defective parts at the factory, the buyer is said to have accepted the exclusion of the maker's liability for personal injuries arising from the breach of the warranty, and to have agreed to the elimination of any other express or implied warranty. An instinctively felt sense of justice cries out against such a sharp bargain. But does the doctrine that a person is bound by his signed agreement, in the absence of fraud, stand in the way of any relief?
. . . . .

The warranty before us is a standardized form designed for mass use. It is imposed upon the automobile consumer. He takes it or leaves it, and he must take it to buy an automobile. No bargaining is engaged in with respect to it. In fact, the dealer through whom it comes to the buyer is without authority to alter it; his function is ministerial—simply to deliver it. The form warranty is not only standard with Chrysler but, as mentioned above, it is the uniform warranty of the Automobile Manufacturers Association. Members of the Association are: General Motors Inc, Ford, Chrysler, Studebaker-Packard, American Motors, (Rambler), Willys Motors, Checker Motors Corp, and International Harvester Company.
. . . . .

The gross inequality of bargaining position occupied by the consumer in the automobile industry is thus apparent. There is no competition among the car makers in the area of the express warranty. Where can the buyer go to negotiate for better protection? Such control and limitation of his remedies are inimical to the public welfare and, at the very least, call for great care by the courts to avoid injustice through application of strict common-law principles of freedom of contract. Because there is no competition among the motor vehicle manufacturers with respect to the scope of protection guaranteed to the buyer, there is no incentive on their part to stimulate goodwill in that field of public relations. Thus, there is lacking a factor existing in more competitive fields, one which tends to guarantee the safe construction of the article sold. Since all competitors operate in the same way, the urge to be careful is not so pressing. See 'Warranties of Kind and Quality', 57 Yale LJ 1389 (1948).

Although the courts, with few exceptions, have been most sensitive to problems presented by contracts resulting from gross disparity in buyer-seller bargaining

positions, they have not articulated a general principle condemning, as 'opposed to public policy, the imposition on the buyer of a skeleton warranty as a means of limiting the responsibility of the manufacturer. They have endeavored thus far to avoid a drastic departure from age-old tenets of freedom of contract by adopting doctrines of strict construction, and notice and knowledgeable assent by the buyer to the attempted exculpation of the seller. 1 Corbin on *Contracts* (1950) 337; 2 Harper & James, *supra,* 1590; Prosser, 'Warranty of Merchantable Quality', 27 Minn L Rev 117 (1932). Accordingly to be found in the cases are statements that disclaimers and the consequent limitation of liability will not be given effect if 'unfairly procured', *International Harvester Co of America v Bean,* 169 SW 549 (Ct App 1914); if not brought to the buyer's attention and he was not made understandingly aware of it, *St Louis Cordage Mills v Western Supply Co,* 154 P 646 (Sup Ct 1916);*Stevenson v BB Kirkland Seed Co,* 180 SE 197 (Sup Ct 1935).
. . . . .

The facts, detailed above, show that on the day of the accident, ten days after delivery, Mrs Henningsen was driving in a normal fashion, on a smooth highway, when unexpectedly the steering wheel and the front wheels of the car went into the bizarre action described. Can it reasonably be said that the circumstances do not warrant an inference of unsuitability for ordinary use against the manufacturer and the dealer? Obviously there is nothing in the proof to indicate in the slightest that the most unusual action of the steering wheel was caused by Mrs Henningsen's operation of the automobile on this day, or by the use of the car between delivery and the happening of the incident. Nor is there anything to suggest that any external force or condition unrelated to the manufacturing or servicing of the car operated as an inducing or even concurring factor.

It is a commonplace of our law that on a motion for dismissal all of the evidence and the inferences therefrom must be taken most favorably to the plaintiff. And if reasonable men studying the proof in that light could conclude that the car was not merchantable, the issue had to be submitted to the jury for determination. Applying that test here, we have no hesitation in holding that the settlement of the question of breach of warranty as to both defendants was properly placed in the hands of the jury. In our judgment, the evidence shown, as a matter of preponderance of probabilities, would justify the conclusion by the ultimate triers of the facts that the accident was caused by a failure of the steering mechanism of the car and that such failure constituted a breach of the warranty of both defendants.

A somewhat similar case is *Knapp v Willys-Ardmore Inc supra,* where liability was predicated upon breach of implied warranty of merchantability. Plaintiff bought a new car from defendant and drove it 107 miles in eight days. During that period it was used only for pleasure and was driven properly and without incident. Immediately before the accident, Mrs Knapp was driving along

US landmark cases

at a moderate speed, when the steering mechanism failed to function and the car suddenly veered to the right over the curb and into a telephone pole. After the collision it was noted that the tie-rod at the right end of the steering assembly had become disconnected and had dropped to the ground. Inspection showed that the rod had been bent and a connecting sleeve or turnbuckle had been broken. A witness who had been driving in the opposite direction testified that he observed the right front wheel 'wobbling' and the car 'seemed to go out of control', over the curb and into the pole. A mechanic gave some testimony from which it might be inferred that the tie-rod had been broken before the impact with the pole. It was held that the facts created a reasonable inference that the car was defective when delivered and that the defect was not caused by subsequent conduct of the plaintiff. The court pointed out that while existence of a defect cannot be found on the basis of mere conjecture or guess, yet it is not necessary to exclude every other possible cause which the ingenuity of counsel might suggest. The finding of breach of an implied warranty of merchantability was held to be circumstantially supportable by the necessary *quantum* of proof.

It may be conceded that the opinion of the automobile expert produced by the plaintiffs in the present case was not entitled to very much probative force. However, his assertion in answer to the hypothetical question that the unusual action of the steering wheel and front wheels must have been due to a mechanical defect or failure of something from the steering wheel down to the front wheels, that 'something down there had to drop off or break loose' to cause the car to act in the manner it did, cannot be rejected as a matter of law. Its evaluation under all of the circumstances was a matter for jury consideration. Defendants argue that the proof of his qualifications was not adequate to warrant the admission of his testimony. But the matter of an expert's competency to testify is primarily for the discretion of the trial court. An appellate tribunal will not interfere unless a clear abuse of discretion appears. *Carbone v Warburton,* 94 A2d 680 (1953). In our view, the experience of the witness, as an automobile repairman and as an appraiser of damaged cars, was such as to preclude a holding by us that the trial court accepted his qualifications without any reasonable basis.

In *M Dietz & Sons Inc v Miller,* 128 A2d 719 (App Div 1957), defendant purchased a new car from a dealer. He drove it only 50 miles when, on the day of the accident while driving in traffic, he applied the brakes in order to stop in back of the Dietz vehicle. The brakes failed completely and Miller ran into the rear of that car. Dietz sued Miller, who cross-claimed against the dealer for negligent installation or inspection of the power brakes. The Appellate Division properly declared that 'even where the rule of *res ipsa loquitur* does not apply, the plaintiff may nevertheless show "defendant's negligence by circumstantial or direct evidence of specific acts from which liability may be inferred." ' And further that: 'The

real issue here is the efficacy of the circumstantial proof to create a fact issue as to defendant's negligence either in installation or inspection of the unit upon installation. There can be no doubt as to the sufficiency of the evidence to justify the finding that there was a power brake failure . . . .'

Although these latter cases sound in negligence, the test for finding a jury question in them is even more stringent. Circumstantial evidence sufficient to create a jury question as to the negligence of a manufacturer or dealer would clearly justify the same result where the issue is breach of warranty. As the late Chief Justice Vanderbilt said, in *Simon v Graham Bakery,* 111 A2d 885, liability would exist notwithstanding all care was used to prevent a breach.

The defense of lack of privity against Mrs Henningsen

Both defendants contend that since there was no privity of contract between them and Mrs Henningsen, she cannot recover for breach of any warranty made by either of them. On the facts, as they were developed, we agree that she was not a party to the purchase agreement. *Faber v Creswick,* 156 A2d 252 (1959). Her right to maintain the action, therefore, depends upon whether she occupies such legal status thereunder as to permit her to take advantage of a breach of defendants' implied warranties.

For the most part the cases that have been considered dealt with the right of the buyer or consumer to maintain an action against the manufacturer where the contract of sale was with a dealer and the buyer had no contractual relationship with the manufacturer. In the present matter, the basic contractual relationship is between Claus Henningsen, Chrysler, and Bloomfield Motors Inc. The precise issue presented is whether Mrs Henningsen, who is not a party to their respective warranties, may claim under them. In our judgment, the principles of those cases and the supporting texts are just as proximately applicable to her situation. We are convinced that the cause of justice in this area of the law can be served only by recognizing that she is such a person who, in the reasonable contemplation of the parties to the warranty, might be expected to become a user of the automobile. Accordingly, her lack of privity does not stand in the way of prosecution of the injury suit against the defendant Chrysler.

The context in which the problem of privity with respect to the dealer must be considered, is much the same. Defendant Bloomfield Motors is chargeable with an implied warranty of merchantability to Claus Henningsen. There is no need to engage in a separate or extended discussion of the question. The legal principles which control are the same in quality. The manufacturer establishes the network of trade and the dealer is a unit utilized in that network to accomplish sales. He is the beneficiary of the same express and implied warranties from the manufacturer as he extends to the buyer of the automobile. If he is sued alone, he

Henningsen v Bloomfield Motors

may implead the manufacturer. *Davis v Radford*, 63 SE2d 822 (Sup Ct 1951). His understanding of the expected use of the car by persons other than the buyer is the same as that of the manufacturer. And so, his claim to the doctrine of privity should rise no higher than that of the manufacturer.

. . . . .

It is important to express the right of Mrs Henningsen to maintain her action in terms of a general principle. To what extent may lack of privity be disregarded in suits on such warranties? In that regard, the *Faber* case points the way. By a parity of reasoning, it is our opinion that an implied warranty of merchantability chargeable to either an automobile manufacturer or a dealer extends to the purchaser of the car, members of his family, and to other persons occupying or using it with his consent. It would be wholly opposed to reality to say that use by such persons is not within the anticipation of parties to such a warranty of reasonable suitability of an automobile for ordinary highway operation. Those persons must be considered within the distributive chain.

Harper and James suggest that this remedy ought to run to members of the public, bystanders, for example, who are in the path of harm from a defective automobile. 2 Harper & James, *supra*, note 6 P 1572. Section 2-318 of the Uniform Commercial Code proposes that the warranty be extended to 'any natural person who is in the family or household of his buyer or who is a guest in his home if it is reasonable to expect that such person may use, consume or be affected by the goods and who is injured in person by breach of the warranty'. And the section provides also that 'A seller may not exclude or limit the operation' of the extension. A footnote thereto says that beyond this provision 'the section is neutral and is not intended to enlarge or restrict the developing case law on whether the seller's warranties, given to his buyer, who resells, extend to other persons in the distributive chain'. Uniform Commercial Code, *supra*, at p 100.

It is not necessary in this case to establish the outside limits of the warranty protection. For present purposes, with respect to automobiles, it suffices to promulgate the principle set forth above.

In his charge as to Mrs Henningsen's right to recover on the implied warranty, the trial court referred to her husband's testimony that he was buying the car for her use, and then instructed the jury that on such facts the warranty extended to her. In view of our holding, obviously the protection of the warranty runs to her as an incident of the sale without regard to such testimony. Accordingly, the contention that the instruction was reversible error must be rejected.

Defendants rely upon certain cases for the proposition that lack of privity of contract bars Mrs Henningsen's recovery. The pertinent ones are *Tomlinson v Armour & Co*, 70A 314; *Schlosser v Goldberg*, 9 A2d 699 (Sup Ct 1939). *Tomlinson v Armour & Co* provides the foundation for the others. It was decided 52 years ago and the principle on which defendants seek support for their case is contained in a short statement which, if applied in the light of the modern marketing conditions, is not inconsistent with the basic substance of the rule we have now espoused. In discussing the legal consequences of a sale of canned ham, Chancellor Pitney said: 'Whether a warranty be express or implied, it is a matter of contract, rendering the maker liable in case of breach, notwithstanding he used all care to prevent a breach, but rendering him liable in ordinary circumstances only to the party with whom he contracted, *or to others for whose benefit the contract was made*'.

In 1908, the need of the community for the making of distinctions growing out of the nature of the contract was not as pressing as it is in this commercial era. A common rule was applied, as indicated by the citation of *Marvin Safe Co v Ward*, (Sup Ct 1884), and *Styles v FR Long Company*, 51 A 710 (Sup Ct 1902), which involved agreements wholly unrelated to the sale of products for consumer use. In this day, given the present situation, it is extremely unlikely that such an enlightened jurist as Chancellor Pitney would not find his expression that 'others for whose benefit the contract was made' could sue for its breach compatible in spirit with the doctrine we deem to be necessary in the interest of justice. In any event, to the extent that *Tomlinson v Armour & Co* and its cited progeny conflict with our ruling, they can no longer be considered the law of this state.

. . . . .

All other grounds of appeal raised by both parties have been examined and we find no reversible error in any of them. Under all of the circumstances outlined above, the judgments in favor of the plaintiffs and against the defendants are affirmed.

US landmark cases

1963 *Greenman v Yuba Power Products*

COMMENTARY

We have now reached the turning point in the development of the law of product liability. Reliance on negligence or on breach of warranty is no longer necessary, and the victim of a defective product in future will be able to base his claim on a new doctrine, strict liability in tort. This is not absolute liability, although at times it seems to approach very closely to liability without fault, but the law is in effect saying that if a product is defective, there need be no investigation into the reason. There is another requirement too; the manufacturer is liable only when he knows that it is to be used without inspection for defects. It is still a defence for a manufacturer to say that he had reasonable cause to rely on somebody else in the chain of distribution to inspect the product, provided, of course, that the defect could have been discovered by such an inspection.

Strict liability did not arrive without warning. Particularly, Justice Traynor himself had said (in the *Escola* case) 19 years previously that it was time to recognise that there was an absolute liability on a manufacturer when a defective product causes injury to human beings. At that time he had also said that liability existed when the manufacturer knew that the product would be used without inspection. However, he did make one change in his statement of the rule. Whereas in 1944 he had spoken of 'absolute liability', in 1963 he said 'strict liability', and we should continue to insist on the distinction. Absolute liability is a term more associated with criminal law than with the law of tort, as when an accused person may be convicted of an offence without the usual requirement of *mens rea*. In tort, strict liability is not unknown, as in the rule in *Rylands v Fletcher* which imposes liability on a person who brings a dangerous thing on his land. If the dangerous thing escapes, there is liability for any harm done, and there is no enquiry into the negligence or otherwise of the landowner. That, of course, is an English decision, but the rule is well known to American lawyers. The similarity of this rule and strict liability in tort is one reason why the acceptance of strict liability was not difficult.

Another warning of strict liability had been seen in 1958 (*Trust v Arden Farms Co*, 324 P2d 583) when the California Supreme Court by a four to three majority rejected a claim for injury caused by the shattering of a milk bottle. The majority held that the plaintiff, who was relying on *res ipsa loquitur*, failed because he had not affirmatively proved that the bottle had remained unchanged since it left the hands of the manufacturer. Justice Traynor was on that court, and repeated his arguments that public policy required a change in the law.

Up to the *Greenman* decision the law could have followed other paths that would have led to the same result as strict liability. There was *res ipsa loquitur* as used in the *Escola* case, and there were the decisions enlarging the scope of warranty. These principles allowed the *Greenman* court to base its decision on the concept of strict liability, but Justice Traynor himself justified the decision on other grounds. He stressed the aspect of public policy, on the social need for a remedy when a person is injured by a defective product. In 1965, Justice Traynor gave a lecture at the University of Tennessee and he started by saying that they had come a long way from *MacPherson v Buick*. The great expansion of a manufacturer's liability for negligence since that case marked 'the transition from industrial revolution to a settled industrial society'. The courts had originally sought to limit the duty of manufacturers (as in the English decision of *Winterbottom v Wright*, see section III later). As the record of injuries grew, and the law refused compensation, the courts changed their attitude, encouraged first by Judge Cardozo in New York and later by Justice Traynor himself in 1963.

At the time of the *Greenman* decision, the American Law Institute was working on a new edition of its Restatement of the Law of Torts, and the force of the decision was such that a new section was inserted. This was the famous section 402A, which now reads:

Special Liability of Seller of Product for Physical Harm to User or Consumer

(1) One who sells any product in a defective condition unreasonably dangerous to the user or consumer or to his property is subject to liability for physical harm thereby caused to the ultimate user or consumer, or to his property, if
(a) the seller is engaged in the business of selling such a product, and
(b) it is expected to and does reach the user or consumer without substantial change in the condition in which it is sold.
(2) The rule stated in subsection (1) applies although
(a) the seller has exercised all possible care in the preparation and sale of his product, and
(b) the user and consumer has not bought the product from or entered into any contractual relation with the seller.

This statement of the rule leaves many points unsettled. For example, the definition of 'product' and liability to a bystander are among the issues that subsequent cases have settled. Moreover, the Restatement of Torts is not a binding authority on state courts, and each state has had to consider whether to adopt the rule and the wording to be accepted. Thus, California has adopted the section without the words 'unreasonably dangerous' and another case we are to discuss, *Cronin v Olson*, is concerned with that point.

The vast majority of states have accepted the idea of strict liability, and most of those have accepted the rule as laid down in section 402A. However, there are some states that do not recognise strict liability, and deal with defective products through negligence and extended warranty theories. This minority of states includes Alabama, Delaware, Massachusetts, Michigan, North Carolina, Virginia and Wyoming. Since the law is never static, the views of state courts and legislatures change from time to time. No legal action should be undertaken without up-to-date advice from a local lawyer.

The editors of the Restatement of Torts, Second, added a number of comments to section 402A, and these comments provide a more detailed picture of the whole concept. The attention given to section 402A has overshadowed section 402B, which has been used on a relatively small number of occasions. It imposes liability for misrepresentation of the character or quality of a product.

JUDGMENT

Supreme Court of California
January 24, 1963

Greenman
versus
Yuba Power Products Inc

Before Chief Justice Gibson and Justices Traynor, Schauer, McComb, Peters, Tobriner and Peek

Traynor, *Justice.* Plaintiff brought this action for damages against the retailer and the manufacturer of a Shopsmith, a combination power tool that could be used as a saw, drill, and wood lathe. He saw a Shopsmith demonstrated by the retailer and studied a brochure prepared by the manufacturer. He decided he wanted a Shopsmith for his home work shop, and his wife bought and gave him one for Christmas in 1955. In 1957 he bought the necessary attachments to use the Shopsmith as a lathe for turning a large piece of wood he wished to make into a chalice. After he had worked on the piece of wood several times without difficulty, it suddenly flew out of the machine and struck him on the forehead, inflicting serious injuries. About ten and half months later, he gave the retailer and the manufacturer written notice of claimed breaches of warranties and filed a complaint against them alleging such breaches and negligence.

After a trial before a jury, the court ruled that there was no evidence that the retailer was negligent or had breached any express warranty and that the manufacturer was not liable for the breach of any implied warranty. Accordingly, it submitted to the jury only the cause of action alleging breach of implied warranties against the retailer and the causes of action alleging negligence and breach of express warranties against the manufacturer. The jury returned a verdict for the retailer

against plaintiff and for plaintiff against the manufacturer in the amount of $65,000. The trial court denied the manufacturer's motion for a new trial and entered judgment on the verdict. The manufacturer and plaintiff appeal. Plaintiff seeks a reversal of the part of the judgment in favor of the retailer, however, only in the event that the part of the judgment against the manufacturer is reversed.

Plaintiff introduced substantial evidence that his injuries were caused by defective design and construction of the Shopsmith. His expert witnesses testified that inadequate set screws were used to hold parts of the machine together so that normal vibration caused the tailstock of the lathe to move away from the piece of wood being turned permitting it to fly out of the lathe. They also testified that there were other more positive ways of fastening the parts of the machine together, the use of which would have prevented the accident. The jury could therefore reasonably have concluded that the manufacturer negligently constructed the Shopsmith. The jury could also reasonably have concluded that statements in the manufacturer's brochure were untrue, that they constituted express warranties,[1] and that plaintiff's injuries were caused by their breach.

The manufacturer contends, however, that plaintiff did not give it notice of breach of warranty within a reasonable time and that therefore his cause of action for breach of warranty is barred by section 1769 of the Civil Code. Since it cannot be determined whether the verdict against it was based on the negligence or warranty cause of action or both, the manufacturer concludes that the error in presenting the warranty cause of action to the jury was prejudicial.

Section 1769 of the Civil Code provides: 'In the absence of express or implied agreement of the parties, acceptance of the goods by the buyer shall not discharge the seller from liability in damages or other legal remedy for breach of any promise or warranty in the contract to sell or the sale. But, if, after acceptance of the goods, the buyer fails to give notice to the seller of the breach of any promise or warranty within a reasonable time after the buyer knows, or ought to know of such breach, the seller shall not be liable therefor.'

Like other provisions of the Uniform Sales Act (Civ Code, sections 1721-1800), section 1769 deals with the rights of the parties to a contract of sale or a sale. It does not provide that notice must be given of the breach of a warranty that arises independently of a contract of sale between the parties. Such warranties are not imposed by the Sales Act, but are the product of

---

[1] In this respect the trial court limited the jury to a consideration of two statements in the manufacturer's brochure. (1) 'WHEN SHOPSMITH IS IN HORIZONTAL POSITION—Rugged construction of frame provides rigid support from end to end. Heavy centerless-ground steel tubing insures perfect alignment of components.' (2) 'SHOPSMITH maintains its accuracy because every component has positive locks that hold adjustments through rough or precision work.'

common law decisions that have recognized them in a variety of situations. (See *Gagne v Bertran*, 275 P2d 15, and authorities cited; *Peterson v Lamb Rubber Co*, 353 P2d 575; *Klein v Duchess Sandwich Co Ltd*, 93 P2d 799; *Burr v Sherwin Williams Co*, 268 P2d 1041; *Souza & McCue Constr Co v Superior Court*, 370 P2d 338.) It is true that in many of these situations the court has invoked the Sales Act definitions of warranties (Civ Code, sections 1732, 1735) in defining the defendant's liability, but it has done so, not because the statutes so required, but because they provide appropriate standards for the court to adopt under the circumstances presented. (See *Clinkscales v Carver*, 136 P2d 777; *Dana v Sutton Motor Sales*, 363 P2d 881.)

The notice requirement of section 1769, however, is not an appropriate one for the court to adopt in actions by injured consumers against manufacturers with whom they have not dealt. (*La Hue v Coca-Cola Bottling*, 314 P2d 421, 422; *Chapman v Brown*, DC 198 FSupp 78.) 'As between the immediate parties to the sale (the notice requirement) is a sound commercial rule, designed to protect the seller against unduly delayed claims for damages. As applied to personal injuries, and notice to a remote seller, it becomes a booby-trap for the unwary. The injured consumer is seldom "steeped in the business practice which justifies the rule", (James, 'Product Liability', 34 Texas L Rev 44, 192, 197) and at least until he has had legal advice it will not occur to him to give notice to one with whom he has had no dealings.' (Prosser, 'Strict Liability to the Consumer', 69 Yale L J 1099, 1130.) It is true that in *Jones v Burgermeister Brewing Corp*, 18 Cal Rptr 311; *Perry v Thrifty Drug Co*, 9 Cal Rptr 50; *Arata v Tonegato*, 314 P2d 130, and *Maecherlein v Sealy Mattress Co*, 302 P2d 331, the court assumed that notice of breach of warranty must be given in an action by a consumer against a manufacturer. Since in those cases, however, the court did not consider the question whether a distinction exists between a warranty based on a contract between the parties and one imposed on a manufacturer not in privity with the consumer, the decisions are not authority for rejecting the rule of the *La Hue* and *Chapman* cases, *supra*. (*Peterson v Lamb Rubber Co*, 353 P2d 575; *People v Banks*, 348 P2d 102.) We conclude, therefore, that even if plaintiff did not give timely notice of breach of warranty to the manufacturer, his cause of action based on the representations contained in the brochure was not barred.

Moreover, to impose strict liability on the manufacturer under the circumstances of this case, it was not necessary for plaintiff to establish an express warranty as defined in section 1732 of the Civil Code. A manufacturer is strictly liable in tort when an article he places on the market, knowing that it is to be used without inspection for defects, proves to have a defect that causes injury to a human being. Recognized first in the case of unwholesome food products, such liability has now been extended to a variety of other products that create as great or greater hazards if defective.

(*Peterson v Lamb Rubber Co* (grinding wheel); *Vallis v Canada Dry Ginger Ale Inc* (bottle); *Jones v Burgermeister Brewing Corp* (bottle); *Gottsdanker v Cutter Laboratories* (vaccine); *McQuaide v Bridgport Brass Co* (insect spray); *Bowles v Zimmer Manufacturing Co* (surgical pin); *Thompson v Reedman* (automobile); *Chapman v Brown* affd *Brown v Chapman* (skirt); *B F Goodrich Co v Hammond* (automobile tire); *Markovich v McKesson and Robbins Inc* (home permanent); *Graham v Bottenfield's Inc* (hair dye); *General Motors Corp v Dodson* (automobile); **Henningsen v Bloomfield Motors Inc* (automobile); *Hinton v Republic Aviation Corporation* (airplane).)

Although in these cases strict liability has usually been based on the theory of an express or implied warranty running from the manufacturer to the plaintiff, the abandonment of the requirement of a contract between them, the recognition that the liability is not assumed by agreement but imposed by law (see *eg Graham v Bottenfield's Inc*, 269 P2d 413; *Rogers v Toni Home Permanent Co*, 147 NE2d 612; *Decker & Sons Inc v Capps*, 164 SW2d 828), and the refusal to permit the manufacturer to define the scope of its own responsibility for defective products (*Henningsen v Bloomfield Motors Inc*; *General Motors Corp v Dodson*) make clear that the liability is not one governed by the law of contract warranties but by the law of strict liability in tort. Accordingly, rules defining and governing warranties that were developed to meet the needs of commercial transactions cannot properly be invoked to govern the manufacturer's liability to those injured by their defective products unless those rules also serve the purposes for which such liability is imposed.

We need not recanvass the reasons for imposing strict liability on the manufacturer. They have been fully articulated in the cases cited above. (See also 2 Harper and James, *Torts*, sections 28.15-28.16 pages 1569-1574; Prosser, 'Strict Liability to the Consumer', 69 Yale L J 1099; **Escola v Coca Cola Bottling Co*, 150 P2d 436, concurring opinion.) The purpose of such liability is to insure that the costs of injuries resulting from defective products are borne by the manufacturers that put such products on the market rather than by the injured persons who are powerless to protect themselves. Sales warranties serve this purpose fitfully at best. (See Prosser, 'Strict Liability to the Consumer', 69 Yale LJ 1099, 1124-1134.) In the present case, for example, plaintiff was able to plead and prove an express warranty only because he read and relied on the representations of the Shopsmith's ruggedness contained in the manufacturer's brochure. Implicit in the machine's presence on the market, however, was a representation that it would safely do the jobs for which it was built. Under these circumstances, it should not be controlling whether plaintiff selected the machine because of the statements in the brochure, or because of the machine's own appearance of excellence that belied the defect lurking beneath the surface, or because he merely assumed that it would safely do the jobs it was built to do. It should not be controlling whether the details of the sales from manufacturer to retailer and from retailer to plaintiff's wife were such that one or more of the implied warranties of the sales act arose. (Civ Code, section 1735.) 'The remedies of injured consumers ought not to be made to depend upon the intricacies of the law of sales.' (*Ketterer v Armour & Co,* DC 200 F322, 323; *Klein v Duchess Sandwich Co,* 93 P2d 799.) To establish the manufacturer's liability it was sufficient that plaintiff proved that he was injured while using the Shopsmith in a way it was intended to be used as a result of a defect in design and manufacture of which plaintiff was not aware that made the Shopsmith unsafe for its intended use.

The manufacturer contends that the trial court erred in refusing to give three instructions requested by it. It appears from the record, however, that the substance of two of the requested instructions was adequately covered by the instructions given and that the third instruction was not supported by the evidence.

The judgment is affirmed.

Chief Justice Gibson and Justices Schauer, McComb, Peters, Tobriner and Peek concur.

1968 *Larsen v General Motors*

COMMENTARY

This is a negligence case, although there is no difficulty about applying its principles in strict liability. It is also a design case, and emphasises the difficulty of establishing liability in design cases without using the language of negligence, even when the action is based on strict liability. The concept of duty is central to the decision, and the issue is whether the duty of an automobile manufacturer extended to persons injured in a collision that was not caused by any defect in the vehicle.

Firstly, there is a collision, caused perhaps by somebody's negligence or even by sheer chance, and secondly there is a collision between an occupant of the car and some part of the interior of the vehicle. It is this 'second collision' that causes additional injuries that would not have been caused if the manufacturer had taken proper care over the design of the car. When injured persons attempted to hold manufacturers liable for these additional injuries, they did not succeed. They were told that the duty of a manufacturer was to make a car safe for its intended use. A collision was not an intended use, and therefore the manufacturer had no duty to an injured person. That was the decision in *Evans v General Motors,* 359 F2d 822, a 1966 case that was regarded for some years as laying down a correct principle.

After ten years, however, statistics and experience proved that most motor cars will be involved in an accident involving personal injury at some time during their existence. This is a melancholy truth that none of us will challenge, and that the law now recognises. Even the law could not argue that an accident was an intended use of a car, and the reasoning adopted by the courts, in *Larsen* and in subsequent cases, is that the test of liability is not 'intended use' but 'foreseeable use'. Collisions can be foreseen, and manufacturers have a duty to reduce as much as they can the consequences of a collision.

In 1977 the principle was applied in *Huff v White Motors,* 565 F2d 104, and the court then said 'the collision, the defect and the injury are interdependent and should be viewed as a combined event. Such an event is the foreseeable risk that a manufacturer should assume. Since collisions for whatever cause are foreseeable events, the scope of liability should be commensurate with the scope of the foreseeable risk'. Collisions are the natural consequences of the intended use of automobiles.

This reasoning has been almost universally adopted, and Mississippi now appears to be the only state that rejects liability for 'second collisions'. The Mississippi Supreme Court has held that the chain of causation was broken when injury was caused by an event for which the manufacturer was not responsible, namely the original accident (*GM v Howard,* 244 So2d 726,

US landmark cases

1971). Although no other state agrees with this reasoning, it would be applied by federal courts in a product liability case under Mississippi law. One federal court has also determined (in *McClung v Ford*, 472 F2d 240, 1973) that West Virginia law would follow *Evans* and not *Larsen*, but no West Virginia court has decided the issue. Although 'second collision' cases are mainly concerned with motor cars, the principle has been applied to other products, such as aircraft (in *McGee v Cessna*, 82 Cal App 1005, 1978).

Some practical difficulties can arise when a manufacturer is liable for second collision injuries. The court will have to determine the extent of the liability and will have to apportion the damages between the manufacturer whose defective design caused additional injuries and the tortfeasor responsible for the first collision. This is a problem familiar to juries in comparative negligence cases, and is an issue of fact for the jury and not an issue of law for the judge.

The general tort principle is that when two or more persons jointly cause an injury, each of the tortfeasors is liable for the entire amount of the damages. This principle has been applied in second collision cases, as in *Horn v G M*, 551 P2d 398, 1976, in which it was held that a manufacturer was liable for all the harm done if the defect was a substantial factor in causing it.

There is also the principle that a manufacturer cannot be held responsible for harm he did not cause, and therefore courts have held that the manufacturer was liable only for the enhancement of the injury caused by the defect for which he was responsible (for example, *De la Concha v Pinero*, 104 So 2d 25, a Florida pre-strict liability case of 1958). This is a question of causation, and generally the plaintiff must show that the injury resulted from the defect. The application of principles in practice is not easy, and the Supreme Court of Oregon laid down an acceptable procedure in *May v Portland Jeep Inc*, 509 P2d 24, a 1973 case, in which a jeep overturned and the plaintiff was pinned underneath. There was a protective roll bar, but 'a jury could reasonably conclude that a major portion of plaintiff's injuries would not have occurred in the absence of the collapse of the bar. There is no way of determining, of course, what the extent of plaintiff's injuries would have been had the roll bar not collapsed. However, we allow juries to make somewhat inexact determinations, such as the extent of pain and suffering and its value in money'.

The general principle, applicable as much in second collision cases as in other torts, is given in the Restatement of Torts, Second, section 433A:
'(1) Damages for harm are to be apportioned among two or more causes where (a) there are distinct harms, or (b) there is a reasonable basis for determining the contribution of each cause to a single harm.
(2) Damage for other harm cannot be apportioned among two or more causes'.

JUDGMENT

United States Court of Appeals, Eighth Circuit
March 11, 1968

Larsen
versus
General Motors Corporation

Before Circuit Judges Blackmun, Gibson and Heaney

Floyd R Gibson, *Circuit Judge.* The driver of an automobile claims injury as a result of an alleged negligent design of the steering assembly of the automobile. The alleged defect in design did not cause the accident, and the manufacturer asserts the law imposes no duty of care in the design of an automobile to make it more safe to occupy in the event of a collision. The trial court agreed, rendering summary judgment in favor of the manufacturer, reported at 274 F Supp 461 (D C Minn 1967). We reverse and remand.

The plaintiff-appellant, Erling David Larsen, received severe bodily injuries while driving, with the consent of the owner, a 1963 Chevrolet Corvair on February 18, 1964 in the state of Michigan. A head-on collision, with the impact occurring on the left front corner of the Corvair, caused a severe rearward thrust of the steering mechanism into the plaintiff's head. The Corvair was manufactured by General Motors Corporation and liability is asserted against General Motors on an alleged design defect in the steering assembly and the placement or attachment of the component parts of the steering assembly to the structure of the Corvair.

The plaintiff does not contend that the design caused the accident but that because of the design he received injuries he would not have otherwise received or, in the alternative, his injuries would not have been as severe. The rearward displacement of the steering shaft on the left frontal impact was much greater on the Corvair than it would be in other cars that were designed to protect against such a rearward displacement. The plaintiff's complaint alleges (1) negligence in design of the steering assembly; (2) negligent failure to warn of the alleged latent or inherently dangerous condition to the user of the steering assembly placement; and (3) breach of express and implied warranties of merchantability of the vehicle's intended use.

General Motors contends it 'has no duty whatsoever to design and manufacture a vehicle . . . . .' which is otherwise 'safe' or 'safer' to occupy during collision impacts,' and since there is no duty there can be no actionable negligence on its part to either design a safe or more safe car or to warn of any inherent or latent defects in design that might make its cars less safe than some other cars manufactured either by it or other manufacturers.

Larsen v General Motors

The District Court for the District of Minnesota rendered summary judgment in favor of General Motors on the basis that there was no common law duty on the manufacturer 'to make a vehicle which would protect the plaintiff from injury in the event of a head-on collision' and dismissed the complaint. A timely appeal was filed. This is a diversity case in a requisite jurisdictional amount and the parties have stipulated that the law of Michigan applies.

Since a summary judgment was rendered on the pleadings and exhibits before the court under Rule 56, Fed R Civ P, we will take the well pled allegations in the complaint at their face value and assume for purposes of discussion and decision that there was a defect in the design of the steering assembly of the Corvair. Then if there are no issues or any discernible theory on which the losing party could recover, a summary judgment is proper. However, a summary judgment proceeding does not provide a very satisfactory approach in tort cases. *Williams v Chick,* 373 F2d 330 (1967).

The District Court found this case to be closely related to the factual situation of *Evans v General Motors Corporation,* 359 F2d 822 (1966), which held in a divided decision that a manufacturer is under no duty to make its automobile 'accident-proof' or 'foolproof' nor to render its vehicle 'more' safe where the danger to be avoided is obvious to all. The District Court discussed other cases, which will be set forth in this opinion, and concluded as follows:
'All of these factors when considered together lead to but one conclusion: The defendant GM's duty toward the public is to design an automobile which is reasonably safe when driven and which contains no latent or hidden defects which could cause an accident and subsequent injury . . . . .
No contention is here made . . . . .
that any design defect caused the accident which allegedly resulted in the plaintiff's injuries. In view of this fact and because this court believes that any standards in this area must be left to the legislature, this court has no alternative but to find that the defendant was not negligent in its design and construction of the 1963 Corvair automobile in that it was under no duty to make a vehicle which would protect the plaintiff from injury in the event of a head-on collision.' The District Court also held that there was no duty to warn since the law only requires a warning when the defects would render the product unsafe for its intended use and that its intended purpose was transportation.

Both parties agree that the question of a manufacturer's duty in the design of an automobile or of any chattel is a question of law for the court. The decisional law is in accord. *Evans v General Motors Corporation, supra; Schemel v General Motors Corporation,* 261 F Supp 134 (S D Ind 1966), aff'd 384 F2d 802 (7 Cir 1967); *Kahn v Chrysler Corporation,* 221 FSupp 677 (SD Tex 1963).

General Motors contends that it has no duty to produce a vehicle in which it is safe to collide or which is accident-proof or incapable of injurious misuse. It views its duty as extending only to producing a vehicle that is reasonably fit for its intended use or for the purpose for which it was made and that is free from hidden defects; and that the intended use of a vehicle and the purpose for which it is manufactured do not include its participation in head-on collisions or any other type of impact, regardless of the manufacturer's ability to foresee that such collisions may occur. General Motors cites as supporting its contention, *Evans v General Motors Corporation, supra; Willis v Chrysler Corporation,* 264 F Supp 1010 (S D Tex 1967); *Shumard v General Motors Corporation,* 270 F Supp 311 (S D Ohio 1967); *Schemel v General Motors Corporation, supra; Campo v Scofield,* 301 NY 468, 95 NE2d 802 (1950).

The plaintiff maintains that General Motors' view of its duty is too narrow and restrictive and that an automobile manufacturer is under a duty to use reasonable care in the design of the automobile to make it safe to the user for its foreseeable use and that its intended use or purpose is for travel on the streets and highways, including the possibility of impact or collision with other vehicles or stationary objects. Plaintiff's reliance is placed on *Ford Motor Company v Zahn,* 265 F2d 729 (1959); *Blitzstein v Ford Motor Company,* 288 F2d 738 (1961); *Spruill v Boyle-Midway Inc,* 308 F2d 79 (1962); *Comstock v General Motors Corporation,* 99 NW2d 627 (1959).

There is a line of cases directly supporting General Motors' contention that negligent design of an automobile is not actionable, where the alleged defective design is not a causative factor in the accident. The latest leading case on this point is *Evans v General Motors Corporation, supra.* A divided court there held that General Motors in designing an 'X' body frame without perimeter support, instead of an allegedly more safe perimeter body frame, was not liable for the death of a user allegedly caused by the designed defect because the defendant's design could not have functioned to avoid the collision. The court reasoned: 'A manufacturer is not under a duty to make his automobile accident-proof or foolproof; nor must he render the vehicle 'more' safe where the danger to be avoided is obvious to all. *Campo v Scofield.* Perhaps it would be desirable to require manufacturers to construct automobiles in which it would be safe to collide, but that would be a legislative function, not an aspect of judicial interpretation of existing law. *Campo v Scofield, supra.* The intended purpose of an automobile does not include its participation in collisions with other objects, despite the manufacturer's ability to foresee the possibility that such collisions may occur.' A strong dissent was written by Judge Kiley in which he contended that General Motors had a duty in designing its automobile to use such care that reasonable protection would be given a user against death or injuries from foreseeable yet unavoidable accidents.

In *General Motors Corporation v Muncy,* 367 F2d

US landmark cases

493 (5 Cir 1966), the court reversed the District Court judgment allowing recovery against General Motors for an allegedly negligent design of an ignition switch, which allowed the key to be removed when the motor was running. The court held that under Texas law there was no liability for a defective design of the ignition switch and also found no actionable negligence in an alleged defective accelerator. No reasons are given for the decision on the ignition switch except that a state case involving the same parties had produced a similar ruling and a voluntary non-suit was taken before judgment was entered. The case was later refiled in the United States District Court. The Texas court in *Muncy v General Motors Corp,* 357 SW2d 430 (Tex Civ App 1962), held there was no showing of negligence as the parties had not shown 'that the car in question was dangerous if used properly and in the manner and for the purpose for which it was intended'; and further held that the car was not being lawfully used under Texas law, which provided that no person in charge of a vehicle shall permit it to stand unattended without first stopping the engine. The court further noted that in the absence of evidence to the contrary it would not presume that General Motors designed the car for use in a manner violative of the law, or that it should have anticipated such illegal use as probable.

In *Shumard v General Motors Corporation,* the United States District Court for the Southern District of Ohio, *supra,* held there was no liability where the alleged design defects in a 1962 Corvair automobile caused it to erupt into flames on impact, killing the plaintiff's decedent. The court said: 'No duty exists to make an automobile fireproof, nor does a manufacturer have to make a product which is 'accident-proof' or 'foolproof'. *Campo v Scofield, supra'* and relied upon the *Evans* case for its holding that: 'The duty of a manufacturer in the design of automobiles does not include designing a 'fireproof' automobile or an automobile in which passengers are guaranteed to be safe from fire. A manufacturer has no duty to design an automobile that will not catch fire under any circumstances. The manufacturer's duty is to design an automobile which will not present a fire hazard during its normal intended operation.' Another United States District Court for the Southern District of Texas in *Kahn v Chrysler Corporation, supra* held that the manufacturer was under no duty to so design its automobiles so that it would be safe for a child to ride his bike into it while it was parked. The child there struck the protruding fins of a 1957 Dodge. Relying on the Texas case of *Muncy v General Motors Corp, supra,* the court stated the manufacturer's duty of care 'to be concomitant with normal use and for the ordinary purpose of the vehicle'. The United States District Court for the Southern District of Texas in *Willis v Chrysler Corporation,* 264 F Supp 1010 (1967), in a Memorandum Opinion followed the rationale of the *Evans* and *Kahn* cases and held that Chrysler Corporation as an automobile manufacturer did not breach an implied warranty of fitness even though the design of the car allegedly allowed it to separate into two sections

as a result of a high-speed collision. The predicate for its decision was that the design of the automobile was reasonably fit for the purpose for which it was intended, and the manufacturer's duty did not extend to designing an accident-proof or foolproof vehicle, nor was it under a duty to design an automobile that would maintain its structural integrity on severe impact, citing the *Gossett* and *Evans* cases among others.

Since General Motors concedes on the negligence count that its duty of care extends to designing and constructing an automobile that is reasonably safe for its intended use of being driven on the roads and highways and that contains no latent or hidden defects which could cause an accident and subsequent injuries, it would be superfluous to review the decisions holding manufacturers liable for negligent construction or design that were the proximate cause of an accident and subsequent injuries. Since ** MacPherson v Buick Motor Co,* 111 NE 1050 (1916), the courts have consistently held a manufacturer liable for negligent construction of an automobile. And also other manufacturers, *Lovejoy v Minneapolis-Moline Power Implement Company,* 79 NW2d 688 (1956) (broken flywheel on a tractor).

The courts, however have been somewhat reluctant to impose liability upon a manufacturer for negligent product design in the automobile field. In *Gossett v Chrysler Corporation,* 359 F2d 84 (1966) the court reversed a judgment based on an alleged defectively designed truck hood latch that allowed the hood to spring open while the vehicle was in motion causing an accident, but did recognize a duty in connection with design. . . . . .

The early case of *Davlin v Henry Ford & Son,* 20 F2d 317 (1927), though it did not permit recovery, did recognize the duty of care in design by stating: 'Its duty was to use reasonable care in employing designs, selecting materials, and making assemblies, in the construction of a tractor, which would fairly meet any emergency of use which could reasonably be anticipated.'. . . . .

Accepting, therefore, the principle that a manufacturer's duty of design and construction extends to producing a product that is reasonably fit for its intended use and free of hidden defects that could render it unsafe for such use, the issue narrows on the proper interpretation of 'intended use'. Automobiles are made for use on the roads and highways in transporting persons and cargo to and from various points., This intended use cannot be carried out without encountering in varying degrees the statistically proved hazard of injury-producing impacts of various types. The manufacturer should not be heard to say that it does not intend its product to be involved in any accident when it can easily foresee and when it knows that the probability over the life of its product is high, that it will be involved in some type of injury-producing accident. O'Connell in his article 'Taming the Automobile', 58 Nw U L Rev 299, 348 (1963) cites that between one-fourth to two-thirds of all automobiles during their use at some time are involved in an accident

Larsen v General Motors

producing injury or death. Other statistics are available showing the frequency and certainty of fatal and injury-producing accidents. It should be recognized that the environment in which a product is used must be taken into consideration by the manufacturer. *Spruill v Boyle-Midway Inc,* 308 F2d 79 (1962).

We think the 'intended use' construction urged by General Motors is much too narrow and unrealistic. Where the manufacturer's negligence in design causes an unreasonable risk to be imposed upon the user of its products, the manufacturer should be liable for the injury caused by its failure to exercise reasonable care in the design. These injuries are readily foreseeable as an incident to the normal and expected use of an automobile. While automobiles are not made for the purpose of colliding with each other, a frequent and inevitable contingency of normal automobile use will result in collisions and injury-producing impacts. No rational basis exists for limiting recovery to situations where the defect in design or manufacture was the causative factor of the accident, as the accident and the resulting injury, usually caused by the so-called 'second collision' of the passenger with the interior part of the automobile, all are foreseeable. Where the injuries or enhanced injuries are due to the manufacturer's failure to use reasonable care to avoid subjecting the user of its products to an unreasonable risk of injury, general negligence principles should be applicable. The sole function of an automobile is not just to provide a means of transportation, it is to provide a means of safe transportation or as safe as is reasonably possible under the present state of the art.

We do agree that under the present state of the art an automobile manufacturer is under no duty to design an accident-proof or foolproof vehicle or even one that floats on water, but such manufacturer is under a duty to use reasonable care in the design of its vehicle to avoid subjecting the user to an unreasonable risk of injury in the event of a collision. Collisions with or without fault of the user are clearly foreseeable by the manufacturer and are statistically inevitable.[1]

The intended use and purpose of an automobile is to travel on the streets and highways, which travel more often than not is in close proximity to other vehicles and at speeds that carry the possibility, probability, and potential of injury-producing impacts. The realities of the intended and actual use are well known to the manufacturer and to the public and these realities should be squarely faced by the manufacturer and the courts. We perceive of no sound reason, either in logic or experience, nor any command in precedent, why the

manufacturer should not be held to a reasonable duty of care in the design of its vehicle consonant with the state of the art to minimize the effect of accidents. The manufacturers are not insurers but should be held to a standard of reasonable care in design to provide a reasonably safe vehicle in which to travel. *Ford Motor Company v Zahn, supra.* Our streets and highways are increasingly hazardous for the intended normal use of travel and transportation. While advances in highway engineering and non-access, dual highways have considerably increased the safety factor on a miles traveled ratio to accidents, the constant increasing number of vehicles gives impetus to the need of designing and constructing a vehicle that is reasonably safe for the purpose of such travel. At least, the unreasonable risk should be eliminated and reasonable steps in design taken to minimize the injury-producing effect of impacts.

This duty of reasonable care in design rests on common law negligence that a manufacturer of an article should use reasonable care in the design and manufacture of his product to eliminate any unreasonable risk of foreseeable injury. The duty of reasonable care in design should be viewed in light of the risk. While all risks cannot be eliminated nor can a crash-proof vehicle be designed under the present state of the art, there are many common-sense factors in design, which are or should be well known to the manufacturer that will minimize or lessen the injurious effects of a collision. The standard of reasonable care is applied in many other negligence situations and should be applied here.

The courts since *MacPherson v Buick Motor Co,* 111 NE 1050 (1916) have held that a manufacturer of automobiles is under a duty to construct a vehicle that is free of latent and hidden defects. We can perceive of no significant difference in imposing a common law duty of a reasonable standard of care in design the same as in construction. A defect in either can cause severe injury or death and a negligent design defect should be actionable. Any design defect not causing the accident would not subject the manufacturer to liability for the entire damage, but the manufacturer should be liable for that portion of the damage or injury caused by the defective design over and above the damage or injury that probably would have occurred as a result of the impact or collision absent the defective design. The manufacturer argues that this is difficult to assess. This is no persuasive answer and, even if difficult, there is no reason to abandon the injured party to his dismal fate as a traffic statistic, when the manufacturer owed, at least, a common law duty of reasonable care in the design and construction of its product. The obstacles of apportionment are not insurmountable.

. . . . .

General Motors in arguing against what it views as an expanded duty of a care in design makes the statement that this duty 'must be considered in its application to all products. Automobile manufacturers cannot be made a special class'. With this we quite agree. We think the

---

[1] National Safety Council, Accident Facts 40 (1966 ed) reports: In 1965 motor vehicle accidents caused 49,000 deaths, 1.8 million disabling injuries. In automobile accidents since the advent of the horseless carriage up to the end of 1965, 1.5 million people have been killed in the United States. In 1966 the annual toll of those killed in automobile accidents rose to 52,500 and 1.9 million suffered disabling injuries.

US landmark cases

duty of the use of reasonable care in design to protect against foreseeable injury to the user of a product and perhaps others injured as an incident of that use should be and is equally applicable to all manufacturers with the customary limitations now applied to protect the manufacturer in case of an unintended and unforeseeable use. The courts have imposed this duty, perhaps more readily against other manufacturers than against the automotive industry.[2]

We, therefore, do not think the automotive industry is being singled out for any special adverse treatment by applying to it general negligence principles in (1) imposing a duty on the manufacturer to use reasonable care in the design of its products to protect against an unreasonable risk of injury or enhancement of injury to a user of the product, and (2) holding that the intended use of an automotive product contemplates its travel on crowded and high speed roads and highways that inevitably subject it to the foreseeable hazards of collisions and impacts. Neither reason, logic, nor controlling precedents compel the courts to make a distinction between negligent design and negligent construction.

The manufacturer's duty to use reasonable care in the design and manufacture of a product to minimize injuries to its users and not to subject its users to an unreasonable risk of injury in the event of a collision or impact should be recognized by the courts. The manufacturers themselves have, in various public utterances in discussing automotive safety, expressed their concern for making safer vehicles.[3] And General Motors admits the foreseeability of accidents which are matters of public and common knowledge over a long period of time. Legal acceptance or imposition of this duty would go far in protecting the user from unreasonable risks. The normal risk of driving must be accepted by the user but there is no need to further penalize the user by subjecting him to an unreasonable risk of injury due to negligence in design.[4]

On the second count of plaintiff's petition alleging negligence in failure to warn of an alleged dangerous

condition in vehicle design the same principles would apply. We think a cause of action is alleged and that under the law the manufacturer has a duty to inspect and to test for designs that would cause an unreasonable risk of foreseeable injury. *Ford Motor Company v Zahn, supra.* The failure to use reasonable care in design or knowledge of a defective design gives rise to the reasonable duty on the manufacturer to warn of this condition.

. . . . .

In *Blitzstein v Ford Motor Company,*288 F2d 738, at p 744 (1961) the court held the evidence was sufficient to present a jury issue on whether the supplier Ford Motor Company was negligent in failing to exercise reasonable care to warn of a dangerous condition caused by designing a non-ventilated motor car trunk in which an undetectable leaky gas tank was located, stating: 'We think that a jury could reasonably have found that the American Ford Company was negligent in marketing a product which was inherently dangerous, of which danger it should have been aware from its long experience in the design and manufacture of automobiles, and that American Ford failed to exercise reasonable care to inform the buying public of this dangerous condition.'

If, because of the alleged undisclosed defect in design of the 1963 Corvair steering assembly, an extra hazard is created over and above the normal hazard, General Motors should be liable for this unreasonable hazard. Admittedly, it would not sell many cars of this particular model if its sales pitch included the cautionary statement that the user is subjected to an extra hazard or unreasonable risk in the event of a head-on collision. But the duty of reasonable care should command a warning of this latent defect that could under certain circumstances accentuate the possibility of severe injury.

. . . . .

For the reasons set forth, we reverse and remand for proceedings not inconsistent with this opinion.

[2]See, *Brandon v Yale & Towne Manufacturing Co,* 342 F2d 519 (1965)—failure to equip a forklift truck with adequate safety devices; *Rosin v International Harvester Company,* 115 NW2d 50 (1962)—a defectively designed inner grease seal that resulted in a brake malfunctioning; *Phillips v Ogle Aluminum Furniture Inc,* 235 P2d 857 (1951)—an inadequately designed chair.

[3]CA Chayne, then vice-president in charge of the engineering staff of defendant General Motors, made a statement in 1956: 'It is always relatively easy to come up with a new design of an old part, or the design of a new feature or part, but until we are able to adequately test this part and have a pretty clear picture of what it will do under the circumstances to which it is subjected, we are exposing ourselves, the users of our products, and frequently others on the highways to risks.'
KA Stonex, Automobile Safety Engineer for General Motors in an article 'Vehicle Aspects of the Highway Safety Problem' in June 1962 said: 'The two-car collision is so important statistically that car structure has to be evaluated under these conditions.'

[4]The *Evans* case has been the subject of a number of law review articles or comments and has generally received adverse comments as being a too restrictive declaration of general negligence principles. See, 80 Harv L Rev 688 (1967) 'Liability of Maker of Chattel'; 32 Iowa L Rev 953 (1967) 'Liability for Negligent Automobile Design'; Nadler and Page, 'Automobile Design and the Judicial Process', 55 Calif L Rev 645 (1967).

1972 *Cronin v Olson*

COMMENTARY

This decision comes nine years after the *Greenman* case, and in that nine years the California courts had gradually enlarged the scope of strict liability. For example, liability had been imposed on retailers (*Vandermark v Ford*, 391 P2d 168, 1964) and bystanders had been allowed to claim (*Elmore v American Motors*, 451 P2d 84, 1969). There had, however, been little judicial comment on the meaning of 'defect', although more and more courts had been willing to base decisions on the wording of section 402A of the Restatement of Torts, Second.

The wording of section 402A had been discussed by its editors over some years, and the decision in *Greenman* had encouraged them to extend strict liability to 'all products', whereas in 1961 they had been content to limit the rule to food products. The wording of 1961 represented the law at that time, and the purpose of the Restatement was not to innovate, but to record the law as it was generally accepted. By 1964, the editors felt that the majority of courts would in fact impose liability for defective products of all types, but they felt that the statement of the law as laid down by Justice Traynor would impose too heavy a burden on manufacturers. It would make them insurers of their products, responsible for all the injuries that might result from the use of a product. Every time a cut was caused by a sharp breadknife, liability would follow.

In order to make matters clear, the words 'unreasonably dangerous' were therefore put into the statement of the law. The editors of the Restatement explained what they meant: 'The article sold must be dangerous to an extent beyond that which would be contemplated by the ordinary consumer who purchases it, with the ordinary knowledge common to the community as to its characteristics'. There were not, however, two separate requirements for strict liability. It was not necessary to show both a defect and a condition of being unreasonably dangerous. It was enough to show that the defect rendered the product unreasonably dangerous.

The reasons for the words 'unreasonably dangerous' do not appear to all lawyers to be completely logical or necessary. The requirement of a defect would be enough to prevent manufacturers from being insurers of their products: they would be liable only when a defect could be shown. Moreover, even then, liability would follow only if the defect had caused harm. The Supreme Court of California shared these doubts about the need for the words, and refused to find that the instructions of the trial court to the jury were wrong because they omitted 'unreasonably dangerous'.

California is not the only state that does not follow the Restatement in requiring 'unreasonable danger'. Pennsylvania and Alaska, for example, do not have the requirement, and at the last count there were eight states that define strict liability in terms of a defective product only. The majority of states require the plaintiff to show that the defect rendered the product 'unreasonably dangerous', and thus have to face some confusion with negligence. According to some lawyers, they also make the plaintiff's task more difficult, but it is likely that juries look first for a defect, and then assume that the defect has made the product unreasonably dangerous. The important point for the plaintiff is that the instructions to the jury include the words 'unreasonably dangerous', because if they are omitted a favourable verdict could be reversed on appeal.

This case illustrates the 'second collision' doctrine. The defect did not cause the accident, but did cause or aggravate the plaintiff's injuries. The court did not accept the defence argument that a vehicle should be safe only for normal driving. An accident is a reasonably foreseeable occurrence, and vehicles should be designed 'with recognition of the realities of their everyday use'.

JUDGMENT

Supreme Court of California
October 17, 1972

Cronin
versus
JBE Olson Corporation

Before Chief Justice Wright and Justices Sullivan, McComb, Peters, Tobriner, Mosk and Burke

Sullivan, *Justice.* In this products liability case, the principal question which we face is whether the injured plaintiff seeking recovery upon the theory of strict liability in tort must establish, among other facts, not only that the product contained a defect which proximately caused his injuries but also that such defective condition made the product unreasonably dangerous to the user or consumer. We have concluded that he need not do so. Accordingly, we find no error in the trial court's refusal to so instruct the jury. Rejecting as without merit various challenges to the sufficiency of the evidence, we affirm the judgment.

On October 3, 1966, plaintiff, a route salesman for Gravem-Inglis Bakery Co (Gravem) of Stockton, was driving a bread delivery truck along a rural road in San Joaquin County. While plaintiff was attempting to pass a pick-up truck ahead of him, its driver made a sudden left turn, causing the pick-up to collide with the plaintiff's truck and forcing the latter off the road and into a ditch. As a result, plaintiff was propelled through the windshield and landed on the ground. The impact broke an aluminium safety hasp which was located just behind the driver's seat and designed to hold the bread trays in place. The loaded trays, driven forward by the abrupt stop and impact of the truck, struck plaintiff in the back and hurled him through the windshield. He sustained serious personal injuries.

The truck, a one-ton Chevrolet stepvan with built-in bread racks, was one of several trucks sold to Gravem in 1957 by defendant Chase Chevrolet Company (Chase), not a party to this appeal. Upon receipt of Gravem's order, Chase purchased the trucks from defendant JBE Olson Corporation (Olson), which acted as sales agent for the assembled vehicle, the chassis, body, and racks of which were manufactured by three subcontractors. The body of the van contained three aisles down which were welded runners extending from the front to the rear of the truck. Each rack held ten bread trays from top to bottom and five trays deep; the trays slid forward into the cab or back through the rear door to facilitate deliveries.

Plaintiff brought the present action against Chase, Olson and General Motors Corporation[1] alleging that the truck was unsafe for its intended use because of defects in its manufacture, in that the metal hasp was exceedingly porous, contained holes, pits and voids, and lacked sufficient tensile strength to withstand the impact. Defendants' answers denied the material allegations of the complaint and asserted the affirmative defense of contributory negligence.[2] Subsequently, upon leave of court, the additional defense of assumption of the risk was asserted.

At the trial, plaintiff's expert testified, in substance, that the metal hasp broke, releasing the bread trays, because it was extremely porous and had a significantly lower tolerance to force than a non-flawed aluminium hasp would have had. The jury returned a verdict in favor of plaintiff and against Olson in the sum of $45,000 but in favor of defendant Chase and against plaintiff.[3] Judgment was entered accordingly. This appeal by Olson followed.

Defendant[4] attacks the sufficiency of the evidence to support the verdict and the trial court's instruction on strict liability. The challenge to the evidence is multi-pronged, claiming in effect that plaintiff produced no

[1]Defendant General Motors Corporation, manufacturer of the chassis, was voluntarily dismissed by plaintiff prior to trial.

[2]The State Compensation Insurance Fund, Gravem's compensation carrier, filed a notice of lien covering the compensation benefits paid to plaintiff and, pursuant to leave of court, filed a complaint in interlocution.

[3]In answer to a special interrogatory the jury unanimously agreed that Gravem was not aware of any defect in the bread racks prior to the accident and hence was not contributorily negligent. This finding had the effect of allowing the lien filed by Gravem's compensation carrier. Contrary to Olson's claim, the evidence supporting the implied finding of a defect in the hasp also supports the finding that Gravem was not negligent.

[4]Hereafter, unless otherwise specified, reference to 'defendant' means Olson, since it is the sole defendant to appeal.

evidence on several essential issues. We first turn to this challenge, considering defendant's arguments in the order presented.

1 *Sufficiency of the evidence*

Defendant first contends that plaintiff failed to show the defective hasp to be the same one originally supplied by the manufacturer. The record contains no evidence as to the use or maintenance of the van from the time it was purchased by Gravem in 1957 until plaintiff began to drive it five years later. Plaintiff admitted that the racks had been modified by the addition of reinforcement bars welded onto a hinge mechanism which the hasp fastened in a closed position to hold the trays in place. But that admission does not derogate from the implied finding that the hasp itself was the original one supplied by the manufacturer. Contrary to defendant's claim that no evidence was introduced on this point, plaintiff's expert witness testified that he saw no indication of any repair of the hasp itself. When there is sufficient evidence to support a factual finding, it is not within the province of an appellate court to reexamine or reweigh it (*Crawford v Southern Pacific Co* (1953) 45 P2d 183).

It is next urged that plaintiff's evidence failed to show any condition of the hasp which could be considered defective. The gist of the argument on this point appears to be that 'defectiveness' cannot be properly determined without proof of some standard set by knowledgeable individuals for the manufacture and use of the particular part under scrutiny and that plaintiff's expert applied 'his own unilateral standard' in giving his opinion that the hasp was defective. In the absence of any appropriate standard, so it is argued, all proof must fail.

The argument lacks merit. Gravem purchased the van and its bread racks from Chase as a unit. Since there were no standard bread racks available, Chase in turn ordered them from Olson according to the latter's blueprint, and left to Olson the manufacture of a safe set of bread racks. Olson admitted through the testimony of its vice president that the purpose of the locking device on the bread rack (of which the hasp was a part) was to hold the trays in place and that it knew that the van was to be driven on public highways. In short, the evidence shows that the intended purpose of the locking device was to keep the bread trays from moving forward into the driver's compartment as a result of any foreseeable movements of the van in highway travel.

The record shows that the hasp, because it was defective, did not fulfill this purpose. Plaintiff's expert testified that the broken hasp was 'extremely porous and extremely defective' as it was full of holes, voids and cracks. These flaws were in the metal itself and resulted in the hasp's lowered tolerance to force. He further stated that this condition could not be attributed to prolonged use. This conclusion was buttressd by the expert's testimony that the break in the hasp was a tensile fracture caused by sudden force rather than a fatigue fracture, which is by nature progressive. The

Cronin v Olson

hasp failed because 'it was just a very, very bad piece of metal. Simply would not stand any force—reasonable force—at all'.

Olson's argument that the van was built only for 'normal' driving is unavailing. We agree that strict liability should not be imposed upon a manufacturer when injury results from a use of its product that is not reasonably foreseeable. Although a collision may not be the 'normal' or intended use of a motor vehicle, vehicle manufacturers must take accidents into consideration as reasonably foreseeable occurences involving their products (*Passwaters v General Motors Corp* (8th Cir 1972) 454 F2d 1270; **Larsen v General Motors Corporation* (8th Cir 1968) 391 F2d 495; 80 Harv L Rev 688, 689 (1967); *contra Evans v General Motors Corporation* (7th Cir 1966) 359 F2d 822, cert den 385 US 836). The design and manufacture of products should not be carried out in an industrial vacuum but with recognition of the realities of their everyday use.

Despite its claim that Gravem used the van beyond its life span, Olson did not show that the van was delivered with any warning that it would not remain safe after seven or eight years. Nor did it show that by reason of age the van was obviously dangerous.

Defendant claims that the hasp was not intended to be used without inspection and repair. However, the expert testimony offered by plaintiff established that the hasp failed because of internal holes, cracks and voids not visible to the naked eye. In any event, the mere failure to discover defects in the product is not a defense in a strict liability case. (*Barth v BF Goodrich Tire Co* (1968) 71 Cal Rptr 306.)

Finally, defendant contends that plaintiff failed to prove proximate causation between the defect in the hasp and the accident. It is urged that the hasp did not cause the collision. Plaintiff, however, does not argue that the hasp caused the accident, but only that its defectiveness was a substantial factor contributing to his injuries. Defendant argues that the fracture of the hasp did not propel plaintiff through the windshield. But plaintiff's expert witness testified that if the hasp had not been porous, it would have withstood the impact and kept the trays in place. The hasp's fragility therefore had a direct, rather than a remote, connection with plaintiff's injuries. There is ample evidence in the record supportive of the jury's implied finding of proximate causation.

2 The instruction on strict liability

Defendant's remaining contention requires us to probe the essential elements of products liability. It is claimed that in instructing the jury as to the issues upon which plaintiff had the burden of proof[5] the trial court erred by submitting a definition of strict liability which failed to include, as defendant requested,[6] the element that the defect found in the product be 'unreasonably danger-ous'. It is urged that without this element, for which Olson finds support in section 402A of the Restatement Second of Torts (1965) and in recent decisions of this court (see *Jiminez v Sears, Roebuck & Co* (1971) 482 P2d 681; *Pike v Frank G Hough Co* (1970) 467 P2d 229), a seller would incur absolute liability for any injury proximately caused by an intended use of a product, regardless of the insignificance of the risk posed by the defect or the fortuity of the resulting harm.

The encapsulation in appropriate jury instructions of the doctrine of strict liability in tort as announced in the decision of this court in **Greenman v Yuba Power Products Inc* (1963) 377 P2d 897 has apparently given rise to some confusion. The instruction given in the case at bench, although drafted by the trial judge, was apparently based upon BAJI No 218-A,[7] the then current instruction on products liability. Prior to this appeal, however, BAJI No 218-A was superseded by BAJI Nos 9.00[8] and 9.01[9] which require a showing that

[5]That instruction reads in pertinent part as follows:
'In this action, the plaintiff has the burden of proving by a preponderance of the evidence all of the facts necessary to prove the following issues as to each defendant seller:
1 That the seller placed the equipment on the market for use under circumstances where he knew that such equipment would be used without inspection for defects;
2 That there was a defect in the manufacture or design of the equipment involved;
3 That the user was not aware of the said defect;
4 That the equipment was being used for the purpose for which it was designed and intended to be used;
5 That the injuries and damages complained of were proximately caused by the said defect;
6 The nature and extent of the injuries and damages sustained by the plaintiff. '

[6]The court refused defendant's instruction which provided in pertinent part that, 'Plaintiff has burden of proving: . . .(2) That the defective condition made it unreasonably dangerous to the user or consumer . . .'

[7]BAJI No 218-A provides: 'The manufacturer (retailer) of an article who places it on the market for use under circumstances where he knows that such articles will be used without inspection for defects, is liable for injuries proximately caused by defects in the manufacture or design of the article of which the user was not aware, provided the article was being used for the purpose for which it was designed and intended to be used.'

[8]BAJI No 9.00 provides: 'The (manufacturer) (retailer) of an article who places it on the market for use under circumstances where he knows that such article will be used without inspection for defects in the particular part, mechanism, or design which is claimed to have been defective is liable for injuries proximately caused by defects in the manufacture or design of the article which caused it to be unreasonably dangerous and unsafe for its intended use and of which the user was not aware, provided the article was being used for the purpose for which it was designed and intended to be used.

'(An article is unreasonably dangerous if it is dangerous to an extent beyond that which would be contemplated by the ordinary consumer who purchases it with the ordinary knowledge common to the community as to its characteristics.)

'The plaintiff has the burden of establishing by a preponderance of the evidence all of the facts necessary to prove each of the foregoing conditions.'

US landmark cases

the defect made the product 'unreasonably dangerous'. Thus, defendant insists that this characteristic of the defect is an essential element of the doctrine.

The history of strict liability in California indicates that the requirement that the defect made the product 'unreasonably dangerous' crept into our jurisprudence without fanfare after its inclusion in section 402A of the Restatement Second of Torts in 1965. The question raised in the instant matter as to whether the requirement is an essential part of the plaintiff's case is one of first impression.

Until our decision in *Greenman v Yuba Power Products Inc, supra,* strict liability for defective products was, in effect, imposed *sub silentio* by extension of the warranty doctrine.[10] As early as 1944, Justice Traynor, concurring in *Escola v Coca Cola Bottling Co* (1944) 150 P2d 436, 440, urged this court to dispense with negligence as the basis of recovery in defective products cases, to discard the fictions of warranty, and to replace them with absolute liability. 'Public policy demands that responsibility be fixed wherever it will most effectively reduce the hazards to life and health inherent in defective products that reach the market.' But the pronouncement of such a rule had to await the *Greenman* case in 1963 in which Justice Traynor wrote for a unanimous court: 'A manufacturer is strictly liable in tort when an article he places on the market, knowing that it is to be used without inspection for defects, proves to have a defect that causes injury to a human being . . . the liability is not one governed by the law of contract warranties but by the law of strict liability in tort.'

Greenman had been injured when a piece of wood on which he was working flew out of his Shopsmith, a combination power tool usable as a saw, drill, and wood lathe. 'To establish the manufacturer's liability it was sufficient that plaintiff proved that he was injured while using the Shopsmith in a way it was intended to be used as a result of a defect in design and manufacture of which plaintiff was not aware[11] that made the Shopsmith unsafe for its intended use.'

During the following decade the *Greenman* rule has been made applicable to retailers (*Vandermark v Ford Motor Co* (1964) 391 P2d 168); bailors and lessors (*Price v Shell Oil Company* (1970) 466 P2d 722); wholesalers and distributors (*Barth v B F Goodrich Tire Co, supra; Cannifax v Hercules Powder Co* (1965) 46 Cal Rptr 552); and sellers of mass-produced homes (*Kriegler v Eichler Homes Inc* (1969) 74 Cal Rptr 749). Its protection has been extended to bystanders (*Elmore v American Motors Corp* (1969) 451 P2d 84). Recovery under the rule for solely economic losses has, however, been withheld (*Seely v White Motor Co* (1965) 403 P2d 145). But throughout the development of the *Greenman* rule we have said very little to explain what we meant in that case by a 'defect' which would give rise to liability if injury were proximately caused thereby.

The addition of section 402A[12] to the Restatement

---

[9]BAJI No 9.01 provides: 'The defendant . . . is not required under the law so to create and deliver its product as to make it accident* proof; however, he is liable to the plaintiff for any injury suffered by him if the plaintiff establishes by a preponderance of the evidence all of the facts necessary to prove each of the following conditions:

'First: The defendant placed the . . . in question on the market for use, and the defendant knew, or in the exercise of reasonable care should have known, that the particular . . . would be used without inspection for defects in the particular part, mechanism or design which is claimed to have been defective;

Second: The . . . was defective in design or manufacture at the time it was placed on the market and delivered;

Third: The plaintiff was unaware of the claimed defect;

Fourth: The claimed defect was a (proximate) (legal) cause of any such injury to the plaintiff occurring while he . . . was being used in the way and for the general purpose for which it was designed and intended, and

Fifth: The defect, if it existed, made the . . . unreasonably dangerous and unsafe for its intended use.

'(An article is unreasonably dangerous if it is dangerous to an extent beyond that which would be contemplated by the ordinary consumer who purchases it with the ordinary knowledge common to the community as to its characteristics.)'

[10]Dean Prosser has provided us with an excellent account of this development. At first the 'implied warranty' of safety was recognized only in cases involving food, drink, and drugs (*Mazetti v Armour & Co* (1913) (prepared meat)). The expansion of the doctrine beyond such products not unexpectedly began with products for intimate bodily use (*Graham v Bottenfield's Inc* (1954) 269 P2d 413 (hair dye)) and animal food (*McAfee v Cargill Inc,* 121 F Supp 5, 6). In 1958 the Michigan Supreme Court allowed recovery based on implied warranty without privity for property damage caused by defective cinder building blocks. (*Spence v Three Rivers Builders & Masonry Supply Inc* (1958) 90 N W 2d 873.) The last vestiges of the privity of contract doctrine, the most common obstacle to recover under the implied warranty theory, vanished quickly after the landmark decision in *Henningsen v Bloomfield's Inc* (1960) 161 AS2d 69, which was followed by most jurisdictions and applied to a variety of products (see generally Prosser, *Law of Torts* (4th ed 1971) pp 650-656; Prosser, 'The Assault Upon the Citadel (Strict Liability to the Consumer)' (1960) 69 Yale L J 1099, 1103-1114).

[11]We construe the 'awareness' requirement today in *Luque v McLean, infra,* 501 P2d 1163.

[12]Section 402A provides: '(1) One who sells any product in a defective condition unreasonably dangerous to the user or consumer or to his property is subject to liability for physical harm thereby caused to the ultimate user or consumer, or to his property, if

(a) the seller is engaged in the business of selling such a product, and

(b) it is expected to and does reach the user or consumer without substantial change in the condition in which it is sold.

(2) The rule stated in subsection (1) applies although

(a) the seller has exercised all possible care in the preparation and sale of his product and

(b) the user or consumer has not bought the product from or entered into any contractual relation with the seller.'

Cronin v Olson

Second of Torts upon its publication in 1965[13] quickly exerted a pervasive influence on the decisional law. Ironically, when this section was first published, it mirrored the law in a limited number of states, see generally Titus, 'Restatement (Second) of Torts Section 402 and the Uniform Commercial Code' (1970) 22 Stan L Rev 713). Since then, however, a substantial majority of jurisdictions have adopted the basic position which it espouses. (Prosser, *Law of Torts, supra,* pp 657-658.)

We have not hesitated to reach conclusions contrary to those set forth in Restatement section 402A (see *Price v Shell Oil Company, supra*), but we and the Courts of Appeal have more frequently adopted than challenged its basic outlines. In numerous cases this court and the Courts of Appeal have referred to the Restatement and the *Greenman* standards in tandem, as if they were for all practical purposes identical.[14] (See, eg *Jiminez v Sears, Roebuck & Co, supra; Pike v Frank G Hough Co, supra; Putensen v Clay Adams Inc* (1970) 91 Cal Rptr 319; *Canifax v Hercules Powder Co, supra.*) But in none of these cases did the decision turn, as it does in the instant case, on whether the jury must decide that the injuries were caused by a 'defective' product or by a product in a 'defective condition unreasonably dangerous'.

Indeed, generally speaking the similarities between the *Greenman* standard and the Restatement formulation are greater than their differences.[15] The literature frequently refers to *Greenman* and Restatement section 402A in the same breath, recognizing their broad expanse of identity without bothering to labor over any subtle distinctions. (See Titus, *supra,* 22 Stan L Rev 713, 720.) More recently, in adopting the *Greenman* rule of strict liability, the Alaska Supreme Court clearly recognized that the jurisdictions which have judicially adopted the doctrine 'are divided between the approaches of *Greenman* and the Restatement . . .' (*Clary v Fifth Avenue Chrysler Center Inc* (Alaska 1969) 454 P2d 244, 247.)

The most inextricable intertwining of the *Greenman* and Restatement standards in our jurisprudence was inevitable, considering the simplicity of *Greenman* and the fuller guidance for many situations offered by the Restatement and its commentary. Nevertheless, the issue now raised requires us to examine and resolve an apparent divergence in the two formulations.

We begin with section 402A itself. According to the official comment to the section, a 'defective condition' is one 'not contemplated by the ultimate consumer, which will be unreasonably dangerous to him'. (Rest 2d Torts, section 402A, comment g.) Comment (i), defining 'unreasonably dangerous', states, 'The article sold must be dangerous to an extent beyond that which would be contemplated by the ordinary consumer who purchases it, with the ordinary knowledge common to the community as to its characteristics'. Examples given in comment (i) make it clear that such innocuous products as sugar and butter, unless contaminated, would not give rise to a strict liability claim merely because the former may be harmful to a diabetic or the latter may aggravate the blood cholesterol level of a person with heart disease. Presumably such dangers are squarely within the contemplation of the ordinary consumer. Prosser, the reporter for the Restatement, suggests that the 'unreasonably dangerous' qualification was added to foreclose the possibility that the manufacturer of a product with inherent possibilities for harm (for example, butter, drugs, whiskey and automobiles) would become 'automatically responsible for all the harm that such things do in the world'. (Prosser, *Strict Liability to the Consumer in California* (1966))

The result of this has been merely to prevent the seller from becoming an insurer of his products with respect to all harm generated by their use. Rather, it has burdened the injured plaintiff with proof of an element which rings of negligence. As a result, if, in view of the trier of fact, the 'ordinary consumer' would have expected the defective condition of a product, the seller is not strictly liable regardless of the expectations of the injured plaintiff. If, for example, the 'ordinary consumer' would have contemplated that Shopsmiths posed a risk of loosening their grip and letting the wood strike the operator, another *Greenman* might be denied recovery. In fact, it has been observed that the Restatement formulation of strict liability in practice rarely leads to a different conclusion than would have been reached under laws of negligence. (Rheingold, 'Proof of Defect in Product Liability Cases' (1971) 38 Tenn L Rev 325, 326; Keeton, 'Products Liability—Some Observations About Allocation of Risks' (1966) 64 Mich L Rev 1329, 1340-1341; Wade, 'Strict Tort Liability of Manufacturers' (1965) 19 SwLJ5, 15; Prosser, *supra,* 69 Yale LJ 1099, 1119; Note, 'Products Liability and Section 402A of the Restatement of Torts' (1966) 55 Geo L J 286, 323; *contra,* Kessler, 'Products Liability' (1967) 76 Yale L J 887, 901.) Yet the very purpose of our pioneering efforts in this field was to relieve the plaintiff from problems of proof inherent in pursuing negligence

---

[13] A draft of section 402A, limited to sales of 'food' (albeit broadly defined) was first introduced in 1961. A revision of the section, adopted in 1962, extended strict liability to products for 'intimate bodily use'. Another emendation in 1964 extended strict liability to 'any product' in line with developments, including *Greenman,* in the intervening years. The Restatement Second of Torts was published in final form in 1965. (Titus, 'Restatement Second of Torts, Section 402 and the Uniform Commercial Code' (1970) 22 Stan L Rev 713.)

[14] It is notable that in the *Pike* case, in which we supposedly 'adopted' 'the standard of strict liability as stated in the Restatement' (*Putensen v Clay Adams Inc* (1970) 91 Cal Rptr 319, 325), we nowhere disavowed *Greenman* nor considered ourselves in conflict with that 'landmark opinion' (*Pike v Frank G Hough Co, supra*).

[15] In an article discussing the definitional and theoretical difficulties involved in applying a 'defective product' standard, the author of the *Greenman* opinion refers to the similarities between *Greenman* and section 402A without pointing out the difference here in controversy. (Traynor, 'The Ways and Meanings of Defective Products and Strict Liability' (1965) 32 Tenn L Rev 363, 366.)

US landmark cases

(*Escola v Coca Cola Bottling Co, supra*) (Traynor J concurring) and warranty remedies, and thereby 'to ensure that the costs of injuries resulting from defective products are borne by the manufacturers . . . ' (*Greenman v Yuba Power Products Inc, supra*, see *Price v Shell Oil Co, supra*.)

Of particular concern is the susceptibility of Restatement section 402A to a literal reading which would require the finder of fact to conclude that the product is, first, defective and, second, unreasonably dangerous. (Note, *supra*, 55 Geo L J 286, 296.) A bifurcated standard is of necessity more difficult to prove than a unitary one. But merely proclaiming that the phrase 'defective condition unreasonably dangerous' requires only a single finding would not purge that phrase of its negligence complexion. We think that a requirement that a plaintiff also prove that the defect made the product 'unreasonably dangerous' places upon him a significantly increased burden and represents a step backward in the area pioneered by this court.

We recognise that the words 'unreasonably dangerous' may also serve the beneficial purpose of preventing the seller from being treated as the insurer of the products. However, we think that such protective end is attained by the necessity of proving that there was a defect in the manufacture or design of the product and that such defect was a proximate cause of the injuries. Although the seller should not be responsible for all injuries involving the use of its products, it should be liable for all injuries proximately caused by any of its products which are adjudged 'defective'.[16]

We can see no difficulty in applying the *Greenman* formulation to the full range of products liability situations, including those involving 'design defects'. A defect may emerge from the mind of the designer as well as from the hand of the workman.

The *Greenman* case itself indicated that 'to establish the manufacturer's liability it was sufficient that plaintiff proved that he was injured while using the Shopsmith in a way it was intended to be used as a result of a defect in *design and manufacture* . . . ', thereby suggesting the difficulty inherent in distinguishing between types of defects. Although it is easier to see the 'defect' in a single imperfectly fashioned product than in an entire line badly conceived, a distinction between manufacturing and design defects is not tenable. (*Pike v Frank G Hough Co, supra; Kessler, supra*, 76 Yale L J 887, 900.)

The most obvious problem we perceive in treating any such distinction is that thereafter it would be advantageous to characterize a defect in one rather than the other category. It is difficult to prove that a product ultimately caused injury because a widget was poorly welded—a defect in manufacture—rather than because it was made of inexpensive metal difficult to weld, chosen by a designer concerned with economy—a defect in design. The proof problem would, of course, be magnified when the article in question was either old or unique, with no easily available basis for comparison. We wish to avoid providing such a battleground for clever counsel. Furthermore, we find no reason why a different standard, and one harder to meet, should apply to defects which plague entire product lines. We recognize that it is more damaging to a manufacturer to have an entire line condemned, so to speak, for a defect in design, than a single product for a defect in manufacture. But the potential economic loss to a manufacturer should not be reflected in a different standard of proof for an injured consumer.

In summary we have concluded that to require an injured plaintiff to prove not only that the product contained a defect but also that such defect made the product unreasonably dangerous to the user or consumer would place a considerably greater burden upon him than that articulated in *Greenman*. We believe the *Greenman* formulation is consonant with the rationale and development of products liability law in California because it provides a clear and simple test for determining whether the injured plaintiff is entitled to recovery. We are not persuaded to the contrary by the formulation of section 402A which inserts the factor of an 'unreasonably dangerous' condition into the equation of products liability.

We conclude that the trial court did not err by refusing to instruct the jury that plaintiff must establish that the defective condition of the product made it unreasonably dangerous to the user or consumer.

The judgment is affirmed.

Chief Justice Wright and Justices McComb, Peters, Tobriner, Mosk and Burke concur.

---

[16]We recognize, of course, the difficulties inherent in giving content to the defectiveness standard. However, as Justice Traynor notes, 'there is now a cluster of useful precedents to supersede the confusing decisions based on indiscriminate invocation of sales and warranty law'. (Traynor, *supra*, 32 Tenn L Rev 363, 373.)

1978 *Barker v Lull Engineering*

COMMENTARY

The year is 1978 and the place is California. This means that 15 years had elapsed since *Greenman* and the courts had been able to establish on many occasions that the law recognised strict liability for defective products. What it had not been able to establish was what was meant by 'defective', particularly since the California decision in *Cronin v Olson*. The California court now had an opportunity to explain what it had really intended by that decision. Although the explanation is expressed in terms of California law, the reasoning of the court would be understood in all the other states.

The problem has its origins in the words of section 402A of the Restatement of Torts Second. In that section liability is said to be based on a 'product in a defective condition unreasonably dangerous', but in *Cronin* the California Supreme Court had held that 'defect' did not necessarily have to be 'unreasonably dangerous'. In *Barker v Lull,* the court came back to that opinion, in order to point out that its disapproval of the 'unreasonably dangerous' requirement did not mean that a jury should not be given some guidance. In fact, we are concerned with the jury instruction that was to be a ground for appeal in a great many future cases. For example, there is *Finn v G D Searle,* a March 1984 decision discussed in *Product Liability International,* June 1984. That was also a California decision, and we must not allow ourselves to assume that all product liability law was developed in that state. But a lot of it was.

In *Barker,* the jury instruction was: 'I instruct you that strict liability for the defect in design of a product is based on a finding that the product was unreasonably dangerous for its intended use, and in turn the unreasonableness of the danger must necessarily be derived from the state of the art at the time of the design. The manufacturer or lessor are not insurers of their products. However, an industry cannot set its own standards.'

The objection to this instruction was the inclusion of the 'unreasonably dangerous' requirement which, of course, conflicted with the *Cronin* ruling. Other words in the instruction could have been challenged, such as the reference to 'state of the art', but the court pointed out that its examination was limited to the portion challenged by the plaintiff. A court of appeal will normally consider only those matters that are brought to its attention by the parties, and the onus on the lawyers is heavy. Cases have been lost because valid points have not been raised. In this case, however, the plaintiff did win his case on the point raised.

The defence argument was that the *Cronin* ruling was limited to manufacturing defects, and should not be applied to design defects. That argument was not accepted, and the law is clear. In California and in the other states that follow California, it is not necessary to show that any type of defect was unreasonably dangerous.

So far as design defects are concerned, a proper instruction is one that gives the jury an alternative standard. Either the product fails to perform as safely as the ordinary consumer would expect, or its dangers outweigh the benefits from its use. When the jury comes to weigh up the dangers and advantages of a product it may be using negligence principles, but all the time it must look at the product itself, and not at the actions of the manufacturer.

JUDGMENT

Supreme Court of California
January 16, 1978

Barker
versus
Lull Engineering Company Inc

Before Acting Chief Justice Tobriner and Justices Mosk, Clark, Richardson, Wright and Sullivan

Tobriner,*Acting Chief Justice.*In August 1970, plaintiff, Ray Barker, was injured at a construction site at the University of California at Santa Cruz while operating a high-lift loader manufactured by defendant Lull Engineering Co and leased to plaintiff's employer by defendant George M Philpott Co Inc. Claiming that his injuries were proximately caused *inter alia* by the alleged defective design of the loader, Barker instituted the present tort action seeking to recover damages for his injuries. The jury returned a verdict in favor of defendants, and plaintiff appeals from the judgment entered upon that verdict, contending primarily that in view of this court's decision in *Cronin v J B E Olson Corp* (1972) 501 P2d 1153, the trial court erred in instructing the jury 'that strict liability for a defect in design of a product is based on a finding that the product was unreasonably dangerous for its intended use . . .'

As we explain, we agree with plaintiff's objection to the challenged instruction and conclude that the judgment must be reversed. In *Cronin,* we reviewed the development of the strict product liability doctrine in California at some length, and concluded that, for a variety of reasons, the 'unreasonably dangerous' element which section 402A of the Restatement Second of Torts had introduced into the definition of a defective product should not be incorporated into a plaintiff's burden of proof in a product liability action in this state. Although defendants maintain that our *Cronin* decision should properly be interpreted as applying only to

US landmark cases

'manufacturing defects' and not to the alleged 'design defects' at issue here, we shall point out that the *Cronin* decision itself refutes any such distinction. Consequently, we conclude that the instruction was erroneous and that the judgment in favor of defendants must be reversed.

In addition, we take this opportunity to attempt to alleviate some confusion that our *Cronin* decision has apparently engendered in the lower courts. Although in *Cronin* we rejected the Restatement's 'unreasonably dangerous' gloss on the defectiveness concept as potentially confusing and unduly restrictive, we shall explain that our *Cronin* decision did not dictate that the term 'defect' be left undefined in jury instructions given in all product liability cases.

As *Cronin* acknowledged, in the past decade and a half California courts have frequently recognized that the defectiveness concept defies a simple, uniform definition applicable to all sectors of the diverse product liability domain. Although in many instances—as when one machine in a million contains a cracked or broken part—the meaning of the term 'defect' will require little or no elaboration, in other instances, as when a product is claimed to be defective because of an unsafe design or an inadequate warning, the contours of the defect concept may not be self-evident. In such a case a trial judge may find it necessary to explain more fully to the jury the legal meaning of 'defect' or 'defective'. We shall explain that *Cronin* in no way precluded such elucidation of the defect concept, but rather contemplated that, in typical common law fashion, the accumulating body of product liability authorities would give guidance for the formulation of a definition.

As numerous recent judicial decisions and academic commentaries have recognized, the formulation of a satisfactory definition of 'design defect' has proven a formidable task; trial judges have repeatedly confronted difficulties in attempting to devise accurate and helpful instructions in design defect cases. Aware of these problems, we have undertaken a review of the past California decisions which have grappled with the design defect issue, and have measured their conclusions against the fundamental policies which underlie the entire strict product liability doctrine.

As we explain in more detail below, we have concluded from this review that a product is defective in design either (1) if the product has failed to perform as safely as an ordinary consumer would expect when used in an intended or reasonably foreseeable manner, or (2) if, in light of the relevant factors discussed below, the benefits of the challenged design outweigh the risk of danger inherent in such design. In addition, we explain how the burden of proof with respect to the latter 'risk-benefit' standard should be allocated.

This dual standard for design defect assures an injured plaintiff protection from products that either fall below ordinary consumer expectations as to safety, or that, on balance, are not as safely designed as they should be. At the same time, the standard permits a manufacturer who has marketed a product which satisfies ordinary consumer expectations to demonstrate the relative complexity of design decisions and the trade-offs that are frequently required in the adoption of alternative designs. Finally, this test reflects our continued adherence to the principle that, in a product liability action, the trier of fact must focus on the *product*, not on the *manufacturer's conduct*, and that the plaintiff need not prove that the manufacturer acted unreasonably or negligently in order to prevail in such an action.

1 The facts of the present case

Plaintiff Barker sustained serious injuries as a result of an accident which occurred while he was operating a Lull High-Lift Loader at a construction site. The loader, manufactured in 1967, is a piece of heavy construction equipment designed to lift loads of up to 5000 pounds to a maximum height of 32 ft. The loader is 23 ft. long, 8 ft. wide and weighs 17,050 pounds; it sits on four large rubber tires which are about the height of a person's chest, and is equipped with four-wheel drive, an automatic transmission with no park position and a hand brake. Loads are lifted by forks similar to the forks of a forklift.

The loader is designed so that the load can be kept level even when the loader is being operated on sloping terrain. The leveling of the load is controlled by a lever located near the steering column, and positioned between the operator's legs. The lever is equipped with a manual lock that can be engaged to prevent accidental slipping of the load level during lifting.

The loader was not equipped with seat belts or a roll bar. A wire and pipe cage over the driver's seat afforded the driver some protection from falling objects. The cab of the loader was located at least nine feet behind the lifting forks.

On the day of the accident the regular operator of the loader, Bill Dalton, did not report for work, and plaintiff, who had received only limited instruction on the operation of the loader from Dalton and who had operated the loader on only a few occasions, was assigned to run the loader in Dalton's place. The accident occurred while plaintiff was attempting to lift a load of lumber to a height of approximately 18 to 20 ft and to place the load on the second story of a building under construction. The lift was a particularly difficult one because the terrain on which the loader rested sloped sharply in several directions.

Witnesses testified that plaintiff approached the structure with the loader, leveled the forks to compensate for the sloping ground and lifted the load to a height variously estimated between 10 and 18 ft. During the course of the lift plaintiff felt some vibration, and, when it appeared to several co-workers that the load was beginning to tip, the workers shouted to plaintiff to jump

Barker v Lull Engineering

from the loader. Plaintiff heeded these warnings and leaped from the loader, but while scrambling away he was struck by a piece of falling lumber and suffered serious injury.

Although the above facts were generally not in dispute, the parties differed markedly in identifying the responsible causes for the accident. Plaintiff contended *inter alia* that the accident was attributable to one or more design defects of the loader.[1] Defendant, in turn, denied that the loader was defective in any respect, and claimed that the accident resulted either from plaintiff's lack of skill or from his misuse of its product. We briefly review the conflicting evidence.

Plaintiff's principal expert witness initially testified that by reason of its relatively narrow base the loader was unstable and had a tendency to roll over when lifting loads to considerable heights; the witness surmised that this instability caused the load to tip in the instant case. The expert declared that to compensate for its instability, the loader should have been equipped with 'outriggers', mechanical arms extending out from the sides of the machine, two in front and two in back, each of which could be operated independently and placed on the ground to lend stability to the loader. Evidence at trial revealed that cranes and some high lift loader models are either regularly equipped with outriggers or offer outriggers as optional equipment. Plaintiff's expert testified that the availability of outriggers would probably have averted the present accident.

The expert additionally testified that the loader was defective in that it was not equipped with a roll bar or seat belts. He stated that such safety devices were essential to protect the operator in the event that the machine rolled over. Plaintiff theorized that the lack of such safety equipment was a proximate cause of his injuries because in the absence of such devices he had no reasonable choice but to leap from the loader as it began to tip. If a seat belt and roll bar had been provided, plaintiff argued, he could have remained in the loader and would not have been struck by the falling lumber.

In addition, plaintiff's witnesses suggested that the accident may have been caused by the defective design of the loader's leveling mechanism. Several witnesses testified that both the absence of an automatic locking device on the leveling lever, and the placement of the leveling lever in a position in which it was extremely vulnerable to inadvertent bumping by the operator of the loader in the course of a lift, were defects which may have produced the accident and injuries in question. Finally, plaintiff's experts testified that the absence of a 'park' position on the loader's transmission, that could have been utilized to avoid the possibility of the loader's

movement during a lift, constituted a further defect in design which may have caused the accident.

Defendants, in response, presented evidence which attempted to refute plaintiff's claims that the loader was defective or that the loader's condition was the cause of the accident. Defendants' experts testified that the loader was not unstable when utilized on the terrain for which it was intended, and that if the accident did occur because of the tipping of the loader it was only because plaintiff had misused the equipment by operating it on steep terrain for which the loader was unsuited.[2] In answer to the claim that the high-lift loader was defective because of a lack of outriggers, defendants' expert testified that outriggers were not necessary when the loader was used for its intended purpose and that no competitive loaders with similar height lifting capacity were equipped with outriggers; the expert conceded, however, that a competitor did offer outriggers as optional equipment on a high-lift loader which was capable of lifting loads to 40, as compared to 32 ft. The expert also testified that the addition of outriggers would simply have given the loader the functional capability of a crane, which was designed for use on all terrain, and that an experienced user of a high-lift loader should recognise that such a loader was not intended as a substitute for a crane.

The defense experts further testified that a roll bar was unnecessary because in view of the bulk of the loader it would not roll completely over. The witnesses also maintained that seat belts would have increased the danger of the loader by impairing the operator's ability to leave the vehicle quickly in case of an emergency. With respect to the claimed defects of the leveling device, the defense experts testified that the positioning of the lever was the safest and most convenient for the operator and that the manual lock on the leveling device provided completely adequate protection. Finally, defendants asserted that the absence of a 'park' position on the transmission should not be considered a defect because none of the transmissions that were manufactured for this type of vehicle included a park position.

In addition to disputing plaintiff's contention as to the defectiveness of the loader, defendants' witnesses testified that the accident probably was caused by the plaintiff's own inexperience and consequent dangerous actions. Defendants maintained that if the lumber had begun to fall during the lift it did so only because plaintiff had failed to lock the leveling device prior to the lift. Defendants alternatively suggested that although the workers thought they saw the lumber begin to tip during

---

[1] Plaintiff additionally contended that his injuries were proximately caused by the absence of adequate warnings and instructions relating to the safe use of the loader. Because the warning issue is not relevant to the issues raised on this appeal, we describe only the facts material to the design defect issue.

[2] In support of this claim, defendants presented the testimony of Bill Dalton, the regular operator of the loader, who testified that he called in sick on the day of the accident because he knew that the loader was not designed to make the lifts scheduled for that day, and he was frightened to make lifts in the area where the accident occurred because of the danger involved. Dalton testified that he informed his supervisor that a crane, rather than a high-lift loader, was required for lifts on such sloping ground, but that the supervisor had not agreed to obtain a crane for such lifts.

US landmark cases

the lift, this tipping was actually only the plaintiff's leveling of the load during the lift. Defendants hypothesized that the lumber actually fell off the loader only after plaintiff had leaped from the machine and that plaintiff was responsible for his own injuries because he had failed to set the hand brake, thereby permitting the loader to roll backwards.

After considering the sharply conflicting testimony reviewed above, the jury by a 10 to 2 vote returned a general verdict in favor of defendants. Plaintiff appeals from the judgment entered upon that verdict.

2 The trial court erred in instructing the jurors that 'strict liability for a defect in design . . . is based on a finding that the product was unreasonably dangerous for its intended use'.

Plaintiff principally contends that the trial court committed prejudicial error in instructing the jury 'that strict liability for a defect in design of a product is based on a finding that the product was unreasonably dangerous for its intended use . . .'[3] Plaintiff maintains that this instruction conflicts directly with this court's decision in *Cronin,* decided subsequently to the instant trial, and mandates a reversal of the judgment. Defendants argue, in response, that our *Cronin* decision should not be applied to product liability actions which involve 'design defects' as distinguished from 'manufacturing defects'.

The plaintiff in *Cronin,* a driver of a bread delivery truck, was seriously injured when, during an accident, a metal hasp which held the truck's bread trays in place broke, permitting the trays to slide forward and propel plaintiff through the truck's windshield. Plaintiff brought a strict liability action against the seller, contending that his injuries were proximately caused by the defective condition of the truck. Evidence at trial established that the metal hasp broke during the accident 'because it was extremely porous and had a significantly lower tolerance to force than a non-flawed aluminium hasp would have had', and, and, on the basis of this evidence, the jury returned a verdict in favor of plaintiff.

On appeal, defendant in *Cronin* argued that the trial court had erred 'by submitting a definition of strict liability which failed to include, as defendant requested, the element that the defect found in the product be "unreasonably dangerous".' Relying upon section 402A

[3]The challenged instruction reads in full: 'I instruct you that strict liability for the defect in design of a product is based on a finding that the product was unreasonably dangerous for its intended use, and in turn the unreasonableness of the danger must necessarily be derived from the state of the art at the time of the design. The manufacturer or lessor are not insurers of their products. However, an industry cannot set its own standards.'

Plaintiff's challenge is limited to the portion of the instruction which provides that 'strict liability for the defect in design of a product is based on a finding that the product was unreasonably dangerous for its intended use', and accordingly we express no opinion as to the propriety of the remaining portions of the instruction.

of the Restatement Second of Torts [4]and a number of California decisions which had utilized the 'unreasonably dangerous' terminology in the product liability context, the defendant in *Cronin* maintained that a product's 'unreasonable dangerousness' was an essential element that a plaintiff must establish in any product liability action.

After undertaking a thorough review of the origins and development of both California product liability doctrine and the Restatement's 'unreasonably dangerous' criterion, we rejected the defendant's contention, concluding 'that to require an injured plaintiff to prove not only that the product contained a defect but also that such defect made the product unreasonably dangerous to the user or consumer would place a considerably greater burden upon him than that articulated in *Greenman v Yuba Power Products Inc* (1963) 377 P2d 897, California's seminal product liability decision . . . We are not persuaded to the contrary by the formulation of section 402A which inserts the factor of an "unreasonably dangerous" condition into the equation of products liability.'

Plaintiff contends that the clear import of his language in *Cronin* is that the 'unreasonably dangerous' terminology of the Restatement should not be utilized in defining defect in product liability actions, and that the trial court consequently erred in submitting an instruction which defined a design defect by reference to the 'unreasonably dangerous' standard.

In attempting to escape the apparent force of *Cronin's* explicit language, defendants observe that the flawed hasp which rendered the truck defective in *Cronin* represented a manufacturing defect rather than a design defect, and they argue that *Cronin's* disapproval of the Restatement's 'unreasonably dangerous' standard should be limited to the manufacturing defect context. Defendants point out that one of the bases for our rejection of the 'unreasonably dangerous' criterion in *Cronin* was our concern that such language, when used in conjunction with the 'defective product' terminology, was susceptible to an interpretation which would place a *dual burden* on an injured plaintiff to prove, first, that a product was defective and, second, that it was additionally unreasonably dangerous. Defendants contend that the 'dual burden' problem is present only in a manufacturing defect context and not in a design defect case.

In elaborating this contention, defendants explain that in a manufacturing defect case, a jury may find a product defective because it deviates from the manufacturer's intended result, but may still decline to impose liability under the Restatement test on the ground that such defect did not render the product unreasonably dangerous. In a design defect case, by contrast, defendants assert that a defect is *defined* by reference to

[4]Section 402A provides *inter alia* that one is strictly liable in tort if he 'sells any product in a defective condition unreasonably dangerous to the user or consumer or to his property . . .'

Barker v Lull Engineering

the 'unreasonably dangerous' standard and, since the two are equivalent, no danger of a dual burden exists. In essence, defendants argue that under the instruction which the trial court gave in the instant case, plaintiff was not required to prove both that the loader was defective and that such defect made the loader unreasonably dangerous, but only that the loader was defectively designed by virtue of its unreasonable dangerousness.

Although defendants may be correct, at least theoretically, in asserting that the so-called 'dual burden' problem is averted when the 'unreasonably dangerous' terminology is used in a design defect case simply as a definition of 'defective condition' or 'defect', defendants overlook the fact that our objection to the 'unreasonably dangerous' terminology in *Cronin* went beyond the 'dual burden' issue, and was based, more fundamentally, on a substantive determination that the Restatement's 'unreasonably dangerous' formulation represented an undue restriction on the application of strict liability principles.

As we noted in *Cronin,* the Restatement draftsmen adopted the 'unreasonably dangerous' language primarily as a means of confining the application of strict tort liability to an article which is 'dangerous to an extent beyond that which would be contemplated by the ordinary consumer who purchases it, with the ordinary knowledge common to the community as to its characteristics'. In *Cronin,* however, we flatly rejected the suggestion that recovery in a products liability action should be permitted *only* if a product is more dangerous than contemplated by the average consumer, refusing to permit the low esteem in which the public might hold a dangerous product to diminish the manufacturer's responsibility for injuries caused by that product. As we pointedly noted in *Cronin,* even if the 'ordinary consumer' may have contemplated that Shopsmith lathes posed a risk of loosening their grip and letting a piece of wood strike the operator 'another Greenman' should not be denied recovery.

Indeed, our decision in *Luque v McLean* (1972) 501 P2d 1163—decided the same day as *Cronin*—aptly reflects our disagreement with the restrictive implications of the Restatement formulation, for in *Luque* we held that a power rotary lawn mower with an unguarded hole could properly be found defective, in spite of the fact that the defect in the product was patent and hence in all probability within the reasonable contemplation of the ordinary consumer.

Thus, our rejection of the use of the 'unreasonably dangerous' terminology in *Cronin* rested in part on a concern that a jury might interpret such an instruction, as the Restatement draftsman had indeed intended, as shielding a defendant from liability so long as the product did not fall below the ordinary consumer's expectations as to the product's safety.[5] As *Luque* demonstrates, the dangers posed by such a misconception by the jury extend to cases involving design defects

as well as to actions involving manufacturing defects: indeed, the danger of confusion is perhaps more pronounced in design cases in which the manufacturer could frequently argue that its product satisfied ordinary consumer expectations since it was identical to other items of the same product line with which the consumer may well have been familiar.

Accordingly, contrary to defendants' contention, the reasoning of *Cronin* does not dictate that that decision be confined to the manufacturing defect context. Indeed, in *Cronin* itself we expressly stated that our holding applied to design defects, as well as to manufacturing defects and in *Henderson v Harnischfeger Corp* (1974) 527 P2d 353, we subsequently confirmed the impropriety of instructing a jury in the language of the 'unreasonably dangerous' standard in a design defect case.[6] Consequently, we conclude that the design defect instruction given in the instant case was erroneous.[7]

3 A trial court may properly formulate instructions to elucidate the 'defect' concept in varying circumstances. In particular, in design defect cases, a court may properly instruct a jury that a product is defective in design if (1) the plaintiff proves that the product failed to perform as safely as an ordinary consumer would expect when used in an intended or reasonably foreseeable manner, or (2) the plaintiff proves that the product's design proximately

[5]This is not to say that the expectations of the ordinary consumer are irrelevant to the determination of whether a product is defective, for as we point out below we believe that ordinary consumer expectations are frequently of direct significance to the defectiveness issue. The flaw in the Restatement's analysis, in our view, is that it treats such consumer expectations as a 'ceiling' on a manufacturer's responsibility under strict liability principles, rather than as a 'floor'. As we shall explain, past California decisions establish that at a minimum a product must meet ordinary consumer expectations as to safety to avoid being found defective.

[6]One commentator has observed that, in addition to the deficiencies in the 'unreasonably dangerous' terminology noted in *Cronin,* the Restatement's language is potentially misleading because it may suggest an idea like ultra-hazardous, or abnormally dangerous, and thus give rise to the impression that the plaintiff must prove that the product was unusually or extremely dangerous. (Wade 'On the Nature of Strict Tort Liability for Products' (1973) 44 Miss L J 825.) We agree with this criticism and believe it constitutes a further reason for refraining from utilizing the 'unreasonably dangerous' terminology in defining a defective product.

[7]Indeed, the challenged instruction was additionally erroneous because it suggested that in evaluating defectiveness, only the 'intended use' of the product is relevant, rather than the product's 'reasonably foreseeable use'. In *Cronin,* we specifically held that the adequacy of a product must be determined in light of its reasonably foreseeable use, declaring that 'the design and manufacture of products should not be carried out in an industrial vacuum but with recognition of the realities of their everyday use' (501 P2d at p 1157.)

Because, in the instant case, the jury may have concluded that the use of the loader by a relatively inexperienced worker was not an 'intended use' of the loader, but was a 'reasonably foreseeable use', this aspect of the instruction may well have prejudiced the plaintiff.

US landmark cases

caused injury and the defendant fails to prove, in light of the relevant factors, that on balance the benefits of the challenged design outweigh the risk of danger inherent in such design.

Defendants contend, however, that if *Cronin* is interpreted as precluding the use of the 'unreasonably dangerous' language in defining a design defect, the jury in all such cases will inevitably be left without any guidance whatsoever in determining whether a product is defective in design or not. (See *Beron v Kramer-Trenton Co* (1975) 402 FSupp 1268.) Amicus California Trial Lawyer Association (CTLA) on behalf of the plaintiff responds by suggesting that the precise intent of our *Cronin* decision was to preclude a trial court from formulating any definition of 'defect' in a product liability case, thus always leaving the definition of defect, as well as the application of such definition, to the jury. As we explain, neither of these contentions represents an accurate portrayal of the intent or effect of our *Cronin* decision.

In *Cronin* we reaffirmed the basic formulation of strict tort liability doctrine set forth in *Greenman:*
'A manufacturer is strictly liable in tort when an article he places on the market, knowing that it is to be used without inspection for defects, proves to have a defect that causes injury to a human being . . .'

We held in *Cronin* that a plaintiff satisfies his burden of proof under *Greenman,* in both a 'manufacturing defect' and 'design defect' context, when he proves the existence of a 'defect' and that such defect was a proximate cause of his injuries. In reaching this conclusion, however, *Cronin* did not purport to hold that the term 'defect' must remain undefined in all contexts (see *Baker v Chrysler Corp* (1976) 127 Cal Rptr 745), and did not preclude a trial court from framing a definition of defect, appropriate to the circumstances of a particular case, to guide the jury as to the standard to be applied in determining whether a product is defective or not.

As this court has recognized on numerous occasions, the term defect as utilized in the strict liability context is neither self-defining nor susceptible to a single definition applicable in all contexts. In *Jiminez v Sears, Roebuck and Co,* 482 P2d 681 for example, we stated: 'A defect may be variously defined, and as yet no definition has been formulated that would resolve all cases or that is universally agreed upon'.

Indeed, in *Cronin* itself, we expressly recognized 'the difficulties inherent in giving content to the defectiveness standard' and suggested that the problem could best be resolved by resort to the 'cluster of useful precedents' which have been developed in the product liability field in the past decade and a half (citing Traynor, 'The Ways and Meanings of Defective Products and Strict Liability' (1965) 32 Tenn L Rev 363.)

Resort to the numerous product liability precedents in California demonstrates that the defect or defectiveness concept has embraced a great variety of injury-producing deficiencies, ranging from products that cause injury because they deviate from the manufacturer's intended result (eg the one soda bottle in ten thousand that explodes without explanation (*Escola v Coca Cola Bottling Co* (1944) 150 P2d 436),) to products which, though 'perfectly' manufactured, are unsafe because of the absence of a safety device (eg a paydozer without rear view mirrors (*Pike v Frank G Hough Co,* 467 P2d 229) and including products that are dangerous because they lack adequate warnings or instructions (eg a telescope that contains inadequate instructions for assembling a 'sun filter' attachment (*Midgley v S S Kresge Co* (1976) 127 Cal Rptr 217)).

Commentators have pointed out that in view of the diversity of product deficiencies to which the defect rubric has been applied, an instruction which requires a plaintiff to prove the existence of a product defect, but which fails to elaborate on the meaning of defect in a particular context, may in some situations prove more misleading than helpful. As Professor Wade has written: The natural application (of the term 'defective') would be limited to the situation in which something went wrong in the manufacturing process, so that the article was defective in the sense that the manufacturer had not intended it to be in that condition. To apply (the term 'defective') also to the case in which a warning is not attached to the chattel or the design turns out to be a bad one or the product is likely to be injurious in its normal condition . . . and to use it without defining it to the jury is almost to ensure that they will be misled.

Wade, 'On the Nature of Strict Tort Liability for Products', *supra,* see also Keeton, 'Product Liability and the Meaning of Defect' (1973) 5 St Mary's L J 30; Hoenig, 'Product Designs and Strict Tort Liability: Is There a Better Approach?' (1976) 8 Sw U L Rev 108; Note (1973) 49 Wash L Rev 231.

Our decision in *Cronin* did not mandate such confusion. Instead, by observing that the problem in defining defect might be alleviated by reference to the 'cluster of useful precedents', we intended to suggest that in drafting and evaluating instructions on this issue in a particular case, trial and appellate courts would be well advised to consider prior authorities involving similar defective product claims.

Since the rendition of our decision in *Cronin,* a number of thoughtful Court of Appeal decisions have wrestled with the problem of devising a comprehensive definition of design defect in light of existing authorities. (See *Hyman v Gordon* (1973) 111 Cal Rptr 262; *Self v General Motors Corp* (1974) 116 Cal Rptr 575; *Baker v Chrysler Corp, supra; Buccery v General Motors Corp* (1976) 132 Cal Rptr 605.) As these decisions demonstrate, the concept of defect raises considerably more difficulties in the design defect context than it does in the manufacturing or production defect context.

In general, a manufacturing or production defect is readily identifiable because a defective product is one

Barker v Lull Engineering

that differs from the manufacturer's intended result or from other ostensibly identical units of the same product line. For example, when a product comes off the assembly line in a substandard condition it has incurred a manufacturing defect. (*Eg Lewis v American Hoist & Derrick Co* (1971) 97 Cal Rptr 798.) A design defect, by contrast, cannot be identified simply by comparing the injury-producing product with the manufacturer's plans or with other units of the same product line, since by definition the plans and all such units will reflect the same design. Rather than applying any sort of deviation-from-the-norm test in determining whether a product is defective in design for strict liability purposes, our cases have employed two alternative criteria in ascertaining, in Justice Traynor's words, whether there is something 'wrong, if not in the manufacturer's manner of production, at least in his product'. (Traynor, 'The Ways and Meanings of Defective Products and Strict Liability', *supra,* 32 Tenn L Rev 363.)

First, our cases establish that a product may be found defective in design if the plaintiff demonstrates that the product failed to perform as safely as an ordinary consumer would expect when used in an intended or reasonably foreseeable manner. This initial standard, somewhat analogous to the Uniform Commercial Code's warranty of fitness and merchantability (Cal U Com Code, section 2314), reflects the warranty heritage upon which California product liability doctrine in part rests. As we noted in *Greenman,* 'implicit in (a product's) presence on the market . . . (is) a representation that it (will) safely do the jobs for which it was built' (377 P2d at p 901.)

When a product fails to satisfy such ordinary consumer expectations as to safety in its intended or reasonably foreseeable operation, a manufacturer is strictly liable for resulting injuries. (*Greenman, supra; Pike v Frank G Hough Co, supra; Hauter v Zogarts* (1975) 534 P2d 377; *Self v General Motors Corp, supra; Culpepper v Volkswagen of America Inc* (1973) 109 Cal Rptr 110; *Van Zee v Bayview Hardware Store* (1968) 74 Cal Rptr 21.) Under this standard, an injured plaintiff will frequently be able to demonstrate the defectiveness of a product by resort to circumstantial evidence, even when the accident itself precludes identification of the specific defect at fault. (*Vandermark v Ford Motor Co.* (1964) 391 P2d 168; *Culpepper v Volkswagen of America Inc, supra; Elmore v American Motors Corp, supra,* 451 P2d 84.)

As Professor Wade has pointed out, however, the expectations of the ordinary consumer cannot be viewed as the exclusive yardstick for evaluating design defectiveness because in many situations . . . the consumer would not know what to expect, because he would have no idea how safe the product could be made. (Wade, 'On the Nature of Strict Tort Liability for Products,' *supra.*)

Numerous California decisions have implicitly recognized this fact and have made clear, through varying linguistic formulations, that a product may be found defective in design, even if it satisfies ordinary consumer expectations, if through hindsight the jury determines that the product's design embodies 'excessive preventable danger', or, in other words, if the jury finds that the risk of danger inherent in the challenged design outweighs the benefits of such design. (*Eg Self v General Motors Corp, supra; Hyman v Gordon, supra; Buccery v General Motors Corp, supra.*)[8]

A review of past cases indicates that in evaluating the adequacy of a product's design pursuant to this latter standard, a jury may consider, among other relevant factors, the gravity of the danger posed by the challenged design, the likelihood that such danger would occur, the mechanical feasibility of a safer alternative design, the financial cost of an improved design, and the adverse consequences to the product and to the consumer that would result from an alternative design. (See *Horn v General Motors Corp* (1976) 551 P2d 398; *Henderson v Harnischfeger Corp, supra,* 527 P2d 353; *Luque v McLean, supra,* 501 P2d 1163.)

Although our cases have thus recognized a variety of considerations that may be relevant to the determination of the adequacy of a product's design, past authorities have generally not devoted much attention to the appropriate allocation of the burden of proof with respect to these matters. (Compare *Self v General Motors Corp, supra* with *Baker v Chrysler Corp, supra.*) The allocation of such burden is particularly significant in this context inasmuch as this court's product liability decisions, from *Greenman* to *Cronin,* have repeatedly emphasized that one of the principal purposes behind the strict product liability doctrine is to relieve an injured plaintiff of many of the onerous evidentiary burdens inherent in a negligence cause of action. Because most of the evidentiary matters which may be relevant to the determination of the adequacy of a product's design under the 'risk-benefit' standard—eg the feasibility and cost of alternative designs—are similar to issues typically presented in a negligent design case and involve technical matters peculiarly within the knowledge of the manufacturer, we conclude that once the plaintiff makes a *prima facie* case showing the injury was proximately caused by the product's design, the burden should appropriately shift to the defendant to prove, in light of the relevant factors, that the product is not defective. Moreover, inasmuch as this conclusion flows from our determination that the fundamental public policies embraced in *Greenman* dictate that a manufacturer who seeks to escape liability for an injury proximately caused by its product's design on a risk-benefit theory should bear the burden of persuading the trier of fact that its product should not be judged defective, the defendant's burden is one affecting the burden of proof, rather than

[8] In the instant case we have no occasion to determine whether a product which entails a substantial risk of harm may be found defective even if no safer alternative design is feasible. As we noted in *Jiminez v Sears, Roebuck & Co, supra,* 482 P2d 681, Justice Traynor has 'suggested that liability might be imposed as to products whose norm is danger'.

US landmark cases

simply the burden of producing evidence. (See Evid Code, section 605; *Cf Harris v Irish Truck Lines* (1974) 521 P2d 481; *Estate of Gelonese* (1974) 111 Cal Rptr 833.)

Thus, to reiterate, a product may be found defective in design, so as to subject a manufacturer to strict liability for resulting injuries, under either of two alternative tests. First, a product may be found defective in design if the plaintiff establishes that the product failed to perform as safely as an ordinary consumer would expect when used in an intended or reasonably foreseeable manner. Second, a product may alternatively be found defective in design if the plaintiff demonstrates that the product's design proximately caused his injury and the defendant fails to establish, in light of the relevant factors, that, on balance, the benefits of the challenged design outweigh the risk of danger inherent in such design.

Although past California decisions have not explicitly articulated the two-pronged definition of design defect which we have elaborated above, other jurisdictions have adopted a somewhat similar, though not identical, dual approach in attempting to devise instructions to guide the jury in design defect cases. (See *Henderson v Ford Motor Co* (Tex 1974) 519 SW2d 87: *Welch v Outboard Marine Corp* (5th Cir 1973) 481 F2d 252.)

As we have indicated, we believe that the test for defective design set out above is appropriate in light of the rationale and limits of the strict liability doctrine, for it subjects a manufacturer to liability whenever there is something 'wrong' with its product's design—either because the product fails to meet ordinary consumer expectations as to safety or because, on balance, the design is not as safe as it should be—while stopping short of making the manufacturer an insurer for all injuries which may result from the use of its product. This test, moreover, explicitly focuses the trier of fact's attention on the adequacy of the product itself, rather than on the manufacturer's conduct, and places the burden on the manufacturer, rather than the plaintiff, to establish that because of the complexity of, and trade-offs implicit in, the design process, an injury-producing product should nevertheless not be found defective.

Amicus CTLA on behalf of the plaintiff, anticipating to some extent the latter half of the design defect standard articulated above, contends that any instruction which directs the jury to 'weigh' or 'balance' a number of factors, or which sets forth a list of competing considerations for the jury to evaluate in determining the existence of a design defect, introduces an element which 'rings of negligence' into the determination of defect, and consequently is inconsistent with our decision in *Cronin*. As amicus interprets the decision, *Cronin* broadly precludes any consideration of 'reasonableness' or 'balancing' in a product liability action.

In the first place, however, in *Cronin* our principal concern was that the 'unreasonably dangerous' lan-

guage of the Restatement test had 'burdened the *injured plaintiff* with proof of an element which rings of negligence' (italics added) (501 P2d at p 1162) and had consequently placed "a considerably greater burden upon (the injured plaintiff) than that articulated in *Greenman".'*

By shifting the burden of proof to the manufacturer to demonstrate that an injury-producing product is not defective in design, the above standard should lighten the plaintiff's burden in conformity with our *Greenman* and *Cronin* decisions.

Secondly, past design defect decisions demonstrate that, as a practical matter, in many instances it is simply impossible to eliminate the balancing or weighing of competing considerations in determining whether a product is defectively designed or not. In *Self v General Motors Corp, supra*, 116 Cal Rptr 575, for example, an automobile passenger, injured when the car in which she was riding exploded during an accident, brought suit against the manufacturer claiming that the car was defective in that the fuel tank had been placed in a particularly vulnerable position in the left rear bumper. One issue in the case, of course, was whether it was technically feasible to locate the fuel tank in a different position which would have averted the explosion in question. But, as the *Self* court recognized, feasibility was not the sole issue, for another relevant consideration was whether an alternative design of the car, while averting the particular accident, would have created a greater risk of injury in other, more common situations.

In similar fashion, weighing the extent of the risks and the advantages posed by alternative designs is inevitable in many design defect cases. As the *Self* court stated: 'We appreciate the need to balance one consideration against another in designing a complicated product so as to achieve reasonable and practical safety under a multitude of varying conditions.'

Inasmuch as the weighing of competing considerations is implicit in many design defect determinations, an instruction which appears to preclude such a weighing process under all circumstances may mislead the jury.

Finally, contrary to the suggestions of amicus CTLA, an instruction which advises the jury that it may evaluate the adequacy of a product's design by weighing the benefits of the challenged design against the risk of danger inherent in such design is not simply the equivalent of an instruction which requires the jury to determine whether the manufacturer was negligent in designing the product. It is true, of course, that in many cases proof that a product is defective in design may also demonstrate that the manufacturer was negligent in choosing such a design. As we have indicated, however, in a strict liability case, as contrasted with a negligent design action, the jury's focus is properly directed to the condition of the product itself, and not to the reasonableness of the manufacturer's conduct. (See *Ault v*

Barker v Lull Engineering

International Harvester (1974) 528 P2d 1148; *Escola v Coca Cola Bottling Co, supra.* (Justice Traynor, concurring).)

Thus, the fact that the manufacturer took reasonable precautions in an attempt to design a safe product or otherwise acted as a reasonably prudent manufacturer would have under the circumstances, while perhaps absolving the manufacturer of liability under a negligence theory, will not preclude the imposition of liability under strict liability principles if, upon hindsight, the trier of fact concludes that the product's design is unsafe to consumers, users, or bystanders. (See *Foglio v Western Auto Supply,* 128 Cal Rptr 545.)

4 Conclusion

The technological revolution has created a society that contains dangers to the individual never before contemplated. The individual must face the threat to life and limb not only from the car on the street or highway but from a massive array of hazardous mechanisms and products. The radical change from a comparatively safe, largely agricultural, society to this industrial unsafe one has been reflected in the decisions that formerly tied liability to the fault of a tortfeasor but now are more concerned with the safety of the individual who suffers the loss. As Dean Keeton has written:

The change in the substantive law as regards the liability of makers of products and other sellers in the marketing chain has been from fault to defect. The plaintiff is no longer required to impugn the maker, but he is required to impugn the product. (Keeton, 'Product Liability and the Meaning of Defect' (1973) 5 St Mary's I I 30, 33.)

If a jury in determining liability for a defect in design is instructed only that it should decide whether or not there is 'a defective design', it may reach to the extreme conclusion that the plaintiff, having suffered injury, should without further showing, recover; on the other hand, it may go to the opposite extreme and conclude that because the product matches the intended design the plaintiff, under no conceivable circumstance, could recover. The submitted definition eschews both extremes and attempts a balanced approach.

We hold that a trial judge may properly instruct the jury that a product is defective in design (1) if the plaintiff demonstrates that the product failed to perform as safely as an ordinary consumer would expect when used in an intended or reasonably forseeable manner, or (2) if the plaintiff proves that the product's design proximately caused his injury and the defendant fails to prove, in light of the relevant factors discussed above, that on balance the benefits of the challenged design outweigh the risk of danger inherent in such design.

Because the jury may have interpreted the erroneous instruction given in the instant case as requiring plaintiff to prove that the high-lift loader was ultrahazardous or more dangerous than the average consumer contemplated, and because the instruction additionally misinformed the jury that the defectiveness of the product must be evaluated in light of the product's 'intended use' rather than its 'reasonably forseeable use', we cannot find that the error was harmless on the facts of this case. In light of this conclusion, we need not address plaintiff's additional claims of error, for such issues may not arise on retrial. The judgment in favor of defendants is reversed.

Justices Mosk, Clark, Richardson, Wright (Retired Chief Justice of California Judicial Council) and Sullivan (Retired Associate Justice of the Supreme Court) concur.

1979 *Smith v ER Squibb & Sons*

COMMENTARY

This case went to the state Supreme Court on two grounds: first, whether the trial judge's instructions to the jury were right, and second, whether it was proper for the court to have excluded evidence about changes made by the manufacturer after the events that caused the injury. There was no dispute about the nature of the defect. The drug contained no impurities, but it could, and did in this case, cause a fatal reaction in some patients. The allegation was that the manufacturer did not give an adequate warning of this possibility, although the jury found that the warning was adequate.

The plaintiff's case was based on two causes of action, negligence and breach of warranty. The trial court took the view that in the circumstances of the case these two causes of action required identical proof, and refused to instruct the jury on the breach of warranty claim. It restricted its charge to the negligence claim, and that claim depended on the reasonableness of the warning. When we speak of 'reasonable' we are in the area of negligence, and are not concerned with the question of whether or not the product matched the specifications of the contract of sale. The breach of warranty claim was superfluous. The Supreme Court affirmed the decision of the lower courts, that an instruction on breach of warranty was not necessary in the circumstances (but in other circumstances might have been).

The other issue, the exclusion of evidence, is connected with the social benefits of product liability litigation. The argument is that if a manufacturer knows subsequent improvements or changes may be used to show that the product must have originally been defective, he will be reluctant to make improvements or changes. That does not mean a plaintiff can never introduce such evidence. He may use subsequent improvements, for example, to show that improvements were possible if the defendant argues that they could not have been made.

The extensive dissenting opinion by Justice Levin centred on the adequacy of the warning, which was not disputed by the majority. He referred to state legislation which provided that evidence might be introduced to show that warnings were in accordance with generally recognised and prevailing non-governmental standards. That provision is much less valuable to a manufacturer than the wording of the Bill as it was originally presented to the legislature. The Bill would have made it a defence to show that the warning conformed with standards.

Justice Levin did not discuss the point that the plaintiff in this case was unusually sensitive to the drug. Neither he nor the majority considered the possibility that a warning might not be required when there was only a slight chance of harm. If the adequacy of a warning is to be judged by the standard of the reasonable man, *ie* the negligence standard, it could be argued that it is not negligent to fail to foresee a remote contingency. Many courts, however, do not go that far, although some require that a manufacturer has a duty to warn only when an 'appreciable number' of persons are likely to be affected. What is an 'appreciable number' depends on the opinions of individual juries, but an example is the Texas case of *Alberto-Culver v Morgan*, 444 SW2d 770, (1965) in which it was held that an average of five complaints for each million bottles of hair dye was not enough to impose liability on the defendant.

In general, the adequacy of a warning is a jury question, depending on the facts of each case. For a general statement of the law we can look to the Comments by the editors of the Restatement of Torts, Second, in which they explained the effect of section 402A:

J. *Directions or warning.* In order to prevent the product from being unreasonably dangerous, the seller may be required to give directions or warning, on the container, as to its use. The seller may reasonably assume that those with common allergies, as for example to eggs or strawberries, will be aware of them, and he is not required to warn against them. Where, however, the product contains an ingredient to which a substantial number of the population are allergic, and the ingredient is one whose danger is not generally known, or if known is one which the consumer would reasonably not expect to find in the product, the seller is required to give warning against it, if he has knowledge, or by the application of reasonable, developed human skill and foresight should have knowledge, of the presence of the ingredient and the danger. Likewise in the case of poisonous drugs, or those unduly dangerous for other reasons, warning as to use may be required.

JUDGMENT

Supreme Court of Michigan
January 10, 1979

Smith
versus
ER Squibb & Sons Inc and others

Before Chief Justice Coleman and Justices Fitzgerald, Ryan, Moody, Williams, Kavanagh and Levin

Coleman, *Chief Justice.* This product liability case arose from the acute anaphylactic (extreme hypersensitivity) reaction resulting in the death of Shirley Smith which occurred when Renografin-60, a product of defendant ER Squibb & Sons Inc, was injected into her blood stream. Such sensitivity is extremely rare and cannot be discovered prior to injection. It is undisputed and clearly reflected in the record that there was no intrinsic defect in the drug.

Smith v ER Squibb

Plaintiff named the drug manufacturer, various doctors and the hospital as defendants in the action. Upon trial by jury, one doctor received a directed verdict on his behalf. The two other doctors, the hospital and the drug manufacturer were successful in obtaining jury verdicts of no cause of action. Nevertheless, plaintiff received monetary settlements from the two doctors and from the hospital after he filed an appeal of the verdicts. The drug manufacturer, ER Squibb & Sons Inc, is the sole remaining defendant.

In the trial court, plaintiff predicated the drug manufacturer's liability upon an alleged failure to provide adequate warnings to the medical profession of the dangers indigenous to Renografin-60 and of the proper precautionary procedures. Although counts of breach of implied warranty and negligence were pled, the trial court refused to instruct the jury concerning the implied warranty claim. Furthermore, proffered evidence of subsequent changes in the literature accompanying the product was held inadmissible.

We granted leave to appeal and limited our inquiry to the following issues of law:
1 Whether it was reversible error for the trial judge to refuse to charge the jury regarding breach of implied warranty, and
2 Whether the trial judge improperly excluded evidence of changes in written material made by the defendant subsequent to 1969.

The Court of Appeals answered both questions in the negative and affirmed the jury's verdict of no cause of action. 245 NW2d 52 (1976).

The finding of the jury that the warnings were adequate is not at issue. We are here confined to questions of law relating to the adequacy of instructions to the jury and of admissibility of certain evidence. We affirm the circuit court and the Court of Appeals.

On April 14, 1969, Shirley Smith was referred to St Joseph Mercy Hospital for an intravenous pyelogram (IVP) by her personal physician, Dr Kozlinski. An IVP is an X-ray of the kidneys which involves the injection of a contrast medium into the veins. The contrast medium serves as a dye by which X-rays can more effectively reveal the operation of the kidneys. The particular contrast medium used was Renografin-60, a 60% iodine solution manufactured by ER Squibb & Sons Inc.

Plaintiff's decedent arrived at the hospital on April 16, 1969 at approximately 12.30pm. After the patient was prepared by a technician, an emergency room physician, Dr Scerhelmi, administered the drug. Dr Scerhelmi injected a one-half cc trial amount and then, slowly, the remainder of the drug. Several minutes subsequent to the injection, Mrs Smith became nauseated—a not uncommon occurrence. After Dr Scerhelmi departed, however, a delayed reaction set in. Foam started to form on her mouth, she had difficulty in breathing and fainted. The radiologist, Dr Dolan, was called. The patient underwent acute anaphylactic shock. All efforts to revive her failed and Shirley Smith died at approximately 2.30pm. The cause of death was determined to be a hypersensitive reaction to Renografin-60.

Each packing case of Renografin-60 contained 25 vials, each vial containing 30cc of the drug. Because of the small size of the vials, no warnings appeared on the labels. However, each vial came with a 'package insert' wrapped around it. At the hospital, these individual vials were taken to and placed in cabinets in the X-ray rooms, while the packing cases and the inserts remained in the pharmacy.

Dr Scerhelmi testified that she had read the Renografin-60 inserts and had read journals on the subject *prior to administering the fatal IVP.* Moreover, she was an experienced physician who had previously given hundreds of IVPs.

The inserts were four pages long and contained information concerning the chemical adverse reactions relative to Renografin-60. The possibility of delayed anaphylactic reactions was stated in the text and further specific recommendations for diagnosis and treatment were set forth in an article (17 pages long) cited in a footnote.

As Dr Dolan said about the Squibb warnings: 'Every single piece of this medicine has it with it. Every intravenous pyelogram has literature with it, contra-indications and reactions. The company has literature in everything. This is the way it's packed. Even if you don't know them, you can read them and know what to expect, what might happen, even without any medical knowledge . . . . .'

As a method of sales promotion primarily, drug manufacturers also commonly inform physicians concerning prescription drugs by two other methods. The information is published in the Physicians Desk Reference to Pharmaceuticals and Biologicals (PDR). This annual volume contains information supplied by drug maufacturers relevant to each product. The 1969 publication of the PDR did not mention the possible adverse effects of Renografin-60.

The other method of conveying information to the medical profession is through 'detail men'. Detail men are sales representatives of the drug companies who extol the virtues of the product while presumably instructing doctors in the proper method of administering the drugs. Squibb's detail man had briefed all radiologists at the hospital prior to Shirley Smith's injection. Dr Scerhelmi was an emergency room physician and not a radiologist so she was not present on these occasions.

The essence of plaintiff's allegations against Squibb is that adequate warnings relative to inherent dangers and necessary precautions were not conveyed to doctors prescribing and using Renografin-60. Such failure is alleged to constitute both a defect in the drug and negligence on the part of the manufacturer.

Recent US cases

The Court of Appeals held that in the context of an alleged failure to provide adequate warnings, breach of implied warranty and negligence involve identical evidence and require proof of exactly the same elements. Although facially contradictory, upon thorough analysis this position becomes both compelling and irrefutable.

A manufacturer of a prescription drug has a legal duty to warn the medical profession, not the patient, of any risks inherent in the use of the drug which the manufacturer knows or should know to exist. *McEwen v Ortho Pharmaceutical Corp,* 528 P2d 522 (1974); *Sterling Drug Inc v Yarrow,* 408 F2d 978, 993 (CA 8, 1969); *Love v Wolf,* 38 Cal Rptr 183 (1964). However, this duty has been held to require warnings to the patient when the prescription drug is administered in a mass immunization program. *Eg Davis v Wyeth Laboratories Inc,* 399 F2d 121 (CA 9, 1968). Determination of whether this duty has been breached in the context of a negligence claim necessitates that the warnings given be examined as to their reasonableness under the circumstances.

Breach of implied warranty, on the other hand, is established when plaintiff proves that a product defect attributable to the manufacturer has a causal relationship to plaintiff's injuries. *Heckel v American Coupling Corp,* 179 NW2d 381 (1970); *Piercefield v Remington Arms Co,* 133 NW2d 129 (1965). It is commonly accepted that inadequate warnings alone can constitute a product defect, whether the theory be implied warranty or strict liability in tort. *Eg Gutowski v M & R Plastics & Coating Inc,* 231 NW2d 456 (1975); *Berkebile v Brantly Helicopter Corp,* 311 A2d 140 (1973); Restatement Torts, 2d, section 402A, comments h-k; Noel, Products Defective Because of Inadequate Directions or Warnings, 23 SW LJ 256 (1969). As noted by the court below, it is also generally recognized 'that implied warranty and negligence are separate and distinct theories of recovery and that under the implied warranty theory it is not necessary to prove negligence'. 245 NW2d 52.

The distinction between the elements of negligence and breach of implied warranty is that in the former plaintiff must prove that the defect was caused by the manufacturer's negligence, whereas under the warranty theory, plaintiff need only establish that the defect was attributable to the manufacturer, regardless of the amount of care utilized by the manufacturer.

However, when the factual issue is not whether the product itself is defective, but is whether the manufacturer has provided adequate warnings, the existence of a product defect and a breach of duty is determined by the same standard—reasonable care under the circumstances. In the context of a product liability case, it has been said that 'the standard by which a jury determines adequacy is the general negligence standard that liability is created by "conduct which falls below the standard established by law for the protection of others

against unreasonably great risk of harm"'. *Gutowski, supra,* quoting from Prosser, *Law of Torts,* 145 (4th Ed). On the facts, therefore, the two theories involve identical facts and require proof of exactly the same elements. This is true because the focus is upon the *adequacy* of the warnings, regardless of the theory of liability.

Although plaintiff is correct when he argues that negligence and implied warranty are separate and distinct theories, it is clear that Renografin-60 could not be defective unless Squibb was negligent. The test for determining whether a legal duty has been breached is whether defendant exercised reasonable care under the circumstances. Determination of whether a product defect exists because of an inadequate warning requires the use of an identical standard. Consequently, when liability turns on the adequacy of a warning, the issue is one of reasonable care, regardless of whether the theory pled is negligence, implied warranty or strict liability in tort. See *eg Gutowski, supra; Basko v Sterling Drug, Inc,* 416 F2d 417 (1969); Kidwell, The Duty to Warn: A Description of the Model of Decision, 53 Texas L.Rev. 1375 (1975); Merrill, Compensation for Prescription Drug Injuries, 59 Va L Rev 1, 31 (1973).

We hold, therefore, that the trial court did not commit reversible error when it refused to instruct the jury on plaintiff's implied warranty theory and submitted the case solely on the negligence claim. Indeed, such an instruction would have been repetitive and unnecessary and could possibly have misled the jury into believing that plaintiff could recover on the warranty count even if Squibb were not negligent. Such is not the law, given this factual setting. See *Skaggs v Clairol Inc,* 85 Cal Rptr 584 (1970) (hearing granted, June 17, 1970, dismissed by stipulation), *Rainbow v Albert Elia Bldg Co,* 373 NYS2d 928 (1975). Duplicative instructions could have created jury confusion and prejudicial error. We believe the trial judge properly exercised his discretion in this matter.

This opinion is limited solely to its facts. We do not suggest that implied warranty and negligence are not independent causes of action. When the factual issue is the adequacy of the warnings given, the legal standard under either theory is one of reasonable care under the circumstances. Note should be made, however, that on *different facts* it could be prejudicial error *not* to give the implied warranty instruction. See *eg Midgeley v S S Kresge Co,* 127 Cal Rptr 217 (1976) (issue of contributory negligence requires instruction on both negligence and strict liability).

Plaintiff contends that the trial court erred when it held that evidence of subsequent changes in the Renografin-60 package inserts and PDR references was inadmissible. The record indicates that Squibb made its warnings and instructions even more explicit in later years. The trial court relied on Michigan's strong policy against admitting evidence of subsequent remedial measures for the purpose of proving negligence.

Smith v ER Squibb

*Crews v General Motors Corp,*253 NW2d 617 (1977), and MRE 407. See also *Judis v Borg-Warner Corp,* 63 NW2d 647 (1954), and *Denolf v Frank L Jurisk Co,* 238 NW2d 1 (1976).

We hold that the trial judge properly excluded the proffered evidence. MRE 407 reads:
'When, after an event, measures are taken which, if taken previously, would have made the event less likely to occur, evidence of the subsequent measures is not admissible to prove negligence or culpable conduct in connection with the event. This rule does not require the exclusion of evidence of subsequent measures when offered for another purpose, such as proving ownership, control, or feasibility of precautionary measures, if controverted, or impeachment.' Also see committee comments.

Exclusion under the rule restates a basic tenet which has long been accepted in Michigan. It encourages persons to improve their products, property, services and customs without risk of prejudicing any court proceeding and consequently delaying implementation of improvements. See *Crews, supra; Denolf, supra; Judis, supra; Grawey v Genesee County Road Commission,* 211 NW2d 68 (1973). Plaintiff's contention does not fall within any exceptions to the rule.

It is irrelevant that this is a product liability case. Plaintiff's argument that the evidence should have been admitted under his implied warranty count ignores the essence of his legal position on these facts. As the Court of Appeals stated:
'Inasmuch as the plaintiff's entire case was built around proof of an inadequate warning, a negligence concept the theoretical distinction between negligence and implied warranty may not be exploited to obviate the policy reasons for the exclusionary rule.' 245 NW2d 52.

Plaintiff sought to have the evidence admitted to buttress his argument that the warnings were inadequate. In light of the recent adoption of MRE 407 and the court's continuing policy, the trial court's action was entirely proper.

The case is decided upon the instructional and evidentiary issues raised by plaintiff and is limited to its facts. We find no prejudicial or legal error on the part of the trial court.

It is conceded that the product was pure, but it is contended that the warning of its possible, if extremely rare, effect upon a hypersensitive person was inadequate. This is a negligence concept. Whether approached on the legal theory of implied warranty or of negligence, the proofs and the jury instructions would be the same in essential part. A duplication of instructions could be not only confusing but possibly misleading. The jury did not find the negligence urged by the plaintiff an essential to both theories. We find no legal error committed by the trial judge. Therefore, we affirm.

We also affirm the decision as to the issue of whether the court erred in precluding evidence of a subsequent change in the warning. The policy against allowing such evidence is well established in Michigan and continued in the new rules of evidence, specifically in MRE 407 which would be applicable in the requested new trial, so reversal on this point would be meaningless as well as improper. We find that the court did not err.

Affirmed.

Justices Fitzgerald, Ryan and Moody concur, and Justices Williams and Kavanagh concur in the result.

Levin,*Justice* (dissenting). A drug manufactured by Squibb was administered to Shirley Smith during a routine hospital procedure. She had an atypical delayed anaphylactic reaction, went into shock and died. The complaint alleged that Squibb did not adequately warn of the possibility of such a reaction, and sought recovery under two theories—implied warranty and negligence.

The trial judge concluded that the plaintiff could not recover on the implied warranty theory, and instructed the jury solely on the negligence theory. The Court of Appeals found it unnecessary to decide whether that was error and affirmed, stating that on the facts of 'this failure to warn case', 'the standard and the proofs necessary to recovery are identical under both theories.' This court, adopting the same reasoning, also affirms.

We all agree that a product is defective unless the 'manufacturer has provided adequate warnings'. The court concludes that in a failure to warn case the adequacy of the warnings is determined by whether the defendant exercised 'reasonable care under the circumstances', the negligence standard. Since plaintiff cannot recover 'unless Squibb was negligent', to have instructed the jury on plaintiff's implied warranty theory 'could possibly have misled the jury into believing that plaintiff could recover on the warranty count even if Squibb were not negligent'.

The court thus holds that in a product liability action for failure to warn the focus of the inquiry is on the *manufacturer's conduct* although in all other product liability cases the focus is on the *fitness of the product.*

To be sure, the standard by which a jury should be instructed to determine whether a product is fit evokes the same concept of 'reasonableness' it is instructed to apply in determining whether a defendant's conduct was negligent. It does not follow that in a failure to warn case the *inquiry* is the same whether the theory is negligence or implied warranty or, as the Court of Appeals put it, it is 'a distinction without a difference'.

A manufacturer's implied warranty may require that it produce a product of higher quality than would result from the exercise of reasonable care; the product must be reasonably fit for the purpose intended. I would hold that the higher standard of quality, reasonable fitness for the intended purpose, applies to the adequacy of

Recent US cases

warnings accompanying the product as well as to the adequacy of the structure or design of the product itself.

The drug was shipped in cases of 25 vials. 'Warning slips were loosely packed within each case but were not attached to the vials themselves and no warning of any kind appeared on the vial labels.' [1]

It was claimed that the warning was inadequate because i) the warning slip was not *attached* by a rubber band or some other means to the vial, ii) the warning slip did not describe *delayed* anaphylactic reaction to the drug or the treatment to be administered for such a reaction, iii) the drug had not been listed in the Physician's Desk Reference, and iv) Squibb's representative had not discussed precautionary measures with the doctor who administered the drug in the instant case (who worked in the emergency room) as he had with other doctors (the radiology staff).

The judge instructed the jury to decide the adequacy of the warnings by an assessment of the reasonableness of Squibb's conduct, the negligence standard, and gave no instruction to consider the reasonableness of the warning itself:
'Now, getting back to the defendant Squibb. At this time, I know that it is not easy for you or anybody else to determine from the case in chief, that is from the witnesses on the witness stand, whether or not they gave the proper warning to the medical profession and was a proximate cause. But consider all of the testimony, consider all of the circumstances and use your common sense in determining: did they *act* the way a prudent drug manufacturer would have acted under the knowledge they had and the circumstances that existed on April 16, 1969. If they *acted* the way a prudent, careful drug manufacturer would have acted by putting the inserts in the box and the inserts referring to various articles to the medical profession, then they didn't do anything wrong.' [2]

---

[1] *Smith v Squibb,* 245 NW2d 52 (1976). The court states that the vial came with a '"package insert wrapped" around it.' The warning slips or package inserts, as they have been variously described, were not, however, shipped wrapped around each vial in such a manner as to insure that they would accompany the vial when it was removed from the shipping container.

[2] The instruction continued:
'On the other hand; if they did not act the way the ordinary drug manufacturer would have acted, under the conditions that existed and the knowledge known on April 16, 1969 and it was a proximate case of the injury and death, because of the lack of warning to the medical profession, then they would be negligent.'
'Negligence is ordinarily defined as what the ordinary prudent person would have done under like or similar circumstances. Or the failure to do what the ordinarily prudent person would have done under like or similar circumstances.'
'I have already told you that a corporation is the same as a person; therefore, it applies to a corporation, did they act the way an ordinarily prudent drug manufacturer would have acted; as you must remember, this case is odd to this extent; there is no claim at this time that the drug, Renografin-60, was not fit for the purpose for which it was used. There is no claim at this time as far as the drug, Renografin-60, is concerned for anything else with the exception of the failure to warn the medical profession.'

The jury was thus instructed that unless it concluded that Squibb was blameworthy the warning was adequate.

Often the answer to a question is determined by the way it is asked. It is one thing to instruct a jury to determine whether the manufacturer is blameworthy or negligent because he failed to conform to a standard of reasonable care; it is quite another to ask if the manufacturer did, in fact, adequately warn.

A jury, convinced that the manufacturer acted in good faith, might decline to find it 'guilty' of negligence. If the question asked were whether the product is reasonably fit for the purpose intended (whether the user can reasonably expect it to be free of the alleged defect), the same jury might conclude that the product was not reasonably fit—in the instant case that the warnings were not adequate.

In a product liability case the jury may find for the plaintiff without deciding that the manufacturer was to blame or at fault. The inquiry is not solely whether the manufacturer has done all that a reasonable manufacturer might have done but, rather, focuses on whether the product is reasonably fit for the purpose intended.

Where, as here, there may be dangers inherent in use of the product and therefore there is a duty to warn of known danger, the inquiry is not whether the manufacturer acted reasonably but whether the warnings actually given are reasonably adequate. Warnings, like structure and design, must measure up to the higher standard of quality implicit in the requirement that the product be reasonably fit for the intended purpose.

The negligence standard looks solely to the defendant's conduct and seeks to determine whether *he acted,* as the judge charged the jury in this case, in conformity to what the law expects of *him.* The implied warranty standard looks, rather, to the product and asks a different question—whether the *product* measures up to the standard which a user may reasonably expect of *it.* The policy of the law is to enforce the consumer's reasonable expectations of the product even though doing so might mean that more is required of the product than reasonable conduct by the manufacturer would produce.

A drug manufacturer is not subject to liability for anaphylactic reaction or for risks it does not know and cannot reasonably be expected to know. It is, however, subject to liability if the means of notification of known risks does not actually notify and the jury concludes that more adequate means of notification can reasonably be expected.

The cases referred to in the opinion of the court do not address the issue—whether warnings can be inade-

Smith v ER Squibb

quate (not reasonably adequate) notwithstanding the reasonable conduct of the manufacturer. [3]

The issue is addressed in *Hamilton v Hardy*, 549 P2d 1099 (1976). Plaintiff suffered a stroke which she claimed was caused by the malpractice of her physician in prescribing an oral contraceptive and the drug manufacturer's negligence and breach of express and implied warranties. A warning of possible adverse reactions was given which plaintiff claimed was inadequate in light of the reports of thrombotic diseases occurring in women taking such contraceptives. The case was submitted to the jury on plaintiff's negligence theory, but the judge 'refused to instruct the jury on the theory of strict liability,' 549 P2d 1102. The verdict was in favor of the manufacturer. The Court of Appeals reversed.

As here, 'the trial court apparently perceived no difference between a negligence claim based on a failure to warn and a strict liability claim based on a failure to warn, and felt instructing on both theories would be duplicitous and confuse the jury.' 549 P2d 1106.

The Colorado Court of Appeals stated that although the scope of the liability of a drug manufacturer (which produces a product that unavoidably causes adverse effects in some people) is determined by a standard of reasonableness, the plaintiff could recover although the jury found that the manufacturer had not been negligent in failing to give more adequate warnings if it concluded that the product was not reasonably fit without more adequate warnings:

'Although we agree the evidence which proves a failure to warn is the same under both theories, we disagree that the theories are identical.... Under strict liability, the test is whether the failure of Searle to adequately warn of the potentially dangerous propensities of its product rendered that product unreasonably dangerous. It is of no import whether this drug manufacturer's warning comported with the warning a reasonably prudent drug manufacturer would have given. "Strict tort liability shifts the focus from the conduct of the manufacturer to the nature of the

product." 2 Frumer & Friedman, *Products Liability,* section 16A [4] [e] 549 P2d 1106-1107.

The court stated the duty of a drug manufacturer thus:
'In general, for there to be recovery under Restatement (Second) Torts, section 402A, a plaintiff must demonstrate that the defective condition of a product makes the product unreasonably dangerous. In the case of prescription drugs, such as Ovulen, which may be "unavoidably unsafe" as that term is used in comment k of section 402A, the requirements of "defective condition" and "unreasonably dangerous" have a different meaning than in the usual 402A sense. Such a drug is made in the way it was intended, contains no impurities, and is in the condition planned, but it proves to be dangerous because it is "incapable of being made safe for (its intended and ordinary use)." Restatement (Second) Torts, section 402A, comment k. As to such products, *if* the product is accompanied by adequate warning, it is not defective and is not *unreasonably* dangerous. However, when not accompanied by an adequate warning, the product is defective, and thus may be unreasonably dangerous. The defect is not the dangerous propensities or side effects of the drug, but the failure to warn. Thus the question to be posed to the jury with regard to the strict liability issue is whether the manufacturer's failure to adequately warn rendered the product unreasonably dangerous without regard to the reasonableness of the failure to warn judged by negligence standards. On remand, the jury should be so instructed.' 549 P2d 1107-1108.

The Oregon Supreme Court has also recognized that although the scope of the manufacturer's liability may be circumscribed by a standard of reasonableness, the plaintiff may nevertheless recover although the manufacturer was not negligent if the trier of fact decides that the warning was not reasonably adequate:

'In a strict liability case we are talking about the condition (dangerousness) of an article which is sold without any warning, while in negligence we are talking about the reasonableness of the manufacturer's actions in selling the article without a warning. The article can have a degree of dangerousness because of a lack of warning which the law of strict liability will not tolerate even though the actions of the seller were entirely reasonable in selling the article without a warning considering what he knew or should have known at the time he sold it.' *Phillips v Kimwood Machine Co,* 525 P2d 1033 (1974).

In sum, a prescription drug may be unavoidably unsafe even though it is made in the way intended, contains no impurities, and is in the condition planned. If such a product is accompanied by adequate warning, it is not defective and is not *unreasonably* dangerous. However, when not accompanied by an adequate warning, the product is defective, and thus may be unreasonably dangerous. The defect is not in the dangerous propensities or side effects of the drug, but the failure to warn.

[3]*McEwen v Ortho Pharmaceutical Corp,*528 P2d 522 (1974), was an action grounded in negligence, not in implied warranty.
In *Basko v Sterling Drug, Inc,* 416 F2d 417 (CA2, 1969), the judge gave the jury a hybrid instruction that the warnings must be proper and that there was a duty to make reasonable efforts to warn. Plaintiff did not complain, as here, that the jury was not instructed on the higher adequacy of the warning standard but, rather, that it had not been properly instructed on the lower, negligence, standard.
In *Sterling Drug, Inc v Yarrow,* 408 F2d 978 (CA8, 1969), the manufacturer complained that it was being held to a standard higher than reasonableness and the court responded that the judge had in fact used the reasonableness standard. It did not decide that reasonable efforts to warn made the warnings actually given adequate.
In *Love v Wolf,* 38 Cal Rptr 183 (1964), the issue was not the adequacy of the warning but whether the manufacturer's conduct tended to negate an otherwise adequate warning.

Recent US cases

The jury was instructed that unless Squibb was negligent it was not subject to liability.

Although the jury concluded that Squibb had acted reasonably in not attaching the warning to the vial, in not providing a more complete warning, in not seeing to it that the drug was listed in the PDR, and in not having its representative discuss adverse effects with hospital staff members other than radiologists, it might nevertheless have concluded that the drug was not reasonably fit for its intended use without warnings more complete than were given.

The jury should have been instructed it could conclude that the product was not reasonably fit for its intended use unless a warning of the life-threatening risk of delayed anaphylactic reaction and of the treatment to be employed in the event of such reaction was *attached* to the vial or in some other manner communicated to physicians administering the drug.

I would reverse and remand for a new trial. [4]

[4] The legislature has recently stated the public policy of this state to be that conformity to industry standards is admissible as evidence in a products liability action. The Act applies to failures to warn as well as to other manufacturing defects. The bill as introduced would have made such conformity a complete defense. The legislature has thereby made parallel conduct by other manufacturers relevant but not a complete defense in a product liability case.

1980 *Sindell v Abbott Laboratories*

COMMENTARY

One of the lawyers who took part in this case called it 'the decision of the year'. There might be some exaggeration about the description, but the decision does represent an attempt to solve an insoluble problem. The court was faced with a classical dilemma; justice and the law were opposed, and that was not because the law was unreasonable or bound by unfortunate precedents. Ever since tort law first took shape, it had been a principle that a person could not be made to pay compensation unless his responsibility for an injury had been proved. The serious and long-lasting effect of DES, however, brought about a situation that could not be covered by this principle. Yet, to depart from it meant possible injustice for the defendant.

In somewhat different circumstances courts have had similar problems to solve in the past. The case most frequently quoted is *Summers v Tice,* 199 P2d 1, in which two hunters were held jointly liable for a shot that injured a third person. Both had fired at the same time, and the decision was that both were jointly liable, unless one of the two could prove that he did not fire the shot that actually caused the injury. That case was different from the DES cases because all of the possible tortfeasors were before the court. The number of manufacturers of DES is so large that a plaintiff could not be sure of suing them all.

Faced with the choice between sending deserving plaintiffs away without a remedy and departing from the basic rules, the *Sindell* court found a solution in the market share principle. The justification for this departure from established principles was that compensation for the harm would come from some at least of those who had profited from the product in the past. That was not a justification that everybody was willing to accept; three of the seven judges that made up the court were strongly opposed.

The harm done by DES is widespread, and a great many claims have been made in the courts of other states. Some courts have devised other theories, variations of the market share theory, such as 'concerted action', 'alternative liability', 'enterprise liability' and 'civil conspiracy'. *Sindell* itself has not been followed enthusiastically, and the attitude of various other states is summarised below:

New York—adopted a 'concerted action' theory in *Bichler v Eli Lilly,* 436 NYS 2d 625, 1981. If persons work together, in concert, to cause a tort they are all liable, and the manufacturers before the New York court were said to have acted together in obtaining approval for DES from the federal Food and Drug Administration.

New Jersey—adopted 'alternative liability' in *Ferrigno v Eli Lilly,* 420 A 2d 1305, 1980.

Sindell v Abbott Laboratories

Florida—insists on the traditional proof that defendant caused the harm (*Morton v Abbott,* 528 F Supp 594, 1982)

Michigan—adopted a modified form of 'alternative liability' in *Abel v Eli Lilly,* 289 NW 2d 20, 1984. The traditional form of alternative liability in California was that expressed in the case of *Summers v Tice* above, which depended on the fact that all potential wrongdoers (only two in that case) were before the court. In this case, there were 16 defendants, and it was not agreed that these 16 manufacturers included all those who were making DES at the relevant time. It was, however, agreed that all of the 16 made DES.

Wisconsin—In *Collins v Eli Lilly,* Wisconsin Supreme Court, January 4, 1984, it was held that a plaintiff could recover from one defendant if it could be proved that the defendant produced or marketed the type of DES taken by the plaintiff's mother. The defendant sued could bring in as co-defendants other manufacturers if it pleased.

These cases all concern DES, but there are other products to which alternative liability or market share can apply. In particular, the issue of identity has arisen in connection with asbestos. In *Thompson v Johns-Manville,* the federal Court of Appeals for the Fifth Circuit held (on March 19, 1984) that alternative liability or market share theories would not be applied in Louisiana. In Florida the market share theory has been adopted, with the condition that the plaintiff must join a substantial number of manufacturers (*Copeland v The Celotex Corporation,* Court of Appeals, Third District, March 6, 1984). This decision contradicts the decision of a US District Court in *Morton v Abbott* above, a DES case decided under Florida law, that state law required traditional proof of identity. In its opinion in the *Copeland* case, the Court of Appeals merely said that in *Morton* the district court found no indication that 'Florida courts would do what we have now done'. In a dissenting opinion, *Morton* was listed as one of the few cases that had followed *Sindell.*

In that dissenting opinion, the point was made that the market share theory had gained only limited acceptance, and that if only a few states follow *Sindell* liability will fall unevenly and in a haphazard manner. Lack of uniformity is one of the charges levelled against product liability in the USA and one of the justifications for a uniform federal statute.

Nb In late 1983, Judith Sindell, the original plaintiff, settled her lawsuit against five DES manufacturers for $20,000.

JUDGMENT

Supreme Court of California
March 20, 1980

Sindell
versus
Abbott Laboratories and others

Before Chief Justice Bird and Justices Mosk, Newman, White, Richardson, Clark and Manuel

Mosk, *Justice.* This case involves a complex problem both timely and significant: may a plaintiff, injured as the result of a drug administered to her mother during pregnancy, who knows the type of drug involved but cannot identify the manufacturer of the precise product, hold liable for her injuries a maker of a drug produced from an identical formula?

Plaintiff Judith Sindell brought an action against 11 drug companies and Does 1 through 100, on behalf of herself and other women similarly situated. The complaint alleges as follows:

Between 1941 and 1971, defendants were engaged in the business of manufacturing, promoting, and marketing diethylstilbesterol (DES), a drug which is a synthetic compound of the female hormone estrogen. The drug was administered to plaintiff's mother and the mothers of the class she represents,[1] for the purpose of preventing miscarriages. In 1947, the Food and Drug Administration authorized the marketing of DES as a miscarriage preventative but only on an experimental basis, with a requirement that the drug contain a warning label to that effect.

DES may cause cancerous vaginal and cervical growths in the daughters exposed to it before birth, because their mothers took the drug during pregnancy. The form of cancer from which these daughters suffer is known as adenocarcinoma, and it manifests itself after a minimum latent period of 10 or 12 years. It is a fast-spreading and deadly disease, and radical surgery is required to prevent it from spreading. DES also causes adenosis, precancerous vaginal and cervical growths which may spread to other areas of the body. The treatment for adenosis is cauterization, surgery, or cryosurgery. Women who suffer from this condition must be monitored by biopsy or colposcopic examination twice a year, a painful and expensive procedure. Thousands of women whose mothers received DES during pregnancy are unaware of the effects of the drug.

In 1971, the Food and Drug Administration ordered defendants to cease marketing and promoting DES for

[1] The plaintiff class alleged consists of 'girls and women who are residents of California and who have been exposed to DES before birth and who may or may not know that fact or the dangers' to which they were exposed. Defendants are also sued as representatives of a class of drug manufacturers which sold DES after 1941.

Recent US cases

the purpose of preventing miscarriages, and to warn physicians and the public that the drug should not be used by pregnant women because of the danger to their unborn children.

During the period defendants marketed DES, they knew or should have known that it was a carcinogenic substance, that there was a grave danger after varying periods of latency it would cause cancerous and precancerous growths in the daughters of the mothers who took it, and that it was ineffective to prevent miscarriage. Nevertheless, defendants continued to advertise and market the drug as a miscarriage preventative. They failed to test DES for efficacy and safety; the tests performed by others, upon which they relied, indicated that it was not safe or effective. In violation of the authorization of the Food and Drug Administration, defendants marketed DES on an unlimited basis rather than as an experimental drug, and they failed to warn of its potential danger. [2]

Because of defendants' advertised assurances that DES was safe and effective to prevent miscarriage, plaintiff was exposed to the drug prior to her birth. She became aware of the danger from such exposure within one year of the time she filed her complaint. As a result of the DES ingested by her mother, plaintiff developed a malignant bladder tumor which was removed by surgery. She suffers from adenosis and must constantly be monitored by biopsy or colposcopy to ensure early warning of further malignancy.

The first cause of action alleges that defendants were jointly and individually negligent in that they manufactured, marketed and promoted DES as a safe and efficacious drug to prevent miscarriage, without adequate testing or warning, and without monitoring or reporting its effects.

A separate cause of action alleges that defendants are jointly liable regardless of which particular brand of DES was ingested by plaintiff's mother because defendants collaborated in marketing, promoting and testing the drug, relied upon each other's tests, and adhered to an industry-wide safety standard. DES was produced from a common and mutually agreed upon formula as a fungible drug interchangeable with other brands of the same product; defendants knew or should have known that it was customary for doctors to prescribe the drug by its generic rather than its brand name and that pharmacists filled prescriptions from whatever brand of the drug happened to be in stock.

Other causes of action are based upon theories of strict liability, violation of express and implied warranties, false and fraudulent representations, misbranding of drugs in violation of federal law, conspiracy and 'lack of consent'.

Each cause of action alleges that defendants are jointly liable because they acted in concert, on the basis of express and implied agreements, and in reliance upon and ratification and exploitation of each other's testing and marketing methods.

Plaintiff seeks compensatory damages of $1 million and punitive damages of $10 million for herself. For the members of her class, she prays for equitable relief in the form of an order that defendants warn physicians and others of the danger of DES and the necessity of performing certain tests to determine the presence of disease caused by the drug, and that they establish free clinics in California to perform such tests.

. . . .

This case is but one of a number filed throughout the country seeking to hold drug manufacturers liable for injuries allegedly resulting from DES prescribed to the plaintiffs' mothers since 1947. [3] According to a note in the *Fordham Law Review,* estimates of the number of women who took the drug during pregnancy range from one and a half million to three million. Hundreds, perhaps thousands, of the daughters of these women suffer from adenocarcinoma, and the incidence of vaginal adenosis among them is 30 to 90%. (Comment, 'DES and a Proposed Theory of Enterprise Liability' (1978) 46 Fordham L Rev 963, 964-967 (hereafter Fordham Comment).) Most of the cases are still pending. With two exceptions, [4] those that have been decided resulted in judgments in favor of the drug company defendants because of the failure of the plaintiffs to identify the manufacturer of the DES prescribed to their mothers. [5] The same result was reached in a recent California case. (*McCreery v Eli Lilly & Co* (1978) 150 Cal Rptr 730.) The present action is another attempt to overcome this obstacle to recovery.

We begin with the proposition that, as a general rule, the imposition of liability depends upon a showing by the plaintiff that his or her injuries were caused by the act of the defendant or by an instrumentality under the defendant's control. The rule applies whether the injury resulted from an accidental event (*eg Shunk v Bosworth* (6th Cir 1964) 334 F2d 309) or from the use of a defective product. (*eg Garcia v Joseph Vince Co* (1978) 148 Cal Rptr 843; and see collection of cases in 51 ALR3d 1344, 1351; I Hursh and Bailey *American Law of Products Liability,* 2d (1974) p125.)

---

[2] It is alleged also that defendants failed to determine if there was any means to avoid or treat the effects of DES upon the daughters of women exposed to it during pregnancy, and failed to monitor the carcinogenic effects of the drug.

[3] DES was marketed under many different trade marks.

[4] In a recent New York case a jury found in the plaintiff's favor in spite of her inability to identify a specific manufacturer of DES. An appeal is pending (*Bichler v Eli Lilly and Co.* (Sup Ct NY 1979).) A Michigan appellate court recently held that plaintiffs had stated a cause of action against several manufacturers of DES even though identification could not be made. (*Abel v Eli Lilly and Co,* decided December 5, 1979). That decision is on appeal to the Supreme Court of Michigan.

[5] *eg Gray v United States* (SD Tex 1978) 445 F Supp 337. In their briefs, defendants refer to a number of other cases in which trial courts have dismissed actions in DES cases on the ground stated above.

Sindell v Abbott Laboratories

There are, however, exceptions to this rule. Plaintiff's complaint suggests several bases upon which defendants may be held liable for her injuries even though she cannot demonstrate the name of the manufacturer which produced the DES actually taken by her mother. The first of these theories, classically illustrated by *Summers v Tice* (1948) 199 P2d 1, places the burden of proof of causation upon tortious defendants in certain circumstances. The second basis of liability emerging from the complaint is that defendants acted in concert to cause injury to plaintiff. There is a third and novel approach to the problem, sometimes called the theory of 'enterprise liability,' but which we prefer to designate by the more accurate term of 'industry-wide' liability, [6] which might obviate the necessity for identifying the manufacturer of the injury-causing drug. We shall conclude that these doctrines, as previously interpreted, may not be applied to hold defendants liable under the allegations of this complaint. However, we shall propose and adopt a fourth basis for permitting the action to be tried, grounded upon an extension of the *Summers* doctrine.

1 Alternative liability theory

Plaintiff places primary reliance upon cases which hold that if a party cannot identify which of two or more defendants caused an injury, the burden of proof may shift to the defendants to show that they were not responsible for the harm. This principle is sometimes referred to as the 'alternative liability' theory.

The celebrated case of *Summers v Tice, supra,* a unanimous opinion of this court, best exemplifies the rule. In *Summers,* the plaintiff was injured when two hunters negligently shot in his direction. It could not be determined which of them had fired the shot which actually caused the injury to the plaintiff's eye, but both defendants were nevertheless held jointly and severally liable for the whole of the damages. We reasoned that both were wrongdoers, both were negligent toward the plaintiff, and that it would be unfair to require plaintiff to isolate the defendant responsible, because if the one pointed out were to escape liability, the other might also, and the plaintiff-victim would be shorn of any remedy. In these circumstances, we held, the burden of proof shifted to the defendants, 'each to absolve himself if he can.' We stated that under these or similar circumstances a defendant is ordinarily in a 'far better position' to offer evidence to determine whether he or another defendant caused the injury.
. . . . .

The rule developed in *Summers* has been embodied in

the Restatement of Torts (section 433B(3)).[7] Indeed, the *Summers* facts are used as an illustration (p447).

Defendants assert that these principles are inapplicable here. First, they insist that a predicate to shifting the burden of proof under *Summers* is that the defendants must have greater access to information regarding the cause of the injuries than the plaintiff, whereas in the present case the reverse appears.

Plaintiff does not claim that defendants are in a better position than she to identify the manufacturer of the drug taken by her mother or, indeed that they have the ability to do so at all, but argues, rather, that *Summers* does not impose such a requirement as a condition to the shifting of the burden of proof. In this respect we believe plaintiff is correct.
. . . . .

Defendants maintain that, while in *Summers* there was a 50% chance that one of the two defendants was responsible for the plaintiff's injuries, here since any one of 200 companies which manufactured DES might have made the product which harmed plaintiff, there is no rational basis upon which to infer that any defendant in this action caused plaintiff's injuries, nor even a reasonable possibility that they were responsible. [8]

These arguments are persuasive if we measure the chance that any one of the defendants supplied the injury-causing drug by the number of possible tortfeasors. In such a context, the possibility that any of the five defendants supplied the DES to plaintiff's mother is so remote that it would be unfair to require each defendant to exonerate itself. There may be a substantial likelihood that none of the five defendants joined in the action made the DES which caused the injury, and that the offending producer not named would escape liability altogether. While we propose, *infra,* an adaption of the rule in *Summers* which will substantially overcome these difficulties, defendants appear to be correct that the rule, as previously applied, cannot relieve plaintiff of

---

[7]Section 433B, subsection (3) of the Restatement provides: 'Where the conduct of two or more actors is tortious, and it is proved that harm has been caused to the plaintiff by only one of them, but there is uncertainty as to which one has caused it, the burden is upon each such actor to prove that he has not caused the harm.' The reason underlying the rule is 'the injustice of permitting proved wrongdoers, who among them have inflicted an injury upon the entirely innocent plaintiff, to escape liability merely because the nature of their conduct and the resulting harm has made it difficult or impossible to prove which of them has caused the harm.'

[8] Defendants claim further that the effect of shifting the burden of proof to them to demonstrate that they did not manufacture the DES which caused the injury would create a rebuttable presumption that one of them made the drug taken by plaintiff's mother, and that this presumption would deny them due process because there is no rational basis for the inference.

---

[6] The term 'enterprise liability' is sometimes used broadly to mean that losses caused by an enterprise should be borne by it. (Klemme, 'Enterprise Liability' (1976) 47 Colo L Rev 153, 158.)

Recent US cases

the burden of proving the identity of the manufacturer which made the drug causing her injuries. [9]

2 Concert of action theory

The second principle upon which plaintiff relies is the so-called 'concert of action' theory. Preliminarily, we briefly describe the procedure a drug manufacturer must follow before placing a drug on the market. Under federal law as it read prior to 1962, a new drug was defined as one 'not generally recognized as . . . safe.' (section 102, 76 Stat 781 (October 10, 1962)) Such a substance could be marketed only if a new drug application had been filed with the Food and Drug Administration and had become 'effective'.[10] If the agency determined that a product was no longer a 'new drug,' ie that it was 'generally recognized as . . . safe,' (21 USCA section 321 (p) (1)) it could be manufactured by any drug company without submitting an application to the agency. According to defendants, 123 new drug applications for DES had been approved by 1952, and in that year DES was declared not to be a 'new drug', thus allowing any manufacturer to produce it without prior testing and without submitting a new drug application to the Food and Drug Administration.

With this background we consider whether the complaint states a claim based upon 'concert of action' among defendants. The elements of this doctrine are prescribed in section 876 of the Restatement of Torts.
. . . . .

Plaintiff contends that her complaint states a cause of action under these principles. She alleges that defendants' wrongful conduct 'is the result of planned and concerted action, express and implied agreements, collaboration in, reliance upon, acquiescence in and

ratification, exploitation and adoption of each other's testing, marketing methods, lack of warnings . . . and other acts or omissions . . . ' and that 'acting individually and in concert, (defendants) promoted, approved, authorized, acquiesced in, and reaped profits from sales' of DES. These allegations, plaintiff claims, state a 'tacit understanding' among defendants to commit a tortious act against her.

In our view, this litany of charges is insufficient to allege a cause of action under the rules stated above. The gravamen of the charge of concert is that defendants failed to adequately test the drug or to give sufficient warning of its dangers and that they relied upon the tests performed by one another and took advantage of each others' promotional and marketing techniques. These allegations do not amount to a charge that there was a tacit understanding or a common plan among defendants to fail to conduct adequate tests or give sufficient warnings, and that they substantially aided and encouraged one another in these omissions.
. . . . .

3 Enterprise liability

A third theory upon which plaintiff relies is the concept of industry-wide liability, or according to the terminology of the parties, 'enterprise liability'. This theory was suggested in *Hall v E I Du Pont de Nemours & Co Inc,* (EDNY 1972) 345 F Supp 353. In that case, plaintiffs were 13 children injured by the explosion of blasting caps in 12 separate incidents which occurred in ten different states betwen 1955 and 1959. The defendants were six blasting cap manufacturers, comprising virtually the entire blasting cap industry in the United States, and their trade association. There were, however, a number of Canadian blasting cap manufacturers which could have supplied the caps. The gravamen of the complaint was that the practice of the industry of omitting a warning on individual blasting caps and of failing to take other safety measures created an unreasonable risk of harm, resulting in the plaintiffs' injuries. The complaint did not identify a particular manufacturer of a cap which caused a particular injury.[11]

The court reasoned as follows: there was evidence that defendants, acting independently, had adhered to an industry-wide standard with regard to the safety features of blasting caps, that they had in effect

---

[9] *Garcia v Joseph Vince Co, supra,* 148 Cal Rptr 843, relied upon by defendants, presents a distinguishable factual situation. The plaintiff in *Garcia* was injured by a defective saber. He was unable to identify which of two manufacturers had produced the weapon because it was commingled with other sabers after the accident. In a suit against both manufacturers, the court refused to apply the *Summers* rationale on the ground that the plaintiff had not shown that either defendant had violated a duty to him. Thus in *Garcia,* only one of the two defendants was alleged to have manufactured a defective product, and the plaintiff's inability to identify which of the two was negligent resulted in a judgment for both defendants.
Here, by contrast, the DES manufactured by all defendants is alleged to be defective, but plaintiff is unable to demonstrate which of the defendants supplied the precise DES which caused her injuries.

[10] A new drug application became 'effective' automatically if the Secretary of Health, Education and Welfare failed within a certain period of time to disapprove the application. If the agency had insufficient information to decide whether the drug was safe or had information that it was unsafe, the application was denied. Section 505, 52 Stat 1052 (June 25, 1938). Since 1962, affirmative approval of an application has been required before a new drug may be marketed. (21 USCA section 355(c)).

[11] We deliberately employ the term 'suggested' to describe the effect of the *Hall* opinion because of the uncertain posture of the decision as authority. The defendants moved to dismiss the action on the ground that the plaintiffs had not stated a claim, and they also sought to sever the claims of the various plaintiffs and transfer them to the district court in the place where each accident occurred. The opinion discusses various possible bases of liability, including industry-wide liability, upon the assumption that there existed a national body of state tort law. (345 F Supp at p360.) At the conclusion of its opinion, the court called for briefs on the choice-of-law issues involved in the case.

Sindell v Abbott Laboratories

delegated some functions of safety investigation and design, such as labelling, to their trade association, and that there was industry-wide cooperation in the manufacture and design of blasting caps. In these circumstances, the evidence supported a conclusion that all the defendants jointly controlled the risk. Thus, if plaintiffs could establish by a preponderance of the evidence that the caps were manufactured by one of the defendants, the burden of proof as to causation would shift to all the defendants. The court noted that this theory of liability applied to industries composed of a small number of units, and that what would be fair and reasonable with regard to an industry of five or ten producers might be manifestly unreasonable if applied to a decentralized industry composed of countless small producers. [12]

Plaintiff attempts to state a cause of action under the rationale of *Hall.* She alleges joint enterprise and collaboration among defendants in the production, marketing, promotion and testing of DES, and 'concerted promulgation and adherence to industry-wide testing, safety, warning and efficacy standards' for the drug. We have concluded above that allegations that defendants relied upon one another's testing and promotion methods do not state a cause of action for concerted conduct to commit a tortious act. Under the theory of industry-wide liability, however, each manufacturer could be liable for all injuries caused by DES by virtue of adherence to an industry-wide standard of safety.

In the Fordham Comment, the industry-wide theory of liability is discussed and refined in the context of its applicability to actions alleging injuries resulting from DES. The author explains causation under that theory as follows, '. . . The industry-wide standard becomes itself the cause of plaintiff's injury, just as defendants' joint plan is the cause of injury in the traditional concert of action plea. Each defendant's adherence perpetuates this standard, which results in the manufacture of the particular, unidentifiable injury-producing product. Therefore, each industry member has contributed to plaintiff's injury.' (Fordham Comment, *supra,* at p997).

The Comment proposes seven requirements for a cause of action based upon industry-wide liability, [13] and suggests that if a plaintiff proves these elements, the burden of proof of causation should be shifted to the defendants, who may exonerate themselves only by showing that their product could not have caused the injury. [14]

We decline to apply this theory in the present case. At least 200 manufacturers produced DES; *Hall,* which involved six manufacturers representing the entire

blasting cap industry in the United States, cautioned against application of the doctrine espoused therein to a large number of producers. (345 F Supp at p378.) Moreover, in *Hall,* the conclusion that the defendants jointly controlled the risk was based upon allegations that they had delegated some functions relating to safety to a trade association. There are no such allegations here, and we have concluded above that plaintiff has failed to allege liability on a concert of action theory.

Equally important, the drug industry is closely regulated by the Food and Drug Administration, which actively controls the testing and manufacture of drugs and the method by which they are marketed, including the contents of warning labels. To a considerable degree, therefore, the standards followed by drug manufacturers are suggested or compelled by the government. Adherence to those standards cannot, of course, absolve a manufacturer of liability to which it would otherwise be subject. (*Stevens v Parke, Davis & Co* (1973) 507 P2d 653.) But since the government plays such a pervasive role in formulating the criteria for the testing and marketing of drugs, it would be unfair to impose upon a manufacturer liability for injuries resulting from the use of a drug which it did not supply simply because it followed the standards of the industry.

If we were confined to the theories of *Summers* and *Hall,* we would be constrained to hold that the judgment must be sustained. Should we require that plaintiff identify the manufacturer which supplied the DES used by her mother or that all DES manufacturers be joined in the action, she would effectively be precluded from any recovery. As defendants candidly admit, there is little

---

[13] The suggested requirements are as follows:
  1 There existed an insufficient, industry-wide standard of safety as to the manufacture of the product.
  2 Plaintiff is not at fault for the absence of evidence identifying the causative agent but, rather, this absence of proof is due to defendant's conduct.
  3 A generically similar defective product was manufactured by all the defendants.
  4 Plaintiff's injury was caused by this defect.
  5 Defendants owed a duty to the class of which plaintiff was a member.
  6 There is clear and convincing evidence that plaintiff's injury was caused by a product made by one of the defendants. For example, the joined defendants accounted for a high percentage of such defective products on the market at the time of plaintiff's injury.
  7 All defendants were tortfeasors.

[14] The Fordham Comment takes exception to one aspect of the theory of industry-wide liability as set forth in *Hall, ie* the conclusion that a plaintiff is only required to show by a preponderance of the evidence that one of the defendants manufactured the product which caused her injury. The Comment suggests that a plaintiff be required to prove by clear and convincing evidence that one of the defendants before the court was responsible and that this standard of proof would require that the plaintiff join in the action the producers of 75 or 80% of the DES prescribed for prevention of miscarriage. It is also suggested that the damages be apportioned among the defendants according to their share of the market for DES. (Fordham Comment, *supra,* pp999-1000.)

---

[12] In discussing strict liability, the *Hall* court mentioned the drug industry stating, 'In cases where manufacturers have more experience, more information, and more control over the risky properties of their products than do drug manufacturers, courts have applied a broader concept of foreseeability which approaches the enterprise liability rationale.' (345 F Supp 353 at p370.)

Recent US cases

likelihood that all the manufacturers who made DES at the time in question are still in business or that they are subject to the jurisdiction of the California courts. There are, however, forceful arguments in favor of holding that plaintiff has a cause of action.

In our contemporary complex industrialized society, advances in science and technology create fungible goods which may harm consumers and which cannot be traced to any specific producer. The response of the courts can be either to adhere rigidly to prior doctrine, denying recovery to those injured by such products, or to fashion remedies to meet these changing needs. Just as Justice Traynor in his landmark concurring opinion in *Escola v Coca Cola Bottling Company* (1944) 150 P2d 436, recognized that in an era of mass production and complex marketing methods the traditional standard of negligence was insufficient to govern the obligations of manufacturer to consumer, so should we acknowledge that some adaptation of the rules of causation and liability may be appropriate in these recurring circumstances. The Restatement comments that modification of the *Summers* rule may be necessary in a situation like that before us.

The most persuasive reason for finding plaintiff states a cause of action is that advanced in *Summers:* as between an innocent plaintiff and negligent defendants, the latter should bear the cost of the injury. Here, as in *Summers*, plaintiff is not at fault in failing to provide evidence of causation, and although the absence of such evidence is not attributable to the defendants either, their conduct in marketing a drug the effects of which are delayed for many years played a significant role in creating the unavailability of proof.

From a broader policy standpoint, defendants are better able to bear the cost of injury resulting from the manufacture of a defective product. As was said by Justice Traynor in *Escola*, 'the cost of an injury and the loss of time or health may be an overwhelming misfortune to the person injured, and a needless one, for the risk of injury can be insured by the manufacturer and distributed among the public as a cost of doing business.' (150 P2d p441; see also Rest 2d Torts, section 402A, comment.) The manufacturer is in the best position to discover and guard against defects in its products and to warn of harmful effects; thus, holding it liable for defects and failure to warn of harmful effects will provide an incentive to product safety. (*Cronin v JBE Olson Corp* (1972) 501 P2d 1153; *Beech Aircraft Corp v Superior Court* (1976) 132 Cal Rptr 541.) These considerations are particularly significant where medication is involved, for the consumer is virtually helpless to protect himself from serious, sometimes permanent, sometimes fatal, injuries caused by deleterious drugs.

Where, as here, all defendants produced a drug from an identical formula and the manufacturer of the DES which caused plaintiff's injuries cannot be identified through no fault of plaintiff, a modification of the rule of *Summers* is warranted. As we have seen, an undiluted

Summers rationale is inappropriate to shift the burden of proof of causation to defendants because if we measure the chance that any particular manufacturer supplied the injury-causing product by the number of producers of DES there is a possibility that none of the five defendants in this case produced the offending substance and that the responsible manufacturer, not named in the action, will escape liability.

But we approach the issue of causation from a different perspective: we hold it to be reasonable in the present context to measure the likelihood that any of the defendants supplied the product which allegedly injured plaintiff by the percentage which the DES sold by each of them for the purpose of preventing miscarriage bears to the entire production of the drug sold by all for that purpose. Plaintiff asserts in her briefs that Eli Lilly and Company and five or six other companies produced 90% of the DES marketed. If at trial this is established to be the fact, then there is a corresponding likelihood that this comparative handful of producers manufactured the DES which caused plaintiff's injuries, and only a 10% likelihood that the offending producer would escape liability. [15]

If plaintiff joins in the action the manufacturers of a substantial share of the DES which her mother might have taken, the injustice of shifting the burden of proof to defendants to demonstrate that they could not have made the substance which injured plaintiff is significantly diminished. While 75 to 80% of the market is suggested as the requirement by the Fordham Comment (at p996), we hold only that a substantial percentage is required.

The presence in the action of a substantial share of the appropriate market also provides a ready means to apportion damages among the defendants. Each defendant will be held liable for the proportion of the judgment represented by its share of that market unless it demonstrates that it could not have made the product which caused plaintiff's injuries. In the present case, as we have seen, one DES manufacturer was dismissed from the action upon filing a declaration that it had not manufactured DES until after plaintiff was born. Once plaintiff has met her burden of joining the required defendants, they in turn may cross-complaint against other DES manufacturers, not joined in the action, which they can allege might have supplied the injury-causing product.

[15] The Fordham Comment explains the connection between percentage of market share and liability as follows: 'If X Manufacturer sold one-fifth of all the DES prescribed for pregnancy and identification could be made in all cases, X would be the sole defendant in approximately one-fifth of all cases and liable for all the damages in those cases. Under alternative liability, X would be joined in all cases in which identification could not be made, but liable for only one-fifth of the total damages in these cases. X would pay the same amount either way. Although the correlation is not, in practice, perfect it is close enough so that defendants' objections on the ground of fairness lose their value.' (Fordham Comment, *supra*, at p994.)

Sindell v Abbott Laboratories

Under this appproach, each manufacturer's liability would approximate its responsibility for the injuries caused by its own products. Some minor discrepancy in the correlation between market share and liability is inevitable; therefore, a defendant may be held liable for a somewhat different percentage of the damage than its share of the appropriate market would justify. It is probably impossible, with the passage of time, to determine market share with mathematical exactitude. But just as a jury cannot be expected to determine the precise relationship between fault and liability in applying the doctrine of comparative fault (*Li v Yellow Cab Co* (1975) 532 P2d 1226) or partial indemnity (*American Motorcycle Assn v Superior Court* (1978) 578 P2d 899), the difficulty of apportioning damages among the defendant producers in exact relation to their market share does not seriously militate against the rule we adopt. As we said in *Summers* with regard to the liability of independent tortfeasors, where a correct division of liability cannot be made 'the trier of fact may make it the best it can.' (199 P2d at p5.)

We are not unmindful of the practical problems involved in defining the market and determining market share, [16]but these are largely matters of proof which properly cannot be determined at the pleading stage of these proceedings. Defendants urge that it would be both unfair and contrary to public policy to hold them liable for plaintiff's injuries in the absence of proof that one of them supplied the drug responsible for the damage. Most of their arguments, however, are based upon the assumption that one manufacturer would be held responsible for the products of another or for those of all other manufacturers if plaintiff ultimately prevails. But under the rule we adopt, each manufacturer's liability for an injury would be approximately equivalent to the damages caused by the DES it manufactured. [17]

The judgments are reversed.

Chief Justice Bird and Justices Newman and White concur.

Richardson, *Justice,* dissenting. I respectfully dissent. In these consolidated cases the majority adopts a wholly new theory which contains these ingredients: The plaintiffs were not alive at the time of the commission of the tortious acts. They sue a generation later. They are permitted to receive substantial damages from multiple defendants without any proof that any defendant caused or even probably caused plaintiffs' injuries.

Although the majority purports to change only the required burden of proof by shifting it from plaintiffs to defendants, the effect of its holding is to guarantee that plaintiffs will prevail on the causation issue because defendants are no more capable of disproving factual causation than plaintiffs are of proving it. 'Market share' liability thus represents a new high water mark in tort law. The ramifications seem almost limitless, a fact which prompted one recent commentator, in criticizing a substantially identical theory, to conclude that 'Elimination of the burden of proof as to identification (of the manufacturer whose drug injured plaintiff) would impose a liability which would exceed absolute liability.' (Coggins, 'Industry-Wide Liability' (1979) 13 Suffolk L Rev 980, 998.) In my view, the majority's departure from traditional tort doctrine is unwise.

. . . . .

The majority now expressly abandons the foregoing traditional requirement of some causal connection between defendants' act and plaintiffs' injury in the creation of its new modified industry-wide tort. Conceptually, the doctrine of absolute liability which heretofore in negligence law has substituted only for the requirement of a breach of defendant's duty of care, under the majority's hand now subsumes the additional necessity of a causal relationship.

. . . . .

Much more significant, however, is the consequence of this unprecedented extension of liability. Recovery is permitted from a handful of defendants *each* of whom *individually* may account for a comparatively small share of the relevant market, so long as the *aggregate* business of those who have been sued is deemed 'substantial.' In other words, a particular defendant may be held proportionately liable *even though mathematically it is much more likely than not that it played no role whatever in causing plaintiffs' injuries.* Plaintiffs have strikingly capsulated their reasoning by insisting ' . . . that while one manufacturer's product may not have injured a particular plaintiff, we can assume that it injured a different plaintiff and all we are talking about is a mere matching of plaintiffs and defendants.' (Counsel's letter (October 16, 1979) p3.) In adopting the foregoing rationale the majority rejects over 100 years of tort law which required that before tort liability was imposed a 'matching' of defendant's conduct and plaintiff's injury was absolutely essential. Furthermore, in bestowing on plaintiffs this new largess the majority sprinkles the rain of liability upon all the joined defendants alike—those who may be tortfeasors and those who may have had nothing at all to do with plaintiffs' injury—and an added bonus is conferred. Plaintiffs are free to pick and choose their targets.

---

[16] Defendants assert that there are no figures available to determine market share, that DES was provided for a number of uses other than to prevent miscarriage and it would be difficult to ascertain what proportion of the drug was used as a miscarriage preventative, and that the establishment of a time frame and area for market share would pose problems.

[17] The dissent concludes by implying the problem will disappear if the Legislature appropriates funds 'for the educaton, identification, and screening of persons exposed to DES.' While such a measure may arguably be helpful in the abstract, it does not address the issue involved here: damages for injuries which have been or will be suffered. Nor, as a principle, do we see any justification for shifting the financial burden for such damages from drug manufacturers to the taxpayers of California.

Recent US cases

The 'market share' thesis may be paraphrased. Plaintiffs have been hurt by *someone* who made DES. Because of the lapse of time no one can prove who made it. Perhaps it was not the named defendants who made it, but they did make some. Although DES was apparently safe at the time it was used, it was subsequently proven unsafe as to some daughters of some users. Plaintiffs have suffered injury and defendants are wealthy. There should be a remedy. Strict products liability is unavailable because the element of causation is lacking. Strike that requirement and label what remains 'alternative' liability, 'industry-wide' liability, or 'market share' liability, proving thereby that if you hit the square peg hard and often enough the round holes will really become square, although you may splinter the board in the process.

The foregoing result is directly contrary to long established tort principles. Once again, in the words of Dean Prosser, the applicable rule is: '(Plaintiff) must introduce evidence which affords a reasonable basis for the conclusion that it is more likely than not that the conduct of the defendant was a substantial factor in bringing about the result. *A mere possibility of such causation is not enough;* and when the matter remains one of pure speculation or conjecture, or the probabilities are at best evenly balanced, it becomes the duty of the court to direct a verdict for the defendant.' (*Prosser, supra,* section 41, at p241, italics added) Under the majority's new reasoning, however, a defendant is fair game if it happens to be engaged in a similar business and causation is *possible,* even though remote.

In passing, I note the majority's dubious use of market share data. It is perfectly proper to use such information to assist in proving, circumstantially, that a particular defendant probably caused plaintiffs' injuries. Circumstantial evidence may be used as a basis for proving the requisite probable causation. The majority, however, authorizes the use of such evidence for an entirely different purpose, namely, to impose and allocate liability among multiple defendants only one of whom *may* have produced the drug which injured plaintiffs. Because this use of market share evidence does not implicate *any* particular defendant, I believe such data are entirely irrelevant and inadmissible, and that the majority errs in such use. In the absence of some statutory authority there is no legal basis for such use.

Although seeming to acknowledge that imposition of liability upon defendants who probably did not cause plaintiffs' injuries is unfair, the majority justifies this inequity on the ground that 'each manufacturer's liability for an injury would be approximately equivalent to the damages caused by the DES it manufactured.' In other words, because each defendant's liability is proportionate to its market share, supposedly 'each manufacturer's liability would approximate its responsibility for the injuries caused by his own products.' The majority dodges the 'practical problems' thereby presented, choosing to describe them as 'matters of proof.'

However, the difficulties, in my view, are not so easily ducked, for they relate not to evidentiary matters but to the fundamental question of liability itself.

Additionally, it is readily apparent that 'market share' liability will fall unevenly and disproportionately upon those manufacturers who are amenable to suit in California. On the assumption that no other state will adopt so radical a departure from traditional tort principles, it may be concluded that under the majority's reasoning those defendants who are brought to trial in this state will bear effective joint responsibility for 100% of plaintiffs' injuries despite the fact that their 'substantial' aggregate market share may be considerably less. This undeniable fact forces the majority to concede that, 'a defendant may be held liable for a somewhat different percentage of the damage than its share of the appropriate market would justify.' With due deference, I suggest that the complete unfairness of such a result in a case involving only five of 200 manufacturers is readily manifest.

Furthermore, several other important policy considerations persuade me that the majority holding is both inequitable and improper. The injustice inherent in the majority's new theory of liability is compounded by the fact that plaintiffs who use it are treated far more favorably than are the plaintiffs in routine tort actions. In most tort cases plaintiff knows the identity of the person who has caused his injuries. In such a case, plaintiff, of course, has no option to seek recovery from an entire industry or a 'substantial' segment thereof, but in the usual instance can recover, if at all, only from the particular defendant causing injury. Such a defendant may or may not be either solvent or amenable to process. Plaintiff in the ordinary tort case must take a chance that defendant can be reached and can respond financially. On what principle should those plaintiffs who wholly fail to prove any causation, an essential element of the traditional tort cause of action, be rewarded by being offered both a wider selection of potential defendants and a greater opportunity for recovery?

The majority attempts to justify its new liability on the ground that defendants herein are 'better able to bear the cost of injury resulting from the manufacture of a defective product.' This 'deep pocket' theory of liability, fastening liability on defendants presumably because they are rich, has understandable popular appeal and might be tolerable in a case disclosing substantially stronger evidence of causation than herein appears. But as a general proposition, a defendant's wealth is an unreliable indicator of fault, and should play no part, at least consciously, in the legal analysis of the problem. In the absence of proof that a particular defendant caused or at least probably caused plaintiff's injuries, a defendant's ability to bear the cost thereof is no more pertinent to the underlying issue of liability than its 'substantial' share of the relevant market. A system priding itself on *'equal* justice under law' does not flower when the *liability* as well as the *damage* aspect of a tort

Sindell v Abbott Laboratories

action is determined by a defendant's wealth. The inevitable consequence of such a result is to create and perpetuate two rules of law—one applicable to wealthy defendants, and another standard pertaining to defendants who are poor or who have modest means. Moreover, considerable doubts have been expressed regarding the ability of the drug industry, and especially its smaller members, to bear the substantial economic costs (from both damage awards and high insurance premiums) inherent in imposing an industry-wide liability. (See *Coggins, supra,* 13 Suffolk L Rev at pp1003-1006, 1010-1011.)

. . . . .

I also suggest that imposition of so sweeping a liability may well prove to be extremely shortsighted from the standpoint of broad social policy. Who is to say whether, and at what time and in what form, the drug industry upon which the majority now fastens this blanket liability, may develop a miracle drug critical to the diagnosis, treatment, or, indeed, cure of the very disease in question? It is counterproductive to inflict civil damages upon *all* manufacturers for the side effects and medical complications which surface in the children of the users a generation after ingestion of the drugs, particularly when, at the time of their use, the drugs met every fair test and medical standard then available and applicable. Such a result requires of the pharmaceutical industry a foresight, prescience and anticipation far beyond the most exacting standards of the relevant scientific disciplines. In effect, the majority requires the pharmaceutical research laboratory to install a piece of new equipment—the psychic's crystal ball.

I am not unmindful of the serious medical consequences of plaintiff's injuries, and the equally serious implications to the class which she purports to represent. In balancing the various policy considerations, however, I also observe that the incidence of vaginal cancer among 'DES daughters' has been variously estimated at one-tenth of 1% to four-tenths of 1%. (13 Suffolk L Rev, *supra,* p999, note 92). These facts raise some penetrating questions. Ninety-nine plus percent of 'DES daughters' have never developed cancer. Must a drug manufacturer to escape this blanket liability wait for a generation of testing before it may disseminate drugs? If a drug has beneficial purposes for the majority of users but harmful side effects are later revealed for a small fraction of consumers, will the manufacturer be absolutely liable? If adverse medical consequences, wholly unknown to the most careful and meticulous of present scientists, surface in *two* or *three* generations, will similar liability be imposed? In my opinion, common sense and reality combine to warn that a 'market share' theory goes too far. Legally, it expects too much.

I believe that the scales of justice tip against imposition of this new liability because of the foregoing elements of unfairness to some defendants who may have had nothing whatever to do with causing any injury, the unwarranted preference created for this particular class of plaintiffs, the violence done to

traditional tort principles by the drastic expansion of liability proposed, the injury threatened to the public interest in continued unrestricted basic medical research as stressed by the Restatement, and the other reasons heretofore expressed.

The majority's decision effectively makes the entire drug industry (or at least its California members) an insurer of all injuries attributable to defective drugs of uncertain or unprovable origin, including those injuries manifesting themselves a generation later, and regardless of whether particular defendants had any part whatever in causing the claimed injury. Respectfully, I think this is unreasonable overreaction for the purpose of achieving what is perceived to be a socially satisfying result.

Finally, I am disturbed by the broad and ominous ramifications of the majority's holding. The law review comment, which is the wellspring of the majority's new theory, conceding the widespread consequences of industry-wide liability, openly acknowledges that 'The DES cases are only the tip of an iceberg,' (Comment, 'DES and a Proposed Theory of Enterprise Liability' (1978) 46 Fordham L Rev 963, 1007.) Although the pharmaceutical drug industry may be the first target of this new sanction, the majority's reasoning has equally threatening application to many other areas of business and commercial activities.

Given the grave and sweeping economic, social and medical effects of 'market share' liability, the policy decision to introduce and define it should rest not with us, but with the legislature which is currently considering not only major statutory reform of California product liability law in general, but the DES problem in particular. (See SB 1392 (1979-1980), which would establish and appropriate funds for the education, identification, and screening of persons exposed to DES, and would prohibit health care and hospital service plans from excluding or limiting coverage to persons exposed to DES.) An alternative proposal for administrative compensation, described as 'a limited version of no-fault products liability' has been suggested by one commentator. (*Coggins, supra,* 13 Suffolk L Rev at pp1019-1021.) Compensation under such a plan would be awarded by an administrative tribunal from funds collected 'via a tax paid by all manufacturers.' In any event, the problem invites a legislative rather than an attempted judicial solution.

I would affirm the judgments of dismissal.

Justices Clark and Manuel concur.

1980 *Wangen v Ford*

COMMENTARY

The opinions in this case analyse in detail the principles governing the award of punitive damages. They are based on Wisconsin law, but refer to decisions in other jurisdictions.

Some of the issues that arise in connection with punitive damages are:
1 It is the plaintiff who has to decide whether to make a claim for punitive damages. A court will not make an award unless there is a claim. It seems that almost as a routine plaintiffs do make such a claim, and attorneys might be open to an action for professional negligence if they did not, but it also seems that awards are made only occasionally.
The main reason for punitive damages is usually said to be the punishment of a defendant who has behaved badly, but it is doubtful whether the predominant motive for punitive damage claims is more than a mere desire to increase as much as possible the amount to be recovered. Both the injured person and his lawyer on a contingency fee basis have a keen interest in the amount of the recovery, and punitive damages merely provide another peg on which to hang a claim.
Thus, courts justify awards of punitive damages on grounds of punishment and deterrence, but the benefit accrues to the plaintiff. There has been some discussion about an alternative procedure, such as making the state the beneficiary of the punitive damage element in a judgment, but there is little expectation of these discussions leading to legislation.

2 Some states relate punitive damages to the award of compensatory damages, but the majority would allow punitive damages even when no compensatable harm has been caused. Nor is the amount of punitive damages generally related to the amount of compensatory damages. This does not mean that the plaintiff can claim punitive damages without proving liability. The defendant must be liable for a tort, such as negligence or strict liability, before there can be any question of punitive damages. It does mean that if liability is established, punitive damages may be awarded even if there is no occasion for compensatory damages.
There is an exception to the general rule. Under the Federal Rules of Evidence a class action is allowed only when each member of the class is able to claim compensatory damages of at least $10,000. Punitive damages in a class action must therefore be limited to cases in which compensatory damages are also claimed.

3 The assessment of punitive damages is a matter for the jury, who should take into account not only the conduct of the defendant but also his wealth.
There is some doubt whether the jury should be told of any previous awards of punitive damages against the defendant.

4 It is outrageous conduct by the defendant that justifies

punitive damages, and there is some inconsistency about the way in which this conduct is proved. The inconsistency is that although punitive damages are expressed as a deterrence and punishment, which are terms appropriate to the criminal law, the conduct is proved by a standard of proof suitable to a civil court. As the Wisconsin court explained, the standard of proof is higher than that required for the tort itself but, even so, it is below the standard that a criminal court would require. It is 'clear, satisfactory and convincing evidence', which is not the same as the 'beyond reasonable doubt' requirement of the criminal law.

JUDGMENT

Wisconsin Supreme Court
June 27, 1980

Wangen and DuVall
versus
Ford Motor Company

Before Justices Abrahamson, Day, Coffey and Hansen

Abrahamson, *Justice.* The central question on appeal is whether punitive damages are recoverable in a product liability suit based on negligence or strict liabilty in tort (sometimes referred to as strict products liability). We conclude that they are recoverable.

1 Facts
This appeal involves two lawsuits which were commenced against Ford Motor Company and others as a result of an automobile accident on July 1, 1975 involving a 1967 Ford Mustang. The cases were consolidated and are before us at the pleading stage; all facts set forth are derived from the pleadings.

The occupants of the 1967 Ford Mustang involved in the accident were Robin DuVall, the driver, Terri Wangen, her sister, Kip Wangen, her brother, and Christopher DuVall, her son. Robin DuVall stopped her 1967 Ford Mustang at an intersection to make a left turn, and a car driven by Patrick J Hawley ran into the rear end of the Mustang. The DuVall Mustang was pushed into the opposite lane of travel where it collided with a car driven by Thomas J Curran. The Mustang's fuel tank ruptured, a fire ensued, and all occupants of the Mustang sustained severe injuries. Christopher DuVall and Kip Wangen died as a result of their injuries.

Two lawsuits were commenced. One is by Terri Wangen and Charles R Wangen, as special administrator of the estates of Christopher DuVall and Kip Wangen, and Charles R Wangen and Ramona M Wangen, individually, against Ford Motor Company, Hawley,

Wangen v Ford

Curran, Robin DuVall and their respective insurance carriers. The second lawsuit is by Robin DuVall against Ford Motor Company, Hawley, Curran and their respective insurance carriers.

Plaintiffs in both lawsuits seek compensatory damages from all named defendants and punitive damages from Ford Motor Company.

The claim for compensatory damages against Ford is based on Ford's alleged negligence in the design, manufacture, assembly, sale and distribution of the 1967 Mustang and on Ford's strict liability in tort arising out of the sale of the 1967 Mustang in a defective condition unreasonably dangerous to users. *Dippel v Sciano,* 155 NW2d 55 (1967).

1 Allegations

The allegations in support of recovery of punitive damages from Ford Motor Company are that Ford knew that the fuel tanks on this and other 1967 Mustangs were dangerously defective before and after the manufacture of the car in question; that corrective design changes were made in models manufactured after this particular model but prior to the date of the instant accident; that Ford failed to warn users of the car of the potential danger both after the danger became apparent and after Ford had changed the design to reduce the danger; that Ford failed to recall, repair or modify the defective vehicles after the defect became apparent in order to avoid the expense of those procedures and to prevent potential lost sales caused by adverse publicity; and that Ford's conduct in failing to warn, repair or recall the known defective vehicles constituted intentional, deliberate, reckless, willful, wanton, gross, callous, malicious and fraudulent disregard for the safety of users of Ford's product.

Ford Motor Company moved to dismiss all allegations in both complaints relating to punitive damages under section 802 06(2)(f), Stats, on the ground that the complaints for punitive damages fail to state a claim against the defendant, Ford Motor Company, upon which relief can be granted. The circuit court denied Ford's motion, concluding that punitive damages may be awarded in product liability cases given a satisfactory evidentiary basis. Review of the circuit court's order was sought, and the court of appeals, in an unpublished decision (May 31, 1979) divided the complaint for punitive damages into five categories of actions and concluded that punitive damages are recoverable in some and not in others. Specifically the court of appeals concluded (1) punitive damages are recoverable in a products liability suit for compensatory damages predicated on strict liability in tort; (2) punitive damages are not recoverable in a product liability suit for compensatory damages predicated on negligence; (3) punitive damages are recoverable in an action which survives the death of the injured person; (4) punitive damages are not recoverable in a wrongful death action; and (5) punitive damages are recoverable by parents in an action for damages for loss of society and companionship of a child but not in an action for damages for loss of the minor's earning capacity and medical expenses. We hold that the complaints state a claim for punitive damages in each of these five categories except number (4), the wrongful death action.

We shall turn first to the question of whether punitive damages are recoverable in a product liability action predicated on negligence or strict liability, and we shall turn then to recovery of punitive damages in a survival action, in a wrongful death action, and in an action by a parent for damages resulting from injury to a child.

2 Punitive damages

Ford Motor Company's argument that punitive damages have no place in product liability cases rests on three grounds: (A) Punitive damages have traditionally been awarded in tort actions in which compensatory damages are premised on defendant's commission of an intentional, personal tort, and recovery of punitive damages should not be allowed in product liability suits in which compensatory damages are premised on the defendant's negligence or on strict liability. (B) The claim for punitive damages characterizing Ford's conduct as willful, deliberate, wanton, malicious, and reckless—all elements of gross negligence—is insufficient because the concept of gross negligence has been abolished in Wisconsin. (C) Punitive damages are unnecessary in product liability cases to effect punishment and deterrence, which are the objectives of imposing punitive damages in the traditional tort action, and the elimination of punitive damages in all products liability cases is in the public interest because the recovery of punitive damages produces economically and socially undesirable results.

A Boundaries of punitive damages

Ford Motor Company asserts that punitive damages are recoverable only in actions based on intentional, personal torts, and are not recoverable in product liability actions which are grounded in negligence or strict liability. Ford argues that the concept of punitive damages is antithetical to the theories of negligence and strict liability because punitive damages are based on the defendant's intentional conduct. Ford's argument is premised on two assumptions: that intentional conduct is the only conduct justifying punitive damages and that the same facts which justify compensatory damages must be sufficient to justify punitive damages. This court has never adopted this view of punitive damages.

Punitive damages are in the nature of 'a demand arising out of a single injurious occurrence,' a 'theory of relief arising out of the same transaction or occurrence,' a 'remedy.' *Wussow v Commercial Mechanisms Inc,* 293 NW2d 897 (1980).See also *Draeger v John Lubotsky Motor Sales Inc,* 202 NW2d 20 (1972).

Recent US cases

This court has rested its analysis of punitive damages not on the classification of the underlying tort justifying compensatory damages but on the nature of the wrongdoer's conduct. Although the usual aggravating circumstances required for the recovery of punitive damages are often found as substantive elements of the tort itself, this court has said a claim for punitive damages may be supported by proof of aggravating circumstances beyond those supporting compensatory damages.

Punitive damages rest on allegations which, if proved, demonstrate a particular kind of conduct on the part of the wrongdoer, which has variously been characterized in our cases as malicious conduct or willful or wanton conduct in reckless disregard of rights or interests.

. . . . .

If there is tortious conduct supporting a claim for compensatory damages, we can find no logical or conceptual difficulty in allowing a claim for punitive damages in a negligence or strict liability action if the plaintiff is able to establish the elements of 'outrageous' conduct justifying punitive damages. A similar conclusion has been reached in the Final Report of the Legal Study of the Interagency Task Force on Product Liability, vol 5 pp. 117-118, and in the reported cases of other jurisdictions which have considered the issue of recovery of punitive damages in product liability actions.

The Alaska Supreme Court, in responding to a defendant's contention that punitive damages have no place in the 'fault-free' context of strict products liability, reached the same conclusion as we do, saying:

We also reject the argument that punitive damages have no place in a strict liability case, although we do agree with appellant that punitive damages ought not be awarded in every products liability case. Where, however, as in the instant case, plaintiff is able to plead and prove that the manufacturer knew that its product was defectively designed and that injuries and deaths had resulted from the design defect, but continued to market the product in reckless disregard of the public's safety, punitive damages may be awarded. See, eg *Gillham v The Admiral Corporation*, 523 F2d 102 (6th Cir 1975), *Toole v Richardson-Merrell, Inc,* 60 Cal Rptr 398 (1967); *Sturm Ruger & Co, Inc v Day*, 594 P2d 38, (Alaska 1979).

This court rejects Ford's argument that as a matter of law, punitive damages cannot be recovered in any product liability case based on strict liability or negligence. We hold that punitive damages are recoverable in a product liability suit if there is proof that the defendant's conduct was 'outrageous.' Awarding punitive damages in a product liability case is a natural, direct outgrowth of basic common law concepts of tort law and punitive damages.

. . . . .

B Deterrent factor

Ford maintains that punitive damages are unnecessary in product liability cases to effect punishment and deterrence, which are the objectives of imposing punitive damages in the traditional tort action and that our outlawing punitive damages in all products liability cases is in the public interest because the recovery of punitive damages would cause economically and socially undesirable consequences.

Ford does not assert that there are no valid policy grounds for awarding punitive damages. Ford does not urge the complete abolition of punitive damages in all tort cases. Ford merely asserts that the accepted justifications for punitive damages, namely, punishment and deterrence, have no application in the product liability context.

. . . . .

This court, although requested to do so, has not been willing to abandon the concept of punitive damages and has on numerous occasions reaffirmed its adherence to the doctrine. *Jones v Fisher,* 166 NW2d 175 (1969) *Fahrenberg v Tengel,* 291 NW2d 516 (1980).

In *Entzminger v Ford Motor Co,* 177 NW2d 899 (1970), this court said that 'despite repeated criticism of the punitive damage rule, this court has adhered to it but has refused to extend the doctrine.' Nevertheless, this court has extended the doctrine, see *Kink v Combs, 135* NW2d 789 (1965); *Anderson v Continental Ins Co,* 271 NW2d 368 (1978). The doctrine of punitive damages was adopted through the Wisconsin judicial process and has grown through the common law process. 'The common law is not immutable, but flexible, and upon its own principles adapts itself to varying conditions.' *Dimick v Schiedt,* 293 US 474, 487 (1935), quoted with approval *Schwanke v Garlt,* 263 NW 176 (1935).

We must acknowledge, and Ford does not argue otherwise, that there are several documented instances of manufacturers who knowingly or recklessly breached the tort rules of product safety.

In *Sturm, Ruger & Co, Inc v Day,* 594 P2d 39, 47 (Alaska 1979), the evidence presented at trial indicated that top officials at Sturm, Ruger knew that the safety and loading notches of their single action revolver presented a danger of accidental discharge because of the propensity of the engaging middle parts to fail or break; that the management of Sturm, Ruger knew that serious injuries had resulted from this deficiency; and that the management procrastinated in changing the basic design, at an increased cost of $1.93 per gun.

In *Gillham v Admiral Corporation,* 523 F2d 102, (6th Cir 1975), the evidence at trial disclosed that fires originated in Admiral color television sets, that Admiral Corporation received a steady stream of complaints about TV set fires, and that Admiral could have remedied the defect and failed to do so. To quote the Missouri Court of Appeals:

The evidence also disclosed that Admiral could feasibly have reduced this fire hazard substantially, or

Wangen v Ford

have eliminated it completely. Materials superior to the paper and wax were available for use as insulation in high voltage transformers long before Admiral designed its transformer in 1963, and these materials were used by other television manufacturers before 1963. Also, Admiral could have installed a fuse in the high voltage circuitry to cut off the electricity in the event of overheating.

The evidence thus demonstrated that when Admiral designed, manufactured and marketed appellant's television set it knew that the set presented a serious fire hazard. Nevertheless, Admiral did not warn prospective purchasers or owners of the danger despite the steady flow of reported fires originating in Admiral color television sets. Nor did Admiral redesign this model or stop marketing it during the period in question.

The evidence also disclosed that the highest officials of Admiral were aware of the fire hazard and its precise source and cause.... Moreover, there was evidence that Admiral officials sought to deceive customers about the fire hazard presented by the color television sets.

In light of this court's repeated reaffirmation of the concept of punitive damages as a civil deterrent to 'outrageous' behavior, and because apparently some businesses have found it in their interests to operate with reckless disregard to consumer safety, this court cannot, in good conscience, prohibit punitive damages in all product liability cases unless there is a strong showing that such prohibition is in the public interest.

Ford, recognizing that the law of punitive damages and product liability are largely judge-made law, the Wisconsin legislature having had little involvement in their development, argues that this court should, as a matter of public policy, eliminate punitive damages in product liability cases because punitive damages are not needed in product liability cases to effect punishment and deterrence, which are the objectives of imposing punitive damages in the traditional tort action, and because our outlawing punitive damages in all product liability cases is in the public interest because the recovery of such damages would cause undesirable economic and social consequences.

i Single plaintiff action

Ford contends that product liability cases differ in nature from the traditional punitive damage tort case in which generally only one plaintiff is involved and in which compensatory damages are relatively small. In product liability cases there are potentially many plaintiffs who will recover compensatory damages. Ford maintains that there has been a substantial increase in the number of product liability cases brought and the amount of damages awarded; that Ford is exposed to multiple, substantial compensatory damage awards; and that the cost of paying products liability claims and buying products liability insurance has become a significant cost of doing business. Ford asserts that in

product liability cases compensatory damages operate as a substantial punishment and deterrence against the manufacture and distribution of unreasonably unsafe products.

The counterargument, which is frequently made to Ford's argument and which we find persuasive, is that the need for deterrence may be particularly appropriate in a product liability case because mere compensatory damages might be insufficient to deter the defendant from further wrongdoing. Some may think it cheaper to pay damages or a forfeiture than to change a business practice. In *Funk v Kerbaugh,* 70 A 953, 954 (1908), the defendant wilfully carried out blasting in such a way as to damage buildings belonging to the plaintiff 'because it was cheaper to pay damages ... than to do work in a different way.' The possibility of the manufacturer paying out more than compensatory damages might very well deter those who would consciously engage in wrongful practices and who would set aside a certain amount of money to compensate the injured consumer. Punishment of manufacturers guilty of intentional or reckless breaches of their obligation might diminish the profitability of misconduct and any unfair competitive advantages such manufacturers might otherwise have.

Ford further argues that, in product liability cases, unlike in the traditional punitive damage tort case, substantial deterrence is provided by pervasive federal regulations of product quality and by the threat of substantial federal civil ($400,000 and $1,500,000 are figures cited by Ford) and criminal penalties ($50,000 and imprisonment are cited by Ford) under various federal statutes. The problem with the argument is that it is made to support Ford's position that punitive damages should be abolished in all product liability cases, not only those involving auto manufacturers. Yet manufacturers of products other than autos may not be subject to the same intensive and extensive regulation as auto manufacturers. And although Ford argues for reliance on administrative controls in this arena, in other arenas businesses understandably argue that they are being overregulated and urge that they be permitted to operate in a marketplace free of government regulation.

Furthermore, Ford offers no hard data to support its position that federal administrative sanctions or judicial sanctions are being vigorously pursued and are adequate deterrents. Even if Ford had such data, the submission would be more appropriate at the trial level than in this court. These data are relevant in attempting to persuade the fact-finder not to impose punitive damages or to bring in a small award.

Ford also argues that punitive damages in a product liability case, unlike in the traditional punitive damage tort case, would not serve the purposes of punishment and deterrence because the public, not the manufacturer, would pay the damages through higher prices for goods. We recognize, as did the court of appeals, an inconsistency between the concept of punitive da-

Recent US cases

mages as a deterrent and the possibility that punitive damages can be passed on to consumers as a cost of production. This court adopted strict liability in tort in product liability cases partly because 'the seller is in the paramount position to distribute the costs of the risks created by the defective product he is selling. He may pass the cost on to the consumer via increased prices.' *Dippel v Sciano,* 37 Wis 2d 443, 450, 155 NW2d 55 (1967). Manufacturers are, however, not always able to pass on to their customers all costs, including multiple punitive damage awards. Ford's contention was ably refuted by the Honorable Thomas H Barland, Circuit Judge, in *Barager v Ford Motor Co* 1977. The *Barager* case, like the instant case, presents the issue whether punitive damages can be claimed in a product liability case. Judge Barland stated:

Finally, Ford argues that even if punitive damages were awarded against it, it would not be punished because it would merely pass on the cost of doing business. That argument flies in the face of all the statements in Ford's annual reports and quarterly statements regarding competitive pricing. It does not follow under economic logic that a punitive damage award will be passed on in whole or in part as a cost of doing business. It may or may not, depending upon Ford's price standing in relation to its competitors and its own financial condition. It could mean lower profits for Ford. It could result in stockholder complaints about a lower profit margin because of punitive damage awards for unsafe cars, thereby spurring Ford on to exercise more care in the safe design of its automobiles. It could result in a greater scrutiny by Ford's management of its auto design from the safety standpoint. All of these changes, with the exception of lower profits or higher costs, if they were to take place, would benefit the public as a whole.

Ford observes that a frequently given justification for punitive damages in the traditional punitive damage tort case is that they encourage redress of wrongs that might otherwise go unpunished; punitive damages provide an incentive to the injured party to sue. Ford argues that punitive damages are wholly unnecessary to encourage the bringing of claims in product liability cases, because compensatory damages provide sufficient incentive to the victim of a product accident to proceed with his claim for compensatory damages. Ford may be right for those instances where injuries are very severe, but is probably wrong for the many product liability cases where injuries are moderate or minor. But even if the injury to each individual is not severe, there is a public need to deter the production of unreasonably unsafe products, and the availability of punitive damages increases the likelihood that the injured customer will sue for recovery.

In summary, we are not persuaded by Ford's argument that punitive damages are unnecessary in product liability cases to effect punishment or deterrence, the objectives of imposing punitive damages in the traditional tort action.

ii Economic consequences

Ford further argues that it is in the public interest for this court to outlaw punitive damages in all product liability cases because allowing the recovery of punitive damages would cause undesirable economic and social consequences.

Ford adopts, to a large extent, the policy objections to allowing punitive damages in a product liability case which were set forth by Judge Friendly in *Roginsky v Richardson-Merrell Inc,* 378 F2d 832 (2d Cir 1967). It should be pointed out, however, that Judge Friendly's expressions of concern were *dicta,* because he concluded that the law of New York permitted the imposition of punitive damages in a product liability case. Professor Owen, in his persuasive article entitled 'Punitive Damages in Products Liability Litigation', 74 Mich L Rev 1258 (1976), systematically examines and refutes the many arguments which have been raised against punitive damages in products liability cases. We shall deal briefly with each of Ford's policy arguments.

Ford argues that if the punitive damages are not passed on to the consumer the innocent shareholder bears the burden. But the loss of investment and the decline in value of investments are risks which investors knowingly undertake, and investors should not enjoy ill-gotten gains. There is a public interest to encourage shareholders and corporate management to exercise closer control over the operations of the entity, and the imposition of punitive damages may serve this interest.

Ford argues that as a practical matter there will be a limit to the amount of punitive damages a manufacturer can pay and to the number of times a manufacturer will be—or should be—punished for the same product. Thus the injured parties who win the race to the courthouse reap 'the bonanza of punitive damages.' The later plaintiffs may receive little or no punitive damages. Ford further asserts that punitive damages are a windfall to the injured party and, if they are to be awarded, they should be awarded to the public. Although Ford's arguments have a certain equitable ring to them, we should not be sidetracked by them. Ford would solve the inequity of awarding punitive damages to some plaintiffs by having this court eliminate all punitive damages and by having us allow the wrongdoer to go unpunished. The supposed unfairness Ford attributes to punitive damages ignores the effort and money required of the early plaintiffs to uncover and prove the misconduct. Later plaintiffs will often be able to use the information gathered by the first plaintiffs and benefit from the early favorable verdicts and settlements. The 'windfall criterion' overlooks that the payment of punitive damages to the injured party is justifiable as a practical matter, because such damages do serve to compensate the injured party for uncompensated expenses, *eg* attorneys' fees and litigation expenses, and that the windfall motivates reluctant plaintiffs to go forward with their claims. If punitive damages were to be paid to the public treasury, fewer wrongdoers would be

Wangen v Ford

punished because the injured would have no inducement to spend the extra time and expense to prove a claim for punitive damages once an action had been brought. The basic question in determining whether punitive damages should be outlawed in product liability cases is not whether some injured party is going to make a profit but whether punitive damages will punish and deter, objectives which are in the public interest.

Ford views its strongest argument as the one that most concerned Judge Friendly in *Roginsky,* namely that large claims for punitive damages in multiple product liability cases cannot be administered fairly to avoid ruinous results to the defendant for a single defect appearing in many products. Judge Friendly saw no way to impose an 'effective ceiling on punitive awards in hundreds of suits in different courts which may result in an aggregate which, when piled on large compensatory damages, could reach catastrophic amounts'.

Professor Owen concludes that 'the threat of bankrupting a manufacturer with punitive damages awards in mass disaster litigation appears to be more theoretical than real.' Nevertheless, we cannot so easily dismiss the risk of catastrophic punitive damages, and we must recognize that the difficulty of measuring and controlling punitive damages awards which exists in any tort case is compounded in product liability cases which may involve inflammatory fact situations, wealthy corporate defendants and multiple lawsuits.

Ford hints of economic disaster if punitive damages are imposed. Ford intimates there is a 'product liability crisis' referring to the *Interagency Task Force on Product Liability: Final report* (Washington: Dept of Commerce, 1977) and *Report of the California Citizens' Commission on Tort Reform, Righting the Liability Balance* (1977). Ford warns that the public will suffer if punitive damages are so high that businesses shut down. But various studies, some of which are relied upon by Ford, conclude that the data do not give credence to the manufacturer's dire predictions.

As to the 'compensatory damage crisis,' the Wisconsin legislative council staff concluded that it is difficult to determine the extent of product liability claims and the scope and nature of the problems of imposing compensatory damages on the manufacturer:

Beginning in June of 1976, a Federal Interagency Task Force began an intensive study of the subject. In November of 1977, it published a *Final Report.* The *Final Report* of the Task Force found that some extraordinary assertions about the product liability problem were not true, such as some insurers' claim that one million product liability claims were filed in 1976. The Task Force concluded that the best 'estimate' of the number of product liability claims filed in 1976 was between 60,000 and 70,000. The Task Force also found that some 'horror' cases related by manufacturers did not exist. On the other hand, the organized plaintiff's bar asserted that there was no product liability problem at

all; the Task Force concluded this assertion also was unfounded. *Appendix A* presents some comparative data on product liability claims and awards drawn from two separate surveys.

The Task Force encountered considerable difficulty in assessing the product liability problem, at least in part, because no single source, governmental or private, has kept statistically reliable data on the number and severity of product liability claims . . . Wisconsin Legislature Council Staff, *Product Liability: An Overview* (1978).

As to the 'punitive damage crisis,' the *Department of Commerce—Model Uniform Product Liability Act,* which was developed based on the reports of the Interagency Task Force on Product Liability, similarly acknowledged that 'while many product sellers have expressed great concern about the economic impact of punitive damages, the 'ISO Closed Claims Survey' suggests that the number of cases in which such damages are imposed is insubstantial. 'ISO Closed Claims Survey' at 183.' 44 Federal Register No 212, p 62748 (October 31, 1979). It appears that the existing facts and figures do not justify the manufacturers' concerns and fears about the economic impact of punitive damages. Nevertheless, the potential danger of multiple punitive and damages awards does exist.

Many of Ford's arguments point to possible problems in our tort system generally, apart from the issue of punitive damages. We need not and cannot in the instant case consider all the possible problems in the existing legal system relating to the entire field of product liability. We must decide only whether Ford is correct in asserting that this court, as a matter of public policy, should hold that in *all* product liability cases punitive damages are an unnecessary and undesirable vehicle for punishment and deterrence.

The very studies cited by Ford relating to product liability acknowledge that although the award of punitive damages presents practical problems, punitive damages 'serve an important function in deterring product sellers from producing, distributing or selling dangerous products' and 'in deterring product sellers from reckless disregard for safety in the production, distribution or sale of dangerous products,' and recommend the retention of punitive damages in product liability cases.

We are persuaded that the problems Ford raises as to punitive damages, especially the problem of controlling multiple awards, can be minimized in this state in the litigation process. We are persuaded that punitive damages may play a vital role in product liability cases and that the role must be shaped, as is the role of all damages awards, to fit the context in which the particular case arises. Judicial controls exist in this state for determining whether the imposition of punitive damages is appropriate in the particular case and for determining the amount of the punitive damages award which will serve the punishment and deterrent objectives of punitive damages, but which will not inflict a penalty on a defendant disproportionate to the defendant's wrong and contrary to the public interest. We believe the judicial controls will provide for fair administration of punitive damage awards in this state.

. . . . .

iii Discretion of jury

Even if the jury is satisfied to a reasonable certainty by evidence that is clear, satisfactory and convincing that the defendant's conduct was 'outrageous,' in Wisconsin, the jury need not award punitive damages. Plaintiff is not entitled to punitive damages as a matter of right. The assessment of punitive damages 'lies entirely in the discretion of the jury, not in any right of the one wronged. Even though the evidence may sustain exemplary damages, still if the jury does not award them it is not error.' *Malco v Midwest Aluminum Sales,* 109 NW2d 516 (1961). The jury's refusal to award punitive damages is not reviewable. The amount awarded can never be unreasonably low. See Ghiardi, 'Punitive Damages in Wisconsin', 60 Marq L Rev 753.

. . . . .

It is incumbent on the parties in the product liability action to produce evidence which enables the jury to reach a proper punitive damages verdict. If they do not, they will be in a poor position to complain about the verdict.

An additional control over punitive damage awards is that the determination of the award in Wisconsin is not left solely to the jury. In Wisconsin the judge has control over excessive punitive awards. In *Malco* this court said:

... It seems to us that once the jury has decided in its discretion to award punitive damages, the amount thereof must be subject to the control of the court. True, the jury need not award any punitive damages, but having done so, the amount thereof should be subject to the court's revision in the same manner as compensatory damages ...

Judge Friendly expressed skepticism in *Roginsky v Richardson-Merrell, Inc* 378 F2d 832, 840 (2d Cir 1967), regarding effective judicial control over multiple punitive awards because 'a state otherwise willing to impose such self-denying limits might be disinclined to do so until assured that others would follow suit.' We do not believe such skepticism of state courts is necessarily deserved, and we are confident that the fair administration of punitive damage awards in the state courts of this country will prove Judge Friendly's fears unfounded. The very arguments which Ford and Judge Friendly make against judicial imposition of punitive damages are the ones repeatedly made against individual state legislative tort reform. These arguments presuppose the need for national legislation or the adoption of a uniform law by all or a majority of states. In view of the undeniably favorable effects of imposing punitive damages, we do not believe this court should abandon the concept of punitive damages in all product liability suits and ask the citizens of this state to wait for a national law or legislative reform in all 50 states.

Although the risk that manufacturers may be subjected to excessive punitive damages is real, the need for punitive damages as a tool for punishment and deterrence is also real. We are persuaded that we should not rule out the possibility of awarding punitive damages in all product liability cases as Ford urges. We believe punitive damages subject to judicial control can be a valuable and effective tool in deterring and punishing misconduct.

C Prima facie case

Having decided that punitive damages are recoverable in a product liability case where there is a showing of malice, vindictiveness, ill-will, or wanton, willful or reckless disregard of plaintiff's rights, we now turn to the plaintiff's complaint to determine if it pleads facts sufficient to support a claim for punitive damages.

On the basis of the facts pleaded and reasonable inferences, the complaint alleges that Ford knew of the defects in the design of the gas tank and filler neck and in the lack of barrier between the gas tank and passenger compartment in the 1967 Mustang and of the fire hazard associated with the design because of tests run by Ford as early as 1964; that for years before this accident Ford knew that these defects were causing serious burn injuries to occupants of these and similar cars; that years before the accident involved in the instant case Ford knew how to correct these defects in ways that would have prevented the plaintiffs' burns, but that Ford intentionally concealed this knowledge from the government and the public; that despite this knowledge Ford deliberately chose not to recall its 1967 Mustangs and not to disclose the defects to the public by the issuance of warnings because Ford wanted to avoid paying the costs of recall and repair and wanted to avoid the accompanying bad publicity; and that Ford's conduct was intentional, reckless, willful, wanton, gross and fraudulent. These facts, if proved by the plaintiff, portray conduct which is willful and wanton and in reckless disregard of the plaintiff's rights. We conclude that the complaint alleges facts sufficient to state a claim for punitive damages in a product liability action predicated on negligence or strict liability.

. . . . .

D Punitive damages limits

Ford argues that even if this court agrees to adopt punitive damages in product liability cases, this court should hold that there can be only one punitive damage award in a given case regardless of the number of injured plaintiffs and that no punitive damages may be awarded if the defendant has previously paid punitive damages in a case arising out of the same alleged wrongful act.

Wangen v Ford

Ford cites *John Mohr & Sons, Inc v Jahnke,* 198 NW2d 363 (1972) to support its argument that multiple punitive damage awards *per se* violate due process. *John Mohr* involved the imposition of both statutory treble damages and punitive damages for the same wrong and is inapposite. Ford's liability in this case is premised on the manufacture of one car but this act may constitute multiple wrongs, and the wrongdoer can be punished for each wrong he inflicted.

. . . . .

In *State v Rabe,* 96 Wis 2d 48, NW2d (1980), we held that the intoxicated driver who negligently operates a motor vehicle and causes several deaths can be punished for each death as a separate offense.

The gravamen of Ford's alleged offense is not only the manufacture and distribution of the car but the injury caused thereby. We are not persuaded that the federal and state constitutions require us to limit punitive damages arising from a single product and a single incident to a single award for punitive damages, and we do not adopt such a rule. We believe that a wrongdoer is protected against oppressive multiple punitive damage awards by the judicial controls we have set forth herein.

For the reasons set forth, we hold that the complaints state a claim for (1) punitive damages in the products liability action predicated on negligence or strict liability in tort; (2) punitive damages in the action which survives the death of the injured person; (3) punitive damages in the actions by the parents for damages for loss of society and companionship of a child and for loss of the minor's earning capacity and medical expenses. We further hold that the complaints fail to state a claim for punitive damages in the wrongful death action.

Day, *Justice* (concurring in part, dissenting in part): I concur in the majority opinion except I dissent from the holding that punitive damages are not available in wrongful death actions. I would hold punitive damages may be assessed in a proper case. The whole theory of punitive damages as set forth in the majority opinion is to serve to punish one who engages in outrageous conduct and as a deterrent to future such conduct by the defendant or by those who might otherwise engage in such conduct.

. . . . .

Coffey, *Justice.* I dissent because the majority has extended application of the concept of punitive damages, established by this court's prior case law, beyond the boundaries set forth in *Entzminger v Ford Motor Co,* 177 NW2d 899 (1970):

Punitive damages are not allowed for a mere breach of contract. . . . or for all torts or for crimes but generally for those personal torts, which are malicious, outrageous or a wanton disregard of personal rights which require the added sanction of a punitive damage to deter others from committing acts against human dignity. . . . The type of cases allowing punitive damages has been cases of assault and battery, slander and libel, seduction,

malicious prosecution, breach of promise, and the like. Despite repeated criticism of the punitive-damage rule, this court has adhered to it but has refused to extend the doctrine. However, in a most recent case, the court did lay down, as an additional requirement, that where no actual malice is shown the character of the offense must have the outrageousness associated with serious crime.

The majority relies on a portion of this quotation. I have included the entire passage.

In this case the majority, contrary to the holding in *Entzminger v Ford Motor Co, supra,* has allowed recovery of punitive damages for a nonpersonal tort. The purpose of a strict liability action is to allow recovery of compensatory damages where injuries are caused by an unreasonably dangerous product without requiring proof of specific acts of negligence. Ghiardi and Koehn, 'Punitive Damages in Strict Liability Cases', 61 Marq L Rev 245 (1977). *Dippel v Sciano,* 37 Wis 2d 443, 155 NW2d 55 (1967). The doctrine of strict liability in tort is in essence a *no fault concept* and it is the condition of the product (whether it is defective and unreasonably dangerous) rather than the conduct of the actor or manufacturer that determines liability. Recovery of punitive damages is based on a finding of *aggravated fault* and thus the conduct of the manufacturer is the sole determinant of liability. Therefore, in a case of strict liability in tort, the conduct of the manufacturer is not at issue, and thus it is singularly inappropriate to allow punitive damages in an action where the standards for recovery of compensatory damages have been so relaxed.

. . . .

There are strong arguments for denying punitive damages in a strict liability case, presenting a substantial problem worthy of the legislature's consideration:

1. Permitting the recovery of punitive damages in product liability cases will have an adverse economic impact and be financially destructive to employees and employers alike. How many times are punitive damages to be awarded for the same act? In this case, the majority would apparently allow punitive damages to be awarded twice, once to the injured minor and once to the parents. The design defect alleged in this case has been the subject of other litigation in many other states. Are the Wisconsin courts to monitor the courts of the other 49 states so as to insure that a Wisconsin court's award of punitive damages does not place an undue burden on the manufacturer and his employees?

. . . . .

2. Punishment and deterrence, the avowed goals of punitive damages, may also be accomplished through the state criminal laws, the federal Consumer Products Safety Act and the state counterpart. Punishment and deterrence are proper goals of the criminal justice system, not the civil tort law.

. . . . .

3. The doctrine of punitive damages does not provide the defendant with the benefits of the constitutional safeguards afforded in criminal proceedings.

. . . . .

4. Punitive damages serve as a bonus, added reward or windfall to the injured party. As a result, the extension of punitive damages to the product liability cases 'will undoubtedly encourage counsel in some cases to pursue *unmeritorious* claims and manufacturers will sometimes have to settle such claims in excess of their fair value because of the risk, however remote, of large jury awards.' Owens, 'Punitive Damages in Products Liability Litigation' 74 Mich L Rev 1257, 1290 (1976).

In light of the above public policy considerations and ramifications, I believe the legislative branch, with its superior fact-finding capabilities, is best able to deal with the question of whether punitive damages should be recovered in a products liability case. As stated in *Kozlowski v John E Smith's Sons Co,* 275 NW2d 915 at 927:

The myriad of problems and solutions in this complex area of products liability law should be the subject of hearings and debates in the legislature in order to balance the scales of justice between the manufacturer and the consumer.

The majority has unwisely usurped the legislative function in this case, and for the above reasons, I must dissent. Let us allow our democracy to function in the manner the framers of our constitution intended. Let each of the three branches of government operate independent of one another. Let no branch usurp or invade the province or responsibility of another. Let not the majority further oil the already turbulent waters of products liability by riding a 'new wave' of social, economic and political improvement. If social welfare experimentation is to be conducted, it should be done by the legislature. The implications for the free enterprise system, and therefore the structure of our economy, are too disturbing to leave a decision of this magnitude to five jurists.

I am authorized to state that Mr Justice Connor T Hansen joins in this dissent.

1980 *LeBouef v Goodyear*

COMMENTARY

This is the report of the Court of Appeals review of a federal district court hearing. The district court case was reported under the name of *Duhon v Goodyear and Ford,* and was the consolidation of two claims, one by Mrs LeBouef Leleux Duhon, who was the mother of the driver of the car that crashed, and the other by Floyd Dugas, a passenger who was severely injured. Mrs Duhon was awarded damages of $37,000, and Mr Dugas just over $36,000. The comparatively moderate level of the awards might possibly reflect the fact that the case was heard without a jury. A jury trial is available in civil matters at the request of either of the parties, and it is rare for a product liability claim to be heard without a jury.

Both Goodyear and Ford were held liable and after the trial Goodyear paid the full amounts awarded. It withdrew from the appeal and its place was taken by its insurers, Travelers Insurance Company.

Goodyear's liability was based upon a defective design, although there was in fact nothing wrong with its tyre except that it was not suitable for speeds above 85 miles per hour. The defect was the failure to warn of this limitation, and according to comment j, section 402A of the Restatement of Torts Second, instructions and warnings form a significant part of a design. This comment is quoted in the note to *Smith v ER Squibb* in connection with the adequacy of warnings. The relevant wording in connection with the *LeBouef* case is: 'In order to prevent the product from being unreasonably dangerous, the seller may be required to give directions or warning, on the container, as to its use'.

The comment includes the words 'unreasonably dangerous', although Louisiana has not specifically adopted section 402A. The state law is based on the civil law of France and it will be noted that the *LeBouef* opinion does not use the words 'strict liability'. The courts in the state think of liability in terms of the violation of a duty, and the opinion does stress the duty of the manufacturer, in this case the duty to warn. The difference is one of definition rather than of meaning, because the defendants were liable for selling a product that was defective, the defect being the absence of a warning.

At the time of the accident the driver was intoxicated, and although at first sight it would seem that a warning would have been disregarded in any case, and that the real cause of the accident was drunken driving, the courts did not take that view. The tyre was defective because there was no warning, and contributory negligence was no defence. If the claim had been made under negligence, without any reference to a defective product, the plaintiff's negligence would have led to the allocation of damages between the opposing parties in accordance with the state's comparative negligence

LeBouef v Goodyear

statute. Assumption of risk is a defence in a product liability claim, and an attempt was made to argue that the passenger could not recover because he had voluntarily assumed the risk of accompanying a drunken driver. Since, however, the drunkenness was held not to be a cause of the accident, that argument did not succeed.

The case is authority for the statement that, at least in Louisiana, the expression 'normal use' includes 'foreseeable use'. This is in line with the decisions on second collisions in which it has been held that the manufacturer of motor cars should foresee the possibilities of accidents. In general, all states will excuse a manufacturer from liability when the product has not been used for a foreseeable purpose and do not limit liability to normal or intended use.

JUDGMENT

United States Court of Appeals, Fifth Circuit
August 11, 1980

LeBouef
versus
The Goodyear Tire & Rubber Company

Travelers Insurance Company
versus
Ford Motor Company

Before Circuit Judges Reavley, Jones and Gee

Reavley, *Circuit Judge.* In the early morning hours of June 6, 1976, Shelby Leleux was killed and his passenger, Floyd Dugas, was seriously injured when the Mercury Cougar driven by Leleux veered off the Louisiana back road on which it had been travelling at over 100 miles per hour and crashed into a cement culvert. The accident occurred when the tread separated from the body of the Cougar's left rear tire. Dugas and Leleux's mother, Lillie Mae Duhon, brought this products liability action against Goodyear Tire & Rubber Company, the manufacturer of the tire, and Ford Motor Company, the maker of the automobile, alleging that the accident was attributable to the products' defective designs and the failure of the defendants to warn of the danger of tread separation at high speeds. The district court, sitting without a jury, agreed and held defendants liable jointly and *in solido*. 451 F Supp 253 (W D La 1978). Ford Motor Company appeals, [1] arguing that: (1) it had no duty to warn of or otherwise to guard

[1] Goodyear also initially filed an attack on the judgment, but has subsequently dismissed its appeal. Its insurer, Travelers Insurance Company, has paid to the plaintiffs the entire amount of the judgment and has now been substituted for them as party plaintiff on appeal.

against the danger of tread separation in situations like that involved here; (2) the district court erred in holding it liable as manufacturer of the tire; and (3) the court should have held Leleux and Dugas to be barred from recovery on the basis of their own conduct in connection with the accident. We affirm.

Facts

In January 1976, Shelby Leleux purchased a new, 1976 Mercury Cougar equipped with a 460 cubic-inch, 425 horsepower engine, and with Goodyear HR78-15 Custom Polysteel Radial tires. The tires were standard equipment for the Cougar, despite the fact that they had actually been designed and tested by Goodyear only for a maximum safe operating speed of around 85 miles per hour, [2] while the Cougar was designed with a capability of attaining speeds greater than 100 miles per hour. Despite the disparity in design capabilities (and at least Ford's knowledge of this), the only 'warning' associated with the use of the tires at high speeds provided by either party, aside from inflation instructions, was a statement in the Cougar owner's manual that 'continuous driving over 90 miles per hour requires using high-speed-capability tires;' the manual did not state whether the tires in question were or were not of high speed caliber.

After the car had been driven about 1,300 miles, the left rear and right front tires developed a low-speed wobble. Because the tires were separately warranted by Goodyear, Leleux arranged to have these tires replaced by a Goodyear dealer, who moved the car's left front tire to the left rear and installed two new tires on the front.

At about 5 am on June 6, 1976 Leleux and Dugas, both of whom had been drinking since 9 pm on the preceding evening, left Kaplan, Louisiana in Leleux's Cougar for a dance in Riceville, about 15 miles away. The road between these towns is a paved, relatively straight, two-way thoroughfare. One mile outside of Kaplan, Leleux accelerated to a speed of at least 100 to 105 miles per hour and maintained that pace. About six minutes later, the tread separated from the carcass of the left rear tire, which had at that point been driven 4,867 miles. The car veered to the left side of the road and remained on the pavement for 219 feet before fading onto the gravel shoulder. Leleux held the car on the shoulder for 67 feet until it left the roadbed, dropping four feet to a field below. From there the car travelled 225 feet and struck a cement culvert, killing Leleux and seriously injuring Dugas. A blood alcohol test revealed that Leleux's blood contained .18% alcohol, well above established standards for intoxication. The separation of tread from the left rear tire was determined later not to have been caused by road hazards or neglected cuts in the tread.

[2] In fact, about 10% of the tires of this type that Goodyear had subjected to test speeds of 95 to 100 miles per hour for 30 minute periods did not survive the test.

Recent US cases

In the ensuing consolidated wrongful death and personal injury actions, the district court, while finding that the tire had not been defectively constructed, held that the use of this tire on the Cougar in the absence of an adequate warning of the danger of tread separation at the high speeds at which both defendants should reasonably have foreseen their products would be used, rendered the car and the tire unreasonably dangerous. The court further found that, while Leleux's excessive speed was a contributing cause of the accident, his intoxication was not. The court rejected this contributory negligence as a bar to recovery and held, finally, that neither plaintiff had voluntarily assumed the risk of the tragedy that befell them.

Scope of duty

Louisiana products liability law, which controls this diversity case, prescribes that the maker of a product may be held liable to one injured due to a defect in that product—whether in design or manufacture, or which results from the lack of adequate warning—that renders the product 'unreasonably dangerous to *normal use.'* Ford contends that the circumstances under which product failure occurred in this case constituted a misuse, outside the 'normal use' of the Cougar and the tires. Therefore, Ford argues that it had no duty to warn or otherwise to guard against the dangers involved here, and that it, consequently, should not have been held liable for injuries flowing from product failure in that setting.

The only aspect of the accident that raises the question of misuse versus normal use is the excessive speed of the Cougar. There is no evidence that the hazards of speed were exacerbated by poor highway pavement or other road hazards, or that the car or tires had otherwise been subjected to abuse on the night of the accident or before. Moreover, aside from the fact that it may have impaired his judgment in deciding to drive at an excessive speed, there is no indication that Leleux's intoxication constituted an independent element of misuse pertinent to this case.

Certainly the operation of the Cougar in excess of 100 miles per hour was not 'normal' in the sense of being a routine or intended use. 'Normal use,' however, is a term of art in the parlance of Louisiana products liability law, delineating the scope of a manufacturer's duty and consequent liability; it encompasses all *reasonably foreseeable* uses of a product. *Rey v Cuccia,* 298 So2d 840, (La 1974) (duty to warn of 'possible hazard' known to manufacturer); *Amco Underwriters of the Audubon Insurance Co v American Radiator & Standard Corp,* 329 So2d 501, 504 (La App 1976) (duty to warn of dangers even from improper use of otherwise non-defective product). See also, *Jones v Menard,* 559 F2d 1282 (5th Cir 1977) (*dictum,* construing Louisiana law to the effect that 'in inadequate warning cases misuse means that the seller had no duty to warn against unforeseeable uses of its products,

while in design cases misuse means that the manufacturer had no duty to design a product so as to prevent injuries arising from unforeseeable uses of that product'). The sports car involved here was marketed with an intended and recognized appeal to youthful drivers. The 425 horsepower engine with which Ford had equipped it provided a capability of speeds over 100 miles per hour, and the car's allure, no doubt exploited in its marketing, lay in no small measure in this power and potential speed. It was not simply foreseeable, but was to be readily expected, that the Cougar would, on occasion, be driven in excess of the 85 mile per hour proven maximum safe operating speed of its Goodyear tires. Consequently, Ford cannot, on the basis of abnormal use, escape its duty either to provide an adequate warning of the specific danger of tread separation at such high speeds or to ameliorate the danger in some other way.

Ford contends, further, that it had no duty to warn—that is, that the car was not 'unreasonably dangerous' without a warning—even if the Cougar was in 'normal use' at the time of the accident, since the danger involved was obvious or at least should have been known to Leleux, who dabbled in amateur stock car racing. *American Insurance Co v Duo Fast Dixie Inc,* 367 So2d 415, 417 (La App 1979) (no duty to warn of obvious danger from improper electrical connection). *Accord, Bradco Oil & Gas Co v Youngstown Sheet & Tube Co,* 532 F2d at 504 (no duty to warn sophisticated purchasers of dangers of which they should be aware). See *Chappuis v Sears, Roebuck & Co,* 358 So2d at 930 (duty to warn 'when the danger is known to the manufacturer and cannot justifiably be expected to be within the knowledge of users generally'). Though Ford correctly states the Louisiana law on this point, the proof in this case does not support the application of that principle. While the hazards generally of high-speed driving would have been as obvious to Leleux as to any other driver, the particular risk in question here—that the tread would separate from a tire and the danger that this would present—would not have been obvious. Moreover, the evidence concerning Leleux's amateur racing background is insufficient to indicate a sophistication on his part regarding tire capabilities such that he, apart from the average purchaser, should have been aware of the danger of tread separation. See *Fincher v Surrette,* 365 So2d 860, 863 (La App 1978). Consequently, Ford was not excused from its duty to warn or otherwise to avert the unreasonable risks from tread separation at high speeds presented by its Cougar automobiles, factory equipped with the Goodyear tires in question.

Ford's liability as manufacturer-assembler

Ford next contends that it should not have been held liable as a manufacturer for the failure of the Goodyear tire since it obviously was not the actual manufacturer and did not represent itself to be such, and since the name of the actual maker, Goodyear, was boldly emblazoned on the tire. It relies for its contention upon

LeBouef v Goodyear

extrapolations from the holdings in *Penn v Inferno Manufacturing Corp,* 199 So2d 210 (La App), and *Aymond v Texaco Inc,* 554 F2d 206 (5th Cir 1977) (applying Louisiana law). In *Penn* the Louisiana court ruled that a company that held a product out as its own, by attaching its label and supplying it for use as a component part in a larger product that it manufactured, was liable to purchasers and users as if it were the manufacturer of that component part, despite the fact that the part had actually been fabricated by another. Conversely, this court in *Aymond* distinguished *Penn* and held that a defendant could not be held liable as manufacturer of the product of another where it had neither marked or otherwise held the item out as its own, nor incorporated it as a component into one of its own products. Ford reasons from these cases that an assembler is not to be held liable under Louisiana products liability law for the failure of a component part of its product, where that component is not held out as the assembler's own, but rather is plainly labelled as the product of another.

Ford's argument misapprehends the import of *Penn* and *Aymond,* as well as the basis upon which its liability is predicated. *Penn* and *Aymond* both involved the question whether one not the actual manufacturer of an item might nonetheless be held responsible for fabrication or design defects of that item. Even if we indulge Ford so far as to accept, *arguendo,* the premise that an assembler is not liable for manufacturing or design flaws in items plainly labelled as the products of others—even though the assembler selected these as components for use in its final creations—this does not carry the day for Ford.

The tire in question was not found to be defective either in design or construction independent of its use on the Cougar; nor is Ford's liability focused on the failure of the tire, alone. It was Ford's selection and utilization of these tires without an adequate warning, on an automobile that it knew was capable of speeds well in excess of those for which the tires had been safety tested and that it should have expected would be driven at such speeds on occasion, that created the unreasonable risk of harm. Thus, Ford is liable in this case, not for the miscarriage of another manufacturer, as was the case in *Penn,* but for its own active role in the assembly of the unreasonably dangerous composite product, the Cougar automobile, and for the failure of that assemblage as a whole through one of its components. 'A manufacturer is no less a manufacturer because his product is composed in part of units manufactured by another.' *Spillers v Montgomery Ward & Co,* 294 So2d 803, 807 (La 1974). *Accord, Ford Motor Co v Mathis,* 322 F2d 267, 274 (5th Cir 1963) (applying Texas law, holding assembler of automobile responsible as manufacturer for all components and totality of automobile).

Defenses

Ford contends, finally, that Leleux's and Dugas' own

fault should have barred recovery in this case. In this vein, Ford first contends that Leleux's contributory fault in driving at more than 100 miles per hour should preclude his mother's recovery.

This court has previously held that contributory negligence is not a defense to a strict products liability claim under Louisiana law. *Rodrigue v Dixilyn Corp,* 620 F2d 537 (5th Cir 1980); *Khoder v AMF Inc,* 539 F2d 1078 (5th Cir 1976). These holdings are bolstered by opinions of the Louisiana appellate courts, holding that recovery is barred by victim fault only in the form of assumption of the risk—that is, voluntary and unreasonable use of a product with full knowledge and appreciation of its defect and the danger involved—as opposed to contributory negligence. *Tri-State Insurance Co v Fidelity & Casualty Insurance Co,* 365 So2d 248 (La 1978) (stating that whether formally characterized as contributory negligence or assumption of risk, victim fault ordinarily will be measured by elements of assumption of risk; denied recovery to one shown to be actually aware of 'defect' and danger).

Insofar as Ford's liability is predicated upon its failure to supply an adequate warning—which, in many ways, is a horse of a different color in Louisiana products liability law—Ford has not demonstrated fault on the part of Leleux sufficient to bar recovery. The Louisiana Supreme Court in *Chappuis v Sears, Roebuck & Co, supra,* indicated that a victim would not be allowed recovery in an action for a manufacturer's failure to warn, where he 'knew, or should have known of the danger, and chose, nevertheless, to use the dangerous instrument.' Although this departs from the traditional formulation of voluntary assumption of the risk by objectifying the element of the victim's knowledge ('*should* have known'), it in no way indicates an intention on the part of the Louisiana Court to expand available defenses to include all forms of contributory negligence. Finally, to reiterate, there is insufficient evidence that Leleux knew or should have been sufficiently aware of tire capabilities to render clearly erroneous the district court's rejection of Leleux's assumption of the risk of tread separation or to compel a finding that even the objective standard of *Chappuis* had been met.

Ford also contends that Dugas may not recover because he knowingly and voluntarily assumed the risk of riding with an intoxicated driver. *Prestenbach v Sentry Insurance Co,* 340 So2d 1331, 1334 (La 1976); *Marcotte v Travelers Insurance Co,* 249 So2d 105, 107 (La 1971). Even if we assume the applicability of this principle to a products liability action, it bars recovery only where the driver's intoxication is a substantial contributing cause of the accident.

The district court found that Leleux's intoxication was not a contributing cause of the accident in this case. Ford attacks this finding, arguing (1) that a sober driver would have held the car on the road longer and the tire, which deflated here only when the car dropped from the roadbed to the field, might not have burst causing complete loss of control; and (2) that, insofar as liability is predicated on failure to warn, Leleux would not have heeded a proper warning in his inebriated state even had it been given.

The brief answer to Ford's contentions is that they are predicated simply on conjecture rather than evidence and, therefore, do not demonstrate the district court's resolution of the question to have been clearly erroneous. As to the first of its arguments, though there was expert testimony that an unintoxicated driver might have been somewhat more successful in holding the car on the highway, there was no indication that the naked carcass of the tire would not also have ruptured simply from additional contact with the pavement. The latter argument, that Leleux would not have heeded an adequate warning, is sheer speculation. One might just as reasonably presume that he would have heeded such a warning that tragic morning or that he might, when he purchased the car, have had it equipped with high-speed capability tires.

Consequently, Ford's arguments having demonstrated no error in the judgment of the district court, that judgment is affirmed.

1981 *Piper Aircraft v Reyno*

COMMENTARY

The issue in this case is jurisdiction and *forum non conveniens*. Jurisdiction means the power of a court to hear and decide a case, and should be considered under two headings:

1. *Subject matter jurisdiction.* Some courts are limited in the type of action they can decide, but product liability cases fall within the powers of courts of general jurisdiction. There are usually two levels of courts of general jurisdiction, the difference being the amount of the claim the court is authorised to decide.

2. *Personal jurisdiction.* A court cannot give a proper judgment unless it has jurisdiction over the persons of the parties; usually, this is the same as saying that valid service of process can be given under the court's rules of procedure. A court has jurisdiction over persons resident in its territory, and over persons who reside elsewhere but either voluntarily submit to jurisdiction or are compelled to submit because of some special circumstance.

US courts will assert jurisdiction over persons doing business in their territory, or who are closely connected with the territory, or who come within the provisions of a 'long-arm' statute. Each state has a long-arm statute, which extends the powers of its courts to persons who commit a tort within the state.

The issue in *Piper v Reyno* is not really one of jurisdiction. It was assumed that the court did have jurisdiction over the parties, and the question was whether that jurisdiction should actually be exercised. A court always has power to refuse to exercise jurisdiction if it considers that the case would more conveniently be tried elsewhere. That is the doctrine of *forum non conveniens*.

The accident giving rise to the case occurred in Scotland, but the plaintiffs wished to bring the matter to an American court, possibly because they would then have a chance of much higher damages. For the same reason, the defendants did not want to go before an American court, and argued that a court in Scotland would be more convenient. For the reasons set out in the opinion of the Supreme Court, the end result was that the defendants' arguments were acceptable.

In this case the plaintiffs were not residents of the state, and in theory it would have made no difference if they had been. In practice, the courts will be less likely to dismiss a case on grounds of *forum non conveniens* when the plaintiffs are domestic residents. One factor that weighs in the decision is the load on local courts, and it is generally thought to be unfair to take up limited court time, and impose the burden of jury service, at the expense of local residents, for the benefit of foreigners. This factor is not so important when the plaintiffs are in fact local residents, especially since the courts see themselves as having a duty to provide a forum for residents of the state.

JUDGMENT

United States Supreme Court
December 8, 1981

Piper Aircraft Company
versus
Reyno

Before Justices Marshall, White, Brennan and Stevens

Marshall, *Justice* delivered the opinion of the court. These cases arise out of an air crash that took place in Scotland. Respondent, acting as representative of the estates of several Scottish citizens killed in the accident, brought wrongful death actions against petitioners in the United States District Court for the Middle District of Pennsylvania. Petitioners moved to dismiss on the ground of *forum non conveniens.* After noting that an alternative forum existed in Scotland, the District Court granted their motions. *Reyno v Piper Aircraft Co,* 479 F Supp 727 (MD Pa 1979). The United States Court of Appeals for the Third Circuit reversed. *Reyno v Piper Aircraft Co,* 630 F2d 149 (CA3 1980). The Court of Appeals based its decision, at least in part, on the ground that dismissal is automatically barred where the law of the alternative forum is less favorable to the plaintiff than the law of the forum chosen by the plaintiff. Because we conclude that the possibility of an unfavorable change in law should not, by itself, bar dismissal, and because we conclude that the District Court did not otherwise abuse its discretion, we reverse.

In July 1976, a small commercial aircraft crashed in the Scottish Highlands during the course of a charter flight from Blackpool to Perth. The pilot and five passengers were killed instantly. The decedents were all Scottish subjects and residents, as are their heirs and next of kin. There were no eye-witnesses to the accident. At the time of the crash the plane was subject to Scottish air traffic control.

The aircraft, a twin engine Piper Aztec, was manufactured in Pennsylvania by petitioner Piper Aircraft Company ('Piper'). The propellers were manufactured in Ohio by petitioner Hartzell Propeller Inc ('Hartzell'). At the time of the crash the aircraft was registered in Great Britain and was owned and maintained by Air Navigation and Trading Co Ltd ('Air Navigation'). It was operated by McDonald Aviation Ltd ('McDonald'), a Scottish air taxi service. Both Air Navigation and McDonald were organized in the United Kingdom. The wreckage of the plane is now in a hangar in Farnborough, England.

The British Department of Trade investigated the accident several months after it occurred. A preliminary report found that the plane crashed after developing a spin, and suggested that mechanical failure in the plane or the propeller was responsible. At Hartzell's request, this report was reviewed by a three-member Review Board, which held a nine-day adversary hearing attended by all interested parties. The Review Board found no evidence of defective equipment and indicated that pilot error may have contributed to the accident. The pilot, who had obtained his commercial pilot's license only three months earlier, was flying over high ground at an altitude considerably lower than the minimum height required by his company's operations manual.

In July 1977, a California probate court appointed respondent Gaynell Reyno administratrix of the estates of the five passengers. Reyno is not related to and does not know any of the decedents or their survivors; she was a legal secretary to the attorney who filed this lawsuit. Several days after her appointment, Reyno commenced separate wrongful death actions against Piper and Hartzell in the Superior Court of California, claiming negligence and strict liability. [1] Air Navigation, McDonald, and the estate of the pilot are not parties to this litigation. The survivors of the five passengers whose estates are represented by Reyno filed a separate action in the United Kingdom against Air Navigation, McDonald, and the pilot's estate. Reyno candidly admits that the action against Piper and Hartzell was filed in the United States because its laws regarding liability, capacity to sue, and damages are more favorable to her position than are those of Scotland. Scottish law does not recognize strict liability in tort. Moreover, it permits wrongful death actions only when brought by a decedent's relatives. The relatives may sue only for 'loss of support and society.'

On petitioners' motion, the suit was removed to the United States District Court for the Central District of California. Piper then moved for transfer to the United States District Court for the Middle District of Pennsylvania, pursuant to 28 USC section 1404(a). Hartzell moved to dismiss for lack of personal jurisdiction, or in the alternative, to transfer. [2] In December 1977, the District Court quashed service on Hartzell and transferred the case to the Middle District of Pennsylvania. Respondent then properly served process on Hartzell.

In May 1978, after the suit had been transferred, both Hartzell and Piper moved to dismiss the action on the ground of *forum non conveniens.* The District Court granted these motions in October 1979. It relied on the

---

[1] Avco-Lycoming Inc, the manufacturer of the plane's engine, was also named as a defendant. It was subsequently dismissed from the suit by stipulation.

[2] The District Court concluded that it could not assert personal jurisdiction over Hartzell consistent with due process. However, it decided not to dismiss Hartzell because the corporation would be amenable to process in Pennsylvania.

Recent US cases

balancing test set forth by this court in *Gulf Oil Corporation v Gilbert*, 330 US 501 (1947) and its companion case, *Koster v Lumbermen's Mut Cas Co*, (1947). In those decisions, the court stated that a plaintiff's choice of forum should rarely be disturbed. However, when an alternative forum has jurisdiction to hear the case, and when trial in the chosen forum would 'establish . . . oppressiveness and vexation to a defendant out of all proportion to plaintiff's convenience,' or when the 'chosen forum (is) inappropriate because of considerations affecting the court's own administrative and legal problems', the court may, in the exercise of its sound discretion, dismiss the case. *Koster, supra*. To guide trial court discretion, the court provided a list of 'private interest factors' affecting the convenience of the litigants, and a list of 'public interest factors' affecting the convenience of the forum. *Gilbert, supra*.

After describing our decisions in *Gilbert* and *Koster*, the District Court analyzed the facts of this case. It began by observing that an alternative forum existed in Scotland; Piper and Hartzell had agreed to submit to the jurisdiction of the Scottish courts and to waive any statute of limitations defense that might be available. It then stated that plaintiff's choice of forum was entitled to little weight. The court recognized that a plaintiff's choice ordinarily deserves substantial deference. It noted, however, that Reyno 'is a representative of foreign citizens and residents seeking a forum in the United States because of the more liberal rules concerning products liability law', and that 'the courts have been less solicitous when the plaintiff is not an American citizen or resident, and particularly, when the foreign citizens seek to benefit from the more liberal tort rules provided for the protection of citizens and residents of the United States.'

The District Court next examined several factors relating to the private interests of the litigants, and determined that these factors strongly pointed towards Scotland as the appropriate forum. Although evidence concerning the design, manufacture, and testing of the plane and propeller is located in the United States, the connections with Scotland are otherwise 'overwhelming'. The real parties in interest are citizens of Scotland, as were all the decedents. Witnesses who could testify regarding the maintenance of the aircraft, the training of the pilot, and the investigation of the accident—all essential to the defense—are in Great Britain. Moreover, all witnesses to damages are located in Scotland. Trial would be aided by familiarity with Scottish topography, and by easy access to the wreckage.

The District Court reasoned that because crucial witnesses and evidence were beyond the reach of compulsory process, and because the defendants would not be able to implead potential Scottish third-party defendants, it would be 'unfair to make Piper and Hartzell proceed to trial in this forum.' The survivors had brought separate actions in Scotland against the pilot,

McDonald, and Air Navigation. 'It would be fairer to all parties and less costly if the entire case was presented to one jury with available testimony from all relevant witnesses.' Although the court recognized that if trial were held in the United States, Piper and Hartzell could file indemnity or contribution actions against the Scottish defendants, it believed that there was a significant risk of inconsistent verdicts. [3]

The District Court concluded that the relevant public interests also pointed strongly towards dismissal. The court determined that Pennsylvania law would apply to Piper and Scottish law to Hartzell if the case were tried in the Middle District of Pennsylvania. As a result, 'trial in this forum would be hopelessly complex and confusing for a jury.' In addition, the court noted that it was unfamiliar with Scottish law and thus would have to rely upon experts from that country. The court also found that the trial would be enormously costly and time-consuming; that it would be unfair to burden citizens with jury duty when the Middle District of Pennsylvania has little connection with the controversy; and that Scotland has a substantial interest in the outcome of the litigation.

In opposing the motions to dismiss, respondent contended that dismissal would be unfair because Scottish law was less favorable. The District Court explicitly rejected this claim. It reasoned that the possibility that dismissal might lead to an unfavorable change in the law did not deserve significant weight; any deficiency in the foreign law was a 'matter to be dealt with in the foreign forum.'

On appeal, the United States Court of Appeals for the Third Circuit reversed and remanded for trial. The decision to reverse appears to be based on two alternative grounds. First, the court held that the District Court abused its discretion in conducting the *Gilbert* analysis. Second, the court held that dismissal is never appropriate where the law of the alternative forum is less favorable to the plaintiff.

The Court of Appeals began its review of the District Court's *Gilbert* analysis by noting that the plaintiff's choice of forum deserved substantial weight, even though the real parties in interest are nonresidents. It then rejected the District Court's balancing of the private interests. It found that Piper and Hartzell had failed adequately to support their claim that key witnesses would be unavailable if trial were held in the United States: they had never specified the witnesses they would call and the testimony these witnesses would provide. The Court of Appeals gave little weight to the fact that Piper and Hartzell would not be able to

---

[3] The District Court explained that inconsistent verdicts might result if petitioners were held liable on the basis of strict liability here, and then required to prove negligence in an indemnity action in Scotland. Moreover even if the same standard of liability applied, there was a danger that different juries would find different facts and produce inconsistent results.

Piper Aircraft v Reyno

implead potential Scottish third-party defendants, reasoning that this difficulty would be 'burdensome' but not 'unfair'. Finally, the court stated that resolution of the suit would not be significantly aided by familiarity with Scottish topography, or by viewing the wreckage.

The Court of Appeals also rejected the District Court's analysis of the public interest factors. It found that the District Court gave undue emphasis to the application of Scottish law: 'the fact that the court is called upon to determine and apply foreign law does not present a legal problem of the sort which would justify the dismissal of a case otherwise properly before the court.' In any event, it believed that Scottish law need not be applied. After conducting its own choice-of-law analysis, the Court of Appeals determined that American law would govern the actions against both Piper and Hartzell. The same choice-of-law analysis apparently led it to conclude that Pennsylvania and Ohio, rather than Scotland, are the jurisdictions with the greatest policy interests in the dispute, and that all other public interest factors favored trial in the United States.

In any event, it appears that the Court of Appeals would have reversed even if the District Court had properly balanced the public and private interests. The court stated:

It is apparent that the dismissal would work a change in the applicable law so that the plaintiff's strict liability claim would be eliminated from the case. But . . . a dismissal for *forum non conveniens,* like a statutory transfer, 'should not, despite its convenience, result in a change in the applicable law.' Only when American law is not applicable, or when the foreign jurisdiction would, as a matter of its own choice of law, give the plaintiff the benefit of the claim to which she is entitled here, would dismissal be justified.'

In other words, the court decided that dismissal is automatically barred if it would lead to a change in the applicable law unfavorable to the plaintiff.

We granted *certiorari* in these cases to consider the questions they raise concerning the proper application of the doctrine of *forum non conveniens,* 450 US 909 (1981).

The Court of Appeals erred in holding that plaintiffs may defeat a motion to dismiss on the ground of *forum non conveniens* merely by showing that the substantive law that would be applied in the alternative forum is less favorable to the plaintiffs than that of the present forum. The possibility of a change in substantive law should ordinarily not be given conclusive or even substantial weight in the *forum non conveniens* inquiry.

. . . . .

The Court of Appeals' approach is not only inconsistent with the purpose of the *forum non conveniens* doctrine, but also poses substantial practical problems. If the possibility of a change in law were given substantial weight, deciding motions to dismiss on the ground of

forum non conveniens would become quite difficult. Choice-of-law analysis would become extremely important, and the courts would frequently be required to interpret the law of foreign jurisdictions. First, the trial court would have to determine what law would apply if the case were tried in the chosen forum, and what law would apply if the case were tried in the alternative forum. It would then have to compare the rights, remedies, and procedures available under the law that would be applied in each forum. Dismissal would be appropriate only if the court concluded that the law applied by the alternative forum is as favorable to the plaintiff as that of the chosen forum. The doctrine of *forum non conveniens,* however, is designed in part to help courts avoid conducting complex exercises in comparative law. As we stated in *Gilbert,* the public interest factors point towards dismissal where the court would be required to 'untangle problems in conflict of laws, and in law foreign to itself.' *Gilbert, supra.*

Upholding the decision of the Court of Appeals would result in other practical problems. At least where the foreign plaintiff named an American manufacturer as defendant, a court could not dismiss the case on grounds of *forum non conveniens* where dismissal might lead to an unfavorable change in law. The American courts, which are already extremely attractive to foreign plaintiffs, [4] would become even more attractive. The flow of litigation into the United States would increase and further congest already crowded courts.

. . . . .

We do not hold that the possibility of an unfavorable change in law should never be a relevant consideration in a *forum non conveniens* inquiry. Of course, if the remedy provided by the alternative forum is so clearly inadequate or unsatisfactory that it is no remedy at all, the unfavorable change in law may be given substantial weight; the district court may conclude that dismissal would not be in the interests of justice. In this case, however, the remedies that would be provided by the Scottish courts do not fall within this category. Although the relatives of the decedents may not be able to rely on a strict liability theory, and although their potential damage award may be smaller, there is no danger that they will be deprived of any remedy or treated unfairly.

---

[4] First, all but six of the 50 American states—Delaware, Massachusetts, Michigan, North Carolina, Virginia, and Wyoming—offer strict liability. Rules roughly equivalent to American strict liability are effective in France, Belgium and Luxembourg. West Germany and Japan have a strict liability statute for pharmaceuticals. However, strict liability remains primarily an American innovation. Second, the tort plaintiff may choose, at least potentially, from among 50 jurisdictions if he decides to file suit in the United States. Each of these jurisdictions applies its own set of malleable choice-of-law rules. Third, jury trials are almost always available in the United States, while they are never provided in civil law jurisdictions. Even in the United Kingdom, most civil actions are not tried before a jury. Fourth, unlike most foreign jurisdictions, American courts allow contingent attorney's fees, and do not tax losing parties with their opponents' attorney's fees. Fifth, discovery is more extensive in American than in foreign courts.

Recent US cases

The Court of Appeals also erred in rejecting the District Court's *Gilbert* analysis. The Court of Appeals stated that more weight should have been given to the plaintiff's choice of forum, and criticized the District Court's analysis of the private and public interests. However, the District Court's decision regarding the deference due plaintiff's choice of forum was appropriate. Furthermore, we do not believe that the District Court abused its discretion in weighing the private and public interests.

The District Court acknowledged that there is ordinarily a strong presumption in favor of the plaintiff's choice of forum, which may be overcome only when the private and public interest factors clearly point towards trial in the alternative forum. It held, however, that the presumption applies with less force when the plaintiff or real parties in interest are foreign.

The District Court's distinction between resident or citizen plaintiffs and foreign plaintiffs is fully justified. In *Koster,* the court indicated that a plaintiff's choice of forum is entitled to greater deference when the plaintiff has chosen the home forum. When the home forum has been chosen, it is reasonable to assume that this choice is convenient. When the plaintiff is foreign, however, this assumption is much less reasonable. Because the central purpose of any *forum non conveniens* inquiry is to ensure that the trial is convenient, a foreign plaintiff's choice deserves less deference.

The *forum non conveniens* determination is committed to the sound discretion of the trial court. It may be reversed only when there has been a clear abuse of discretion; where the court has considered all relevant public and private interest factors, and where its balancing of these factors is reasonable, its decision deserves substantial deference. Here, the Court of Appeals expressly acknowledged that the standard of review was one of abuse of discretion. In examining the District Court's analysis of the public and private interests, however, the Court of Appeals seems to have lost sight of this rule, and substituted its own judgment for that of the District Court.

In analyzing the private interest factors, the District Court stated that the connections with Scotland are 'overwhelming.' *Reyno v Piper Aircraft Co,* 479 F Supp 727, 732 (MD Pa 1979). This characterization may be somewhat exaggerated. Particularly with respect to the question of relative ease of access to sources of proof, the private interests point in both directions. As respondent emphasizes, records concerning the design, manufacture, and testing of the propeller and plane are located in the United States. She would have greater access to sources of proof relevant to her strict liability and negligence theories if trial were held here.[5] However,

[5] In the future, where similar problems are presented, district courts might dismiss subject to the condition that defendant corporations agree to provide the records relevant to the plaintiff's claims.

the District Court did not act unreasonably in concluding that fewer evidentiary problems would be posed if the trial were held in Scotland. A large proportion of the relevant evidence is located in Great Britain.

The Court of Appeals found that the problems of proof could not be given any weight because Piper and Hartzell failed to describe with specificity the evidence they would not be able to obtain if trial were held in the United States. It suggested that defendants seeking *forum non conveniens* dismissal must submit affidavits identifying the witnesses they would call and the testimony these witnesses would provide if the trial were held in the alternative forum. Such detail is not necessary. Piper and Hartzell have moved for dismissal precisely because many crucial witnesses are located beyond the reach of compulsory process, and thus are difficult to identify or interview. Requiring extensive investigation would defeat the purpose of their motion. Of course, defendants must provide enough information to enable the District Court to balance the parties' interests. Our examination of the record convinces us that sufficient information was provided here. Both Piper and Hartzell submitted affidavits describing the evidentiary problems they would face if the trial were held in the United States.

The District Court correctly concluded that the problems posed by the inability to implead potential third party defendants clearly supported holding the trial in Scotland. Joinder of the pilot's estate, Air Navigation, and McDonald is crucial to the presentation of petitioners' defense. If Piper and Hartzell can show that the accident was caused not by a design defect, but rather by the negligence of the pilot, the plane's owners, or the charter company, they will be relieved of all liability. It is true, of course, that if Hartzell and Piper were found liable after a trial in the United States, they could institute an action for indemnity or contribution against these parties in Scotland. It would be far more convenient, however, to resolve all claims in one trial. The Court of Appeals rejected this argument. Forcing petitioners to rely on actions for indemnity or contributions would be 'burdensome' but not 'unfair.' Finding that trial in the plaintiff's chosen forum would be burdensome, however, is sufficient to support dismissal on grounds of *forum non conveniens.*[6]

The District Court's review of the factors relating to the public interest was also reasonable. On the basis of its choice-of-law analysis, it concluded that if the case were tried in the Middle District of Pennsylvania, Pennsylvania law would apply to Piper and Scottish law to Hartzell. It stated that a trial involving two sets of laws would be confusing to the jury. It also noted its own lack of familiarity with Scottish law. Consideration of these problems was clearly appropriate under *Gilbert;* in that case we explicitly held that the need to apply foreign law pointed towards dismissal. The Court of Appeals found

[6] See *Pain v United Technologies Corp,* 637 F2d 775 (relying on similar argument in approving dismissal of action arising out of helicopter crash that took place in Norway).

that the District Court's choice-of-law analysis was incorrect, and that American law would apply to both Hartzell and Piper. Thus, lack of familiarity with foreign law would not be a problem. Even if the Court of Appeals' conclusion is correct, however, all other public interest factors favored trial in Scotland.

Scotland has a very strong interest in this litigation. The accident occurred in its airspace. All of the decedents were Scottish. Apart from Piper and Hartzell, all potential plaintiffs and defendants are either Scottish or English. As we stated in *Gilbert,* there is 'a local interest in having localized controversies decided at home.' Respondent argues that American citizens have an interest in ensuring that American manufacturers are deterred from producing defective products, and that additional deterrence might be obtained if Piper and Hartzell were tried in the United States, where they could be sued on the basis of both negligence and strict liability. However, the incremental deterrence that would be gained if this trial were held in an American court is likely to be insignificant. The American interest in this accident is simply not sufficient to justify the enormous commitment of judicial time and resources that would inevitably be required if the case were to be tried here.

The Court of Appeals erred in holding that the possibility of an unfavorable change in law bars dismissal on the ground of *forum non conveniens.* It also erred in rejecting the District Court's *Gilbert* analysis. The District Court properly decided that the presumption in favor of the respondent's forum choice applied with less than maximum force because the real parties in interest are foreign. It did not act unreasonably in deciding that the private interests pointed towards trial in Scotland. Nor did it act unreasonably in deciding that the public interests favored trial in Scotland. Thus, the judgment of the Court of Appeals is reversed.

White, *Justice,* concurring in part and dissenting in part. I join Parts I and II of the court's opinion. However, like Justice Brennan and Justice Stevens, I would not proceed to deal with the issues addressed in Part III. To that extent, I am in dissent.

Stevens, *Justice,* with whom Justice Brennan joins, dissenting. In no. 80-848, only one question is presented for review to this court:

'Whether, in an action in federal district court brought by foreign plaintiffs against American defendants, the plaintiffs may defeat a motion to dismiss on the ground of *forum non conveniens* merely by showing that the substantive law that would be applied if the case were litigated in the district court is more favorable to them than the law that would be applied by the courts of their own nation.'

In no. 80-883, the court limited its grant of *certiorari,* see 450 US 909, to the same question:

'Must a motion to dismiss on grounds of *forum non conveniens* be denied whenever the law of the alternate forum is less favorable to recovery than that which would be applied by the district court?'

I agree that this question should be answered in the negative. Having decided that question, I would simply remand the case to the Court of Appeals for further consideration of the question whether the District Court correctly decided that Pennsylvania was not a convenient forum in which to litigate a claim against a Pennsylvania company that a plane was defectively designed and manufactured in Pennsylvania.

Recent US cases

1982 *Beshada v Johns-Manville*

COMMENTARY

This is an important decision for litigants in New Jersey courts, although it is by no means certain that the courts of other states will follow it. It imposes virtual absolute liability when the defect is failure to warn because the state Supreme Court refused to accept the defence that the manufacturers had no means of knowing the danger of the product. If a claim is made under strict liability, the basis for damages is that the product is defective, the defect being the absence of a warning. It is not material that the manufacturers could not, according to the state of the art at the time of sale, have known of the need for a warning.

If a claim is made under negligence, the position is different. Then the test is whether the manufacturer has been negligent, and that depends on the knowledge he had, or should have had.

It seems clear from the opinion that the court was influenced by considerations of public policy. It regarded product liability as a means to risk spreading and accident avoidance. The 'unruly horse' of public policy has perhaps led the court beyond the boundaries that other courts would respect.

State of the art has long been a controversial issue, partly because there is no definition acceptable to all parties, and partly because of the difficulty of the unknown danger, unknown in the sense that nobody could have known about it at the time of manufacture. The proposed federal Products Liability Act would, if it is ever passed, establish state of the art as a defence, which means that a manufacturer would not be liable for harm that he could not have suspected. Such a rule would leave without a remedy the person who is injured by the unknown and unsuspected danger, and it is in the interests of such persons that the New Jersey court has gone the other way.

Some states have passed product liability laws that specifically allow a state of the art defence. These are Arizona, Indiana, Nebraska, New Hampshire. Two states, Colorado and Kentucky, provide that a product made in accordance with the prevailing knowledge at the time would be presumed not to be defective, but the presumption is rebuttable. Four states provide that it is a defence to prove compliance with federal or state statutes or administrative regulations. These are Arkansas, Kansas, North Dakota and Tennessee. Lastly, there are two states, Michigan and Washington, which provide that evidence of state of the art is admissible in product liability cases.

A generally acceptable definition of state of the art is 'the best technology reasonably available at the time the product was first sold to any person not engaged in the business of selling that product' (from the Nebraska Act of 1978); or 'the state of scientific and technological knowledge available to the manufacturer or seller at the time the product was placed on the market' (Tennessee Products Liability Act of 1978).

JUDGMENT

Supreme Court of New Jersey
July 7, 1982

Beshada
versus
Johns-Manville Products Corporation

Before Justices Pashman, Handler, Pollock, O'Hern and Sullivan and Judge Matthews

Pashman, *Justice.* The sole question here is whether defendants in a product liability case based on strict liability for failure to warn may raise a 'state of the art' defense. Defendants assert that the danger of which they failed to warn was undiscovered at the time the product was marketed and that it was undiscoverable given the state of scientific knowledge at that time. The case comes to us on appeal from the trial court's denial of plaintiffs' motion to strike the state of the art defense. For the reasons stated below, we reverse the trial court judgment and strike the defense.

These six consolidated cases are personal injury and wrongful death actions brought against manufacturers and distributors of asbestos products. Plaintiffs are workers, or survivors of deceased workers, who claim to have been exposed to asbestos for varying periods of time. They allege that as a result of that exposure they contracted asbestosis (a non-malignant scarring of the lungs), mesothelioma (a rare cancer of the lining of the chest, the pleura, or the lining of the abdomen, the peritoneum) and other asbestos-related illnesses.

These cases involve asbestos exposure dating back perhaps as far as the 1930s. The suits are first arising now because of the long latent period between exposure and the discernible symptoms of asbestosis and mesothelioma. See *Borel v Fibreboard Paper Products Corporation,* 493 F2d 1076, 1083 (5th Cir 1973). Plaintiffs have raised a variety of legal theories to support their claims for damages. The important claim, for purposes of this appeal, is strict liability for failure to warn. Prior to the 1960s, defendants' products allegedly contained no warning of their hazardous nature. Defendants respond by asserting the state of the art defense. They allege that no one knew or could have known that asbestos was dangerous when it was marketed.

There is a substantial factual dispute about what defendants knew and when they knew it. A trial judge in the Eastern District of Texas, the forum for numerous

Beshada v Johns-Manville

asbestos-related cases, has concluded that 'knowledge of the danger can be attributed to the industry as early as the mid-1930s . . .' *Hardy v Johns-Manville Sales Corp*, 509 F Supp 1352, 1355 (ED Texas 1981). Defendants respond, however, that it was not until the 1960s that the medical profession in the United States recognized that a potential health hazard arose from the use of insulation products containing asbestos. Before that time, according to defendants, the danger from asbestos was believed limited to workers in asbestos textile mills, who were exposed to much higher concentrations of asbestos dust than were the workers at other sites, such as shipyards. Defendants claim that it was not discovered until recently that the much smaller concentrations those workers faced were also hazardous.

We need not resolve the factual issues raised. For purposes of plaintiffs' motion to strike the defense, we assume the defendants' version of the facts. The issue is whether the medical community's presumed unawareness of the dangers of asbestos is a defense to plaintiffs' claims.

As noted, this case involves six consolidated cases. *Jarusewicz v Johns-Manville* is a suit by 18 workers who were employed by Jersey Central Power and Light Company for various periods between 1930 and 1981, all of whom allege that they used asbestos, asbestos products or asbestos materials in the course of their work. They allege that they were given no warning, handling instructions or safety equipment to protect them from the dangers of asbestos. *Beshada v Johns-Manville* is a suit by 21 current or former pipefitters employed at Hercules Inc between 1935 and the present, who allege that they worked with and around insulation products containing asbestos, *Biazewicz v Johns-Manville* and *Hann v Johns-Manville* involve respectively 12 and six employees of Research Cottrell Inc between 1936 and 1979. Plaintiff in *Beckwith v Johns-Manville* is the widow of an electrician, Earl Beckwith, who was exposed to finished asbestos products during his work. She alleges that her husband's exposure to asbestos caused various illnesses which resulted in his death. Finally, *Crilley v Cork* is a wrongful death action by the widow of James Crilley, who died allegedly as a result of occupational exposure to insulation products containing asbestos.

A single trial judge has been specially assigned to hear all asbestos-related litigation in Middlesex County. On September 9, 1981, counsel for plaintiffs in four of the cases filed a Motion for Partial Summary Judgment seeking to strike the state of the art defense. Subsequently, plaintiffs in the other two cases joined the motion.

Plaintiffs based their motion on *Freund v Cellofilm Properties Inc*, 432 A2d 925 (1981), our most recent case concerning product liability. In *Freund*, Justice Handler elaborated the difference between negligence and strict liability in a failure to warn case. He explained that in strict liability cases knowledge of the dangerous-

ness of the product is imputed to defendants. Plaintiff need not prove that defendant knew or should have known of its dangerousness. The only issue is whether the product distributed by defendant was reasonably safe. Plaintiffs urge that *Freund* disposed of the state of the art issue. Since defendant's knowledge of the dangers of the product is presumed, it is irrelevant whether the existence of such dangers was scientifically discoverable. Defendants respond that *Freund* imputes to defendants only 'existing knowledge, the technical knowledge available at the time of manufacture.'

The trial judge denied the motion to strike. Reading *Freund* in conjunction with prior cases, *Suter v San Angelo Foundry & Machine Company*, 406 A2d 140 (1979) and *Torsiello v Whitehall Laboratories*, 398 A2d 132 (App Div 1979), the judge concluded that *Freund* merely created a rebuttable presumption that defendants had knowledge of the dangers of their product. That presumption could be overcome by proof that the knowledge at issue was 'unknowable' at the time of manufacture.

Plaintiff sought leave from the Appellate Division to appeal the trial court's interlocutory order and filed a motion with this court for direct certification. The Appellate Division denied plaintiffs' motion for leave to appeal. In all but the *Crilley* case, plaintiffs moved before this court for leave to appeal the Appellate Division order. We granted their motion on February 25, 1982 and subsequently granted plaintiff Crilley's late motion for leave to appeal.

Our inquiry starts with the principles laid down in *Freund v Cellofilm Properties Inc, supra, Suter v San Angelo Foundry & Machine Company, supra*, and *Cepeda v Cumberland Engineering Company Inc*, 386 A2d 816 (1978). In *Suter*, we summarized the principle of strict liability as follows:
If at the time the seller distributes a product, it is not reasonably fit, suitable and safe for its intended or reasonably foreseeable purposes so that users or others who may be expected to come in contact with the product are injured as a result thereof, then the seller shall be responsible for the ensuing damages.

The determination of whether a product is 'reasonably fit, suitable and safe' depends on a comparison of its risks and its utility (risk-utility equation).

Central to this theory is the risk-utility equation for determining liability. The theory is that only safe products should be marketed—a safe product being one whose utility outweighs its inherent risk, provided that risk has been reduced to the greatest extent possible consistent with the product's continued utility. (*Freund*, 432 A2d 925)

In *Cepeda*, we explained that in the context of design defect liability, strict liability is identical to liability for negligence, with one important *caveat:* 'The only qualification is as to the requisite of foreseeability by the

Recent US cases

manufacturer of the dangerous propensity of the chattel manifested at the trial—this being imputed to the manufacturer.' In so holding, we adopted the explication of strict liability offered by Dean Wade:

The time has now come to be forthright in using a tort way of thinking and tort terminology (in cases of strict liability in tort). There are several ways of doing it, and it is not difficult. The simplest and easiest way, it would seem, is to assume that the defendant knew of the dangerous condition of the product and ask whether he was then negligent in putting it on the market or supplying it to someone else. In other words, the scienter is supplied as a matter of law, and there is no need for the plaintiff to prove its existence as a matter of fact. Once given this notice of the dangerous condition of the chattel, the question then becomes whether the defendant was negligent to people who might be harmed by that condition if they came into contact with it or were in the vicinity of it. Another way of saying this is to ask whether the magnitude of the risk created by the dangerous condition of the product was outweighed by the social utility attained by putting it out in this fashion. (Wade, 'On the Nature of Strict Tort Liability for Products,' 44 Miss LJ 825, 834-35 (1973), quoted in *Cepeda,* 386 A2d 816.)

Stated differently, negligence is conduct-oriented, asking whether defendant's actions were reasonable; strict liability is product-oriented, asking whether the product was reasonably safe for its foreseeable purposes.

'Warning' cases constitute one category of strict liability cases. Their relation to the strict liability principles set forth above can best be analyzed by focusing on the definition of safe products found in footnote 1 of *Freund.* For purposes of analysis, we can distinguish two tests for determining whether a product is safe: (1) does its utility outweigh its risk? and (2) if so, has that risk been reduced to the greatest extent possible consistent with the product's utility? The first question looks to the product as it was in fact marketed. If that product caused more harm than good, it was not reasonably fit for its intended purposes. We can therefore impose strict liability for the injuries it caused without having to determine whether it could have been rendered safer. The second aspect of strict liability, however, requires that the risk from the product be reduced to the greatest extent possible without hindering its utility. Whether or not the product passes the initial risk-utility test, it is not reasonably safe if the same product could have been made or marketed more safely.

Warning cases are of this second type. When plaintiffs urge that a product is hazardous because it lacks a warning, they typically look to the second test, saying in effect that regardless of the overall cost-benefit calculation the product is unsafe because a warning could make it safer at virtually no added cost and without limiting its utility. *Freund* recognized this, noting that in cases alleging 'an inadequate warning as to safe use, the utility of the product, as counter-balanced against the risks of its use, is rarely at issue.'

Freund is our leading case on strict liability for failure to warn. In *Freund,* Justice Handler applied the principles set forth above, initially laid down in *Suter* and *Cepeda,* to warning cases. The issue there was whether there is any difference between negligence and strict liability in warning cases. We stated unequivocally that there is. That difference is the same difference that we noted in *Suter* and *Cepeda* concerning other design defect cases:

when a plaintiff sues under strict liability, there is no need to prove that the manufacturer knew or should have known of any dangerous propensities of its product—such knowledge is imputed to the manufacturer (*Freund v Cellofilm Properties Inc.*)

Thus, we held in *Freund* that it was reversible error for the trial judge to instruct the jury only with a negligence charge.

With these basic principles of design defect strict liability in New Jersey as our framework for analysis, we turn now to a discussion of the state of the art defense.

As it relates to warning cases, the state of the art defense asserts that distributors of products can be held liable only for injuries resulting from dangers that were scientifically discoverable at the time the product was distributed. Defendants argue that the question of whether the product can be made safer must be limited to consideration of the available technology at the time the product was distributed. Liability would be absolute, defendants argue, if it could be imposed on the basis of a subsequently discovered means to make the product safer since technology will always be developing new ways to make products safer. Such a rule, they assert, would make manufacturers liable whenever their products cause harm, whether or not they are reasonably fit for their foreseeable purposes.

Defendants conceptualize the scientific unknowability of the dangerous propensities of a product as a technological barrier to making the product safer by providing warnings. Thus, a warning was not 'possible' within the meaning of the *Freund* requirement that risk be reduced 'to the greatest extent possible.'

In urging this position, defendants must somehow distinguish the *Freund* holding that knowledge of the dangers of the product is imputed to defendants as a matter of law. A state of the art defense would contravene that by requiring plaintiffs to prove at least that knowledge of the dangers was scientifically available at the time of manufacture.

Defendants argue that *Freund* did not specify precisely what knowledge is imputed to defendants. They construe *Freund* to impute only that degree of knowledge of the product's dangerousness that existed at the time of manufacture or distribution.

While we agree that *Freund* did not explicitly address this question, the principles laid down in *Freund* and our prior cases contradict defendants' position. Essentially,

Beshada v Johns-Manville

state of the art is a negligence defense. It seeks to explain why defendants are not culpable for failing to provide a warning. They assert, in effect, that because they could not have known the product was dangerous, they acted reasonably in marketing it without a warning. But in strict liability cases, culpability is irrelevant. The product was unsafe. That it was unsafe because of the state of technology does not change the fact that it was unsafe. Strict liability focuses on the product, not the fault of the manufacturer. 'If the conduct is unreasonably dangerous, then there should be strict liability without reference to what excuse defendant might give for being unaware of the danger.' (Keeton, 48 Tex L Rev at 408.)

When the defendants argue that it is unreasonable to impose a duty on them to warn of the unknowable, they misconstrue both the purpose and effect of strict liability. By imposing strict liability, we are not requiring defendants to have done something that is impossible. In this sense, the phrase 'duty to warn' is misleading. It implies negligence concepts with their attendant focus on the reasonableness of defendant's behavior. However, a major concern of strict liability—ignored by defendants—is the conclusion that if a product was in fact defective, the distributor of the product should compensate its victims for the misfortune that it inflicted on them.

If we accepted defendants' argument, we would create a distinction among fact situations that defies common sense. Under the defendants' reading of *Freund,* defendant would be liable for failure to warn if the danger was knowable even if defendants were not negligent in failing to discover it. Defendants would suffer no liability, however, if the danger was undiscoverable. But, as Dean Keeton explains, if a defendant is to be held liable for a risk that is discoverable by some genius but beyond the defendant's capacity to do so, why should he not also be liable for a risk that was just as great but was not discoverable by anyone? (Keeton, 48 Tex L Rev at 409)

We are buttressed in our conclusion that the state of the art defense is inconsistent with *Freund* by the recent decision of Judge Ackerman in *Marcucci v Johns-Manville Sales Corp,* (DNJ February 19, 1982), in which he applied New Jersey law to strike defendants' state of the art defense.

The most important inquiry, however, is whether imposition of liability for failure to warn of dangers which were undiscoverable at the time of manufacture will advance the goals and policies sought to be achieved by our strict liability rules. We believe that it will.

Risk spreading

One of the most important arguments generally advanced for imposing strict liability is that the manufacturers and distributors of defective products can best allocate the costs of the injuries resulting from those products. The premise is that the price of a product should reflect all of its costs, including the cost of injuries caused by the product. This can best be accomplished by imposing liability on the manufacturer and distributors. Those persons can insure against liability and incorporate the cost of the insurance in the price of the product. In this way, the costs of the product will be borne by those who profit from it: the manufacturers and distributors who profit from its sale and the buyers who profit from its use. 'It should be a cost of doing business that in the course of doing that business an unreasonable risk was created.' Keeton, 48 Tex L Rev at 408. See Prosser, *The Law of Torts,* section 75 p 495 (4th Ed 1971).

Defendants argue that this policy is not forwarded by imposition of liability for unknowable hazards. Since such hazards by definition are not predicted, the price of the hazardous product will not be adjusted to reflect the costs of the injuries it will produce. Rather, defendants state, the cost 'will be borne by the public at large and reflected in a general, across the board increase in premiums to compensate for unanticipated risks.' There is some truth in this assertion, but it is not a bad result.

First, the same argument can be made as to hazards which are deemed scientifically knowable but of which the manufacturers are unaware. Yet it is well established under our tort law that strict liability is imposed even for defects which were unknown to the manufacturer. It is precisely the imputation of knowledge to the defendant that distinguishes strict liability from negligence. Defendants advance no argument as to why risk spreading works better for unknown risks than for unknowable risks.

Second, spreading the costs of injuries among all those who produce, distribute and purchase manufactured products is far preferable to imposing it on the innocent victims who suffer illnesses and disability from defective products. This basic normative premise is at the center of our strict liability rules. It is unchanged by the state of scientific knowledge at the time of manufacture.

Finally, contrary to defendants' assertion, this rule will not cause the price and production level of manufactured products to diverge from the so-called economically efficient level. Rather, the rule will force the price of any particular product to reflect the cost of insuring against the possibility that the product will turn out to be defective.

Accident avoidance

In *Suter,* we stated: Strict liability in a sense is but an attempt to minimize the costs of accidents and to consider who should bear those costs. See the discussion in *Calabresi & Horschoff,* 'Toward a Test for Strict Liability in Torts,' 81 Yale LJ 1055 (1972), in which the authors suggest that the strict liability issue is to decide which party is the 'cheapest cost avoider' or who is in the best position to make the cost-benefit analysis between accident costs and accident avoidance costs and to act on that decision once it is made. Using this approach, it is obvious that the manufacturer rather than the factory employee is 'in the better position both to judge whether avoidance costs would exceed foreseeable accident costs and to act on that judgment.'

Defendants urge that this argument has no force as to hazards which by definition were undiscoverable. Defendants have treated the level of technological knowledge at a given time as an independent variable not affected by defendants' conduct. But this view ignores the important role of industry in product safety research. The 'state of the art' at a given time is partly determined by how much industry invests in safety research. By imposing on manufacturers the costs of failure to discover hazards, we create an incentive for them to invest more actively in safety research.

Fact finding process
The analysis thus far has assumed that it is possible to define what constitutes 'undiscoverable' knowledge and that it will be reasonably possible to determine what knowledge was technologically discoverable at a given time. In fact, both assumptions are highly questionable. The vast confusion that is virtually certain to arise from any attempt to deal in a trial setting with the concept of scientific knowability constitutes a strong reason for avoiding the concept altogether by striking the state of the art defense.

Scientific knowability, as we understand it, refers not to what in fact was known at the time, but to what *could have been* known at the time. In other words, even if no scientist had actually formed the belief that asbestos was dangerous, the hazards would be deemed 'knowable' if a scientist could have formed that belief by applying research or performing tests that were available at the time. Proof of what could have been known will inevitably be complicated, costly, confusing and time-consuming. Each side will have to produce experts in the history of science and technology to speculate as to what knowledge was feasible in a given year. We doubt that juries will be capable of even understanding the concept of scientific knowability, much less be able to resolve such a complex issue. Moreover, we should resist legal rules that will so greatly add to the costs both sides incur in trying a case.

The concept of knowability is complicated further by the fact, noted above, that the level of investment in safety research by manufacturers is one determinant of the state of the art at any given time. Fairness suggests that manufacturers not be excused from liability because their prior inadequate investment in safety rendered the hazards of their product unknowable. Thus, a judgment will have to be made as to whether defendants' investment in safety research in the years preceding distribution of the product was adequate. If not, the experts in the history of technology will have to testify as to what would have been knowable at the time of distribution if manufacturers had spent the proper amount on safety in prior years. To state the issue is to fully understand the great difficulties it would engender in a courtroom.

In addition, discussion of state of the art could easily confuse juries into believing that blameworthiness is at issue. Juries might mistakenly translate the confused concept of state of the art into the simple question of whether it was defendants' fault that they did not know of the hazards of asbestos. But that would be negligence, not strict liability.

For precisely this reason, Professor Keeton has urged that negligence concepts be carefully avoided in strict liability cases. 'My principal thesis is and has been that theories of negligence should be avoided altogether in the products liability area in order to simplify the law, and that if the sale of a product is made under circumstances that would subject someone to an unreasonable risk in fact, liability for harm resulting from those risks should follow.' (Keeton, 48 Tex L Rev at 409.)

For the reasons expressed above, we conclude that plaintiffs' position is consistent with our holding in *Freund* and prior cases and will achieve the various policies underlying strict liability. The burden of illness from dangerous products such as asbestos should be placed upon those who profit from its production and, more generally, upon society at large, which reaps the benefits of the various products our economy manufactures. That burden should not be imposed exclusively on the innocent victim. Although victims must in any case suffer the pain involved, they should be spared the burdensome financial consequences of unfit products. At the same time, we believe this position will serve the salutary goals of increasing product safety research and simplifying tort trials.

Defendants have argued that it is unreasonable to impose a duty on them to warn of the unknowable. Failure to warn of a risk which one could not have known existed is not unreasonable conduct. But this argument is based on negligence principles. We are not saying what defendants should have done. That is negligence. We are saying that defendants' products were not reasonably safe because they did not have a warning. Without a warning, users of the product were unaware of its hazards and could not protect themselves from injury. We impose strict liability because it is unfair for the distributors of a defective product not to compensate its victims. As between those innocent victims and the distributors, it is the distributors—and the public which consumes their products—which should bear the unforeseen costs of the product.

The judgment of the trial court is reversed; the plaintiff's motion to strike the state of the art defense is granted.

Justices Pashman, Handler, Pollock, O'Hern and Sullivan, and Judge Matthews vote for reversal

Owens v Allis-Chalmers

1982 *Owens v Allis-Chalmers*

COMMENTARY

In our comment on *Larsen* we said that the second collision doctrine (or 'crashworthiness') was not restricted to motor vehicles. This case shows that the doctrine could be applied to fork lifts, although on the facts of the case that point did not have to be decided. Since the design was held not to be unreasonably dangerous, the question of liability did not arise.

The case also draws our attention to the importance of procedure. The trial judge ended the hearing when the plaintiff had produced her evidence, and gave a decision in favour of the defendant without calling on it to answer the claims. That is not an uncommon procedure, because it saves the time of the overburdened courts, but a directed verdict can be given only when there is no real doubt. The question for the court is whether, even if all the plaintiff says is true, there is any basis for liability. If there is an issue to be decided, the case must proceed. As may be expected, whenever a directed verdict is given, there is usually an appeal, on the grounds that there was actually an issue of fact for the jury.

In this case, the evidence produced by the plaintiff did not satisfy the judge that there was any question of a design defect. In fact, one judge in the Court of Appeals said there was no evidence that the injury had been caused by any defective product. So what should the plaintiff have done? According to the Court of Appeals, she should have produced evidence to show that the product did not conform with government or industry standards. As an alternative, she should have shown that the product was dangerous in a way that would not be obvious to the potential user, and no adequate warning was given of that danger.

The case was decided under Michigan law, which does not recognise strict liability in tort. The appeals court said that the requirements for strict liability were the same as those for breach of warranty, and that the strict liability count was therefore 'a mere redundancy'. One of the objections to breach of warranty as a cause of action has been the absence of privity in many cases, although in product liability cases the courts tend to take a lenient view of the requirement. The Michigan Commercial Code extends the benefit of a warranty to 'any natural person who is in the family or household of the buyer, or who is a guest in his home', but even this wording would not apply in this case. None of the three courts that heard the case seems to have made any mention of privity. The wording of the Commercial Code emphasises the close connection between product liability and consumer protection. It is not helpful in workplace accidents.

Michigan legislation also deals with compliance with industry standards. The state statute of 1978 (code section 600-2496) allows the admission of evidence that a design complied with standards at the time the product was made or delivered. In Michigan, therefore, there is no controversy about the state of the art defence.

Whereas American courts frequently base their decisions on public policy, in this case the Court of Appeals was anxious to disclaim the role of policy maker. It was not, the court said, a judicial function to determine questions of design on policy grounds. The legislatures must play their part, and the law was no longer on 'the frontiers of product liability legislation'. The state Supreme Court did not agree that in this particular case there was no question for a court to answer. The question was whether a fork lift without a seat belt or other 'driver restraint' was unreasonably dangerous. The plaintiff had not proved it was.

JUDGMENT

Supreme Court of Michigan
November 23, 1982

Owens
versus
Allis-Chalmers Corporation

Before Justices Coleman, Kavanagh, Williams, Levin, Moody, Fitzgerald and Ryan

Coleman, *Justice.* In this products liability case, plaintiff appeals from a directed verdict granted in the circuit court and affirmed in the Court of Appeals. She argues that the testimony of her expert witness created a question of fact for the jury. We disagree, and affirm the decision of the trial court, but for reasons different from those of the Court of Appeals.

Leave to appeal was granted in order to consider the following questions:

1. Does a manufacturer's compliance with industry or governmental standards in a products liability action preclude the jury from determining whether such conduct was reasonable?

2. Is the test for assessing a manufacturer's liability to persons injured by its product whether the risk is unreasonable and foreseeable by the manufacturer, and not whether the risk is patent or obvious?

After the briefs were filed and oral arguments were heard, the court requested the parties to file supplemental briefs addressing the following added issues:

3. Did the trial court err, in light of MRE 705, in holding that the testimony of plaintiff's expert witness did not create a question of fact for the jury?

Recent US cases

4. Does a manufacturer of a vehicle have a duty to design and manufacture its products so as to eliminate any unreasonable risk of foreseeable injury to the occupants as a result of a collision for which the manufacturer may not be responsible?

Plaintiff's husband had been a qualified forklift driver at Great Lakes Steel for four or five years prior to September 30, 1970. He reported to work shortly after midnight on that date and was assigned to the location where he would be working for the evening. A short time later, other employees found that he had been in an accident en route to his assignment. No one witnessed the accident. For undetermined reasons, the forklift which he was operating had traveled off the roadway, struck a concrete-filled post, and turned over on its side. There were no skidmarks, and the post was knocked over to a 33-degree angle. Plaintiff's husband was pinned under the overhead protective guard on the forklift and was dead when discovered. After the accident, the forklift was tested and found to be in perfect mechanical order. The road was one regularly traveled by forklift drivers. There had been no complaints about the road condition, nor had there been any prior accident.

The physician called to the scene found that the decedent had suffered a fractured skull, which seemed to the doctor to be the most plausible cause of death. However, it could not be determined at the scene whether a heart attack or other physical failure preceded the accident. An autopsy was ordered but was not offered into evidence prior to the conclusion of plaintiff's proofs and the directed verdict of the trial court. Plaintiff's motion *in limine* to suppress the autopsy report of 0.32% alcohol in the decedent's urine was denied by the trial judge.

Plaintiff sued the manufacturer of the forklift, Allis-Chalmers Corporation, utilizing theories of negligence, implied warranty, and strict liability. At trial she sought, *inter alia*, to prove that defendant's negligence or some defect in the vehicle had caused the accident and that the stability of the forklift had not been properly tested. She also sought to prove that the design of the forklift was defective for failing to provide some sort of factory-installed driver restraint that would have prevented the decedent's ejection during the rollover and, hence, would have prevented his being pinned under the overhead guard.

However, on appeal, plaintiff does not challenge that portion of the trial court's directed verdict which found no evidence that either the forklift's collision with the post or the rollover was caused by a defect in the forklift or the manufacturer's negligence. She did appeal the denial of her motion *in limine* to the Court of Appeals but does not pursue that issue in her appeal to this court.

The issue she presents to us is whether she established a *prima facie* case that the forklift was defectively designed because of its failure to include some sort of driver restraint as standard equipment.

In seeking to prove defective or negligent design, the plaintiff relied on the testimony of one expert witness, Joseph Harris. Mr Harris was employed as an independent consulting physicist, and previously had worked for General Motors for 12 years in the area of vehicle safety. He had never designed a forklift, nor any part of one, and had not worked in conjunction with their manufacture. He had operated one during a summer about 30 years prior to trial, but not since. Apart from preparing for this litigation, the record is not clear concerning whether any of his work in the area of vehicle safety had related specifically to forklifts. He testified, however, that a forklift was just another type of vehicle to which much of his work on vehicles in general would be applicable.

Plaintiff's expert gave his opinion that a rollover was a foreseeable type of forklift accident. He also stated that it was foreseeable that a forklift driver could be pinned under the overhead protective guard in the event of a rollover. The overhead protective guard, which consisted of four posts and an overhead screen, is a safety device used on forklifts in order to prevent objects from falling on the driver's head. Mr Harris recognized the guard as being a proper safety device, but testified that when it is used some sort of driver restraint should be utilized to keep the driver from being ejected through the open sides of the forklift in the event of a rollover.

He suggested four types of driver restraints that might have been effective: first, a seat belt; second, a cage-type enclosure; third, a bar like those used on carnival rides; and fourth, an encapsulating seat which would have arms that to some extent would restrict a driver's movement. He gave his opinion that had a driver restraint been used the decedent might still have been injured, but he might not have been crushed.

The cage-type enclosure which he suggested was offered by the defendant and other forklift manufacturers as an option. It had been offered to plaintiff's employer, but was not purchased.

Plaintiff's expert testified that he was not aware of any law, safety regulation, standard, or policy that required or suggested the use of driver restraints on forklifts. He also did not know of any manufacturer which provided seat belts or any driver restraints as standard equipment.[1] He had not seen driver restraints on the kind of forklift involved in this accident.

Evidence was admitted that union employees at decedent's workplace indicated after decedent's death that they would not wear seat belts if they were provided because they considered it more dangerous to be trapped in a forklift during a rollover. They would not be able to jump free. Many kinds of 'protective' devices were tested and found to be more dangerous than the model used.

[1] Apart from the cage-enclosure option, the only time he had seen a forklift equipped with any of the proposed restraints was when he had worked at General Motors and had noticed that two huge forklifts that were used to transport cars had seat belts.

Owens v Allis-Chalmers

At the close of plaintiff's proofs, the defendant moved for a directed verdict, arguing, *inter alia*, that the record lacked any basis for the expert witness's assertion that driver restraints were needed, and that something more than the witness's mere unsubstantiated assertion was necessary to send this case to the jury. The plaintiff argued that on the basis of the expert's testimony, the question whether the design was defective should go to the jury on a strict liability theory.

Circuit Judge Horace W Gilmore determined that neither a negligent design theory nor a strict liability theory was supported by the record. He assumed that the rule of *Rutherford v Chrysler Motors Corp,* 231 NW2d 413 (1975), and *Larsen v General Motors Corp,* 391 F2d 495 (1968), would apply to the forklift industry and stated: '(These cases do) not mean that the industry has to design a totally crash-proof, injury-proof forklift. (They mean) that the manufacturer has a duty to design and manufacture so as to eliminate any unreasonable risk of foreseeable injury to its occupants as a result of a collision. Now I find nothing in this record other than again the bold assertions of Mr Harris without supporting data of any standard whatever or any showing that you could say there is an unreasonable risk of foreseeable injury of this kind because of the design of this vehicle. It just is not on this record.'

The plaintiff appealed the directed verdict to the Court of Appeals. The Court of Appeals affirmed, but on grounds different from those utilized by the trial judge. *Owens v Allis-Chalmers Corp,* 268 NW2d 291 (1978). The majority concluded that 'for a plaintiff to establish a question of fact as to a manufacturer's breach of duty in design defect products liability litigation, evidence of the following must be presented:

(1) That the particular design was not in conformity with industry design standards, design guidelines established by an authoritative voluntary association, *or* design criteria set by legislative or other governmental regulation; *or*

(2) That the design choice of the manufacturer carries with it a *latent* risk of injury *and* the manufacturer has *not* adequately communicated the nature of that risk to potential users of the product.'
Judge Kaufman wrote a concurring opinion in which he concluded that 'a careful reading of the transcript reveals that there was no testimony whatsoever that the injury was caused by any defective product'.

The first two questions asked of the parties upon granting leave to appeal were those framed by plaintiff and were related to the Court of Appeals opinion. The parties were directed to address first, the significance in a products liability case of a manufacturer's compliance with governmental and industrial standards, and second, whether the test for a manufacturer's liability depends upon whether the risks are unreasonable and foreseeable, regardless of whether they are patent and obvious. We will first address these questions as they relate to products liability actions in general and then consider whether the Court of Appeals rationale supports a departure in design defect cases from the general rules.

This court has previously held that compliance with governmental and industrial standards does not preclude a trier of fact from finding certain conduct to be negligent. The holding in *Marietta v Cliff's Ridge Inc,* 189 NW2d 208 (1971), cited with approval in *Hill v Husky Briquetting Inc,* 223 NW2d 290 (1974), remains as precedent.

As stated in *Marietta, supra:*
'The customary usage and practice of the industry is relevant evidence to be used in determining whether or not (the) standard (of reasonable care) has been met. Such usage cannot, however, be determinative of the standard.'

Judge Learned Hand eloquently stated the rule when he wrote:
'Indeed, in most cases reasonable prudence is in fact common prudence; but strictly it is never its measure; a whole calling may have unduly lagged in the adoption of new and available devices. It never may set its own tests, however persuasive be its usages.' *The T J Hooper,* 60 F2d 737, 740 (CA 2, 1932).

We note that our legislature has recently enacted a statute which provides that industrial and governmental standards are admissible in products liability actions, MCL section 600 2946; MSA section 27A 2946. The statute does not provide that such standards are conclusive. The defendant, in arguing that plaintiff did not present a *prima facie* case, does not challenge the rule that compliance with governmental and industrial standards is admissible as evidence but is not conclusive as to whether the defendant was negligent or the product was defective. We reaffirm that position.

Apart from those instances in which the design of a product does not conform with governmental or industrial standards, the only other design defect cases in which liability would attach under the Court of Appeals holding would be those cases in which 'the design choice of the manufacturer carries with it a *latent* risk of injury *and* the manufacturer has *not* adequately communicated the nature of that risk to potential users of the product.' 268 NW2d 291. The limitations adopted by the Court of Appeals would preclude liability in any case in which the risk is patent and obvious, unless there was non-compliance with industrial or governmental standards. Defendant, however, does not argue in favor of the Court of Appeals holding insofar as it would exclude liability for all patent and obvious dangers where there was compliance with industrial standards, but instead argues for the more limited proposition that when the dangers are patent and obvious, there is no duty to warn. We note, however, that the language in one of our prior products liability actions would tend to support the proposition that liability does not attach when the dangers are patent and obvious.

Recent US cases

In *Fisher v Johnson Milk Co Inc,* 174 NW2d 752 (1970), the defendant sold plaintiff a wire carrier for milk bottles. When he was carrying milk bottles in the wire carrier, he slipped on some ice. The bottom of the carrier struck the sidewalk and the bottles broke. In extending his hand to break his fall, the plaintiff cut it on glass from the broken bottles. He sued the defendant claiming, *inter alia,* that defendant was negligent in not placing a false bottom on the milk carrier and that defendant had breached its implied warranty of merchantability by selling an unsafe product. The trial court granted summary judgment and this court affirmed:

'There was no inherent, hidden or concealed defect in the wire carrier. Its manner of construction, how the bottles would rest in it, and what might happen if it were dropped, upright, on a hard surface below, with the possibility that the contained bottles might break, was plain enough to be seen by anyone including a patent attorney (the plaintiff) as well as a milk dealer. There is no duty to warn or protect against dangers obvious to all.' *Fisher,* 174 NW2d 752.

. . . . .

Our Court of Appeals has essentially limited the language in our decision in *Fisher* by the fact that *Fisher* involved a simple product or tool. We believe that such a limitation is proper. Obvious risks may be unreasonable risks, and there is no justification for departing from general negligence and breach of implied warranty principles merely because the dangers are patent.

This is not to say that the obviousness of the danger is irrelevant. As in *Fisher,* the obviousness of the risks that inhere in some simple tools or products is a factor contributing to the conclusion that such products are not unreasonably dangerous. The test, however, is not whether the risks are obvious, but whether the risks were unreasonable in light of the foreseeable injuries.

. . . . .

This case provides a noteworthy illustration of why the asserted problem does not justify the solution adopted in the Court of Appeals. Although this is not a 'duty to warn' case, nor a case in which there has been a departure from governmental or industrial standards, it does present a focused question.

The factual inquiry demanded is whether a forklift is unreasonably dangerous when it fails to include a factory-installed driver restraint, such as a seat belt. Obviously, to attach a seat belt to a forklift would not require major changes in the design, utility, or costs of a forklift. When considering whether it was unreasonable not to attach a seat belt to a forklift as standard equipment, one is not confronted with the open-ended question whether another product, somewhat alike and somewhat different from the product under scrutiny, should instead have been manufactured.

Additionally, because one form of driver restraint *was available* as an option ie the cage enclosure, there was the manageable question whether this available restraint should have been installed as standard equip-

ment. Although we find that the plaintiff has not made a *prima facie* showing, as will be discussed below, our affirmance of the directed verdict is not based on the premise that the issue presented was too open-ended to be competently adjudicated.

Because we have determined that the Court of Appeals decision does not provide appropriate standards upon which to affirm the directed verdict, we must now proceed to consider whether the directed verdict was nevertheless proper. We initially granted leave to appeal limited to the two questions related to the holding of the Court of Appeals, but after oral arguments we requested the parties to file supplemental briefs which would include consideration of two additional questions.

These questions were issue (3), whether the testimony of plaintiff's expert witness created a question for the jury in light of MRE 705, and issue (4), whether the manufacturer of a vehicle has 'a duty to design and manufacture his products so as to eliminate any reasonable risk of foreseeable injury to the occupants as a result of a collision for which the manufacturer may not be responsible'.

We conclude that the directed verdict was proper because plaintiff failed to present a *prima facie* case of either negligence or a defective product. Because resolution of the questions we posed after oral arguments is found, after study of the entire matter, unnecessary to our affirmance of the directed verdict, we address issues three and four in only summary fashion.

Consideration of the effect of MRE 705 is not necessary to our decision because the rule did not take effect until long after the directed verdict was entered in this case. The court followed the practice in effect at the time of trial.

The question of the applicability of the 'crashworthiness' doctrine to the forklift manufacturing industry is likewise not necessary to our decision because, assuming applicability of the *Larsen* crashworthiness test in order to posture the evidence in the light most favorable to the plaintiff as we pass upon the directed verdict issue, plaintiff did not show that the design of the forklift was unreasonably dangerous in light of the foreseeable risks of injury. Therefore, the applicability of the 'crashworthiness' test to forklift vehicles is not decided.

Our conclusion that the plaintiff did not present a *prima facie* case is based on the lack of evidence concerning both the magnitude of the risks involved and the reasonableness of the proposed alternative design. Although from the testimony of plaintiff's expert one might infer that a forklift rollover and the injuries resulting from being pinned under the overhead protective guard were foreseeable, neither his testimony nor any other evidence on the record gave any indication how likely such an event might be. In conjunction with this uncertainty, the record also produces no indication

Owens v Allis-Chalmers

how the use of any of the driver restraints would affect a forklift operator's ability to do his or her job or the operator's safety in other circumstances.

The nature of a forklift operator's work is not a function concerning which the court is able to take judicial notice. We must look to the record to determine what showing was made that any of the proposed driver restraints would be compatible with the nature of a forklift operator's work. Especially in a case such as this, where the magnitude of the risks is quite uncertain because it is dependent upon the unknown incidence of forklift rollovers, an examination of the effects of any proposed alternative design must bear a heavy burden in determining whether the chosen design was unreasonably dangerous.

Little evidence was provided on these points. The only evidence concerning the nature of a forklift operator's work was one statement made by plaintiff's expert on cross-examination that he did not know whether most forklift drivers would be in the forklift the better part of their working day or whether they would be in and out of it. He said he had seen both types of operations. Concerning the effects of any of the proposed driver's restraints, the only testimony was a statement by the expert that certain types of seat belts allow some freedom of movement and would only lock when jerked. Regarding whether seat belts would be used, the expert did not testify about the industry in question, but the workers at decedent's workplace indicated that they would not wear seat belts if they were provided. No evidence was provided concerning the effects of the use of the other restraints, and no cost estimates were provided for any of the restraints.

Viewing the evidence in a light most favorable to the plaintiff, we cannot conclude that plaintiff established a *prima facie* case for either negligence or a defective product. Even if this court could take judicial notice that the costs involved in attaching a seat belt or other designated restraint to a forklift would not be great, we cannot take judicial notice that their use by forklift drivers would be likely, practical, or more safe. Neither the costs nor the effects of the other restraints were established.

Significantly, the defendant did offer the cage enclosure, which was one of the suggested restraints, as an option. The question then becomes whether such a cage enclosure should have been installed as standard equipment. Although plaintiff's expert acknowledged that some drivers are frequently in and out of their vehicles, there was no testimony concerning the effects of a cage upon the driver's ability to perform his or her work. There also was no factual testimony concerning the safety of an operator in a cage enclosure in a rollover or in any foreseeable accidents or emergencies other than roll-overs. In short, we find no support in the record for the conclusion that the manufacturer, as opposed to the employer, would be in a better position

to conclude that the cage enclosure should be installed as standard equipment.

In the entirety of plaintiff's proofs, there is no data or other factual evidence concerning the magnitude of the risks involved, the utility or relative safety of the proposed alternatives, or evidence otherwise concerning the 'unreasonableness' of risks arising from failure to install driver restraints on the subject forklift model as standard equipment.

Manufacturers are not insurers that 'in every instance and under all circumstances no injury will result from the use' of their products. *El DuPont de Nemours & Co v Baridon,* 73 F2d 26 (1934).

Therefore, we find that the trial court did not err. The plaintiff's evidence did not raise an issue of fact concerning any unreasonable risk at the time of the design or manufacture of the vehicle.

We affirm.

Justices Kavanagh, Williams, Levin, Moody, Fitzgerald and Ryan concur.

1983 *McKay v Rockwell*

COMMENTARY

The background to this case is sovereign immunity, a principle developed in the early days of the common law and incorporated into American law. Over the years the immunity of governments has been steadily eroded, to the point that the USA abandoned most of its immunities by passing the Federal Tort Claims Act in 1946. There are exceptions to the Act, and in some cases sovereign immunity remains unchanged. Among these exceptions is a claim by a member of the armed forces against the Government.

The case most quoted in connection with government immunity is *Feres v US,* a Supreme Court decision in 1950, in which the court held that a soldier could not sue for harm caused by the negligence of his commanding officer. The issue in *McKay* is whether this immunity extends to a contractor working for the Government. If a contractor is responsible there can be no indemnity from the Government (*Stencel Aero Engineering Corp v US* 1977).

The *McKay* court was persuaded that a supplier of military equipment may not be liable under section 402A for a design defect. It is responsible for a manufacturing defect, and its immunity for a design defect applies only when the Government established or approved the specifications under which the equipment was manufactured. Moreover, the contractor must warn the Government of any dangers that the latter might not know about.

We have seen in previous cases that courts have developed the principles of product liability for reasons of public policy. In this case, the same reasons are used to hold that in certain conditions there is no liability. The factors of risk spreading and deterrence are not present, and the victims would receive compensation under the Veterans' Benefits legislation. To award compensation under section 402A would be a double compensation, although that in itself is not a legal reason for denying liability. Any payments under the Veterans' Act would not be from the same source, and the law in most states is that damages should not be reduced by receipts from collateral sources. The defendant is not to benefit from the plaintiff's good fortune or foresight in providing insurance for himself.

A government supplier is given immunity only when he follows a specification established or approved by the Government, and it will be seen from the dissenting opinion that there can be some difficulty about this condition. The dissent would grant immunity only when the contractor was compelled to work to government specifications, but other courts may not go to the limit of compulsion. The test would be who is responsible for the specifications.

This case is relevant to the current litigation over Agent Orange. It seems that a voluntary settlement may be made, but one estimate is that the average amount could be no more than $10,000, and not all those who have a claim may be satisfied with that amount. The litigation may not be over, and there is still the question of the Government's liability. According to *Stencel* quoted above, the Government cannot be made to indemnify manufacturers who have to pay damages to third parties, but the extent of the Agent Orange disaster is such that Congress may well have to intervene. Before the Federal Tort Claims Act, it was not uncommon for Congress to pass Acts granting compensation in individual cases. In the 76th Congress, from 1939 to 1940, 262 Acts were passed for individual compensation arising out of torts committed by government employees.

In January 1984, the Supreme Court refused to review this decision.

JUDGMENT

United States Court of Appeals, Ninth Circuit
April 20, 1983

McKay
versus
Rockwell International Corporation

Before Circuit Judges Sneed and Alarcon and District Judge Hardy

Sneed, *Circuit Judge.* These are consolidated wrongful death actions arising out of two unrelated crashes of RA-5C naval aircraft in the waters off the coast of Florida. The widows of the two Navy pilots killed in the crashes seek damages from Rockwell International Corp ('Rockwell'), the manufacturers of the RA-5C aircraft and its ejection system. The district court held that Rockwell was liable for the pilots' deaths because of defects in the aircraft's ejection system. Both the widows and Rockwell have appealed.

In this case we confront the question under what circumstances, if any, the doctrine of strict liability in tort, as set forth in section 402A of the Second Restatement of Torts, should be extended to cover manufacturers of military equipment that proves to be defective in design and injures members of the armed forces who are on active duty. We must also address the question whether, under the circumstances of this case, sections 388 and 389 of the Second Restatement impose liability on Rockwell. For the reasons set forth below we reverse the judgment of the district court and remand for further proceedings.

McKay v Rockwell

1 Facts

Rockwell, under contract with the United States Navy, began development in the mid-1950s of an aircraft capable of sustained flight at altitudes of up to 75,000 feet, and with a potential speed of two and a half times the speed of sound. In the early 1960s, the Navy decided to redesign the aircraft as a supersonic carrier-based reconnaissance aircraft, designated the RA-5C 'Vigilante.' The RA-5C was put into use by the Navy in 1962 and was used extensively in Vietnam.

Both the RA-5C aircraft involved in the accidents out of which these cases arise were equipped with the HS-1A escape system. This system was a modified version of an earlier escape system in use in the RA-5C aircraft. The HS-1A system operated by physically restraining the crew in their seats, and then ejecting them ballistically into the airstream by means of a rocket thrust. After ejection, a drogue chute would initiate the opening of a 28 foot parachute to enable the crewmen to descend safely to the ground.

On March 5, 1974, Navy Lieutenant Frank Carson was killed during a daytime training mission when the RA-5C aircraft he piloted caught fire and he was forced to eject from the aircraft. Navy Lieutenant Commander Malcolm McKay was killed on August 13, 1974, after ejecting from a burning RA-5C aircraft during a night training mission. Autopsies of the two pilots revealed that their deaths were probably caused by injuries sustained during ejection.

Plaintiffs filed civil actions in the United States District Court for the Central District of California, seeking recovery of damages for the death of plaintiffs' decedents under theories of negligence, breach of warranty, and wrongful death.

The cases were consolidated for trial and after an evidentiary hearing, the district court determined that it had admiralty jurisdiction over the actions pursuant to the Death on the High Seas Act, 46 USC sections 761-767. The district court found that Rockwell properly was liable for the design of the HS-1A escape system under the principles of tort law set forth in sections 388, 389 and 402A of the Second Restatement of Torts. The court declined to impose liability under these principles for the design of the RA-5C aircraft. It entered judgment after a trial on the merits in favor of plaintiff Carson for $385,703 and in favor of plaintiff McKay for $325,850. Carson and McKay seek review of the measure and amount of damages awarded in their respective judgments. Rockwell also appeals, contending that military suppliers should not be liable to servicemen for injuries caused by defects in military hardware. Our disposition of Rockwell's appeal makes it unnecessary to address the appeals of Carson and McKay.

2 Liability under section 402A of the Second Restatement of Torts

The district court, as stated above, held that Rockwell was liable under section 402A of the Second Restatement of Torts for defects in the design of the HS-1A escape system. We applied the principles of this section in admiralty in *Pan-Alaska Fisheries Inc v Marine Construction & Design Co*, 565 F2d 1129 (9th Cir 1978). But in *Pan-Alaska* we did not hold that strict liability applies for all purposes and for all defendants. Section 402A is not a federal statute. It should be applied only when the purposes it seeks to serve dictate its application. When that is not the case it has no independent force. To apply it merely because it is there is to abdicate judicial responsibility.

Mindful of this responsibility, we conclude that only under the limited circumstances we shall enumerate below should a manufacturer be held strictly liable in tort for injuries to a serviceman on active duty caused by design defects in military equipment.

A *Feres-Stencel doctrine*

We commence our analysis with *Feres v United States*, 340 US 135 (1950). In that case the Supreme Court held that the United States is not subject to liability under the Federal Tort Claims Act, 28 USC section 2674, to a member of the armed forces who sustains an injury while on active duty. The scope of governmental immunity was broadened recently in *Stencel Aero Engineering Corp v United States*, 431 US 666 (1977). There, the court held that the Federal Tort Claims Act precludes the United States from indemnifying a third party for damages paid by it to a member of the armed forces who is injured during military service. The *Stencel* court explained that allowing indemnity would subject the United States to varying degrees of liability, depending on the situs of the accident, would require the United States to pay indirectly to the serviceman what the Veterans' Benefits Act forbids it to pay directly, and would interfere with military discipline. *Id* at 672-73, 97 SCt at 2058-59.

Thus, under the circumstances of these cases, the United States would be immune both from direct tort liability as well as from the obligation of indemnifying Rockwell for damages it might be required to pay.

B *Government contractor defense*

Given the immunities of the United States in cases such as these, the question arises whether a supplier of military equipment should be required to shoulder directly and immediately the entire burden of the liability to an injured serviceman. Some courts, when confronted with this issue, have relied on the so-called government contractor defense. This rule, first articulated by the Supreme Court in *Yearsley v WA Ross Construction Co*, 309 US 18 (1940), protects a government contractor from liability for acts done by him while complying with government specifications during execution of performance of a contract with the United States. See *Myers v United States*, 323 F2d 580, 583 (9th Cir 1963). The rule has been applied when the

United States is immune from suit. *Dolphin Gardens Inc v United States,* 243 F Supp 824, 827 (D Conn 1965).

While the government contractor defense covered at first only construction projects, it has recently been applied by several courts to military equipment design defect cases. See Note, 23 BCL Rev 1025, 1055-64 (1982). For example, in *Sanner v Ford Motor Co,* 144 NJ Super 1 364 A2d 43 (1976), *aff'd,* 154 NJ Super 407, 381 A2d 805 (1977), *cert denied,* 75 NJ 616, 384 A2d 846 (1978), the court held that when a manufacturer produces a jeep in compliance with government specifications, the manufacturer cannot be held strictly liable for defects in the government's design specifications. Similarly, in *Casabianca v Casabianca,* 104 Misc 2d 348, 428 NYS2d 400 (1980), the manufacturer of kitchen equipment made for the Army and in accordance with Army specifications was held not to be subject to liability for defects in the equipment. Finally, in *In Re Agent Orange Product Liability Litigation,* 534 F Supp 1046 (EDNY 1982), the court approved a government contractor defense for manufacturers of a chemical defoliant where the government set or ratified performance specifications for a product, the manufacturer met those specifications, and warned the Government of known dangers from using the product. *Id* at 1055. See also *Littlehale v El DuPont de Nemours & Co,* 268 F Supp 791 (SDNY 1966), (no duty to print warnings on blasting caps where not required by Navy specifications).

The reasons for applying the government contractor defense to suppliers of military equipment with design defects approved by the government parallel those supporting the *Feres-Stencel* doctrine. First, the Supreme Court emphasized in *Stencel* that the United States cannot be directly or indirectly liable to servicemen injured by defective military products. But holding the supplier liable in government contractor cases without regard to the extent of government involvement in fixing the product's design and specifications would subvert the *Feres-Stencel* rule since military suppliers, despite the government's immunity, would pass the cost of accidents off to the United States through cost overrun provisions in equipment contracts, through reflecting the price of liability insurance in the contracts, or through higher prices in later equipment sales.
. . . . .
Second, to hold military suppliers liable for defective designs where the United States set or approved the design specifications would thrust the judiciary into the making of military decisions. Although judges must decide cases arising from fields of endeavor of which they know little, their otherwise omnicompetence confronts its limits in military matters. At this point, it must be acknowledged, separation of powers becomes a proper concern.
. . . . .
Third, it should be noted that in setting specifications for military equipment, the United States is required by the exigencies of our defense effort to push technology towards its limits and thereby to incur risks beyond those that would be acceptable for ordinary consumer goods. A supplier is frequently unable to negotiate with the United States to eliminate those risks. As one court put it: Where, as here, manufacturers claim to have been compelled by federal law to produce a weapon of war without ability to negotiate specifications, contract prices or terms, the potential for unfairly imposing liability becomes great. Without the government contract defense a manufacturer capable of producing military goods for government use would face the untenable position of choosing between severe penalties for failing to supply products necessary to conduct a war, and producing what the government requires but at a contract price that makes no provision for the need to insure against potential liability for design flaws in the government's plans. *In Re Agent Orange Product Liability Litigation,* 506 F Supp at 794.

Finally, a government contractor defense provides incentives for suppliers of military equipment to work closely with and to consult the military authorities in the development and testing of equipment. The defense therefore encourages fixing the locus of responsibility for military equipment design with more precision than is possible under a system where the government contractor rule is not allowed.
. . . . .
To summarize, we hold that under the *Feres-Stencel* doctrine and the government contractor rule, a supplier of military equipment is not subject to section 402A liability for a design defect where: (1) the United States is immune from liability under *Feres* and *Stencel,* (2) the supplier proves that the United States established, or approved, reasonably precise specifications for the allegedly defective military equipment, (3) the equipment conformed to those specifications, and (4) the supplier warned the United States about patent errors in the government's specifications or about dangers involved in the use of the equipment that were known to the supplier but not to the United States. The imposition of this duty to warn of known defects is necessary to enable the United States to balance the risks and benefits inherent in the use of the equipment. *Cf In Re Agent Orange Product Liability Litigation,* 534 F Supp at 1055:
We recognize that the term 'military equipment' is somewhat imprecise, and that at some point lines will have to be drawn. We need not do so here. The line, however, lies somewhere between an ordinary consumer product purchased by the armed forces—a can of beans, for example—and the escape system of a Navy RA-5C reconnaissance aircraft. The latter falls within the term while the former does not.
We also note that the rule enunciated here does not relieve suppliers of military equipment of liability for defects in the manufacture of that equipment. To hold otherwise would remove the incentive from manufacturers to use all cost-justified means to conform to government specifications in the manufacture of military equipment.

McKay v Rockwell

C *Policy considerations in the imposition of strict liability*

The reasons for imposing strict liability as set forth in section 402A are inapplicable when the elements of our holding exist. Courts and commentators have identified four principal reasons for imposing strict liability on an accident producing activity—enterprise liability, market deterrence, compensation, and implied representation of safety, See Note, 33 Stan L Rev 535, 536 & n7 (1981). We shall consider each.

i *Enterprise liability*

Under the enterprise liability rationale, when a product's price reflects the cost of accidents caused by the use of the product, that price will rise. Increased prices will then discourage consumers from purchasing risky products, and thereby lower accident costs to society. See Klemme, *The Enterprise Liability Theory of Torts*, 47 U Colo L Rev 153, 158 (1976). *Cf Pan-Alaska Fisheries*, 565 F2d at 1135.

However, the rationale rests on two assumptions. These are that consumers underestimate the risks involved in a product's use, and will therefore overconsume the product unless the product's price reflects the cost of accidents, and that demand for a product is elastic—that is, that it will decrease as the product's price rises.

Neither of these assumptions applies in the usual case to sales of military equipment to the government. First, the armed forces are aware of most, although sometimes not all, the risks involved in using military equipment. They undertake a constant program of testing and evaluating such equipment. Higher prices would not affect significantly their awareness of the safety risks involved in the use of the equipment. In addition, within broad limits demand is not elastic for military equipment. Rather, government purchases of military equipment are planned in advance, and are based on considerations of military and political strategy, as well as on the government's assessment of the risks and benefits involved in the use of the equipment. Thus, including the cost of accidents in the price of sales to the military would probably have little or no effect on product sales. Meeting adequately the needs of national defense, not accident costs, is the ultimate standard by which purchases of military equipment must be measured.

ii *Market deterrence*

A second reason for imposing strict liability is to deter manufacturers from marketing unsafe products by encouraging the use of cost-justified safety features. See W Prosser, *The Law of Torts* section 4 at 23 (4th ed 1971). The safer the product, the argument runs, the lower the cost of accidents. This should reduce the product's price which, in turn, should increase the sales of the product.

But in the case of military equipment, as noted above, the demand for such equipment is quite inelastic. Moreover, the government, the sole purchaser of most military equipment, has both the ability to recognize safety problems in military equipment and to negotiate with suppliers to remedy those problems. It constantly balances the safety of the article against the imperatives of national defense. Strict liability would no doubt increase defense costs but would do little not already being done to increase the use of safety features in military equipment. See *In Re Agent Orange Product Liability Litigation*, 506 F Supp at 793. Increased defense costs, on the other hand, will diminish either other expenditures, public or private, or the level of national defense, if the level of total expenditures for that purpose were to be held constant.

iii *Compensation*

A third justification for strict liability is that it provides compensation for victims of accidents caused by defective products. Restatement (Second) of Torts section 402A, comment c. In the case of injured military personnel, however, the Veterans' Benefits Act provides what the Supreme Court called 'a generous military compensation scheme,' and 'a swift, efficient remedy.' *Stencel*, 431 US at 672-73. Thus, the serviceman or his family will not go uncompensated, unlike the case of an ordinary consumer injured by a defective product. It is true, of course, that strict liability would increase that compensation, but it can hardly be said that any such increase was anticipated at the time of enlistment.

iv *Implied representation*

Finally, it has been reasoned that by marketing a product, a supplier makes an implied representation that the product, if put to its intended use, will not be unreasonably dangerous and will meet the safety standard expected of similar products. If the product proves to be defective, consumers should receive compensation for the disappointment of their reasonable expectations of safety. Restatement (Second) of Torts section 402A, comment i.

Members of the armed forces are not ordinary consumers with respect to military equipment. Their 'reasonable expectations of safety' are much lower than those of ordinary consumers. They recognize when they join the armed forces that they may be exposed to grave risks of danger, such as having to bail out of a disabled aircraft. This is part of the job. The nation sometimes demands their very lives. This is an immutable feature of their calling. To regard them as ordinary consumers would demean and dishonor the high station in public esteem to which, because of their exposure to danger, they are justly entitled.

D. *Application of our holding to the facts of these cases*

The application of our holding to the facts of these cases requires that we reverse and remand the judgments

Recent US cases

below. It is clear, and we so hold, that in these cases the United States is immune from liability for the design of the HS-1A ejection system under *Feres* and *Stencel*. Moreover, the District Court held that the defect in the system was its design, not its failure to conform to government specifications. Finally, there is no allegation that Rockwell failed to warn the United States of dangers known to Rockwell but not to the Navy.

The present record, however, does not permit us to say with assurance that the United States set or approved reasonably detailed specifications for the HS-1A system. On the one hand, Rockwell alleges that the United States was deeply involved in the process of designing and approving the system. On the other hand, plaintiffs-appellants contend that the United States did little more than send Rockwell a letter asking them to come up with a new ejection system and agree to purchase Rockwell's completed design.

We remand these cases to the District Court to determine whether the United States set or approved reasonably detailed specifications for the HS-1A ejection system. If the District Court finds that the involvement of the United States was limited in the manner the plaintiffs-appellants assert—that is, if the United States neither set specifications for the system (other than general outlines of what type of system it required) nor approved Rockwell's final reasonably detailed specifications (by examining and agreeing to a detailed description of the workings of the system)— then Rockwell is subject to strict liability under the rule set forth in section 402A. We note that Rockwell, the supplier, has the burden of proving by a preponderance of the evidence that the United States established, or approved, reasonably precise specifications for the ejection system.

3. *Liability under section 389 of the Second Restatement of Torts*
. . . . .
Military personnel frequently have been sent to their deaths by the incompetence of others. Hardly a page of history lacks an example or two. We do not suggest that is the case here. However, should it be so those who serve the United States in an active military capacity are assured their survivors will receive some compensation. We merely hold that it is not for this court to increase that compensation in the manner plaintiffs-appellants suggest.

The judgment of the District Court is reversed and these cases remanded for proceedings consistent with this opinion. These holdings, to repeat, make it unnecessary for us to consider the appeals by the plaintiffs-appellants.

Alarcon, *Circuit Judge,* dissenting. I respectfully dissent. Neither the *Feres-Stencel* doctrine nor the government contractor defense protects Rockwell from liability in this case. As demonstrated by the discussion below, a remand on this issue is unnecessary and the

District Court's finding of liability should be affirmed. To the extent that the damage awards have been reduced for failure to apply the collateral source rule, the decision should be reversed and the original amounts awarded.

Finally, the failure to grant prejudgment interest or damages for loss of services is discussed and instructions for the consideration of these issues on remand are given.

Feres-Stencel

The majority's reliance on these opinions for authority in this context is misplaced. Neither opinion addresses, limits, nor precludes contractor liability to military personnel who are injured while using defectively designed and unsafe equipment.
. . . . .
While there is no doubt that some of these liability costs will find their way into overall bid costs, this is to a certain extent inevitable. The free market system, however, insures that this cost transfer will be minimized. Just as some manufacturers are better at minimizing the cost of overhead, others will be better at producing safe designs and avoiding liability. Bid price competition and the cost of liability provide incentives to minimize both. Footnote eight of the *Stencel* opinion concedes this system's existence and recognizes that one way or another, all costs incident to manufacture get passed on to the customer, whether or not it is the Government. As long as our economy continues as a free market system this court should refrain from denying its realities.

The above analysis, of course, does not apply to all government contractors, for not all of them contract at arms length with the Government. In those situations where compulsion exists, in one form or another, the contractor should be immune from suit. Public policy, however, requires that this immunity be extended only in those cases where liability will not encourage safer design or lower costs.

Government contractor defense

In its analysis of this defense, the majority has chosen to disregard the aforementioned public policy limitation. The four elements of the defense summarized in the opinion too easily allow contractors to shift responsibility for the safety of their designs on to the Government. Under the majority's four part test, any contractor who submits designs to the Military and secures approval for them is immune from unsafe design liability. This goes too far.
. . . . .
The approval of the government contractor defense in the *In Re Agent Orange Products Liability Litigation,* 506 F Supp 762 (EDNY 1980), *reh den,* 534 F Supp 1046 (EDNY 1982) opinion, also involved manufacturers who alleged that they were compelled during 'time of war' to produce supplies according to specifications

McKay v Rockwell

developed and provided by the Military. 506 F Supp at 794-95. Although that case has yet to come to trial, the court established the elements of the government contractor defense which the chemical companies must prove. There, the court stated, that 'one of the elements of the defense is that the product in issue be one for which the government established the design and specific characteristics.' 584 F Supp at 1056. Furthermore, 'if it should appear that the contract set forth merely a 'performance specification', as opposed to a specified product, then the government contract defense would be far more restricted than as described here.' *Id.* It is clear from these statements that the *Agent Orange* court recognizes and requires control or compulsion as an element of the defense.

. . . . .

Finally, the majority suggests that to treat military personnel 'as ordinary consumers would demean and dishonor the high station in public esteem to which, because of their exposure to danger, they are justly entitled.' *Ante* at 453. While all can agree that military personnel are entitled to the high honor and esteem in which they are held, I take issue with the majority's description of its source.

Military personnel are honored and esteemed because they are willing to fight for their country and risk their lives doing so. They are not so respected because they are sometimes forced by their calling to use unsatisfactory or unsafe equipment. It is the Military's, Rockwell's and this court's duty to insure that our servicemen are provided with reliable and safe equipment. Just as the Military can make any parachute packer take one that he has just folded and make him jump with it, the court should require that Rockwell stand behind the products for which it voluntarily contracts and provides at a profit. To extend the contractor defense in the way the majority suggests will only result in more unsafe and unreliable equipment. To do so would unnecessarily increase the danger which our military personnel face so patriotically.

The remand

Applying the holdings and reasoning of *O'Keefe, Brown, Merritt* and *Agent Orange* to the instant case demonstrates that a remand on the issue of liability is unnecessary. As mentioned earlier, although Rockwell raised the government contractor defense in a motion for summary judgment, it failed to put on evidence in support of that defense at trial. Rockwell does not point to any testimony or evidence in the record which shows that it was compelled by the Military to build the ejection system in a particular manner. On the other hand, the District Court opinion is replete with references which demonstrate that the trial judge found Rockwell, not the Military, to be the designer of the ejection system. Furthermore, Rockwell's reliance on *Kropp v Douglas Aircraft,* 329 F Supp 447 (EDNY 1971) for a description of their ejection seat design process demonstrates that they are not entitled to the defense. In *Kropp,* the design

process was described as beginning 'rather informally with an idea or suggestion which may emanate either from the manufacturer or the Government, usually the latter.' *Id* at 456. This description closely parallels the 'performance specification' situation described in *Agent Orange.* There, the court held that the government contractor defense was 'far more restricted.' See *Agent Orange,* 534 F Supp at 1056. It also reflects Boeing's behavior in *O'Keefe,* where a failure to show 'the defendant was totally oblivious and/or aloof from the genesis of the design specifications in the first place' precluded the defense. See *O'Keefe,* 335 F Supp at 1124. Finally, *Brown* shows that inspection and approval of a design by the Military does not in any way dismiss the primary responsibility of the contractor who creates the design. See *Brown,* 291 F2d at 317.

The purpose of the remand, proposed by the majority, is to discover whether or not the Government set or approved 'reasonably detailed specifications for the HS-1A system.' *Ante* at 453. As shown by the discussion above, however, it is compulsion to follow *Government* plans, not Government approval of contractor plans, which entitles Rockwell to immunity. Even if we assume, *arguendo,* that a detailed set of plans created by Rockwell were submitted and then approved, the lack of compulsion would prevent the Government from assuming responsibility for the safety or adequacy of Rockwell's design. Because Rockwell has failed to prove or allege that it was compelled to produce the HS-1A system, a remand is unnecessary. Without evidence of the compulsion element, the Ninth Circuit has held and should continue to hold as a matter of law, that the defense is unavailable. See *Merritt,* 295 F2d at 16. If the majority continues to insist on a remand, then, in addition to the four elements set out in the opinion, Rockwell should be required to prove, as a fifth element of the defense, that it was compelled by the Government to produce the ejection system in a manner which failed to protect the crewman's head and neck from injury.

While I believe that a remand on the liability issue is unnecessary, I do believe that other issues, not discussed by the majority, require reversal and further consideration by the District Court . . . . .

Recent US cases

1984 *Green v Firestone*

COMMENTARY

The large number of mergers and takeovers now taking place has brought into prominence the issue of successor liability. As this case shows, Illinois courts are not eager to extend the liability of acquiring corporations, but other states are more inclined to hold successor corporations liable for defects in products manufactured by their predecessors. There is a conflict between the wish to find a remedy for an injured person and the traditional requirement that liability should be placed on the person who put the product into the stream of commerce.

In dealing with the issue the courts have first of all looked at conventional corporation law principles, under which an acquiring corporation would not assume the liabilities of the selling corporation unless there had been a specific agreement to assume liabilities. Even without a specific agreement, traditional corporation law principles would impose liability in certain situations, namely (1) the transaction amounted to a consolidation or merger of the two corporations, (2) the new corporation was in fact a continuation of the old, and (3) the transaction was tainted with fraud.

These rules did not help in many product liability cases, and in 1976 the Michigan Supreme Court extended their scope by holding that liability would be imposed on a successor corporation where there was a 'basic continuity'. Evidence of a basic continuity would be provided by the retention of key employees, the use of the predecessor's assets or the use of its name (*Turner v Bituminous Casualty*, 244 NW2d 873).

A further extension was made in the following year, when the California court developed the 'product line' theory (*Ray v Alad*, 560 P2d 3 1977). Liability will be imposed on a successor corporation that continues the same product line as the predecessor. This theory has not received universal acceptance, although it has been adopted by New Jersey in *Ramirez v Amsted*, New Jersey Supreme Court, June 18 1981. The New Jersey court based its decision on the product line theory, even though it noted that the defendant had expressly declined to assume liability in the takeover agreement.

On the other hand, Florida and Nebraska have refused to follow suit. In *Bernard v Kee Manufacturing* (Florida Supreme Court, January 28 1982) the court spoke of the threat to small businesses if liability was imposed on the product-line theory. It considered that liability should rest with the manufacturer who put the product into the stream of commerce. In *Jones v Johnson Machine and Press Co* (January 4 1982), the Nebraska Supreme Court also held that liability should be imposed on the person putting a product into the stream of commerce. Of course, in all cases the original manufacturer is liable, but usually the only source of compensation is in fact the successor corporation. The Nebraska

court said that the successor corporation in the case before it should not be liable because it had 'neither invited use of its predecessor's product nor represented to the public that the product is safe or suitable for use'.

Another theory of liability was unsuccessfully put forward in *Meisel v M & N Modern Hydraulic Press* (May 27 1982), in which the Washington Supreme Court rejected the 'corporate disregard' theory. The argument was that the successor and predecessor corporations should be treated as one enterprise, and their individual corporate identities ignored for that purpose. The court said that corporate identity should be disregarded only when it was used to evade a duty or commit a fraud. The facts did not support such an argument. Also on the facts the court declined to follow the California decision in *Ray v Alad*, thus leaving open the question whether it would adopt the product line theory on different facts.

JUDGMENT

Illinois Appellate Court, Second District
February 29, 1984

Green
versus
The Firestone Tire and Rubber Co Inc and Sensation Mower Inc

Before Justices Hopf and Van Deusen and Presiding Justice Seidenfeld

Hopf, *Justice.* Plaintiff Edwin N Green brought this action against Sensation Mower Inc and Firestone Tire and Rubber Co Inc (Firestone) alleging one count of breach of warranty and one count of negligence against each of the two corporations. Plaintiff sustained injuries while operating a lawnmower allegedly manufactured by Sensation Mower Inc and sold by McCornack Tire & Service Inc of St Charles, Illinois. It is claimed that Sensation Corporation is a successor to Sensation Mower Inc and that Firestone is a successor to McCornack Tire. Sensation Corporation and Firestone filed motions for summary judgment which were granted Plaintiff appeals.

On appeal plaintiff contends that the trial court erred in granting summary judgment for defendants. During oral argument plaintiff acknowledged that in count I of his complaint he was attempting to extend the theory of products liability to a negligence claim against a predecessor corporation. Plaintiff supplies us with no authority supporting such a theory, and we know of none.

Green v Firestone

Viewed from another perspective, the central issue raised on appeal concerns the liability of successor corporations under the case of *Hernandez v Johnson Press Corp* (1979) 388 NE2d 778, where plaintiff was injured by a punch press and brought an action against the corporation which manufactured the press and its successor corporation. The *Hernandez* court set forth the general rule in Illinois regarding the liability of a successor corporation. Except for certain specified circumstances, a successor corporation is not liable for the debts and liabilities of the transferor. In the case at bar the trial court held that the defendants, which both occupied the position of successor corporations, did not fall within the exceptions set forth by *Hernandez*. On appeal, plaintiff argued that the trial court erred in granting summary judgments because the facts presented in the instant case fall within those exceptions. In the alternative, plaintiff urges that the Illinois law relied on by the trial court is incorrect, and that there is a trend in other states which establishes a strict liability rationale. Plaintiff urges the time has arrived for Illinois to follow this new theory.

The facts of this case show that in June or July 1969, the plaintiff's father-in-law purchased a lawnmower alleged to have been manufactured by Sensation Mower Inc. The mower was purchased from McCornack Tire & Service Inc in St Charles. Later that year, on September 14, Firestone purchased the assets of McCornack Tire & Service Inc. Shortly after the purchase plaintiff's father-in-law died and plaintiff became the owner of the lawnmower. Over the course of the next ten years he used the lawnmower on a regular basis until the time of the accident.

On May 25 1980, plaintiff was injured while mowing his yard. He was pulling the mower with him as he backed up to trim an area of grass. He backed into a tree stump, fell backwards, and as he fell his foot came in contact with the blade of the lawnmower.

Ownership of the company which manufactured plaintiff's lawnmower was transferred a number of times between the date of the sale and the date of the injury. Plaintiff's complaint named both Sensation Mower Inc and Firestone as party-defendants. Sensation Mower Inc was in existence prior to 1968 and manufactured, among other things, lawnmowers. In 1968 Sensation Mower Inc sold certain of its assets to Sensation Manufacturing Company. The sales agreement is not a part of the record in the case at bar, and the precise date of sale is unknown. Subsequently, on August 1 1972, Sensation Manufacturing Company entered into an agreement to sell the assets of that corporation to Sidells Warehouse of Denver Inc, a Nebraska corporation, nominee for the Sensation Corporation, a Nebraska corporation to be formed. The agreement became effective on August 1 1972. The articles of incorporation were subsequently filed with the Nebraska Secretary of State. The new company came to be known as Sensation Inc.

The vice-president of Sensation Corporation, Albert Schinker, filed an affidavit in support of Sensation's motion for summary judgment. In that affidavit Schinker indicated the lawnmower identified in the complaint was manufactured in 1968 or 1969 by either Sensation Mower Inc or by Sensation Manufacturing Company. He did not know which company made the mower because the precise date of manufacture had not been established. He indicated that the production of that model of that lawnmower was discontinued in 1969 and Sensation Corporation did not come into existence until 1972. Therefore it was urged Sensation was not in any way involved with the design, manufacture or sale of the lawnmower identified in the complaint. The affidavit also set forth certain provisions of the agreement for the sale of assets entered into by Sidells Warehouse of Denver Inc, a Nebraska corporation, as nominee for the Sensation Corporation, the corporation that was formed. The portion of that sales agreement which distributed the debts and liabilities of the corporation provided that certain responsibilities regarding liability insurance were made by each party. This provision is quoted in the first issue discussed below. The agreement also indicated that the sale of assets was a cash sale rather than transfer of stock. The Schinker affidavit also stated no present or former stockholders, directors, or officers of Sensation Inc, had ever been stockholders, directors or officers of Sensation Mower Inc, or of Sensation Manufacturing Company.

At the hearing on Sensation Inc's motion for summary judgment plaintiff contended that defendant-corporation was a 'mere continuation of its predecessor corporation, Sensation Manufacturing.' After arguments the trial court decided that there was no genuine issue of fact presented in the briefs or affidavits. The court found that under the *Hernandez* case there was no showing in the facts presented to show an assumption of the predecessor corporation's debts by the successor corporation. The court held that the sales agreement did not provide for an assumption of debts, and because none of the exceptions set forth in *Hernandez* were present, it granted the motion for summary judgment.

Defendant, Firestone Tire & Rubber Co Inc, was granted summary judgment for largely the same reasons as those just discussed. The lawnmower in issue was originally purchased from McCornack Tire & Service Inc, (McCornack) who was not named as a defendant. Approximately three months after the purchase of the lawnmower, on September 14 1969, McCornack was sold to Firestone. That transaction was made pursuant to a sales agreement which provided:

5. McCornack will assume full liability and pay any and all taxes, unemployment compensation contributions, workmen's compensation claims or premiums and all other obligations of whatsoever kind or nature arising from the operation of the Company's business prior to the effective date. It is understood that personal property taxes assessed prior to the effective date of this Agreement shall be paid by the Company and are not to be prorated.

Recent US cases

The deposition of Warren Kammerer who, along with Robert McCornack, was one of the owners of McCornack, indicated that the sale of McCornack Tire was a cash sale. Robert McCornack had no involvement in the new Firestone store. Warren Kammerer was rehired as store manager and became president and 49% owner of Firestone. Firestone retained ownership of the rest of the shares of the corporation. Firestone contends that the operation of the store differs greatly from what it was as McCornack Tire. The new business was required to follow the procedures and policies of Firestone and report to Firestone's zone office. Although some of the original employees of McCornack Tire were retained, not all were rehired.

Most important is the fact that the Firestone store sold different products from McCornack Tire. Specifically the new business was directed by Firestone to not sell Sensation products, which included their line of lawnmowers.

After the hearing on Firestone's motion for summary judgment the trial court noted that there was no genuine issue of fact, that Firestone was the purchaser of the assets of McCornack Tire and that the sale date was September 14 1969. The court noted that it was a cash sale and no exchange of stock was made. Plaintiff made no counter-affidavit of this allegation and although plaintiff sought to bring the case within the exceptions of the *Hernandez* case the court held the facts were not applicable to those exceptions. The court noted that although the mower in issue had been taken into the Firestone store for servicing there was no structural or mechanical failure involved and therefore there was no showing of negligence on the part of defendant. Thus, it granted Firestone's motion for summary judgment as well as Sensation Inc's.

Plaintiff's initial contention on appeal is that his case falls within the exceptions to the general rule that successor corporations are not liable for the liabilities of their predecessor.

The general rule in Illinois has been that when a company sells its assets to another company, the new company is not liable for the debts and liabilities of the old company merely by reason of its succession. *Alexander v State Savings & Trust Co.* (1935) 281 Ill App 88, 96.

However, there are exceptions to the non-liability rule. Several recognized exceptions have been set forth: (1) where there is an express or implied agreement of assumption; (2) where the transaction amounts to a consolidation or merger of the purchaser or seller corporation; (3) where the purchaser is merely a continuation of the seller; or (4) where the transaction is for the fraudulent purpose of escaping liability for the seller's obligations. (*Leannais v Cincinnati Inc,* (7th Cir 1977)).

Plaintiff urges that the first of these exceptions is applicable here. He argues that the language in the sales

agreement between Sensation Manufacturing and Sensation Inc, (as quoted below) provides that buyer agreed to include seller as a named assured for a period of five years from the closing date. Plaintiff urges that this was an assumption, either express or implied, by Sensation Corporation of its predecessor's liability. The clause in issue provides:
'C. Seller covenants that it has had in effect a products liability insurance policy covering liabilities for defective products sold through closing date. Thereafter and continuing for a period of five (5) years from closing date, buyer agrees to include seller as an additional named assured in all products liability insurance policies and to furnish seller with copies of such policies. Should adding seller as additional insured result in additional cost to buyer, seller agrees to pay such additional cost.'

This language indicates that Sensation Corporation, the buyer, agreed to include Sensation Manufacturing as named assured after the closing date. However, there is a difference between agreeing to include a predecessor corporation as a named assured and agreeing to assume the liabilities of that corporation. It could be argued that the seller wanted to have liability insurance maintained in its name expressly because buyer was not assuming liability.

In any event, Sensation Corporation urges that the quoted language should be construed to mean that it was Sensation Manufacturing that agreed to provide insurance for products sold up until the closing date. Because the product sold, the lawnmower, was sold prior to that date, Sensation Manufacturing, not the defendant Sensation Corporation, assumed liability. Factually, this argument is on solid ground. Thus, we believe the trial court was correct in ruling there was no assumption of liability or genuine issue as to a material fact on this point.
. . . . .
The next issue raised by plaintiff on appeal involves the *Hernandez* exceptions as they apply to Firestone. Here, plaintiff argues, the facts surrounding the sale of McCornack Tire to Firestone show a *de facto* merger between successor and predecessor corporations. Secondly, plaintiff argues, Firestone is a mere continuation of its predecessor.

In determining whether there was a *de facto* merger between corporations the *Hernandez* court stated that if there are no facts indicating 'continuity of management, personnel, physical location, assets, and general business operations *** or continuity of shareholders or an exchange of stock' (*Hernandez v Johnson Press Corp* (1979) 388 NE2d 778, 780), no *de facto* merger exists.

Management of the corporation did change when Firestone purchased McCornack Tire. Robert McCornack, who had been co-owner and co-manager of the business, had no involvement in the new business. The other co-owner and co-manager, Warren Kammerer, stayed on, but was responsible to the Firestone zone office. Thus, it appears there was some disruption in the

Green v Firestone

management. With regard to business operations, it should be noted that when Firestone assumed control, the business could no longer sell Sensation mowers.

The transaction failed to meet the second test for a *de facto* merger described in *Hernandez*. It requires a 'continuity of shareholders which results from the purchasing corporation paying for the acquired assets with shares of its own stock, this stock ultimately coming to be held by the shareholders of the seller corporation so that they become a constituent part of the purchasing corporation.'
. . . . .

Applying the principles of *Hernandez* to the facts of the case at bar, we do not believe Firestone was a continuation of McCornack Tire such that it is liable for the latter's alleged torts.

Plaintiff's final contention is that the application of the reasoning set forth in *Hernandez* makes it very difficult to hold a successor corporation liable for the torts of its predecessor, and that this can create a harsh result. Plaintiff urges that a products liability view of corporate mergers, rather than a corporate law view, is the more enlightened approach.

Plaintiff discusses a Michigan case that adopted the product liabilities approach, *Turner v Bituminous Casualty Co* (1976) 244 NW2d 873. The *Turner* court recognized that strict products liability was intended to put the burden for the cost of liability on those who could best cushion the impact of the liability. Thus, to impose liability on a successor corporation was a preferred alternative to leaving a plaintiff without a remedy. *Turner* would substantially lesen the requirements for proof of a *de facto* merger. Although there is some equity to cases which follow the 'product line' approach (see *Ray v Alad Corp* (1977) 560 P2d 3.), they have not been followed.

Illinois courts have not followed the strict liability approach because it could place the burden on one who did not place an injury-causing product in the stream of commerce, thereby putting the burden on one who did not create the risk of harm. *Domine v Fulton Iron Works* (1979) 395 NE2d 19.

This same policy argument was raised in the recent case of *Gonzalez v Rock Wool Engineering & Equipment Co* (1983) 453 NE2d 792, where the court refused to adopt the 'product line' approach to successor liability, noting that one who has done nothing to place a product in the stream of commerce is outside the producing and marketing chain. The court found no liability for a successor corporation, despite the fact that the successor had continued its predecessor's product line.

In *Nguyen v Johnson Machine & Press Corp* (1982) 433 NE2d 1104, the court found that one who has done nothing to create a risk of injury cannot usually be burdened with the duty of preventing that injury.

However, the court noted, if a successor corporation learns of a defect in its predecessor's product, it may have a duty to warn of those defects. While this is a softened approach to the situation, the *Nguyen* court balanced the conflicting interests of corporate law with strict liability principles and found no sufficient justification for changing basic principles of corporate law. The court stressed the importance of the requirement that there be a continuity of shareholders, for without that, it would not be 'just to require the successor corporation to assume the liabilities of the predecessor when it has already paid a substantial price for the assets of the predecessor.' The court also mentioned that a change in the law in this area should come from the legislature.

Thus, while it is clear that the courts have been struggling with this issue none have adopted the strict product liability approach. We do not believe the circumstances presented here should lead to a different conclusion. Therefore the trial court properly found the facts presented did not fall within the exceptions to the general rule of nonliability of a successor corporation.

For the reasons stated, we hold that the trial court did not err in dismissing plaintiff's complaint.

The circuit court of Kane County is affirmed.

Seidenfeld PJ and Van Deusen J, concur.

The development of product liability law in the UK

Until comparatively recently, a law student seeking enlightenment on the UK law relating to liability for defective products would have been hard put to find in any text book a heading entitled 'Product Liability'. It was not treated as a topic in its own right, but rather as an area for consideration under the different headings of contract law, and liability arising in negligence.

The fact that not only has this book been published, but has now been preceded by a number of studies of the UK law on product liability shows how far things have changed in the eight years or so since product liability became a 'live' issue in English legal and industrial circles with the publication in 1976 of the draft EEC directive proposing the introduction of strict liability for defective products.

Having introduced the subject as an essentially modern one, it may seem somewhat quixotic to then choose as the first landmark case one which was decided as long ago as 1842. However *Winterbottom v Wright* combines a clear statement of the doctrine of privity of contract, and its application in the pre-*Donoghue v Stevenson* days, with another element which seems to be a forerunner of much product liability litigation in later years, the four-wheeled means of transport.

Donoghue v Stevenson is of course the definitive landmark case in the development of UK law, in establishing the manufacturer's duty to the ultimate consumer to take care, and looking back from 1984 we can see that *Daniels v White*, which has caused much concern over the years, was really a temporary hiccup in the chain of cases which developed from *Donoghue*.

Grant v Australian Knitting Mills established the important principle that the defect must be hidden from the consumer, which point was to be reinforced again later in a decision which went against the plaintiff in *Crow v Barford*.

Hill v James Crowe (Cases) Ltd extends the liability of the manufacturer in *Donoghue* to defects in a container or packaging rather than to just an end product, and in circumstances where the manufacturer should have foreseen injuries arising, albeit from an abnormal use.

Of the more recent cases dating from 1978, the theme is on the whole the practical application of the *Donoghue* principles. In *Walton v BL* for example, the issue is whether the manufacturer's failure to institute a recall amounted to a breach of the duty to take care; and in *Matthews v Tretol* the question is whether the duty owed to the applicators of a dangerous process had been adequately discharged by the warnings given.

In *Castree v Squibb*, the duty of care of distributors as well as manufacturers in respect of defective products is underlined, while in *Lexmead v Lewis*—perhaps a classic product liability case—the liability of the whole chain of those involved in a tragic road accident is

examined—the manufacturer/designer, the wholesaler, the retailer and the negligent end user.

The three most recent cases selected have their own particularly interesting features. *Junior Books*—if interpreted broadly—considerably extends the scope of a product liability action in negligence by awarding damages for commercial losses when no physical injury or risk of physical injury was involved—and raises the question of whether it will 'open the floodgates' or should be treated only as a special case on its facts. *Mitchell v Finney Lock Seeds* (the 'cabbage seed case') is based on contract rather than negligence but is of great interest in its discussion of the effectiveness of exclusion clauses, and the final dismissal of the doctrine of fundamental breach. Co-incidentally, it was also one of the last cases to be considered in the Court of Appeal by one of the greatest English judges, Lord Denning.

The remaining case selected to illustrate developments in UK product liability law from 1978 to 1983, *Berliner v Sun Alliance*, brings together two of the practical issues facing manufacturers and distributors today—selling to the United States of America and the question of insurance. It seem particularly appropriate for inclusion in this volume of American and English cases because, despite the recent developments in English law (as illustrated in *Junior Books*), we have no doubt that there is a feeling of being in limbo when viewing the present UK scene. The EEC directive remains bogged down in Brussels, and the present British Government appears unwilling to take any independent initiative to implement the proposals of the Law Commissions. Although the initial horror at some of the alleged (and probably highly apocryphal) excesses of the American system has died away, developments in the USA remain of great practical *current* importance for manufacturers involved in exporting there. Similarly, whilst the lawyers argue about the extent of the duty to take care, the duty to warn and the benefits or otherwise of strict liability, the businessman still has the practical issue to face of ensuring that he has adequate insurance to cover liability for his defective products here and now, regardless of the fine detail of the legal arguments, which will no doubt continue for some time.

As study of the first part of this casebook relating to American law reminds us, US law relating to product liability is—depending on your point of view of course—either the signpost pointing the way for future improvements in the consumer's lot in Europe, or an experience to be avoided at all costs.

English law on product liability is still developing, and in many respects is certainly underdeveloped compared with the USA. However, as reading these cases shows, we have come a long way since *Winterbottom v Wright*, and perhaps we are now not so far away in practice from strict liability as those lobbying for change would have us believe.

SECTION III — UK landmark cases

1842 *Winterbottom v Wright*

COMMENTARY

Until the middle of the 19th century, the law of contract dominated the issue of liability for products which turned out to be defective. Privity of contract was the rule, and only the direct purchaser could sue the seller if the goods turned out to have a defect which caused injury or loss with two limited exceptions where someone other than the direct purchaser might have a cause of action. One was where fraudulent representations about the goods were made by the seller, which he intended should be relied on by others. The second was where the goods sold were by their nature dangerous.

These principles had been illustrated in the earlier case of *Langridge v Levy* where a man bought a gun from a gunsmith for his son, which subsequently exploded and caused the latter severe injuries. It was held that the seller was liable to pay the son damages even though he had not been a party to the contract, because the seller had fraudulently represented the gun to be safe knowing that it was not. Further, as a supplier of an inherently dangerous product, *ie* a gun, he should be liable to anyone injured by its defective state.

The case of *Winterbottom v Wright* decided in 1842 made it clear that at this stage the courts would go no further in giving rights of redress to plaintiffs not connected with the original contract.

The driver of the mail coach was not entitled to recover compensation for his injuries caused by the defective construction of the coach because he had no contract with the manufacturer. As in later cases, the judicial view was clearly that it was better to err on the side of caution than to open the floodgates to large amounts of litigation. As one of the judges remarked 'The only safe rule is to confine the right to recover to those who enter into the contract: if we go one step beyond that, there is no reason why we should not go fifty'.

The plaintiff of course had argued that the case fell within the principles of *Langridge v Levy*, suggesting that the defendant had entered into a contract to supply an article (*ie* the coach) which, if it had defects of construction, would be inherently dangerous, and which by its nature and normal use was likely to be driven by a coachman. He drew the parallel with *Langridge v Levy* that, although the contract there was made by the father on behalf of his son, who was a minor, there was no evidence that the gunsmith knew of that particular son's existence. It was also argued that there had been fraud on the part of the defendant, who had represented that the coach was in a proper state for use when in fact due to its defect it was not.

On both of these points the defendant failed. The court was unanimous in holding that it would be wrong and undesirable to extend the *Langridge v Levy*

principles, thus confirming the privity of contract rule and closing the door on further developments of the law to give remedies to a third party. An American commentator[1] has said of this case that 'it was misinterpreted as limiting a manufacturer's liability for his negligence in manufacture to persons with whom the manufacturer had contractual relations, and produced a century-long struggle to square products liability with economic development'.

[1] Cornelius W Gillam, 'Products Liability in the Automobile Industry. A Study in Strict Liability and Social Control'

JUDGMENT

Court of Exchequer
June 6, 1842

Winterbottom
versus
Wright

Before Lord Abinger, Chief Baron, Baron Alderson, Baron Gurney and Baron Rolfe

Case. The declaration stated, that the defendant was a contractor for the supply of mail-coaches, and had in that character contracted for hire and reward with the Postmaster-General, to provide the mail-coach for the purpose of conveying the mail-bags from Hartford, in the county of Chester, to Holyhead: That the defendant, under and by virtue of the said contract, had agreed with the said Postmaster-General that the said mail-coach should, during the said contract, be kept in a fit, proper, safe, and secure state and condition for the said purpose, and took upon himself, to wit, under and by virtue of the said contract, the sole and exclusive duty, charge, care, and burden of the repairs, state, and condition of the said mail-coach; and it had become and was the sole and exclusive duty of the defendant, to wit, under and by virtue of his said contract, to keep and maintain the said mail-coach in a fit, proper, safe, and secure state and condition for the purpose aforesaid: That Nathaniel Atkinson and other persons, having notice of the said contract, were under contract with the Postmaster-General to convey the said mail-coach from Hartford to Holyhead, and to supply horses and coachmen for that purpose, and also not, on any pretence whatever, to use or employ any other coach or carriage whatever than such as should be so provided, directed, and appointed by the Postmaster-General: That the plaintiff, being a mail-coachman, and thereby obtaining his livelihood, and whilst the said several contracts were in force, having notice thereof, and trusting to and confiding in the contract made between the defendant and the Postmaster-General, and believing that the said coach was in a fit, safe, secure, and proper state and condition for the purpose aforesaid,

Winterbottom v Wright

and not knowing and having no means of knowing to the contrary thereof, hired himself to the said Nathaniel Atkinson and his co-contractors as mail-coachman, to drive and take the conduct of the said mail-coach, which but for the said contract of the defendant he would not have done. The declaration then averred, that the defendant so improperly and negligently conducted himself, and so utterly disregarded his aforesaid contract, and so wholly neglected and failed to perform his duty in this behalf, that heretofore, to wit, on the 8th of August, 1840, whilst the plaintiff, as such mail-coachman so hired, was driving the said mail-coach from Hartford to Holyhead, the same coach, being a mail-coach found and provided by the defendant under his said contract, and the defendant then acting under his said contract, and having the means of knowing and then well knowing all the aforesaid premises, the said mail-coach being then in a frail, weak, and infirm, and dangerous state and condition, to wit, by and through certain latent defects in the state and condition thereof, and unsafe and unfit for the use and purpose aforesaid, and from no other cause, circumstance, matter or thing whatsoever, gave way and broke down, whereby the plaintiff was thrown from his seat, and in consequence of injuries then received, had become lamed for life.

To this declaration the defendant pleaded several pleas, to two of which there were demurrers; but as the court gave no opinion as to their validity, it is not necessary to state them.

Peacock, who appeared in support of the demurrers, having argued against the sufficiency of the pleas—

Byles, for the defendant, objected that the declaration was bad in substance. This is an action brought, not against Atkinson and his co-contractors, who were the employers of the plaintiff, but against the person employed by the Postmaster-General, and totally unconnected with them or with the plaintiff. Now it is a general rule, that wherever a wrong arises merely out of the breach of a contract, which is the case on the face of this declaration, whether the form in which the action is conceived be *ex contractu* or *ex delicto*, the party who made the contract alone can sue: *Tollit v Sherstone* (5 M & W 283). If the rule were otherwise, and privity of contract were not requisite, there would be no limit to such actions. If the plaintiff may, as in this case, run through the length of three contracts, he may run through any number or series of them; and the most alarming consequences would follow the adoption of such a principle. For example, every one of the sufferers, by such an accident as that which recently happened on the Versailles railway, might have his action against the manufacturer of the defective axle. So, if the chaincable of an East Indiaman were to break, and the vessel went aground, every person affected, either in person or property, by the accident, might have an action against the manufacturer, and perhaps against every seller also of the iron. Again, suppose a gentleman's coachman were injured by the breaking down of his carriage, if this action be maintainable, he might bring his action against

the smith or the coachmaker, although he could not sue his master, who is the party contracting with him: *Priestley v Fowler* (3 M & W 1). There is no precedent to be found of such a declaration, except one in 8 Wentworth, 397, which has been deemed very questionable. *Rapson v Cubitt* (9 M & W 710) is an authority to show that the party injured by the negligence of another cannot go beyond the party who did the injury, unless he can establish that the latter stood in the relation of a servant to the party sued. In *Witte v Hague* (2 Dowl & Ry 33), where the plaintiff sued for an injury produced by the explosion of a steam-engine boiler, the defendant was personally present managing the boiler at the time of the accident. *Levy v Langridge* (4 M & W 337) will probably be referred to on the other side. But that case was expressly decided on the ground that the defendant, who sold the gun by which the plaintiff was injured, although he did not personally contract with the plaintiff, who was a minor, knew that it was bought to be used by him. Here there is no allegation that the defendant knew that the coach was to be driven by the plaintiff. There, moreover, fraud was alleged in the declaration, and found by the jury: and there too, the cause of injury was a weapon of a dangerous nature, and the defendant was alleged to have had notice of the defect in its construction. Nothing of that sort appears upon this declaration.

Peacock, *contra*. This case is within the principle of the decision in *Levy v Langridge*. Here the defendant entered into a contract with a public officer to supply an article which, if imperfectly constructed, was necessarily dangerous, and which, from its nature and the use for which it was destined, was necessarily to be driven by a coachman. That is sufficient to bring the case within the rule established by *Levy v Langridge*. In that case the contract made by the father of the plaintiff with the defendant was made on behalf of himself and his family generally, and there was nothing to show that the defendant was aware even of the existence of the particular son who was injured. Suppose a party made a contract with government for a supply of muskets, one of which, from its misconstruction, burst and injured a soldier: there it is clear that the use of the weapon by a soldier would have been contemplated, although not by the particular individual who received the injury, and could it be said, since the decision in *Levy v Langridge*, that he could not maintain an action against the contractor? So, if a coachmaker, employed to put on the wheels of a carriage, did it so negligently that one of them flew off, and a child of the owner were thereby injured, the damage being the natural and immediate consequence of his negligence, he would surely be responsible. So, if a party entered into a contract to repair a church, a workhouse, or other public building, and did it so insufficiently that a person attending the former, or a pauper in the latter, were injured by the falling of a stone, he could not maintain an action against any other person than the contractor; but against him he must surely have a remedy. It is like the case of a contractor who negligently leaves open a

UK landmark cases

sewer, whereby a person passing along the street is injured. It is clear that no action could be maintained against the Postmaster-General: *Hall v Smith* (2 Bing 156), *Humphreys v Mears* (1 Man & R 187), *Priestly v Fowler*. But here the declaration alleges the accident to have happened through the defendant's negligence and want of care. The plaintiff had no opportunity of seeing that the carriage was sound and secure. (Alderson, B. The decision in *Levy v Langridge* proceeds upon the ground of the knowledge and fraud of the defendant.) Here also there was fraud: the defendant represented the coach to be in a proper state for use, and whether he represented that which was false within his knowledge, or a fact as true which he did not know to be so, it was equally a fraud in point of law, for which he is responsible.

Lord Abinger, CB. I am clearly of opinion that the defendant is entitled to our judgment. We ought not to permit a doubt to rest upon this subject, for our doing so might be the means of letting in upon us an infinity of actions. This is an action of the first impression, and it has been brought in spite of the precautions which were taken, in the judgment of this court in the case of *Levy v Langridge,* to obviate any notion that such an action could be maintained. We ought not to attempt to extend the principle of that decision, which, although it has been cited in support of this action, wholly fails as an authority in its favour; for there the gun was bought for the use of the son, the plaintiff in that action, who could not make the bargain himself, but was really and substantially the party contracting. Here the action is brought simply because the defendant was a contractor with a third person; and it is contended that thereupon he became liable to every body who might use the carriage. If there had been any ground for such an action, there certainly would have been some precedent of it; but with the exception of actions against innkeepers, and some few other persons, no case of a similar nature has occurred in practice. That is a strong circumstance, and is of itself a great authority against its maintenance. It is however contended, that this contract being made on the behalf of the public by the Postmaster-General, no action could be maintained against him, and therefore the plaintiff must have a remedy against the defendant. But that is by no means a necessary consequence—he may be remediless altogether. There is no privity of contract between these parties; and if the plaintiff can sue, every passenger, or even any person passing along the road, who was injured by the upsetting of the coach, might bring a similar action. Unless we confine the operation of such contracts as this to the parties who entered into them, the most absurd and outrageous consequences, to which I can see no limit, would ensue. Where a party becomes responsible to the public, by undertaking a public duty, he is liable, though the injury may have arisen from the negligence of his servant or agent. So, in cases of public nuisances, whether the act was done by the party as a servant, or in any other capacity, you are liable to an action at the suit of any person who suffers. Those, however, are cases where

the real ground of the liability is the public duty, or the commission of the public nuisance. There is also a class of cases in which the law permits a contract to be turned into a tort; but unless there has been some public duty undertaken, or public nuisance committed, they are all cases in which an action might have been maintained upon the contract. Thus, a carrier may be sued either in assumpsit or case; but there is no instance in which a party, who was not privy to the contract entered into with him, can maintain any such action. The plaintiff in this case could not have brought an action on the contract; if he could have done so, what would have been his situation, supposing the Postmaster-General had released the defendant? That would, at all events, have defeated his claim altogether. By permitting this action, we should be working this injustice, that after the defendant had done everything to the satisfaction of his employer, and after all matters between them had been adjusted, and all accounts settled on the footing of their contract, we should subject them to be ripped open by this action of tort being brought against him.

Baron Alderson. I am of the same opinion. The contract in this case was made with the Postmaster-General alone; and the case is just the same as if he had come to the defendant and ordered a carriage, and handed it at once over to Atkinson. If we were to hold that the plaintiff could sue in such a case, there is no point at which such actions would stop. The only safe rule is to confine the right to recover to those who enter into the contract: if we go one step beyond that, there is no reason why we should not go fifty. The only real argument in favour of the action is, that this is a case of hardship; but that might have been obviated, if the plaintiff had made himself a party to the contract. Then it is urged that it falls within the principle of the case of *Levy v Langridge*. But the principle of that case was simply this, that the father having bought the gun for the very purpose of being used by the plaintiff, the defendant made representations by which he was induced to use it. There a distinct fraud was committed on the plaintiff; the falsehood of the representation was also alleged to have been within the knowledge of the defendant who made it, and he was properly held liable for the consequences. How are the facts of that case applicable to those of the present? Where is the allegation of misrepresentation or fraud in this declaration? It shows nothing of the kind. Our judgment must therefore be for the defendant.

Baron Gurney concurred.

Baron Rolfe. The breach of the defendant's duty, stated in this declaration is his omission to keep the carriage in a safe condition; and when we examine the mode in which that duty is alleged to have arisen, we find a statement that the defendant took upon himself, to wit, under and by virtue of the said contract, the sole and exclusive duty, charge, care, and burden of the repairs, state and condition of the said mail-coach, and, during all the time aforesaid, it had become and was the sole and exclusive duty of the defendant, to wit, under and by virtue of his said contract, to keep and maintain the said mail-coach in a fit, proper, safe, and secure state and condition. The duty, therefore, is shown to have arisen solely from the contract; and the fallacy consists in the use of that word 'duty'. If a duty to the Postmaster-General be meant, that is true; but if a duty to the plaintiff be intended (and in that sense the word is evidently used), there was none. This is one of those unfortunate cases in which there certainly has been *damnum,* but it is *damnum absque injuria;* it is, no doubt, a hardship upon the plaintiff to be without a remedy, but by that consideration we ought not to be influenced. Hard cases, it has been frequently observed, are apt to introduce bad law.

Judgment for the defendant.

1932 *Donoghue v Stevenson*
COMMENTARY

This is perhaps the most significant of all landmark cases in the development of the modern law of product liability in the UK, although it was in fact a Scottish case. The principle established has never been questioned and it has since been adopted and expanded all over the world in a whole series of cases.

Lord Atkin underlined the importance of the case when he remarked to his judicial colleagues in his judgment 'I do not think a more important problem has occupied your Lordships in your judicial capacity, important both because of its bearing on public health and because of the practical test which it applies to the system of law under which it arises.'

Prior to 1932 it was, as we have seen, extremely doubtful that there was any liability on the part of the manufacturer of goods to the ultimate consumer or user with whom he had no relationship in contract, unless the goods were dangerous *per se,* or he was aware that the goods were dangerous. An earlier attempt to make the seller of goods liable in negligence to someone other than the direct purchaser in *George v Skivington* (1869) LR 5 Exch 1 had not been followed in other cases and had been criticised. However, by 1932 the judicial climate had changed and this House of Lords decision established the principle that the manufacturer of a product owes a duty of care to the ultimate consumer or user. As Lord Wright remarked in the later case of *Grant v Australian Knitting Mills* (see next case) the decision treats 'negligence, where there is a duty to take care, as a specific tort in itself, and not simply as an element in some more complex relationship or in some specialised breach of duty.' It also established that the absence of privity of contract between the parties did not preclude liability in tort.

The scope of this liability was defined by Lord Atkin as follows—'a manufacturer of products which he sells in such a form as to show that he intends them to reach the ultimate consumer in the form in which they left him with no reasonable possibility of intermediate examination and with the knowledge that the absence of reasonable care in the preparation or putting up of the products will result in an injury to the consumer's life or property, owes a duty to the consumer to take reasonable care.'

Although a landmark case, the original effect of the decision was limited. Later cases have extended these limits and considerably increased the scope of the principles laid down.

In the *Donoghue* case, the duty was taken to extend to the manufacturers of 'food, medicine or the like', as the heading to the case report states. This limitation was, as we shall see, to be quickly extended to apply to all types of products. Similarly, 'consumer' has been extended to mean 'ultimate user' and 'in the form in

UK landmark cases

which they left him' has been extended to mean not just in the same package or container, but subject to the same defect.

A limitation in *Donoghue* which has, however, remained unchanged until very recently[1] was that the defect in the product must be one that may result in injury to the consumer's life or property. The element of 'no reasonable possibility of intermediate examination' has given rise to difficulties in later cases. Clearly, in the case of a bottle of ginger beer, the possibility of examination by the consumer was fairly remote but in later cases this element has come under scrutiny. For example, an opportunity to examine the goods may have been offered but not taken, or the examination may not have revealed the defect, or the plaintiff, having examined and found the defect, has used the goods anyway.

The duty to take care

The case also established the nature of the duty to take care with Lord Atkin's famous explanation of what has been called 'the neighbour principle'. This is so important that it is worth extracting from the text of the judgment.

'The rule that you are to love your neighbour becomes in law, you must not injure your neighbour; and the lawyer's question "Who is my neighbour?" receives a restricted reply. You must take reasonable care to avoid acts or omissions which you can reasonably foresee would be likely to injure your neighbour. Who, then, in law is my neighbour? The answer seems to be—persons who are so closely and directly affected by my act that I ought reasonably to have had them in contemplation as being so affected when I am directing my mind to the acts or omissions which are called in question.'

The onus of proving negligence rests with the plaintiff. In this case the decision of the House of Lords rested on the basis that the plaintiff could prove the facts 'as averred'. It is interesting to note that, in fact, we do not know whether the case would have been won on this basis, as following the House of Lords judgment the case was settled.

[1] See *Junior Books Ltd v Veitchi* in section IV

JUDGMENT

House of Lords
May 26, 1932

Donoghue
versus
Stevenson

Before Lord Buckmaster, Lord Atkin, Lord Tomlin, Lord Thankerton and Lord Macmillan

Lord Buckmaster (read by Lord Tomlin). My Lords, the facts of this case are simple. On August 26, 1928, the appellant drank a bottle of ginger-beer, manufactured by the respondent, which a friend had bought from a retailer and given to her. The bottle contained the decomposed remains of a snail which were not, and could not be, detected until the greater part of the contents of the bottle had been consumed. As a result she alleged, and at this stage her allegations must be accepted as true, that she suffered from shock and severe gastro-enteritis. She accordingly instituted the proceedings against the manufacturer which have given rise to this appeal.

The foundation of her case is that the respondent, as the manufacturer of an article intended for consumption and contained in a receptacle which prevented inspection, owed a duty to her as consumer of the article to take care that there was no noxious element in the goods, that he neglected such duty and is consequently liable for any damage caused by such neglect. After certain amendments, which are now immaterial, the case came before the Lord Ordinary, who rejected the plea in law of the respondent and allowed a proof. His interlocutor was recalled by the Second Division of the Court of Session, from whose judgment this appeal has been brought.

Before examining the merits two comments are desirable: (1) that the appellant's case rests solely on the ground of a tort based not on fraud but on negligence; and (2) that throughout the appeal the case has been argued on the basis, undisputed by the Second Division and never questioned by counsel for the appellant or by any of your Lordships, that the English and the Scots law on the subject are identical.

It is therefore upon the English law alone that I have considered the matter, and in my opinion it is on the English law alone that in the circumstances we ought to proceed.

The law applicable is the common law, and, though its principles are capable of application to meet new conditions not contemplated when the law was laid down, these principles cannot be changed nor can additions be made to them because any particular meritorious case seems outside their ambit.

Now the common law must be sought in law books by writers of authority and in judgments of the judges entrusted with its administration. The law books give no assistance, because the work of living authors, however deservedly eminent, cannot be used as authority, though the opinions they express may demand attention; and the ancient books do not assist. I turn, therefore, to the decided cases to see if they can be construed so as to support the appellant's case. One of the earliest is the case of *Langridge v Levy* (2 M&W 519, 4 M&W 337). It is a case often quoted and variously explained. There a man sold a gun which he knew was dangerous for the use of the purchaser's son. The gun

Donoghue v Stevenson

exploded in the son's hands, and he was held to have a right of action in tort against the gunmaker. How far it is from the present case can be seen from the judgment of Parke B who, in delivering the judgment of the court, used these words: 'We should pause before we made a precedent by our decision which would be an authority for an action against the vendors, even of such instruments and articles as are dangerous in themselves, at the suit of any person whomsoever into whose hands they might happen to pass, and who should be injured thereby'; and in *Longmeid v Holliday*(6 Ex 761) the same eminent judge points out that the earlier case was based on a fraudulent misstatement, and he expressly repudiates the view that it has any wider application. The case of *Langridge v Levy,* therefore, can be dismissed from consideration with the comment that it is rather surprising it has so often been cited for a proposition it cannot support.

The case of **Winterbottom v Wright*(10M&W109) is, on the other hand, an authority that is closely applicable. Owing to negligence in the construction of a carriage it broke down, and a stranger to the manufacturer and sale sought to recover damages for injuries which he alleged were due to negligence in the work, and it was held that he had no cause of action either in tort or arising out of contract. This case seems to me to show that the manufacturer of any article is not liable to a third party injured by negligent construction, for there can be nothing in the character of a coach to place it in a special category. It may be noted, also, that in this case Alderson B said: 'The only safe rule is to confine the right to recover to those who enter into the contract; if we go one step beyond that, there is no reason why we should not go fifty.'

Longmeid v Holliday was the case of a defective lamp sold to a man whose wife was injured by its explosion. The vendor of the lamp, against whom the action was brought, was not the manufacturer, so that the case is not exactly parallel to the present, but the statement of Parke B in his judgment covers the case of manufacturer, for he said: 'It would be going much too far to say, that so much care is required in the ordinary intercourse of life between one individual and another, that, if a machine not in its nature dangerous, ... but which might become so by a latent defect entirely unknown, although discoverable by the exercise of ordinary care, should be lent or given by one person, even by the person who manufactured it, to another, the former should be answerable to the latter for a subsequent damage accruing by the use of it.' It is true that he uses the words 'lent or given' and omits the word 'sold', but if the duty be entirely independent of contract and is a duty owed to a third person, it seems to me to be the same whether the article be originally given or sold. The fact in the present case that the ginger-beer originally left the premises of the manufacturer on a purchase, as was probably the case, cannot add to his duty, if such existed, to take care in its preparation.

It has been suggested that the statement of Parke B

does not cover the case of negligent construction, but the omission to exercise reasonable care in the discovery of a defect in the manufacture of an article where the duty of examination exists is just as negligent as the negligent construction itself.

The general principle of these cases is stated by Lord Sumner in the case of*Blacker v Lake & Elliot* (106 LT 533) in these terms: 'The breach of the defendant's contract with A to use care and skill in and about the manufacture or repair of an article does not of itself give any cause of action to B when he is injured by reason of the article proving to be defective.'

From this general rule there are two well known exceptions: (1) In the case of an article dangerous in itself; and (2) where the article not in itself dangerous is in fact dangerous, by reason of some defect or for any other reason, and this is known to the manufacturer. Until the case of *George v Skivington* (LR 5 Ex1) I know of no further modification of the general rule.

As to (1), in the case of things dangerous in themselves, there is, in the words of Lord Dunedin, 'a peculiar duty to take precaution imposed upon those who send forth or install such articles when it is necessarily the case that other parties will come within their proximity': *Dominion Natural Gas Co v Collins & Perkins* [1909] AC 640. And as to (2), this depends on the fact that the knowledge of the danger creates the obligation to warn, and its concealment is in the nature of fraud. In this case no one can suggest that ginger-beer was an article dangerous in itself, and the words of Lord Dunedin show that the duty attaches only to such articles, for I read the words 'a peculiar duty' as meaning a duty peculiar to the special class of subject mentioned.

. . . . .

In *Earl v Lubbock* [1905] 1KB 253, the plaintiff had been injured by a wheel coming off a van which he was driving for his employer and which it was the duty of the defendant under contract with such employer to keep in repair. The county court judge and the Divisional Court both held that even if negligence was proved the action would not lie. It was held by the Court of Appeal that the defendant was under no duty to the plaintiff and that there was no cause of action.

In *Bates v Batey and Co* [1913] 3KB 351, the defendants, ginger-beer manufacturers, were held not liable to a consumer (who had purchased from a retailer one of their bottles) for injury occasioned by the bottle bursting as a result of a defect of which the defendants did not know, but which by the exercise of reasonable care they could have discovered. In reaching this conclusion Mr Justice Horridge stated that he thought the judgments of Baron Parke in *Longmeid v Holliday* (*supra*), of Lords Justices Cotton and Bowen in *Heaven v Pender* (11 QBD 503), of Lord Justice Stirling in *Earl v Lubbock* (*supra*), and of Mr Justice Hamilton in *Blacker v Lake & Elliot* (*supra*), made it clear that the plaintiff was not entitled to recover, and that he had not felt himself bound by *George v Skivington* (*supra*).

UK landmark cases

So far, therefore, as the case of *George v Skivington* (*supra*) and the *dicta* in *Heaven v Pender* (*supra*) are concerned, it is, in my opinion, better that they should be buried so securely that their perturbed spirits shall no longer vex the law.

One further case mentioned in argument may be referred to, certainly not by way of authority but to gain assistance by considering how similar cases are dealt with by eminent judges of the United States. That such cases can have no close application and no authority is clear, for though the source of the law in the two countries may be the same its current may well flow in different channels. The case referred to is that of *Thomas v Winchester* (6 NY 397). There a chemist issued poison in answer to a request for a harmless drug, and he was held responsible to a third party injured by his neglect.

It appears to me that the decision might well rest on the principle that he in fact sold a drug dangerous in itself, none the less so because he was asked to sell something else, and on this view the case does not advance the matter.

In another case of * *MacPherson v Buick Motor Company* (217 NY 382), where a manufacturer of a defective motor-car was held liable for damages at the instance of a third party, the learned judge appears to base his judgment on the view that a motor-car might reasonably be regarded as a dangerous article.

In my view, therefore, the authorities are against the appellant's contention, and apart from authority it is difficult to see how any common law proposition can be formulated to support her claim.

The principle contended for must be this: that the manufacturer or indeed the repairer of any article, apart entirely from contract, owes a duty to any person by whom the article is lawfully used to see that it has been carefully constructed. All rights in contract must be excluded from consideration of this principle, for such rights undoubtedly exist in successive steps from the original manufacturer, down to the ultimate purchaser, embraced in the general rule that an article is warranted as reasonably fit for the purpose for which it is sold. Nor can the doctrine be confined to cases where inspection is difficult or impossible to introduce. This conception is simply to misapply to tort doctrines applicable to sale and purchase.

The principle of tort lies completely outside the region where such considerations apply, and the duty, if it exists, must extend to every person who in lawful circumstances, uses the article made. There can be no special duty attaching to the manufacture of food, apart from those implied by contract or imposed by statute. If such a duty exists it seems to me it must cover the construction of every article, and I cannot see any reason why it should not apply to the construction of a house. If one step, why not fifty? Yet if a house be, as it sometimes is, negligently built, and in consequence of that negligence the ceiling falls and injures the occupier or any one else, no action against the builder exists according to the English law, although I believe such a right did exist according to the laws of Babylon. Were such a principle known and recognized, it seems to me impossible, having regard to the numerous cases that must have arisen to persons injured by its disregard, that with the exception of *George v Skivington* (*supra*) no case directly involving the principle has ever succeeded in the courts, and were it well known and accepted much of the discussion of the earlier cases would have been a waste of time.

In *Mullen v Barr & Co* [1929] SC 461, a case indistinguishable from the present, except upon the ground that a mouse is not a snail, and necessarily adopted by the Second Division in their judgment, Lord Anderson says this at page 479:- 'In a case like the present, where the goods of the defenders are widely distributed throughout Scotland, it would seem little short of outrageous to make them responsible to members of the public for the condition of the contents of every bottle which issues from their works. It is obvious that, if such responsibility attached to the defenders, they might be called on to meet claims of damages which they could not possibly investigate or answer.'

In agreeing, as I do, with the judgment of Lord Anderson, I desire to add that I find it hard to dissent from the emphatic nature of the language with which his judgment is clothed. I am of opinion that this appeal should be dismissed, and I beg to move your Lordships accordingly.

Lord Atkin. My Lords, the sole question for determination in this case is legal: do the averments made by the pursuer in her pleading, if true, disclose a cause of action? I need not restate the particular facts. The question is whether the manufacturer of an article of drink sold by him to a distributor in circumstances which prevent the distributor or the ultimate purchaser or consumer from discovering by inspection any defect is under any legal duty to the ultimate purchaser or consumer to take reasonable care that the article is free from defect likely to cause injury to health. I do not think a more important problem has occupied your Lordships in your judicial capacity, important both because of its bearing on public health and because of the practical test which it applies to the system of law under which it arises. The case has to be determined in accordance with Scots law, but it has been a matter of agreement between the experienced counsel who argued this case, and it appears to be the basis of the judgments of the learned judges of the Court of Session, that for the purposes of determining this problem the law of Scotland and the law of England are the same. I speak with little authority on this point, but my own research, such as it is, satisfies me that the principles of the law of Scotland on such a question as the present are identical with those of English law, and I discuss the issue on that footing. The law of both countries appears to be that in order to support an action for damages for negligence

Donoghue v Stevenson

the complainant has to show that he has been injured by the breach of a duty owed to him in the circumstances by the defendant to take reasonable care to avoid such injury. In the present case we are not concerned with the breach of the duty; if a duty exists, that would be a question of fact which is sufficiently averred and for the present purposes must be assumed. We are solely concerned with the question whether as a matter of law in the circumstances alleged the defender owed any duty to the pursuer to take care.

It is remarkable how difficult it is to find in the English authorities statements of general application defining the relations between parties that give rise to the duty. The courts are concerned with the particular relations which come before them in actual litigation, and it is sufficient to say whether the duty exists in those circumstances. The result is that the courts have been engaged upon an elaborate classification of duties as they exist in respect of property, whether real or personal, with further divisions as to ownership, occupation or control, and distinctions based on the particular relations of the one side or the other, whether manufacturer, salesman or landlord, customer, tenant, stranger, and so on. In this way it can be ascertained at any time whether the law recognizes a duty, but only where the case can be referred to some particular species which has been examined and classified. And yet the duty which is common to all the cases where liability is established must logically be based upon some element common to the cases where it is found to exist. To seek a complete logical definition of the general principle is probably to go beyond the function of the judge, for the more general the definition the more likely it is to omit essentials or introduce non-essentials. The attempt was made by Lord Esher in *Heaven v Pender* in a definition to which I will later refer. As framed it was demonstrably too wide, though it appears to me, if properly limited, to be capable of affording a valuable practical guide.

At present I content myself with pointing out that in English law there must be and is some general conception of relations giving rise to a duty of care, of which the particular cases found in the books are but instances. The liability for negligence, whether you style it such or treat it as in other systems as a species of *culpa,* is no doubt based upon a general public sentiment of moral wrongdoing for which the offender must pay. But acts or omissions which any moral code would censure cannot in a practical world be treated so as to give a right to every person injured by them to demand relief. In this way rules of law arise which limit the range of complainants and the extent of their remedy. The rule that you are to love your neighbour becomes in law you must not injure your neighbour, and the lawyer's questions Who is my neighbour? receives a restricted reply. You must take reasonable care to avoid acts or omissions which you can reasonably foresee would be likely to injure your neighbour. Who then, in law, is my neighbour? The answer seems to be persons who are so closely and directly affected by my act that I ought reasonably to have them in contemplation as being so affected when I am directing my mind to the acts or omissions which are called in question. This appears to me to be the doctrine of *Heaven v Pender (supra)* as laid down by Lord Esher when it is limited by the notion of proximity introduced by Lord Esher himself and Lord Justice A L Smith in *Le Lievre or Dennes v Gould* [1893] 1QB 491. Lord Esher, at page 497, says: 'That case established that, under certain circumstances, one man may owe a duty to another, even though there is no contract between them. If one man is near to another, or is near to the property of another, a duty lies upon him not to do that which may cause a personal injury to that other, or may injure his property.' So Lord Justice A L Smith says: 'The decision of *Heaven v Pender (supra)* was founded upon the principle that a duty to take due care did arise when the person or property of one was in such proximity to the person or property of another that, if due care was not taken, damage might be done by the one to the other.' I think that this sufficiently states the truth if proximity be not confined to mere physical proximity, but be used, as I think it was intended, to extend to such close and direct relations that the act complained of directly affects a person whom the person alleged to be bound to take care would know would be directly affected by his careless act. That this is the sense in which nearness or 'proximity' was intended by Lord Esher is obvious from his own illustration in *Heaven v Pender (supra,* at p 510) of the application of his doctrine to the sale of goods. 'This' (*ie* the rule he has just formulated) 'includes the case of goods supplied to be used immediately by a particular person or persons, or one of a class of persons, where it would be obvious to the person supplying, if he thought, that the goods would in all probability be used at once by such persons before a reasonable opportunity for discovering any defect which might exist, and where the thing supplied would be of such a nature that a neglect of ordinary care or skill as to its condition or the manner of supplying it would probably cause danger to the person or property of the person for whose use it was supplied, and who was about to use it. It would exclude a case in which the goods are supplied under circumstances in which it would be a chance by whom they would be used, or whether they would be used or not, or whether they would be used before there would probably be means of observing any defect, or where the goods would be of such a nature that a want of care or skill as to their condition or the manner of supplying them would not probably produce danger of injury to person or property.' I draw particular attention to the fact that Lord Esher emphasizes the necessity of goods having to be used immediately and used at once before a reasonable opportunity of inspection. This is obviously to exclude the possibility of goods having their condition altered by lapse of time, and to call attention to the proximate relationship, which may be too remote where inspection even by the person using, certainly by an intermediate person, may reasonably be interposed. With this necessary qualification of proximate relationship, as explained

UK landmark cases

in *Le Lievre or Dennes v Gould* (*supra*), I think the judgment of Lord Esher expresses the law of England. Without the qualification, I think that the majority of the court in *Heaven v Pender* (*supra*) were justified in thinking that the principle was expressed in too general terms. There will, no doubt, arise cases where it will be difficult to determine whether the contemplated relationship is so close that the duty arises. But in the class of case now before the court I cannot conceive any difficulty to arise. A manufacturer puts up an article of food in a container which he knows will be opened by the actual consumer. There can be no inspection by any purchaser and no reasonable preliminary inspection by the consumer. Negligently in the course of preparation he allows the contents to be mixed with poison. It is said that the law of England and Scotland is that the poisoned consumer has no remedy against the negligent manufacturer. My Lords, if this were the result of the authorities, I should consider the result a grave defect in the law and so contrary to principle that I should hesitate long before following any decision to that effect which had not the authority of this House. I would point out that in the assumed state of the authorities not only would the consumer have no remedy against the manufacturer, he would have none against any one else, for in the circumstances alleged there would be no evidence of negligence against anyone other than the manufacturer, and except in the case of a consumer who was also a purchaser no contract and no warranty of fitness, and in the case of the purchase of a specific article under its patent or trade name, which might well be the case in the purchase of some articles of food or drink, no warranty protecting even the purchaser-consumer. There are other instances than of articles of food and drink where goods are sold intended to be used immediately by the consumer, such as many forms of goods sold for cleaning purposes, when the same liability must exist. The doctrine supported by the decision below would not only deny a remedy to the consumer who was injured by consuming bottled beer or chocolates poisoned by the negligence of the manufacturer, but also to the user of what should be a harmless proprietary medicine, an ointment, a soap, a cleaning fluid or cleaning powder. I confine myself to articles of common household use, where everyone, including the manufacturer, knows that the articles will be used by persons other than the actual ultimate purchaser—namely, by members of his family and his servants, and, in some cases, his guests. My Lords, I do not think so ill of our jurisprudence as to suppose that its principles are so remote from the ordinary needs of civilized society and the ordinary claims which it makes upon its members as to deny a legal remedy where there is so obviously a social wrong.

It will be found, I think, on examination, that there is no case in which the circumstances have been such as I have just suggested where the liability has been negatived. There are numerous cases where the relations were much more remote where the duty has been held not to exist. There are also *dicta* in such cases which go further than was necessary for the determination of the particular issues, and which have caused the difficulty experienced by the courts below. I venture to say that in the branch of the law which deals with civil wrongs, dependent in England, at any rate, entirely upon the application by judges of general principles also formulated by judges, it is of particular importance to guard against the danger of stating propositions of law in wider terms than is necessary, lest essential factors be omitted in the wider survey and the inherent adaptability of English law be unduly restricted. For this reason it is very necessary, in considering reported cases in the law of torts, that the actual decision alone should carry authority, proper weight, of course, being given to the *dicta* of the judges.

. . . . .

The last case I need refer to is *Bates v Batey and Co Limited* [1913] 3 K B 351, where manufacturers of ginger beer were sued by a plaintiff who had been injured by the bursting of a bottle of ginger beer bought from a shopkeeper who had obtained it from the manufacturers. The manufacturers had bought the actual bottle from its maker, but were found by the jury to have been negligent in not taking proper means to discover whether the bottle was defective or not. Mr Justice Horridge found that a bottle of ginger beer was not dangerous in itself, that this defective bottle was in fact dangerous, but, as the defendants did not know it was dangerous, they were not liable, though by the exercise of reasonable care they could have discovered the defect. This case differs from the present only by reason of the fact that it was not the manufacturers of the ginger beer who caused the defect in the bottle, but, on the assumption that the jury were right in finding a lack of reasonable care in not examining the bottle, I should have come to the conclusion that, as the manufacturers must have contemplated the bottle being handled immediately by the consumer, they owed a duty to him to take care that he should not be injured externally by explosion, just as I think they owed a duty to him to take care that he should not be injured internally by poison or other noxious thing. My Lords, I do not find it necessary to discuss at length the cases dealing with duties where a thing is dangerous, or, in the narrower category, belongs to a class of things which are dangerous in themselves.

. . . . .

In the most recent case, *Bottomley v Bannister* [1932] 1 KB 458, an action under Lord Campbell's Act, the deceased man, the father of the plaintiff, had taken an unfurnished house from the defendants, who had installed a gas boiler with a special gas burner which, if properly regulated, required no flue. The father and his wife were killed by fumes from the apparatus. The case was determined on the ground that the apparatus was part of the realty and that the landlord did not know of the danger, but there is a discussion of the case on the supposition that it was a chattel. Lord Justice Greer states with truth that it is not easy to reconcile all the authorities, and that there is no authority binding on the

Donoghue v Stevenson

Court of Appeal that a person selling an article which he did not know to be dangerous can be held liable to a person with whom he has made no contract, by reason of the fact that reasonable inquiries might have enabled him to discover that the article was in fact dangerous. When the danger is in fact occasioned by his own lack of care, then in cases of proximate relationship this case will, I trust, supply the deficiency.

It is always satisfaction to an English lawyer to be able to test his application of fundamental principles of the common law by the development of the same doctrines by the lawyers of the courts of the United States. In that country I find that the law appears to be well established in the sense which I have indicated. The mouse had emerged from the ginger-beer bottle in the United States before it appeared in Scotland, but there it brought a liability upon the manufacturer. I must not in this long judgment do more than refer to the illuminating judgment of Judge Cardozo in *McPherson v Buick Motor Company*, in the New York Court of Appeals (217 NY 382), in which he states the principles of the law as I should desire to state them and reviews the authorities in states other than his own. Whether the principle which he affirms would apply to the particular facts of that case in this country would be a question for consideration if the case arose. It might be that the course of business, by giving opportunities of examination to the immediate purchaser or otherwise, prevented the relation between manufacturer and the user of the car from being so close as to create a duty. But the American decision would undoubtedly lead to a decision in favour of the pursuer in the present case.

My Lords, if your Lordships accept the view that the appellant's pleading discloses a relevant cause of action, you will be affirming the proposition that by Scots and English law alike a manufacturer of products which he sells in such a form as to show that he intends them to reach the ultimate consumer in the form in which they left him, with no reasonable possiblity of intermediate examination, and with the knowledge that the absence of reasonable care in the preparation or putting up of the products is likely to result in injury to the consumer's life or property, owes a duty to the consumer to take that reasonable care. It is a proposition that I venture to say no one in Scotland or England who was not a lawyer would for one moment doubt. It will be an advantage to make it clear that the law in this matter, as in most others, is in accordance with sound common sense. I think that this appeal should be allowed.

Lord Tomlin. My Lords, I have had an opportunity of considering the opinion prepared by my noble and learned friend Lord Buckmaster, which I have already read. As the reasoning of that opinion and the conclusions reached therein accord in every respect with my own views, I propose to say only a few words.

First, I think that if the appellant is to succeed it must be upon the proposition that every manufacturer or repairer of any article is under a duty to every one who

may thereafter legitimately use the article to exercise due care in the manufacture or repair. It is logically impossible to stop short of this point. There can be no distinction between food and any other article. Moreover the fact that an article of food is sent out in a sealed container can have no relevancy on the question of duty. It is only a factor which may render it easier to bring negligence home to the manufacturer.

Secondly, I desire to say that, in my opinion, the decision in *Winterbottom v Wright* is directly in point against the appellant.

The examination of the report makes it, I think, plain, (1) that negligence was alleged and was the basis of the claim, and (2) that the wide proposition which I have indicated was that for which the plaintiff was contending. The declaration averred (*inter alia*) that the defendant 'so improperly and negligently conducted himself' that the accident complained of happened. The plaintiff's counsel said: 'Here the declaration alleges the accident to have happened through the defendant's negligence and want of care.' The alarming consequences of accepting the validity of this proposition were pointed out by the defendant's counsel, who said: 'For example, every one of the sufferers by such an accident as that which recently happened on the Versailles Railway might have his action against the manufacturer of the defective axle.'

That the action, which was in case, embraced a cause of action in tort is I think implicit in its form and appears from the concluding sentence of Lord Abinger's judgment, which was in these terms: 'By permitting this action, we should be working this injustice, that after the defendant had done everything to the satisfaction of his employer, and after all matters between them had been adjusted, and all accounts settled on the footing of their contract, we should subject them to be ripped open by this action of tort being brought against him.'

I will only add to what has been already said by my noble and learned friend Lord Buckmaster with regard to the decisions and *dicta* relied upon by the appellant, and the other relevant reported cases, that I am unable to explain how the cases of dangerous articles can have been treated as 'exceptions' if the appellant's contention is well founded. Upon the view which I take of the matter the reported cases, some directly, others impliedly, negative the existence as part of the common law of England of any principle affording support to the appellant's claim, and therefore there is, in my opinion, no material from which it is legitimate for your Lordships' House to deduce such a principle.

Lord Thankerton. My Lords, in this action the appellant claims reparation from the respondent in respect of illness and other injurious effects resulting from the presence of a decomposed snail in a bottle of ginger beer, which is alleged to have been manufactured by the respondent, and which was partially consumed by her, it having been ordered by a friend on her behalf in a café in Paisley.

UK landmark cases

The action is based on negligence, and the only question in this appeal is whether, taking the appellant's averments *pro veritate,* they disclose a case relevant in law, so as to entitle her to have them remitted for proof. The Lord Ordinary allowed a proof, but, on a reclaiming note for the respondent, the Second Division of the Court of Session recalled the Lord Ordinary's interlocutor and dismissed the action, following their decision in the recent cases of *Mullen v Barr and Co* and *McGowan v Barr and Co* [1929] S C 461.

The appellant's case is that the bottle was sealed with a metal cap, and was made of dark opaque glass, which not only excluded access to the contents before consumption if the contents were to retain their aerated condition, but also excluded the possibility of visual examination of the contents from outside; and that on the side of the bottle there was pasted a label containing the name and address of the respondent, who was the manufacturer. She states that the shopkeeper who supplied the ginger beer opened it and poured some of its contents into a tumbler, which contained some ice cream, and that she drank some of the contents of the tumbler; that her friend then lifted the bottle and was pouring the remainder of the contents into the tumbler when a snail which had been, unknown to her, her friend, or the shopkeeper, in the bottle, and was in a state of decomposition, floated out of the bottle.

The duties which the appellant accuses the respondent of having neglected may be summarized as follows: (*a*) that the ginger beer was manufactured by the respondent or his servants to be sold as an article of drink to members of the public (including the appellant), and that accordingly it was his duty to exercise the greatest care in order that snails should not get into the bottles, render the ginger beer dangerous and harmful, and be sold with the ginger beer; (*b*) a duty to provide a system of working his business which would not allow snails to get into the sealed bottles, and in particular would not allow the bottles when washed to stand in places to which snails had access; (*c*) a duty to provide an efficient system of inspection, which would prevent snails from getting into the sealed bottles; and (*d*) a duty to provide clear bottles, so as to facilitate the said system of inspection.

There can be no doubt, in my opinion, that equally in the law of Scotland and of England it lies upon the party claiming redress in such a case to show that there was some relation of duty between her and the defender which required the defender to exercise due and reasonable care for her safety. It is not at all necessary that there should be any direct contract between them, because the action is not based upon contract but upon negligence; but it is necessary for the pursuer in such an action to show there was a duty owed to her by the defender, because a man cannot be charged with negligence if he has no obligation to exercise diligence. The question in each case is whether the pursuer has established, or, in the stage of the present appeal, has relevantly averred, such facts as involve the existence of such a relation of duty.

We are not dealing here with a case of what is called an article *per se* dangerous or one which was known by the defender to be dangerous, in which cases a special duty of protection or adequate warning is placed upon the person who uses or distributes it. The present case is that of a manufacturer and a consumer, with whom he has no contractual relation, of an article which the manufacturer did not know to be dangerous, and, unless the consumer can establish a special relationship with the manufacturer, it is clear, in my opinion, that neither the law of Scotland nor the law of England will hold that the manufacturer has any duty towards the consumer to exercise diligence. In such a case the remedy of the consumer, if any, will lie against the intervening party from whom he has procured the article. I am aware that the American courts, in the decisions referred to by my noble and learned friend Lord Macmillan, have taken a view more favourable to the consumer.

The special circumstances, from which the appellant claims that such a relationship of duty should be inferred, may, I think, be stated thus—namely, that the respondent, in placing his manufactured article of drink upon the market, has intentionally so excluded interference with, or examination of, the article by any intermediate handler of the goods between himself and the consumer that he has, of his own accord, brought himself into direct relationship with the consumer, with the result that the consumer is entitled to rely upon the exercise of diligence by the manufacturer to secure that the article shall not be harmful to the consumer. If that contention be sound, the consumer, on her showing that the article has reached her intact, and that she has been injured by the harmful nature of the article owing to the failure of the manufacturer to take reasonable care in its preparation before its enclosure in the sealed vessel, will be entitled to reparation from the manufacturer.

In my opinion, the existence of a legal duty under such circumstances is in conformity with the principles of both the law of Scotland and the law of England. The English cases demonstrate how impossible it is finally to catalogue, amid the ever-varying types of human relationships, those relationships in which a duty to exercise care arises apart from contract, and each of these cases relates to its own set of circumstances, out of which it was claimed that the duty had arisen. In none of these cases were the circumstances identical with the present case as regards that which I regard as the essential element in this case—namely, the manufacturer's own action in bringing himself into direct relationship with the party injured. I have had the privilege of considering the discussion of these authorities by my noble and learned friend Lord Atkin in the judgment which he has just delivered, and I so entirely agree with it that I cannot usefully add anything to it.

An interesting illustration of similar circumstances is to be found in *Gordon v McHardy* (6 F 210), in which

Donoghue v Stevenson

the pursuer sought to recover damages from a retail grocer on account of the death of his son by ptomaine poisoning, caused by eating tinned salmon purchased from the defender. The pursuer averred that the tin, when sold, was dented, but he did not suggest that the grocer had cut through the metal and allowed air to get in, or had otherwise caused injury to the contents. The action was held irrelevant, the Lord Justice Clerk remarking, 'I do not see how the defender could have examined the tin of salmon which he is alleged to have sold without destroying the very condition which the manufacturer had established in order to preserve the contents, the tin not being intended to be opened until immediately before use.' Apparently in that case the manufacturers' label was off the tin when sold, and they had not been identified. I should be sorry to think that the meticulous care of the manufacturer to exclude interference or inspection by the grocer in that case should relieve the grocer of any responsibility to the consumer without any corresponding assumption of duty by the manufacturer.

My Lords, I am of opinion that the contention of the appellant is sound and that she has relevantly averred a relationship of duty as between the respondent and herself, as also that her averments of the respondent's neglect of that duty are relevant.

The cases of *Mullen* and *McGowan* [1929] S C 461, which the learned judges of the Second Division followed in the present case, related to facts similar in every respect except that the foreign matter was a decomposed mouse. In these cases the same court— Lord Hunter dissenting—held that the manufacturer owed no duty to the consumer. The view of the majority was that the English authorities excluded the existence of such a duty, but Lord Ormidale would otherwise have been prepared to come to a contrary conclusion. Lord Hunter's opinion seems to be in conformity with the view which I have expressed above.

My conclusion rests upon the facts averred in this case, and would apparently also have applied in the cases of *Mullen* and *McGowan* (*supra*), in which, however, there had been a proof before answer, and there was also a question as to whether the pursuers had proved their averments.

I am therefore of opinion that the appeal should be allowed and the case should be remitted for proof, as the pursuer did not ask for an issue.

Lord Macmillan. My Lords, the incident which in its legal bearings your Lordships are called upon to consider in this appeal was in itself of a trivial character, though the consequences to the appellant, as she describes them, were serious enough. It appears from the appellant's allegations that on an evening in August 1928, she and a friend visited a café in Paisley, where her friend ordered for her some ice cream and a bottle of ginger beer. These were supplied by the shopkeeper, who opened the ginger-beer bottle and poured some of the contents over the ice cream which was contained in a tumbler. The appellant drank part of the mixture and her friend then proceeded to pour the remaining contents of the bottle into the tumbler. As she was doing so a decomposed snail floated out with the ginger beer. In consequence of her having drunk part of the contaminated contents of the bottle the appellant alleges that she contracted a serious illness. The bottle is stated to have been of dark opaque glass, so that the condition of the contents could not be ascertained by inspection, and to have been closed with a metal cap, while on the side was a label bearing the name of the respondent, who was the manufacturer of the ginger beer, of which the shopkeeper was merely the retailer.

The allegations of negligence on which the appellant founds her action against the respondent may be shortly summarized. She says that the ginger beer was manufactured by the respondent for sale as an article of drink to members of the public, including herself; that the presence of a decomposing snail in ginger beer renders the ginger beer harmful and dangerous to those consuming it; and that it was the duty of the respondent to exercise his process of manufacture with sufficient care to prevent snails from getting into or remaining in the bottles which he filled with ginger beer. The appellant attacks the respondent's system of conducting his business, alleging that he kept his bottles in premises to which snails had access and that he failed to have his bottles properly inspected for the presence of foreign matter before he filled them.

The respondent challenged the relevancy of the appellant's averments and, taking them *pro veritate,* as for this purpose he was bound to do, pleaded that they disclosed no ground of legal liability on his part to the appellant.

The Lord Ordinary repelled the respondent's plea to the relevancy and allowed the parties a proof of their averments, but on a reclaiming note their Lordships of the Second Division (Lord Hunter dissenting, or, perhaps more accurately, protesting) dismissed the action, and in doing so followed their decision in the previous cases of *Mullen v Barr and Co* and *McGowan v Barr and Co* [1929] S C 461. The only difference in fact between those cases and the present case is that it was a mouse and not a snail which was found in the ginger beer. The present appeal is consequently in effect against the decision in these previous cases, which I now proceed to examine.

. . . . .

This summary survey is sufficient to show what more detailed study confirms, that the current of authority has by no means always set in the same direction. In addition to *George v Skivington* (*supra*) there is the American case of *Thomas v Winchester* (6 NY 397), which has met with considerable acceptance in this country and which is distinctly on the side of the appellant. There a chemist carelessly issued in response to an order for extract of dandelion, a bottle containing belladonna which he labelled extract of dandelion, with the consequence that a third party who took a dose from the bottle suffered severely. The chemist was held responsible. This case is quoted by Lord Dunedin in giving the judgment of the Privy Council in *Dominion Natural Gas Company Limited v Collins* [1909] A C 640 as an instance of liability to third parties, and I think it was a sound decision.

In the American courts the law has advanced considerably in the development of the principle exemplified in *Thomas v Winchester*. In one of the latest cases in the United States, *MacPherson v Buick Motor Company* (217 NY 382), the plaintiff, who had purchased from a retailer a motor-car, manufactured by the defendant company, was injured in consequence of a defect in the construction of the car and was held entitled to recover damages from the manufacturer. Judge Cardozo, the very eminent Chief Judge of the New York Court of Appeals, and now an Associate Justice of the United States Supreme Court, thus stated the law: 'There is no claim that the defendant knew of the defect and wilfully concealed it. . . . The charge is one not of fraud but of negligence. The question to be determined is whether the defendant owed a duty of care and vigilance to anyone but the immediate purchaser. . . The principle of *Thomas v Winchester* is not limited to poisons, explosives, and things of like nature, to things which in their normal operations are implements of destruction. If the nature of a thing is such that it is reasonably certain to place life and limb in peril when negligently made, it is then a thing of danger. Its nature gives warning of the consequences to be expected. If to the element of danger there is added knowledge that the thing will be used by persons other than the purchaser, and used without new tests, then, irrespective of contract, the manufacturer of this thing of danger is under a duty to make it carefully.'

The prolonged discussion of English and American cases into which I have been led might well dispose your Lordships to think that I have forgotten that the present is a Scottish appeal, which must be decided according to Scots law. But this discussion has been rendered inevitable by the course of the argument at your Lordships' bar, which, as I have said, proceeded on the footing that the law applicable to the case was the same in England and Scotland. Having regard to the inconclusive state of the authorities in the courts below, and to the fact that the important question involved is now before your Lordships for the first time, I think it desirable to consider the matter from the point of view of the principles applicable to this branch of law which are admittedly common to both English and Scottish jurisprudence.

The law takes no cognizance of carelessness in the abstract. It concerns itself with carelessness only where there is a duty to take care and where failure in that duty has caused damage. In such circumstances carelessness assumes the legal quality of negligence and entails the consequences in law of negligence. What then are the circumstances which give rise to this duty to take care? In the daily contacts of social and business life human beings are thrown into or place themselves in an infinite variety of relationships with their fellows, and the law can refer only to the standards of the reasonable man in order to determine whether any particular relationship gives rise to a duty to take care as between those who stand in that relationship to each other. The grounds of action may be as various and manifold as human errancy, and the conception of legal responsibility may develop in adaptation to altering social conditions and standards. The criterion of judgment must adjust and adapt itself to the changing circumstances of life. The categories of negligence are never closed. The cardinal principle of liability is that the party complained of should owe to the party complaining a duty to take care and that the party complaining should be able to prove that he has suffered damage in consequence of a breach of that duty. Where there is room for diversity of view is in determining what circumstances will establish such a relationship between the parties as to give rise on the one side to a duty to take care and on the other side to a right to have care taken.

To descend from these generalities to the circumstances of the present case I do not think that any reasonable man or any 12 reasonable men would hesitate to hold that if the appellant establishes her allegations the respondent has exhibited carelessness in the conduct of his business. For a manufacturer of aerated water to store his empty bottles in a place where snails can get access to them and to fill his bottles without taking any adequate precautions by inspection or otherwise to ensure that they contain no deleterious foreign matter may reasonably be characterized as carelessness without applying too exacting a standard. But, as I have pointed out, it is not enough to prove the respondent to be careless in his process of manufacture. The question is, Does he owe a duty to take care, and to whom does he owe that duty? Now I have no hesitation in affirming that a person who for gain engages in the business of manufacturing articles of food and drink intended for consumption by members of the public in the form in which he issues them is under a duty to take care in the manufacture of these articles. That duty, in my opinion, he owes to those whom he intends to consume his products. He manufactures his commodities for human consumption; he intends and contemplates that they shall be consumed. By reason of that very fact he places himself in a relationship with all the potential consumers of his commodities, and that relationship which he assumes and desires for his own ends imposes upon him a duty to take care to avoid injuring them. He owes them a duty not to convert by his own carelessness an article which he issues to them as wholesome and innocent into an article which is dangerous to life and health. It is sometimes said that liability can arise only where a reasonable man would have foreseen and could have avoided the consequences of his act or omission. In the present case the respondent, when he manufactured his ginger beer, had

Donoghue v Stevenson

directly in contemplation that it would be consumed by members of the public; can it be said that he could not be expected as a reasonable man to foresee that if he conducted his process of manufacture carelessly he might injure those whom he expected and desired to consume his ginger beer? The possibility of injury so arising seems to me in no sense so remote as to excuse him from foreseeing it. Suppose that a baker through carelessness allows a large quantity of arsenic to be mixed with a batch of his bread, with the result that those who subsequently eat it are poisoned, could he be heard to say that he owed no duty to the consumers of his bread to take care that it was free from poison, and that, as he did not know that any poison had got into it, his only liability was for breach of warranty under his contract of sale to those who actually bought the poisoned bread from him? Observe that I have said 'through carelessness' and thus excluded the case of a pure accident such as may happen where every care is taken. I cannot believe, and I do not believe, that neither in the law of England nor in the law of Scotland is there redress for such a case. The state of facts I have figured might well give rise to a criminal charge, and the civil consequence of such carelessness can scarcely be less wide than its criminal consequences. Yet the principle of the decision appealed from is that the manufacturer of food products intended by him for human consumption does not owe to the consumers whom he has in view any duty of care, not even the duty to take care that he does not poison them.

My Lords, the recognition by counsel that the law of Scotland applicable to the case was the same as the law of England implied that there was no special doctrine of Scots law which either the appellant or the respondent could invoke to support her or his case, and your Lordships have thus been relieved of the necessity of a separate consideration of the law of Scotland. For myself I am satisfied that there is no specialty of Scots law involved and that the case may safely be decided on principles common to both systems. I am happy to think that in their relation to the practical problem of everyday life which this appeal presents the legal systems of the two countries are in no way at variance and that the principles of both alike are sufficiently consonant with justice and common sense to admit of the claim which the appellant seeks to establish.

I am anxious to emphasize that the princple of judgment which commends itself to me does not give rise to the sort of objection stated by Baron Parke in *Longmeid v Holliday* where he said 'But it would be going much too far to say that so much care is required in the ordinary intercourse of life between one individual and another that, if a machine not in its nature dangerous—a carriage for instance—but which might become so by a latent effect entirely unknown, although discoverable by the exercise of ordinary care, should be lent or given by one person, even by the person who manufactured it, to another, the former should be answerable to the latter for a subsequent damage accruing by the use of it.' I read this passage rather as a note of warning that the standard of care exacted in the dealings of human beings with one another must not be pitched too high, than as giving any countenance to the view that negligence may be exhibited with impunity. It must always be a question of circumstances whether the carelessness amounts to negligence and whether the injury is not too remote from the carelessness. I can readily conceive that where a manufacturer has parted with his product and it has passed into other hands it may well be exposed to vicissitudes which may render it defective or noxious and for which the manufacturer could not in any view be held to be to blame. It may be a good general rule to regard responsibility as ceasing when control ceases. So also where between the manufacturer and the user there is interposed a party who has the means and opportunity of examining the manufacturer's product before he reissues it to the actual user. But where, as in the present case, the article of consumption is so prepared as to be intended to reach the consumer in the condition in which it leaves the manufacturer and the manufacturer takes steps to ensure this by sealing or otherwise closing the container, so that the contents cannot be tampered with, I regard his control as remaining effective until the article reaches the consumer and the container is opened by him. The intervention of any exterior agency is intended to be excluded, and was in fact in the present case excluded. It is doubtful whether in such a case there is any redress against the retailer, *Gordon v McHardy* (6 F 210).

The burden of proof must always be upon the injured party to establish that the defect which caused the injury was present in the article when it left the hands of the party whom he sues, that the defect was occasioned by the carelessness of that party, and that the circumstances are such as to cast upon the defender a duty to take care not to injure the pursuer. There is no presumption of negligence in such a case as the present, nor is there any justification for applying the maxim *res ipsa loquitur*. Negligence must be both averred and proved. The appellant accepts this burden of proof and, in my opinion, she is entitled to have an opportunity of discharging it if she can. I am accordingly of opinion that this appeal should be allowed, the judgment of the Second Division of the Court of Session reversed, and the judgment of the Lord Ordinary restored.

UK landmark cases

1935 *Grant v Australian Knitting Mills*

COMMENTARY

From Scotland in 1932 to Australia in 1935, and switching our thoughts from foreign bodies in ginger beer to sulphites in underpants, brings us to the next major landmark of *Grant v Australian Knitting Mills,* an appeal case from the Australian High Court heard by the Privy Council.

Here the court was considering the case of the appellant who had contracted dermatitis due to wearing woollen underwear containing excess sulphites that had been left in during the process of manufacture. In its decision, the Privy Council affirmed that the liability of the manufacturer in tort is independent of any liability in contract (the retailer was also liable in contract under the implied terms of the Sale of Goods Act); and that as the presence of the sulphites in the clothing was a hidden defect which could not be detected on any reasonable examination, and that the garment was being worn exactly as intended by the manufacturer, the latter owed a duty of care to the appellant which had been broken.

In overturning the High Court of Australia's judgment that the manufacturer of the underpants was not liable, the Privy Council applied the principles set out in *Donoghue,* and further extended them. Thus the principle in *Donoghue* that the goods in question should reach the consumer in the same sealed package or container in which they left the manufacturer was held not to be of the essence: it was sufficient to show only that the goods reached the consumer subject to the same defect. The offending underwear was sent out by the defendants in paper packets containing six sets, of which only two were sold by the retailer to Dr Grant, and yet the manufacturer was still liable.

On the question of intermediate examination, the Privy Council was able to be quite firm that the presence of the damaging sulphites in the pants was a hidden defect just as much as the decomposing snail in the opaque bottle. They could not be detected by any reasonable examination and nor was it reasonable to claim, as the manufacturer did, that the sulphites could be removed by washing. As Lord Wright remarked 'the garments were made by the manufacturer for the purpose of being worn exactly as they were worn in fact by the appellant: it was not contemplated that they should be first washed'. However, the Privy Council confirmed that an intermediate examination of the goods that did reveal the defect would prevent *Donoghue* being applied—'The man who consumes or uses a thing which he knows to be noxious cannot complain in respect of whatever mischief follows, because it follows from his own conscious volition in choosing to incur the risk or certainty of mischance'.

The manufacturer finally tried to establish that he had indeed fulfilled the duty to take care established by

Donoghue. He pointed to the processing of the wool which involved both the chemical removal of other chemicals used in the process, and washing designed to ensure that no excesses of chemicals were left in the finished product. He protested that over four million of these garments had been treated by a similar process over the previous six years, with no record of any other complaints being made. However, the evidence of one of the workmen involved in the cleaning process was they knew they had to be very careful that there was no excess of one chemical or another, and that if there was, it was bound to be somebody's fault.

The manufacturer's final argument has a somewhat prescient ring 50 years later—that the extension in any respect at all of the principle in *Donoghue* would in effect open the floodgates to the indefinite extension of manufacturer's liability. Their Lordships displayed equal prescience in their robust response that many difficult problems were likely to arise before the precise limits of *Donoghue* were defined, but that they were content to rule that this case fell clearly within those principles.

JUDGMENT

House of Lords (Privy Council)
October 21, 1935

Grant
versus
Australian Knitting Mills Ltd and others

Before Viscount Hailsham, LC,
Lord Blanesburgh, Lord Macmillan,
Lord Wright and Sir Lancelot Sanderson

Lord Wright. The appellant is a fully qualified medical man practising at Adelaide in South Australia. He brought his action against the respondents, claiming damages on the ground that he had contracted dermatitis by reason of the improper condition of underwear purchased by him from the respondents, John Martin & Co Ltd, and manufactured by the respondents, the Australian Knitting Mills Ltd. The case was tried by Sir George Murray, Chief Justice of South Australia, who, after a trial lasting for 20 days, gave judgment for the appellant against both respondents for £2,450 and costs. On appeal the High Court of Australia set aside that judgment by a majority. Evatt J dissented, and agreed in the result with the Chief Justice though he differed in regard to the Sale of Goods Act, 1895. Of the majority, the reasoning of Dixon J, with whom McTiernan J concurred, was in effect that the evidence was not sufficient to make it safe to find for the appellant. Starke J, who accepted substantially all the detailed findings of the Chief Justice, differed from him on his general conclusions of liability based on these findings.

Grant v Australian Knitting Mills

The appellant's claim was that the disease was caused by the presence in the cuffs or ankle ends of the underpants which he purchased and wore, of an irritating chemical, namely, free sulphite, the presence of which was due to negligence in manufacture, and also involved on the part of the respondents, John Martin & Co Ltd, a breach of the relevant implied conditions under the Sale of Goods Act.

The underwear, consisting of two pairs of underpants and two singlets, was bought by the appellant at the shop of the respondents, John Martin & Co Ltd, who dealt in such goods, and who will be hereafter referred to as 'the retailers', on June 3, 1931. The retailers had in ordinary course at some previous date purchased them with other stock from the respondents, the Australian Knitting Mills Ltd, who will be referred to as the manufacturers; the garments were of that class of the manufacturers' make known as Golden Fleece. The appellant put on one suit on the morning of Sunday, June 28th, 1931; by the evening of that day he felt itching on the ankles but no objective symptoms appeared until the next day, when a redness appeared on each ankle in front over an area of about 2.1/2 inches by 1.1/2 inches. The appellant treated himself with calomine lotion, but the irritation was such that he scratched the places till he bled. On Sunday, July 5, he changed his underwear and put on the other set which he had purchased from the retailers; the first set was washed and when the appellant changed his garments again on the following Sunday he put on the washed set and sent the others to the wash; he changed again on July 12. Though his skin trouble was getting worse, he did not attribute it to the underwear, but on July 13 he consulted a dermatologist, Dr Upton, who advised him to discard the underwear, which he did, returning the garments to the retailers with the intimation that they had given him dermatitis; by that time one set had been washed twice and the other set once. The appellant's condition got worse and worse; he was confined to bed from July 21 for 17 weeks; the rash became generalised and very acute. In November he became convalescent and went to New Zealand to recuperate. He returned in the following February, and felt sufficiently recovered to resume his practice, but soon had a relapse, and by March his condition was so serious that he went in April into hospital, where he remained until July. Meantime, in April 1932, he commenced this action, which was tried in and after November of that year. Dr Upton was his medical attendant throughout and explained in detail at the trial the course of the illness and the treatment he adopted. Dr de Crespigny also attended the appellant from and after July 22, 1931, and gave evidence at the trial. The illness was most severe, involving acute suffering, and at times Dr Upton feared that his patient might die.

It is impossible here to examine in detail the minute and conflicting evidence of fact and of expert opinion given at the trial: all that evidence was meticulously discussed at the hearing of the appeal before the Board. It is only possible to state briefly the conclusions at which their Lordships, after careful consideration, have arrived.

In the first place, their Lordships are of opinion that the disease was of external origin. Much of the medical evidence was directed to supporting or refuting the contention, strenuously advanced on behalf of the respondents, that the dermatitis was internally produced and was of the type described as herpetiformis, which is generally regarded as of internal origin. That contention may now be taken to have failed: it has been rejected by the Chief Justice at the trial, and in the High Court by Starke and Evatt JJ and, in effect also, by Dixon and McTiernan JJ.

. . . . .

Evidence was given on behalf of the manufacturers as to the processes used in the manufacture of these garments. The webs of wool were put through six different processes: of these the second, third and fourth, were the most significant for this case. The second was for shrinking, and involved treatment of the web with a solution of calcium hypochloride and hydrochloric acid. The third process was to remove these chemicals by a solution of bisulphite of soda, and the fourth process was to neutralise the bisulphite by means of bicarbonate of soda; the fifth process was for washing, and the sixth was a drying and finishing process. If the fourth process did not neutralise the added bisulphite, free sulphites would remain, which the subsequent washing might not entirely remove. The manufacturers' evidence was that the process was properly applied to the wool from which these garments were made, and if properly applied was bound to be effective. The foreman scourer, Smith, was not called at the trial, where his absence was made matter of comment, but Ashworth, one of the scourers, gave evidence and, among other things, said that they had to be very careful that there was no excess of one chemical or the other. If there were an excess of some sort or the other, it would be bound to be somebody's fault. The washing off was to clear out as much of the traces of the previous process as possible. But something might go wrong, some one might be negligent, and as a result some bisulphite of soda which had been introduced might not have been got rid of. The cuffs of the pants were ribbed and were made of a different web separately treated. The appellant's advisers had at the trial no independent information as to the actual process adopted in respect of these garments, or even when they were made, and, by petition, they asked for leave to adduce further evidence which would go to show, as they suggested, that the process deposed to was not adopted by the manufacturers until after June 3, 1931. Their Lordships, however, feel themselves in a position to dispose of the appeal on the evidence as it stands, taking due account of the fact that the manufacturers' secretary was called and deposed that in the previous six years the manufacturers had treated by a similar process 4,737,600 of these garments, which they had sold to drapers throughout Australia, and he had no recollection of any complaints, which, if made, would in ordinary course have come under his notice. Dr Hargreaves, an analytical chemist, on the instructions of the manufacturers analysed specimen garments, subjecting them to tests which would extract any sulphur adherent to the wool as well as free sulphites, if any were present, and found only negligible quantities. Against this evidence was that of Professor Hicks, who agitated in unheated water for two minutes a singlet of the manufacturers' Golden Fleece make, purchased in November, 1932, and found that the aqueous extract contained a percentage by weight of sulphite of .11, which, in his opinion, was free in the fabric and readily soluble in cold water. The significance of this experiment seems to be that however well designed the manufacturers' proved system may be to eliminate deleterious substances it may not invariably work according to plan. Some employee may blunder.

. . . . .

That conclusion means that the disease contracted, and the damage suffered by the appellant, were caused by the defective condition of the garments which the retailers sold to him, and which the manufacturers made and put forth for retail and indiscriminate sale. The Chief Justice gave judgment against both respondents, against the retailers on the contract of sale, and against the manufacturers in tort, on the basis of the decision in the House of Lords in *Donoghue v Stevenson*. The liability of each respondent depends on a different cause of action, though it is for the same damage. It is not claimed that the appellant should recover his damage twice over; no objection is raised on the part of the respondents to the form of the judgment, which was against both respondents for a single amount.

So far as concerns the retailers, Mr Greene conceded that if it were held that the garments contained improper chemicals and caused the disease, the retailers were liable for breach of implied warranty, or rather condition, under section 14 of the South Australia Sale of Goods Act, 1895, which is identical with section 14 of the English Sale of Goods Act, 1893. The section is in the following terms:-

'14. Subject to the provisions of this Act, and of any Statute in that behalf, there is no implied warranty or condition as to the quality or fitness for any particular purpose of goods supplied under a contract of sale, except as follows—

I. Where the buyer, expressly or by implication, makes known to the seller the particular purpose for which the goods are required so as to show that the buyer relies on the seller's skill or judgment, and the goods are of a description which it is in the course of the seller's business to supply (whether he be the manufacturer or not), there is an implied condition that the goods shall be reasonably fit for such purpose: Provided that in the case of a contract for the sale of a specified article under its patent or other trade name, there is no implied condition as to its fitness for any particular purpose:

II. Where goods are bought by description from a seller who deals in goods of that description (whether

he be the manufacturer or not), there is an implied condition that the goods shall be of merchantable quality: Provided that if the buyer has examined the goods, there shall be no implied condition as regards defects which such examination ought to have revealed:

III. An implied warranty or condition as to quality or fitness for a particular purpose may be annexed by the usage of trade:

IV. An express warranty or condition does not negative a warranty or condition implied by this Act unless inconsistent therewith.'

He limited his admission to liability under exception (ii), but their Lordships are of opinion that liability is made out under both exception (i) and exception (ii) to section 14, and feel that they should so state out of deference to the conflicting views expressed in the court below. Section 14 begins by a general enunciation of the old rule of *caveat emptor*, and proceeds to state by way of exception two implied conditions by which it has been said the old rule has been changed to the rule of *caveat venditor:* the change has been rendered necessary by the conditions of modern commerce and trade.

. . . . .

The first exception, if its terms are satisfied, entitles the buyer to the benefit of an implied condition that the goods are reasonably fit for the purpose for which the goods are supplied, but only if that purpose is made known to the seller 'so as to show that the buyer relies on the seller's skill or judgment.'

. . . . .

With great deference to Dixon J, their Lordships think that the requirements of exception (i) were complied with. The conversation at the shop in which the appellant discussed questions of price and of the different makes did not affect the fact that he was substantially relying on the retailers to supply him with a correct article.

The second exception in a case like this in truth overlaps in its application the first exception; whatever else merchantable may mean, it does mean that the article sold, if only meant for one particular use in ordinary course, is fit for that use; merchantable does not mean that the thing is saleable in the market simply because it looks all right; it is not merchantable in that event if it has defects unfitting it for its only proper use but not apparent on ordinary examination: that is clear from the proviso, which shows that the implied condition only applies to defects not reasonably discoverable to the buyer on such examination as he made or could make. The appellant was satisfied by the appearance of the underpants; he could not detect, and had no reason to suspect, the hidden presence of the sulphites: the garments were saleable in the sense that the appellant, or any one similarly situated and who did not know of their defect, would readily buy them: but they were not merchantable in the statutory sense because

Grant v Australian Knitting Mills

their defect rendered them unfit to be worn next the skin. It may be that after sufficient washing that defect would have disappeared; but the statute requires the goods to be merchantable in the state in which they were sold and delivered; in this connection a defect which could easily be cured is as serious as a defect that would not yield to treatment.

. . . . .

The retailers, accordingly, in their Lordships' judgment are liable in contract: so far as they are concerned, no question of negligence is relevant to the liability in contract. But when the position of the manufacturers is considered, different questions arise: there is no privity of contract between the appellant and the manufacturers: between them the liability, if any, must be in tort, and the gist of the cause of action is negligence. The facts set out in the foregoing show, in their Lordships' judgment, negligence in manufacture. According to the evidence, the method of manufacture was correct: the danger of excess sulphites being left was recognised and was guarded against: the process was intended to be fool proof. If excess sulphites were left in the garment, that could only be because some one was at fault. The appellant is not required to lay his finger on the exact person in all the chain who was responsible, or to specify what he did wrong. Negligence is found as a matter of inference from the existence of the defects taken in connection with all the known circumstances: even if the manufacturers could by apt evidence have rebutted that inference they have not done so.

On this basis, the damage suffered by the appellant was caused in fact (because the interposition of the retailers may for this purpose in the circumstances of the case be disregarded) by the negligent or improper way in which the manufacturers made the garments. But this mere sequence of cause and effect is not enough in law to constitute a cause of action in negligence, which is a complex concept, involving a duty as between the parties to take care, as well as a breach of that duty and resulting damage. It might be said that here was no relationship between the parties at all: the manufacturers, it might be said, parted once and for all with the garments when they sold them to the retailers, and were therefore not concerned with their future history, except in so far as under their contract with the retailers they might come under some liability: at no time, it might be said, had they any knowledge of the existence of the appellant: the only peg on which it might be sought to support a relationship of duty was the fact that the appellant had actually worn the garments, but he had done so because he had acquired them by a purchase from the retailers, who were at that time the owners of the goods by a sale which had vested the property in the retailers and divested both property and control from the manufacturers. It was said there could be no legal relationships in the matter save those under the two contracts between the respective parties to those contracts, the one between the manufacturers and the retailers and the other between the retailers and the appellant. These contractual relationships (it might be said) covered the whole field and excluded any question of tort liability: there was no duty other than the contractual duties.

This argument was based on the contention that the present case fell outside the decision of the House of Lords in Donoghue's case. Their Lordships, like the judges in the courts in Australia, will follow that decision, and the only question here can be what that authority decides and whether this case comes within its principles. In Donoghue's case the defendants were manufacturers of ginger-beer, which they bottled: the pursuer had been given one of their bottles by a friend who had purchased it from a retailer who in turn had purchased from the defendants. There was no relationship between pursuer and defenders except that arising from the fact that she consumed the ginger-beer they had made and bottled. The bottle was opaque, so that it was impossible to see that it contained the decomposed remains of a snail: it was sealed and stoppered so that it could not be tampered with until it was opened in order that the contents should be drunk. The House of Lords held these facts established in law a duty to take care as between the defenders and the pursuer.

Their Lordships think that the principle of the decision is summed up in the words of Lord Atkin: 'A manufacturer of products, which he sells in such a form as to show that he intends them to reach the ultimate consumer in the form in which they left him with no reasonable possibility of intermediate examination, and with the knowledge that the absence of reasonable care in the preparation or putting up of the products will result in an injury to the consumer's life or property, owes a duty to the consumer to take that reasonable care.'

This statement is in accord with the opinions expressed by Lord Thankerton and Lord Macmillan, who in principle agreed with Lord Atkin.

In order to ascertain whether the principle applies to the present case, it is necessary to define what the decision involves, and consider the points of distinction relied upon before their Lordships.

It is clear that the decision treats negligence, where there is a duty to take care, as a specific tort in itself, and not simply as an element in some more complex relationship or in some specialized breach of duty, and still less as having any dependence on contract. All that is necessary as a step to establish the tort of actionable negligence is to define the precise relationship from which the duty to take care is to be deduced. It is, however, essential in English law that the duty should be established: the mere fact that a man is injured by another's act gives in itself no cause of action: if the act is deliberate, the party injured will have no claim in law even though the injury is intentional, so long as the other party is merely exercising a legal right: if the act involves lack of due care, again no case of actionable negligence will arise unless the duty to be careful exists. In Donoghue's case the duty was deduced simply from the facts relied on—namely, that the injured party was one

UK landmark cases

of a class for whose use, in the contemplation and intention of the makers the article was issued to the world, and the article was used by that party in the state in which it was prepared and issued without it being changed in any way and without there being any warning of, or means of detecting, the hidden danger: there was, it is true, no personal intercourse between the maker and the user.

. . . . .

It is obvious that the principles thus laid down involve a duty based on the simple facts detailed above, a duty quite unaffected by any contracts dealing with the thing, for instance, of sale by maker to retailer, and again by retailer to consumer or to the consumer's friend.

It may be said that the duty is difficult to define, because when the act of negligence in manufacture occurs there was no specific person towards whom the duty could be said to exist: the thing might never be used: it might be destroyed by accident, or it might be scrapped, or in many ways fail to come into use in the normal way: in other words the duty cannot at the time of manufacture be other than potential or contingent, and only can become vested by the fact of actual use by a particular person. But the same theoretical difficulty has been disregarded in cases like *Heaven v Pender* or in the case of things dangerous *per se* or known to be dangerous, where third parties have been held entitled to recover on the principles explained in *Dominion Natural Gas Co Ltd v Collins & Perkins*. In *Donoghue's* case the thing was dangerous in fact, though the danger was hidden, and the thing was dangerous only because of want of care in making it; as Lord Atkin points out in *Donoghue* the distinction between things inherently dangerous and things only dangerous because of negligent manufacture cannot be regarded as significant for the purpose of the questions here involved.

One further point may be noted. The principle of *Donoghue's* case can only be applied where the defect is hidden and unknown to the consumer, otherwise the directness of cause and effect is absent: the man who consumes or uses a thing which he knows to be noxious cannot complain in respect of whatever mischief follows, because it follows from his own conscious volition in choosing to incur the risk or certainty of mischance.

If the foregoing are the essential features of *Donoghue's* case they are also to be found, in their Lordships' judgment, in the present case. The presence of the deleterious chemical in the pants, due to negligence in manufacture, was a hidden and latent defect, just as much as were the remains of the snail in the opaque bottle: it could not be detected by any examination that could reasonably be made. Nothing happened between the making of the garments and their being worn to change their condition. The garments were made by the manufacturers for the purpose of being worn exactly as they were worn in fact by the appellant: it was not contemplated that they should be first washed. It is immaterial that the appellant has a claim in contract against the retailers, because that is a quite independent cause of action, based on different considerations, even though the damage may be the same. Equally irrelevant is any question of liability between the retailers and the manufacturers on the contract of sale between them. The tort liability is independent of any question of contract.

It was argued, but not perhaps very strongly, that *Donoghue* was a case of food or drink to be consumed internally, whereas the pants here were to be worn externally. No distinction, however, can be logically drawn for this purpose between a noxious thing taken internally and a noxious thing applied externally: the garments were made to be worn next the skin: indeed Lord Atkin specifically puts as examples of what is covered by the principle he is enunciating things operating externally, such as 'an ointment, a soap, a cleaning fluid or cleaning powder'.

Mr Greene, however, sought to distinguish *Donoghue's* case from the present on the ground that in the former the makers of the ginger-beer had retained 'control' over it in the sense that they had placed it in stoppered and sealed bottles, so that it would not be tampered with until it was opened to be drunk, whereas the garments in question were merely put into paper packets, each containing six sets, which in ordinary course would be taken down by the shop keeper and opened, and the contents handled and disposed of separately, so that they would be exposed to the air. He contended that though there was no reason to think that the garments when sold to the appellant were in any other condition, least of all as regards sulphur contents, than when sold to the retailers by the manufacturers, still the mere possibility and not the fact of their condition having been changed was sufficient to distinguish *Donoghue's* case: there was no 'control' because nothing was done by the manufacturers to exclude the possibility of any tampering while the goods were on their way to the user. Their Lordships do not accept that contention. The decision in *Donoghue* did not depend on the bottle being stoppered and sealed: the essential point in this regard was that the article should reach the consumer or user subject to the same defect as it had when it left the manufacturer. That this was true of the garment is in their Lordships' opinion beyond question. At most there might in other cases be a greater difficulty of proof of the fact.

Mr Greene further contended on behalf of the manufacturers that if the decision in *Donoghue* were extended even a hair's-breadth, no line could be drawn, and a manufacturer's liability would be extended indefinitely. He put as an illustration the case of a foundry which had cast a rudder to be fitted on a liner: he assumed that it was fitted and the steamer sailed the seas for some years: but the rudder had a latent defect due to faulty and negligent casting, and one day it broke, with the result that the vessel was wrecked, with great loss of life and damage to property. He argued that if

Donoghue were extended beyond its precise facts, the maker of the rudder would be held liable for damages of an indefinite amount, after an indefinite time, and to claimants indeterminate until the event. But it is clear that such a state of things would involve many considerations far removed from the simple facts of this case. So many contingencies must have intervened between the lack of care on the part of the makers and the casualty that it may be that the law would apply, as it does in proper cases, not always according to strict logic, the rule that cause and effect must not be too remote: in any case the element of directness would obviously be lacking. Lord Atkin deals with that sort of question in *Donoghue,* where he refers to *Earl v Lubbock:* he quotes the common-sense opinion of Mathew LJ: 'It is impossible to accept such a wide proposition, and, indeed, it is difficult to see how, if it were the law, trade could be carried on.'

In their Lordships' opinion it is enough for them to decide this case on its actual facts. No doubt many difficult problems will arise before the precise limits of the principle are defined: many qualifying conditions and many complications of fact may in the future come before the courts for decision. It is enough now to say that their Lordships hold the present case to come within the principle of *Donoghue's* case, and they think that the judgment of the Chief Justice was right in the result and should be restored as against both respondents, and that the appeal should be allowed, with costs here and in the courts below.

. . . . .

1938 *Daniels v White*

COMMENTARY

The judgment in this case has been widely criticised, and the view frequently expressed that, were the case to be tried again today, the decision would go the other way. It remains nonetheless a graphic illustration of the inequities of limiting a manufacturer's liability for a defective product to his liability in contract, and the decision in this case is now most often referred to by those who want to illustrate the shortcomings of the present UK law on liability for defective products. This is perhaps unfortunate in view of the judicial criticisms that have been directed at it, and the fact that the case itself never went to appeal.

The fact that the lemonade in the bottle had become contaminated with carbolic acid, had been purchased by Mr Daniels from Mrs Tarbard, and then immediately opened and drunk by both Mr and Mrs Daniels was not in dispute. This case therefore turned on the issue of the interpretation of the duty of care owed by the manufacturer, and the extent to which his duty can be discharged by a 'foolproof' process of manufacture. As Mr Justice Lewis said, 'The duty owed to the consumer by the manufacturer is not to ensure his goods are perfect. All he has to do is to take reasonable care to see that no injury is done to the consumer'.

Although the court was satisfied that the process adopted by the defendants for examining, cleaning and preparing the lemonade bottles for refilling was indeed foolproof and that the manufacturer had discharged his duty to take reasonable care, it seems likely that what is 'reasonable' is going to depend both on the general standards of care in manufacturing processes prevailing at the time, and the likely result of any lack of care. Measured by these criteria it seems surprising, even nearly 50 years ago, that the judge should be satisfied that a process consisting of the returned bottles being smelt and given a brief visual examination followed by a wash should be a sufficiently 'reasonable' standard to enable the manufacturer's duty to be discharged.

Apart from the perhaps unreliable aspects of *Daniels v White,* it nevertheless still has importance today as an illustration of the present state of English law in a situation involving personal injuries caused by a defective product.

Whereas Mr Daniels could recover damages for his injuries from the retailer of the lemonade under the provisions of section 14(2) of the 1893 Sale of Goods Act (as it was a sale of goods by description), Mrs Daniels who was not a party to the contract would have to show that there had been negligence by the manufacturer in order to bring her claim within the principles laid down in *Donoghue.*

JUDGMENT

King's Bench Division
November 3, 1938

Daniels and Daniels
versus
R White & Sons Ltd and Tarbard

Before Mr Justice Lewis

Mr Justice Lewis. The first plaintiff, Mr Daniels, is a street trader. He hawks and trades in secondhand clothing and secondhand furniture. Mr Daniels claims damages for negligence against R White & Sons Ltd, who are manufacturers and bottlers of, amongst other things, lemonade.

The second plaintiff, his wife, also claims damages for negligence against R White & Sons Ltd. The negligence alleged is that the defendants, in breach of the duty which they owed to the plaintiffs, supplied a bottle of lemonade which in fact contained carbolic acid. The bottle of lemonade was in fact obtained by the male plaintiff from a Mrs Tarbard, the licensee of a public-house known as the Falcon Arms, Falcon Terrace, Battersea, in the county of London. Both plaintiffs allege as against the first defendants, who are, as I say, manufacturers and bottlers, that they did not exercise reasonable care as manufacturers to prevent injury being done to the consumers or purchasers of their wares. The male plaintiff also sues Mrs Tarbard, from whom the bottle of lemonade was actually obtained, alleging, first of all, that under the Sale of Goods Act, in the circumstances there was an implied warranty that the lemonade was reasonably fit for the purpose of drinking, that it contained no deleterious and noxious matter, and/or that it was of merchantable quality, relying, as I read that plea, upon the Sale of Goods Act, 1893, section 14 (1), (2).

On July 23, the male plaintiff, who was a customer of the Falcon Arms, went into the Falcon Arms at about 7 pm with a jug, in order to purchase a jug of beer, and, as he said, a bottle of R White's lemonade, which is the lemonade made and bottled by the first defendants. He says that he prefers that particular lemonade, and that it was his usual order. He is a perfectly sober gentleman, and no suggestion of any kind is made against him. On the evidence given by himself, and also on that given by Mrs Tarbard, it is quite clear that sometimes three times a week he used to go in the evening for a jug of beer and a bottle of lemonade.

'On this occasion' he said, 'I asked for R White's lemonade.' Mrs Tarbard corroborated that, and said 'Oh yes, he came in, and he asked for R White's lemonade'. I accept that evidence. Having obtained his jug of beer and his bottle of lemonade, he then proceeded quite a short distance to his own home. It was a very hot day. On arriving home, the first thing he did was to take out

the stopper of the lemonade bottle, having first of all torn away the paper label which was stuck over the top of the bottle, which paper label I find was intact when it was sold to him. Having opened the bottle, he then poured a little lemonade into the jug of beer. He also poured some of the lemonade into a glass, which his wife then immediately drank, and he also drank some lemonade. He did not drink out of the jug of beer into which, as I say, a little of the lemonade had been poured, but he said he was very thirsty, and he had a drink. Both husband and wife drank almost simultaneously, and they both immediately realised that there was something burning in the liquid which they had taken, and they at once thought they had been poisoned. I need not go into the details, but in fact it was estimated, on an analysis of what remained in the bottle, that that bottle of lemonade contained 38 grains of carbolic acid, and that would amount to half a teaspoonful. The remains of the contents of the bottle, when analysed, were 4.2oz and in that 4.2oz there were 8 grains of carbolic acid. The analyst has worked it out as a mathematical calculation, and has therefore estimated that there were in the bottle at the time 38 grains of carbolic acid.

That was the case for the plaintiffs, and at the end of the plaintiffs' case a submission that there was no case to answer was made to me by counsel for the first defendants. The position was this. After a certain discussion for the purpose of the submission, it was said that they had to assume and accept that here was a bottle which, when purchased, quite properly had its stopper in, and also had the label pasted over the top but which, on the evidence called by the plaintiffs at that stage, contained carbolic acid, and that, as a result of drinking the contents of the bottle, the two plaintiffs had suffered damage. That, said counsel for the first defendants—and he said it quite accurately—is the only evidence in the case. He prayed in aid a statement which is to be found at the end of the opinion of Lord Macmillan in *Donoghue v Stevenson* in which, said counsel, Lord Macmillan was saying that those facts are not sufficient to establish a *prima facie* case. Lord Macmillan said 'The burden of proof must always be upon the injured party to establish that the defect which caused the injury was present in the article when it left the hands of the party whom he sues, that the defect was occasioned by the carelessness of that party, and that the circumstances are such as to cast upon the defender a duty to take care not to injure the pursuer. There is no presumption of negligence in such a case as the present, nor is there any justification for applying the maxim *res ipsa loquitur*. Negligence must be both averred and proved. The appellant accepts this burden of proof, and in my opinion she is entitled to have an opportunity of discharging it if she can.'

It was argued by counsel that Lord Macmillan was saying that it is not sufficient to say: Here is an article which is defective and has caused injury to the plaintiff. It is not sufficient to say that carbolic acid is not found in bottles of lemonade unless someone has blundered. The

Daniels v White

plaintiff must go further, and must prove that the carbolic acid has got into the bottle because the defendant has not taken reasonable care to keep it out.

I do not propose to discuss the point at length—it would not become me to critcise Lord Macmillan—but I think it is said that was *obiter,* and was not necessary for the decision of that case in their Lordships' House, and that the only question which they were deciding then was: What was the duty owed by a manufacturer of certain consumable goods to an ultimate purchaser or consumer? It was not necessary to go into the facts of that particular case, because the case had never been before the courts on the facts at all, and it is therefore suggested by counsel for the plaintiff that Lord Macmillan did not mean to include all such cases in the passage to which I have referred. He points out that it would cast a very great onus upon the consumer who has been poisoned in a case where an article is enclosed in a container sealed up and rendered quite impossible of interference when it leaves the factory, and which, when opened, is found to be poisoned. It is said that, in such a condition of things, the plaintiff cannot possibly, in 99 cases out of 100, say anything more than this: 'Here is a sealed container, and it is so sealed that it cannot be possibly opened or tampered with. It purports to contain food for human consumption, and it turns out to be full of poison. I cannot go to the factory and say, "You did not do something which you ought to have done, or you did something which you ought not to have done." That ought to be a sufficiently *prima facie* case on the doctrine of *res ipsa loquitur.'*

I did not stop the case, because I thought that it was right to hear what the defendants had to say. Counsel for the plaintiffs addressed me, and, as he always does, dealt most efficiently with the facts of the case and the evidence. He said that the defendants, upon the hypothesis that they had to rebut any inference of negligence which there might be, had entirely failed to do so. I do not take that view. I have to remember that the duty owed to the consumer, or the ultimate purchaser, by the manufacturer is not to ensure that his goods are perfect. All he has to do is to take reasonable care to see that no injury is done to the consumer or ultimate purchaser. In other words, his duty is to take reasonable care to see that there exists no defect that is likely to cause such injury.

I listened yesterday to a description of the machinery and the method used in these works in dealing with these bottles. The empty bottles are brought in, I dare say, from many parts of London. They are brought, it is true, into the same building and into the same room where the washing and filling of bottles is eventually done. Mr Busse has questioned the propriety of a state of things in which bottles which may come from anywhere, and which may contain poisonous matter, are in the same room in which the washing and the filling takes place. What happens is this. The bottles are brought in. There is a trolley alongside the girl who has to sort out the bottles. It is her duty to look at the bottles

and smell them, and, if she finds any bottle with an unpleasant smell, either from poison or from anything else, that bottle is immediately put on the trolley, and at the end of the day is taken away and broken, so as not to be used again. The girl having satisfied herself by her sense of smell and by the general look of the bottle that the bottle is innocuous, it then goes to the washing machine, and there, I am quite satisfied, that bottle has the most thorough washing that any bottle could have. It is washed at least three times. It has a 30-seconds' rinse first of all in hot water. Then it has another rinse in caustic soda at a heat of 130 deg F. Then it has another rinse in exactly the same process in cold water from the main. The bottles, while this is happening, are inverted— namely, with their necks down—and the washing is done under pressure by a jet. It stands to reason that, if one of these bottles by any chance escapes the nose of the lady who smells it first of all, it is then placed upside down on the carrier which conveys these bottles to the washing and, if there were half-a-teaspoonful, or, indeed, any amount, of liquid in the bottle, it would of course fall out before the bottle was ever washed at all. During the washing process the bottle is not handled at all, and, when it comes to the end of the carrier washed, the only handling it then receives is to remove it from the carrier and to place it on the machine which fills it. Then it is taken off and the stopper put on.

That method has been described as foolproof, and it seems to me a little difficult to say that, if people supply a foolproof method of cleaning, washing and filling bottles, they have not taken all reasonable care to prevent defects in their commodity. The only way in which it might be said that the foolproof machine was not sufficient was if it could be shown that the people who were working it were so incompetent that they did not give the foolproof machine a chance. It is pointed out quite rightly by Mr Busse that the question of supervision comes in. If you have 16 girls doing this process with no supervision of their work, of course all kinds of accidents may happen. A bottle may get to the filler without ever having been washed at all. A girl may upset a bottle just after it has been filled. She finds, let us say, that two teaspoonfuls of the liquid have been poured out. She has to fill it up from somewhere, so she walks along to the trolley were the dirty bottles have been put, picks up the first bottle she sees there, and pours the contents into the lemonade. Of course, that would be a rather curious thing for anyone to do, but it is a possible thing to happen if there is no supervision in this process.

I am satisfied in this case that there is supervision. I have had called before me the works manager who has charge of all three factories. That means, of course, that he is not at one factory the whole time, but he has described to me what takes place in this particular factory, and I am satisfied that there is quite adequate supervision. Even if the true view be that there was here a case for the defendants to answer, I am quite satisfied that they have answered it, and that the plaintiffs, as a result, have entirely failed to prove to my satisfaction that the defendant company were guilty of a breach of their duty towards the plaintiffs—namely, a duty to take reasonable care to see that there should be no defect which might injure the plaintiffs. For that reason, I think that the plaintiffs' claim against the first defendants fails. I have not forgotten, as Mr Busse in his argument pointed out, that there was called from this factory nobody who was doing the mixing, and no foreman. I am quite satisfied, however, on the evidence before me, that the work of this factory is carried on under proper supervision, and, therefore, that there has been no failure of the duty owed by the defendant company to the plaintiffs.

With regard to the other defendant, I confess that there is one consideration which ought really perhaps to be taken into account, and that is this. She was, of course, entirely innocent and blameless in the matter. She had received the bottle three days before from the first defendants, and she sold it over the counter to the husband, and the husband, of course, is the only one who has any rights in contract and breach of warranty against her. There is no issue of fact between the husband and Mrs Tarbard. They entirely agree as to what happened—namely, that Mr Daniels came into the public-house, the licensed premises, and said, 'I want a bottle of R White's lemonade', and R White's lemonade was what she gave him. The question which arises is, on those facts, the bottle in fact containing carbolic acid, and the lemonade, therefore, not being of merchantable quality, whether or not the second defendant is liable.

To my mind, it is quite clear that she is not liable under section 14 (1) of the Act, because Mr Daniels did not rely upon her skill and judgment at all. He asked for and obtained exactly what he wanted. If a man goes in and asks for a bottle of R White's lemonade, or somebody's particular brand of beer, he is not relying upon the skill and judgment of the person who serves it to him. In spite of the argument which has been put forward by counsel for the second defendant, I have some difficulty in seeing—particularly in view of the cases which have been cited to me, and more particularly *Morelli v Fitch & Gibbons*—why this was not a case of sale by description within the Sale of Goods Act 1893, section 14 (2). If it is a case of goods sold by description by a seller who deals in goods of that description, there is an implied condition that the goods shall be of merchantable quality. Unfortunately for Mrs Tarbard, through no fault of hers, the goods were not of merchantable quality. It was suggested by Mr Block that there was an opportunity of examination so as to bring the matter within the proviso to section 14 (2) of the Act, and he cited an authority to me, but I do not think that that authority takes him the length which he would wish it to do. I therefore find that this was a sale by description, and therefore hold—with some regret, because it is rather hard on Mrs Tarbard, who is a perfectly innocent person in the matter—that she is liable for the injury sustained by Mr Daniels through drinking this bottle of lemonade. However, that, as I understand it, is the law,

and therefore I think that there must be judgment for Mr Daniels, who is the only person who can recover against Mrs Tarbard.

Judgment for the male plaintiff against the second defendant for £21 15s, and judgment for the first defendants against both plaintiffs.

1963 *Crow v Barford*

COMMENTARY

The plaintiff in this case seems to have been in a classic 'heads you win—tails I lose' situation. Either the risk of injury from the rotary grass cutter was foreseeable both to the manufacturer and to the plaintiff, or it was not reasonably foreseeable at all as a risk. In either case, the plaintiff could not succeed in his action. In the first situation, he would fail because of the principle of *Donoghue v Stevenson* that the defect had to be both hidden and unknown in order for the duty of reasonable care to apply; in the second situation he would fail because if the risk was not foreseeable there would be no breach of duty of care by the manufacturer.

Lord Wright, in commenting on the need for the defect to be hidden and unknown to the consumer in the case of *Grant v Australian Knitting Mills,* said 'The principle of *Donoghue's* case can only be applied where the defect is hidden and unknown to the consumer, otherwise the directness of cause and effect is absent: the man who consumes or uses a thing which he knows to be noxious cannot complain in respect of whatever mischief follows, because it follows from his own conscious volition in choosing to incur the risk of certainty or mischance.'

The principle can give rise to hard cases as was demonstrated, not only in this case, but also in the earlier case of *Farr v Butters Bros* [1932] 2 KB 606. A crane manufacturer sent out a crane in parts which was intended to be assembled by the purchaser. The plaintiff's foreman realised that the crane was defective, but nevertheless he assembled it, used it and was killed as a result. It was held in the subsequent action that the foreman had voluntarily taken the risk knowing of the defect, and therefore was not able to claim against the defendants. In another case, however, involving the unloading of an unsafe load, where the plaintiff recognised the danger but unloaded it anyway because there was no other alternative, he was able to recover damages in respect of the resulting injury he suffered. Presumably it would have been open to the plaintiff in this case to have similarly argued that having recognised the potential danger of the operator's foot slipping when starting the machine, he had no choice but to take that risk in order to operate it.

This point leads on to the whole question of the foreseeability of the risk which was, as the court put it, the other horn of the plaintiff's dilemma. The court's views are interesting in respect of the designer's potential liability for a defective design. The plaintiff's main argument was not that the physical design of the machine was itself defective, but the existence of the danger that someone's foot might slip and be injured when starting the machine. The trial judge had been quite unequivocal on this point: 'I do not think that in the early part of 1959, the first defendants (the manufacturers of the rotary grass cutter) could reasonably have foreseen the likelihood of an accident such as the plaintiff sustained, or indeed that there was any foreseeable risk of danger. In my judgment it is really going altogether too far to suggest that a manufacturer fails in his duty to the public if, in the early days of manufacture of a machine of this sort, he fails to anticipate that an operator might be wearing wellington boots; he might slip or overbalance, he might pull the machine in such a way that his foot in a wellington boot would get into the aperture'. 'Clearly this issue of foreseeability is going to be decided on the facts of each case. It is at least arguable that in this particular case such a risk was in fact foreseeable, as Lord Diplock appears to be suggesting when he comments on the 'aperture as large as life . . . the knives . . . and . . . the starting handle'.

To summarise the effect of this case on designers' liability, it seems to be (1) that if the risk of injury is not reasonably foreseeable, the designer cannot be liable and (2) that if the risk of injury is reasonably foreseeable and obvious to the consumer, the designer will not be liable.

JUDGMENT

Court of Appeal
April 8, 1963

Crow
versus
Barford (Agricultural) Limited and H B Holttum & Company Limited

Before Lord Justices Willmer, Upjohn and Diplock

Lord Justice Diplock. This is an appeal from the judgment of Mr Justice Hinchcliffe given at the Cambridge Assizes in November 1962. The plaintiff, who is a farmer, purchased in 1958 a machine known as a new Barford 18-inch Rotomo, which was a rotary grass cutter. He purchased the machine from the second defendants, who were dealers in and retailers of machinery of that kind, describing themselves as light tractor specialists. The machine was manufactured by the first defendants, Barford (Agricultural) Limited. It was of the ordinary design of a rotary grass cutter with revolving blades which were covered by an iron case or shield, and it was operated by a Villiers 2-stroke motor. The motor ran the blades; the machine itself was pushed and not power-driven in that sense. The guard for the blades had an aperture for expelling the grass as it was cut, which was on the right-hand side of the machine. The engine, which was on top of the machine, had a recoil starter handle, which had to be pulled in order to start the engine. The recoil starter handle was also on the right-hand side of the machine, and the normal way of starting the motor was to put one's left hand upon the

UK landmark cases

handle of the machine, one's right hand on the starter, and one's right foot on the iron casing to the side and to the rear of the aperture.

Mr Crow bought this machine after considering various other machines of different makes, and after a demonstration when Mr Holttum, employed by the second defendants, brought it to his farm and showed him how it worked. At that demonstration Mr Crow inspected the machine, and in particular inspected the knives; and it must have been evident on any such inspection not only what the aperture was for, but also what was plain for everyone to see, where the starter handle was, that the knives revolved within one-eighth of an inch or so of the opening of the aperture, and that it would obviously be very dangerous if a foot or a hand or any part of the human body got into the aperture while the knives were revolving.

The machine was delivered in December 1958, and towards Easter 1959, when the grass began to grow, Mr Crow desired to use it for cutting his grass. He used it on one or two occasions prior to the accident, and on those occasions it started easily enough. But on Easter Saturday (which was March 28, 1959) it did not start when he wished to start it. He had it at that time on some concrete in the yard on his farm, I think. He discovered by examining it that there was an air lock in the petrol feed, and, having cured that, he tried again to start it. It was difficult to start, and he had to pull the handle of the recoil starter a number of times, doing it in the way in which he had been shown to do it by Mr Holttum, by holding the handle of the machine with his left hand, grasping the starter with his right hand, and with his right foot on the casing by the side of the aperture towards the rear of the machine. Unfortunately, the last time that he pulled the starting handle, the engine started, and in some way which he was unable to explain, his right foot slipped, it went into the aperture, and as a result two of his toes were cut off, a most unfortunate accident.

He brings this action against the manufacturers and the retailers of the machine, against the manufacturers for negligence and breach of duty in 'manufacturing and distributing without giving any warning of its true nature an article, namely, the mower which was dangerous in itself, or alternatively in failing to take reasonable care in the design or manufacture of the mower to prevent the purchaser and user thereof, namely, the plaintiff, being exposed to the danger of his foot being caught by the blades on starting up the same'. He sued the second defendants, the retailers, for breach of the implied warranty of merchantable quality contained in the Sale of Goods Act 1893, section 14 (2).

I deal first with the claim against the manufacturers, for that was put upon the grounds of the decision in * Donoghue v Stevenson [1932] AC 562, on the duty of a manufacturer to use reasonable care in the preparation and putting up of goods which he puts upon the market and which he knows are 'likely to reach the ultimate consumer in the form in which they left him with no reasonable possibility of intermediate examination, and with the knowledge that the absence of reasonable care in the preparation or putting up of the product will result in an injury to the consumer's life or property'. The principle in Donoghue v Stevenson which lays that duty upon a manufacturer is subject to this limitation set out in the case of * Grant v Australian Knitting Mills [1936] AC 85, that the principle can be applied only where the defect is hidden and unknown to the customer or consumer; that is set out in the headnote and is in fact a quotation from page 120 of the opinion of their Lordships in that Privy Council case. The requirement is dichotomous: the defect must be hidden as well as unknown to the consumer.

I pause, therefore, to ask: What is the defect which there is said to be in this machine? The answer seems to be that the aperture and the starter handle were on the same side of the machine; that in order to start it, it was proper (though it may not have been necessary) to put your right foot on the casing not far from the aperture, and that so to do involved a danger that your foot might slip and get into the aperture. That defect, or at any rate the physical design of the machine, was in no sense hidden. It was perfectly obvious on looking at the machine that there was the aperture as large as life, there were the knives, and there was the starting handle. It was quite obvious that if you were going to use the machine and start the blades revolving, it would be very dangerous indeed to allow your foot or any part of your body to get in the aperture. So that so far as the physical design of the machine is concerned, and in so far as that design was a defect of the machine, in no sense can it be said to be hidden. Prima facie, therefore, it is a defect to which the rule in Donoghue v Stevenson does not apply.

Mr Martin Jukes has sought to put it in this way. He says that the physical design of the machine which is obvious is not the defect. What is the defect is the danger that someone's foot might slip when starting the machine in the usual way for starting it. I think that is a misuse of the word 'defect' in the Donoghue v Stevenson rule. But assuming, if one may, that a danger of that kind which was a consequence of the design could be a 'defect' within the Donoghue v Stevenson rule, it could be so only if two conditions were fulfilled: (1) that the manufacturer should foresee the risk of danger to the user; that it should be reasonably foreseeable; and (2)—for this is the meaning of the expression that the defect must be hidden—that the user of the machine could not reasonably foresee the risk. As I put to Mr Jukes in the course of his argument, it seems to me that the plaintiff in this case is in a dilemma. Either the risk of the foot slipping in the circumstances in which it did slip in the unfortunate case of Mr Crow was not reasonably foreseeable, or it was. The learned judge, who saw the machine and the demonstration and heard the witnesses, expressed the view at the end of his judgment: 'I do not think that in the early part of 1959 the first defendants could reasonably have foreseen the likelihood of an accident such as the plaintiff sustained, or indeed that there was any foreseeable risk of danger. In my judgment it is really going altogether too far to suggest that a manufacturer fails in his duty to the public if, in the early days of manufacture of a machine of this sort, he fails to anticipate that an operator might be wearing wellington boots; he might slip or over-balance; he might pull the machine in such a way that his foot in a wellington boot would get into the aperture.'

If the learned judge is right (and that seems very much a matter for the trial judge) then the risk was not a foreseeable risk and there was no lack of care on the part of the manufacturers in marketing a machine of this kind.

The alternative horn of the dilemma—assuming that the learned judge was wrong, and that this risk was a foreseeable one—is that it is a risk (whatever view you take of the likelihood of its occurrence) which is perfectly apparent when you look at the machine in order to form a judgment as to its likelihood or otherwise. The possibility of its happening, and the way in which it could happen, is perfectly obvious, and as obvious to the plaintiff and to Mr Holttum and the retailer as it was to the manufacturer. Therefore, if it was a risk sufficiently likely to be foreseeable, it could not amount to a hidden defect so as to place on the manufacturer the duty to avoid marketing a machine in which that risk was present. So far as the action against the manufacturers is concerned, it appears to me that this appeal must fail.

As regards the action against the retailers, which was based upon the implied condition of merchantable quality contained in the Sale of Goods Act 1893, I should perhaps read it from section 14 (2): 'Where goods are bought by description from a seller who deals in goods of that description (whether he be the manufacturer or not)'—that was the case of the second defendants—'there is an implied condition that the goods shall be of merchantable quality; Provided that if the buyer has examined the goods, there shall be no implied condition as regards defects which such examination ought to have revealed'. What I have said in relation to the liability of the manufacturer would involve that the proviso applies in this case if it were right to say (which I do not accept) that this machine was not of merchantable quality.

In my opinion this appeal against both defendants fails.

Lord Justice Willmer. I have reached the same conclusion, and as I agree entirely with what my Lord has just said, I see no reason to add anything further thereto.

Lord Justice Upjohn. I also agree.

Appeal dismissed with costs.

1977 *Hill v James Crowe (Cases)*

COMMENTARY

This case further develops the law from the position in *Donoghue v Stevenson*. Now liability can also be incurred for a defect in a container or packaging as well as in an end product, and in circumstances where the use of that packaging might be thought somewhat abnormal.

In reaching its decision as to whether the packing case was defectively made and whether therefore the manufacturer had been negligent, the court also seems to be showing a readiness to act on circumstantial evidence rather than determining if *res ipsa loquitur* rules should be applied.

Indeed it can be argued that this case is eloquent evidence that English law is not really as underdeveloped in relation to product liability as it has been frequently said to be; that the notorious judgment in the *Daniels v White* case is now totally discredited and those who base their argument for a fundamental change in English law on that case are in fact exaggerating the problems that confront a plaintiff in seeking to recover damages in tort from a manufacturer for injuries caused by a defective product.

Certainly, at first sight the liability of the manufacturer of the packing case does seem rather surprising when the doctrine of foreseeability in *Donoghue v Stevenson* is applied.

The maxim that 'English law does not recognise a duty in the air, so to speak; that is, a duty to undertake that no one shall suffer from one's carelessness' (per Lord Justice Greer in *Bottomley v Bannister* [1932] 1 KB 458) seems to be a particularly relevant one. However, on closer examination of the facts, it does seem that despite the apparent abnormal use of the product it was foreseeable that a lorry driver would stand on packing cases when loading his lorry, and that if the case gave way he would be injured. The evidence of the foreman of the packing case manufacturer was that the case, if properly made, would support the weight of four people, and would easily have borne the weight of a large man standing in the centre. The judge seems to have had no difficulty in finding that the injuries to Mr Hill were therefore foreseeable as a consequence of the packing case being badly made.

On the issue of negligence the defendants had argued that, on the basis of *Daniels v White,* they were able to show both adequate supervision and a safe system of work and at first instance had satisfied the trial judge that this discharged their duty of care. In rejecting this argument, Mr Justice MacKenna appeared fairly to put the last nail in the coffin of *Daniels v White* by holding that the manufacturer's liability in negligence depended only on vicarious liability for the negligence of workmen in the manufacture of the packing case, and that *Daniels v White* had been wrongly decided.

The lesson from this decision for manufacturers seems to be that the test of foreseeability must be applied even to situations which might be regarded as abnormal use of the product, and that claims for damages arising from negligent manufacture may succeed in circumstances where, even a few years ago, this would have been thought unlikely.

JUDGMENT

Queen's Bench Division
May 11 and 12, 1977

Hill
versus
James Crowe (Cases) Limited

Before Mr Justice MacKenna

Mr Justice MacKenna. On January 25, 1973, Mr Hill was working as a lorry driver employed by AA Kent Ltd. His work took him that day to a warehouse owned by Newbold Shipping Services at Silvertown in the East End of London, where he had to load onto his lorry a number of packed wooden cases and also cartons containing television sets. A forklift truck, operated by one of Newbold's men, lifted the cases onto the floor of the lorry, where Mr Hill moved them into a suitable position. The cases covered the floor of the lorry, which was then ready to receive the cartons which would be also brought to him by the truck. He was standing on one of the cases waiting for the first load of cartons when he fell to the ground, injuring his ankle and, more seriously, his right hand.

He brings this action against James Crowe (Cases) Ltd whom I shall call 'Crowe', claiming that his accident was caused by their negligence. Crowe are in business as packers of goods for shipment overseas, and in the course of this business they manufacture wooden cases. They had made at least one of the cases which had been loaded onto Mr Hill's lorry to carry a quantity of household goods from London to Lagos in West Africa for delivery to Miss Ronke Allison. Mr Hill alleges that just before he fell he had been standing on the end of this case when some of the boards stove in, causing him to lose his balance and fall. He says that the case was badly nailed. The fact of his accident, he argues, by itself proves bad manufacture, and if it does not he says that he has proved by the testimony of a credible witness that not enough nails were used to fasten the boards. Crowe, he says, owed a duty to those who were likely to come in contact with the case in transit, to make it strong enough to withstand the foreseeable hazards of its journey; and one of these was the likelihood of persons standing on it in the course of loading who might be injured if the boards caved in. They had neglected this duty, and their

negligence was the cause of this accident for which they are liable in damages.

On liability there are four issues: (1) Did Mr Hill fall because the boards of the packing case he was standing on caved in? If so, (2) Was the packing case badly made? If so, (3) Ought the maker to have foreseen that if it were badly made persons in Mr Hill's position might suffer injury in some such way as Mr Hill was injured and to have taken care to make it properly, so that their failure to do so was in law negligence? If so, (4) Had the case on which Mr Hill was standing been made by Crowe?

I have no hesitation in answering all these questions in Mr Hill's favour.

There were three important witnesses: (1) Mr Hill; (2) Mr Youles, another driver in Crowe's employment; and (3) Mr Taylor, the manager of Newbold's warehouse. Mr Hill described how he had loaded the cases onto the deck of the lorry and was waiting for the forklift truck to return with the cartons. He was standing on the upturned end of one of the cases near the back of the lorry.
Something gave in (he said). It may have been one of the struts. I lost my balance. I did a somersault.
A little later in his evidence he said:
I don't know if part of the wood broke. All I know is something went from under my foot. The case was stowed properly. If it had moved it would have fallen onto the lorry. I don't know what broke.

Mr Youles said that he was going to help Mr Hill with the load; that he had gone to the side of the lorry to help him when he saw him fall. He described the position of the case on the lorry resting on one of its two ends. He examined it after the accident. Two or three of the boards had caved in at the end on which Mr Hill had been standing. There were, he said, no nails in these boards. He had talked to the driver of the forklift truck about repairing the case—this was after the accident— and the driver had said 'Leave it'.

Mr Hill and Mr Youles each gave Mr Hill's solicitor a written account of the accident shortly after it had happened, which was in substance the same as the witness's evidence in court. I quote from Mr Youles', written in reply to the solicitor's letter of March 1, 1973, that is about five weeks after the day of the accident, which was January 25. He wrote:
I finished loading my lorry at Trans Storage (which seems to have been a warehouse near Newbold's) and was walking over to assist Mr Hill complete his loading when the case Mr Hill had stepped on stove in, Mr Hill tumbled off his lorry and could not get off the ground. An ambulance was called and Mr Hill was taken to hospital. I looked at the broken case and noted the struts were secured by only a few nails.
Mr Youles said that after the accident he had driven Mr Hill's lorry to the docks, where the load, including the case in question, had been given to the port authority.

Hill v James Crowe (Cases)

Documents were produced by Crowe which showed the receipt by the authority of a case of personal effects marked 'R Allison, Nigeria General Insurance, Lagos, Nigeria'. Its language reproduces that of a shipping note prepared by Crowe on January 24 when they had sent the case to the warehouse. Crowe also produced a bill of lading for the case, dated February 16, 1973. Neither the receipt nor the bill of lading mentions any defect of the case, which they would have been likely to do if it had been in a damaged condition. A statement of Miss Allison was put in evidence which she had made in 1976, and in which she said that the case had been received by her intact without any trace of damage or repair.

Three questions were left unanswered when this case was adjourned some weeks ago. Was it really Crowe's case to be sent to Miss Allison at Lagos on which Mr Hill had been standing? If so, how had Mr Hill been able to identify the case as hers, which he had done in the particulars of the statement of claim given to Crowe in 1975, which had identified the case as Miss Allison's by its shipping marks? How did the authority, the ship's master, Miss Allison fail to notice its damaged condition if it were the case whose boards had caved in, and which, if Mr Youles' evidence were complete and accurate, had apparently not been repaired?

The answers to these questions were given yesterday by Mr Taylor, an impressive witness whose evidence I accept without any reserve whatever. I have already mentioned that he was the manager of Newbold's Silvertown warehouse. He was at the warehouse on January 25 when the accident happened. He had not seen it happen, but had been told about it. He went to the scene and saw Mr Hill on the ground beside his lorry. He saw a broken case. One of the battens was loose. It had been pushed down. 'Allison' was the name on this case. He spoke to Mr Smith, a director of his company, who told him to record the accident, which he did in the diary which he kept at the warehouse. D2, the sheet for January 25, has been put in evidence. It contains this entry:
Stokes driver accident—ankle and wrist J Hill c/o A Kent.
Allison Lagos c/s. Mr Smith advised.
I should say that Mr Hill's lorry was owned by a firm called Kent which had let it on hire with its driver to Stokes.

Mr Taylor told me that some time later the case was sent to the docks.
Before it left (he said), we would have had it repaired. I'd have asked one of the warehouse lads to do it. We wouldn't charge for it. It wouldn't take long to do.
That was his evidence-in-chief. In cross-examination he said that he was quite sure that it had been repaired. He told me that Mr Hill had come to him at the warehouse soon after the accident. His hand was still in bandages. Mr Hill had asked him for particulars about the packing case, which he gave him in writing. These were the document P8. I quote from it:

Case was received from James Crowe Ltd, Corway Road, W4 24/1/73 marked R Allison, Lagos. Size: 121x73x96 centimetres, 129 kilograms.
Mr Hill's solicitors wrote to Mr Taylor on March 1, 1973, asking for information about the accident. He and his foreman replied in a letter signed by both of them and dated April 4, 1973. It was put in under the Civil Evidence Act. I quote from it: 'On the 25th January Mr J Hill, driver for A Kent Hauliers, was loading groupage traffic for Lagos. To receive the last case, a TV in a wooden case, Mr Hill stood on a case the end of which stove in, causing him to lose his balance and to fall from the lorry. As a result of his fall Mr Hill sustained injury to his wrist and ankle.'

There is, of course, an apparent conflict between Mr Youles' evidence and that of Mr Taylor. Mr Youles had given me to understand by implication, if not expressly, that the damaged case had not been repaired. If Mr Taylor were right, which I am satisfied he was, the case had been repaired. I was asked, because of this error in Mr Youles' evidence, to reject the whole of it. I do not. He struck me as an honest witness. He may well have been telling the truth when he said that the truck driver had answered his suggestion about repairing the case with the words 'Leave it'. Mr Taylor, it is clear, decided otherwise, and it is possible either that Mr Youles did not know of Mr Taylor's decision or that he has since forgotten it.

Crowe called two witnesses on liability: Mr Crowe himself and Mr Shrubb, employed in the bill of lading department of Killick Martin's. Mr Shrubb told me about the practice of the port of London in dealing with damaged goods. If the case had been damaged, the authority, he said, would not have accepted it until it had been recooped. Mr Crowe told me of the high standards of workmanship and of supervision at his company's workshop, where they had been making packing cases for 14 years and supplying what he called the complete cif service for nine years. He had no recollection of the making of the case which went to Miss Allison. If it had been properly nailed, which he was sure it had been if it was one of his company's manufacture, it would have supported the weight of four people. It would have easily borne the weight of a large man standing on the centre. The company, he said, had made many of these cases and had never had a complaint like this. Their standards of workmanship and of supervision were high. Mr Youles had spoken of the boards stoving in for a distance of 9in. It was, Mr Crowe thought, inconceivable that there would be that extent of dunnage or empty space at the end of the case. These cases were made to measure, and it would be wasteful to make one which was too large for its contents.

In spite of Mr Crowe's evidence, I find that the accident happened while Mr Hill was standing on the packing case which Crowe had made; that it was caused by the end caving in; and that it caved in because it had been very badly nailed. If the case can be brought within the rule in *Donoghue v Stevenson, liability is established. I think that it can. It resembles a case in the Court of Appeal in which I was briefed many years ago, which was not reported and whose name I have forgotten. Sir Wilfred Greene, who was then Master of the Rolls, presided. The appeal, which came from the Northern Circuit, was in an action brought by a stevedore against the company which had packed the goods he was handling. The goods were heavy, and the packing consisted of, or at least included, pieces of wire bound round the outside of the package. It was the practice of the stevedores to handle the goods by means of the wire. One of the packages had been badly wired, and the wire had come off while the plaintiff was handling it, so that he lost his balance, fell and injured himself. He lost in the court of first instance, but his appeal was allowed. The Court of Appeal held that the defendants who had put on the wire should have foreseen the possibility that a stevedore handling the package might be injured if the wire had not been properly fastened. I see no difference in principle between the defendants' liability in that case and Crowe's liability in this.

Mr Serota, for Crowe, relied on the case of *Daniels v White & Sons* [1938] 4 All ER 258. The plaintiff in that case had bought at a public house a sealed bottle of lemonade made by the defendant manufacturers and sold by them to the public house. The bottle contained, in addition to the lemonade, a quantity of carbolic acid which it was contended had caused injury to the plaintiff, who sued the manufacturers. His action failed. The manufacturers satisfied Mr Justice Lewis, the trial judge, that they had a good system of work in their factory and provided adequate supervision. He said, at page 263: 'I am quite satisfied, however, on the evidence before me, that the work at this factory was carried on under proper supervision, and therefore that there has been no failure of the duty owed by the defendant company to the plaintiff.'

With respect, I do not think that this was a sufficient reason for dismissing the claim. The manufacturer's liability in negligence did not depend on proof that he had either a bad system of work or that his supervision was inadequate. He might also be vicariously liable for the negligence of his workmen in the course of their employment. If the plaintiff's injury were a reasonably foreseeable consequence of such negligence, the manufacturer's liability would be established under *Donoghue v Stevenson*. *Daniels v White & Sons* has been criticised, I think justly, in *Charlesworth on Negligence* (5th edition), at page 398, and I do not propose to follow it.

1978 *Walton v British Leyland*

COMMENTARY

This case examines the standard of the duty of care owed by a manufacturer to users of his product in circumstances where a defect was known to the manufacturer but was not a matter of public knowledge. In practical terms, it provides an eloquent illustration of the dilemma facing manufacturers when a fault is identified affecting a number of products—whether or not to institute a recall campaign. As Mr Justice Willis recognised ' . . . manufacturers have to steer a course between alarming the public unnecessarily and so damaging the reputation of their products, and observing their duty of care towards those whom they are in a position to protect from dangers of which they and they alone are aware.' The failure of the manufacturer to undertake a recall campaign was held to be a breach of the duty of care, and the company was consequently liable for damages for the accident that occurred as a direct result of the known product defect.

It was accepted that the driver of the car who lost control and hit the motorway central reservation when a rear wheel came off as a result of bearing failure had not been negligent in any way. The case therefore turned on the apportionment of blame between the manufacturer, the selling dealer who had carried out certain servicing work, and a third dealer who had worked on the car on other occasions.

From the evidence, it seems that the manufacturer had been aware of a problem affecting the rear hub assembly of cars of this particular model for at least two and a half years before this accident occurred.

It had been recognised that incorrect adjustment could lead to overtightening, with consequent over-heating and bearing failure, which in turn could lead to the loss of a wheel. Advice had been circulated to the authorised dealer network drawing attention to the way in which the new type of rear hub bearings should be adjusted and the importance of 'end float'. Despite this, numerous cases of bearing failure including instances of 'wheel adrift' had been reported, and in September 1974 a decision was taken to fit a modified retaining washer on the rear wheels to stop the wheels coming off in the event that the bearings failed.

The court dismissed the arguments put forward on behalf of the manufacturer that he had in effect discharged his duty of care adequately when, having concluded that there was no defect in assembly, he introduced the modified washer and alerted his own dealer to the problem. To do so and accept the manufacturer's argument that the problem leading to the accident was caused by mechanics carelessly or ignorantly overtightening the bearings and not allowing sufficient 'end float' to avoid the seizing up, would have passed the burden of negligence to one or both of the two dealers who had carried out servicing work on the car in question.

In the case of the authorised dealer, who had also been the original selling dealer, there was evidence that he had indeed taken notice of the bulletins from the manufacturer, and when attending to the plaintiff's complaint about noisy wheel bearings had fitted the larger recommended washer to the other rear wheel.

The judge rejected arguments that the dealer should at that time have fitted the larger washer to both wheels as he took the view that the service bulletin did not give clear advice on this point. The other defendant garage was not an authorised dealer, and therefore was unaware of the bulletins issued by the manufacturer. As to whether staff should have noticed in working on the car subsequent to its visit to the authorised dealer that a larger washer had been fitted on one side than on the other, and thereby elected to make further checks and enquiries, the judge took the view that the company's own duty of care did not extend this far.

In dismissing all the other factors which may have contributed to the accident, and finding the manufacturer alone liable, Mr Justice Willis summarised the extent of their duty as follows: 'It was, in my view, their duty to ensure that all cars still in stock and unsold by the time the washer palliative was proven were fitted with this safety feature device before sale.'

This case not only illustrates the extent of the duty of care required of a manufacturer, but also indicates ways in which that duty may be fulfilled—to discharge or at least reduce the liability arising from that duty.

The manufacturer could have taken steps after modifying new models to ensure that all vehicles in stock and unsold should be modified before sale.

The manufacturer could have taken steps to warn all dealers, not just franchised ones, in unequivocal terms of the danger and the action to be taken.

The manufacturer could have instituted a recall campaign to ensure that all vehicles in service were modified without delay.

JUDGMENT

Queen's Bench Division
July 12, 1978

Victor and Margaret Walton
versus
British Leyland (UK) Limited, Dutton Forshaw
(North East) Limited and Blue House Lane
Garage Limited

Before Mr Justice Willis

Mr Justice Willis. The facts and tragic results of the accident which gave rise to this claim are not in dispute

Recent UK cases

and can be shortly stated. Mr and Mrs Victor Walton, the plaintiffs, were on holiday in this country from Australia. During the evening of April 22, 1976 they were travelling northwards on the M1 motorway as passengers in an Austin Allegro motor car, owned and driven by the first plaintiff's brother, Mr Albert Walton. At a point near Newport Pagnell when the car was travelling at 50-60 mph the *rear nearside wheel* came off, the driver lost control and the vehicle collided with the central crash barrier. Both plaintiffs are elderly, in their sixties. Miraculously the first plaintiff, who is a handicapped person, escaped with minor injuries; his wife was thrown from the car, she suffered catastrophic injuries which it is not necessary to detail and has been left a quadriplegic.

Although both the first and second defendants saw fit in their pleadings to allege negligence on the part of the driver, Albert Walton, those allegations were properly withdrawn by counsel on the first day of the trial; during the course of the case by the first defendant, an agreement *inter partes* was announced that both plaintiffs are entitled to recover their damages in full—the sums to be assessed later—subject to a reservation immaterial to these proceedings, for the negligence of one or more or all the defendants. From that point my sole task has been to decide whether one of the three defendants is solely to blame or, if more than one, to apportion the degrees of negligence. The Allegro, as a new range to replace the Austin 1300, had been introduced in May 1973. The car in question was manufactured by Leyland and left their works in February 1974. Its immediate history is unrecorded by the evidence, save that it must be assumed to have remained in the possession and under the control of a franchise holder or authorised Leyland dealer until it was sold as a new car by Duttons to Mr Walton, its first owner, on November 1, 1974.

It is now necessary to go back somewhat in the history of the Allegro. A significant alteration in its design compared with *eg* the Maxi and 1300 range was the introduction of tapered roller bearings in the rear hub assembly which had to be adjusted in a different way from earlier models fitted with roller bearings. The Marina was designed in a similar way. This was a bearing designed by the well-known firm of Timken, and it is fitted to a great many makes of car world wide; it is a tried method and no criticism is sought to be made of Leyland for using it in the Marina and Allegro. Its proper adjustment involves what is technically described as 'end float', to produce a certain amount of play in the wheel which is apparent upon its rotation and rocking after it has been properly adjusted.

According to the documents I have seen, the first rumblings that all was not well with the rear hub assembly of the Allegro had been heard by Leyland by at least October 1973, and probably earlier. On the 17th of that month, Leyland circulated a Product Bulletin to the service managers of (*inter alios*) all their accredited dealers, with a request to pass the information therein to all workshop personnel. This drew attention to the change in the method of adjusting the new rear hub bearing and emphasised the importance of correct end float and the risk of bearings seizing up if enough end float was not provided.

The information contained in this bulletin (as in certain later ones) was, according to a note on the document, to be treated as confidential by the recipients. It seems to have been a very ineffective method of averting the gathering storm.

It does not appear that any similar bulletins on this topic were issued until August 9, 1974, when a diagrammatic illustration of the importance of the difference between torque tightening (for ball bearings) and end float (for roller bearings) was issued, with a similar distribution. This was followed by a bulletin of September 25, 1974 to all dealers (and some others whom it is immaterial to try to identify) in which the recipients were told that all cars produced since a certain chassis number (in fact, since about September 16, 1974) incorporated a larger retaining washer in the rear hub assembly 'to improve bearing security', and urging the importance of fitting such washers 'when servicing the rear hub bearings or brakes of earlier vehicles'. I shall have to return to this document together with a letter from Leyland, dated October 24, which followed it addressed to 'All distributors and retail dealers (cars) UK for the attention of their managing directors and service managers'. In the background, Leyland realised they had a very serious problem on their hands with, and in the context of the problem *only with,* the Allegro. Speaking with the experience of an engineer with Leyland and its various predecessors since 1940, Mr de Lassalle, the only company witness, could recall nothing similar in scope and seriousness. By December 12, 1973 some diagnosis of the problem had been made, and on that day a 'major' modification to the Allegro was authorised, namely a new special washer 'to provide an additional bearing retention safety feature'.

The alarming story of what was happening to Allegros in this country and abroad can be gleaned in part from Leyland's 'product problem progress card'. The problem was identified as 'rear wheel bearing failure—wheel adrift'; it runs from an entry on December 17, 1973, with many entries month by month through 1974 as the evidence accumulated until its conclusion in early March 1975.

I only propose to select entries to illustrate the scale of the problem as it was presented to Leyland.

In the month to August 22, not less than ten cases of bearing failures, some with wheels adrift, had been reported from the Continent. By September 5, a total of 50 cases of failure had been reported to Leyland. By October 26, no less than '100 cases of wheel adrift to date' are recorded as having been reported, *ie* 50 more in seven weeks. In January 1975, three further failures were reported 'thought to be due to corrosion'. A further case from this cause is entered on February 7.

Walton v British Leyland

Leyland were naturally anxious to identify, if they could, the cause of so many bearing failures, many involving wheels coming off, or adrift, if there is any sensible difference. I could discover none. Lives were plainly at risk, but so were sales, and a solution or at least a palliative had to be found urgently. It is clear from the documents and the evidence of Mr de Lassalle that early on in Leyland's investigation the expert consensus was to put the blame for the bearing failure on mechanics, careless or unfamiliar with the new technique of end float adjustment, and so producing overtightening. This in turn would lead to overheating, then to bearing collapse and, in the worst cases, to wheels coming off. The design was satisfactory, there was little evidence of corrosion being the cause, proper adjustment and greasing of the bearing was accepted as having been correctly done at the factory, and so the conclusion was reached that the fault lay with mechanics when working on the brakes or other parts of the rear hub assembly, and particularly at 12,000 miles service when the brakes had to be attended to. This conclusion appears to leave quite unexplained why similar problems did not appear to affect Marinas which had made their début a little earlier, and were fitted with similar roller bearings. At least, on September 10, 1974 the deputy chairman, Mr Barber, was urgently writing a letter to senior officials about a serious Allegro accident in Italy, saying (inter alia) 'I am still not satisfied with the solution to the loss of rear wheels on the Allegro. The larger washer will certainly stop the wheels coming off in some cases but there has been at least one example of the hub itself fracturing and the larger washer obviously cannot help when that happens. To my untutored eye, it looks as if the bearing is not up to the job. Will you please have this investigated.'

The reference to the larger washer is explained by the tests which had been carried out during the summer. These assumed the cause of failure basically to be due to negligent mechanics, and involved the simulation of such negligence by deliberately overtightening and testing to failure. The tests were not designed, therefore, to diagnose the cause of bearing failure but to try to find a palliative to avert the worst results should bearing failure occur. The proposal finally adopted to remedy the assumed basic cause was a limited education programme directed to mechanics working in distributors' garages.

Meantime the tests had satisfied most of Leyland's experts (but not Mr de Lassalle) that the worst potential and possibly fatal consequences of roller bearing failure could be mitigated by incorporating a larger diameter washer. With the above exception, all the experts before me agreed that the larger washer, while not preventing hub bearing failure, would prevent the wheel coming off and give a driver sufficient warning to enable him with luck to control or regain control of his car and so avoid the sort of disaster which befell the plaintiffs. This was the test conclusion expressed on October 2, 1974. 'The (larger) washer is effective in preventing the wheel from coming adrift when bearing failure occurs.' The decision

to incorporate the larger washer had been effective on Allegros since September 16: the Princess model was modified to provide this *ab initio*, and the Allegro dealers had been alerted.

It is, however, necessary to advert to the letter of September 16, 1974 from Mr Griffin, the chief engineer, advising Mr Perry and Mr King how to reply to Mr Barber's memorandum referred to above:

'Rear Hubs and Bearings
The design was introduced to satisfy performance demands at lower cost, and it is true to state that provided design requirements are adhered to no problem would be experienced. Unfortunately the design is not idiot proof and will therefore continuously involve risk. The risk becomes greater as vehicles become older and evermore carelessly maintained. *Had we incorporated the large washer from the commencement the risk would have been tolerable. . . .* Enginering have considered the possibility of recall action but do not favour it owing to the fact that it would *damage the product,* and historically the response is too low to guarantee fixing the problem and thereby remove our liability.'

('Damage the product' is agreed to be a euphemism for 'be bad for sales'.)

The extent to which the public at large was given any inkling of the true state of affairs was a television programme on October 14, 1974 having reference to a single case of a wheel 'becoming detached' and a press release next day which read 'We have had a small number of rear wheel bearing failures reported and the evidence shows that failure can be brought about by corrosion arising from water ingress and/or maladjustment during vehicle servicing. Action has already been taken to correct any irregularities in new vehicle production and any cases arising in service are being dealt with as necessary.'

This form of commercial camouflage of the true state of affairs was no doubt thought to be justified in the circumstances.

Meantime, on October 17, 1974 Engineering and Service were recommending that a recall campaign at a cost of £300,000 was not justified, that an intensive education campaign to 'franchise outlets' should be mounted and that authority should be given for fitting the larger washer when attention was being given to the rear hub or rear brake servicing. 'This should protect the customer against subsequent malpractice.'

I have thought it right to set out as briefly as I can, from such documents as I have seen, which are plainly incomplete, what information was available to Leyland about the appalling record of 'wheels adrift' on the Allegro, the problem as they saw it and the steps they took to try to remedy or palliate it, and considerations which seem to have influenced the course they took. I have done so because all these events occurred prior to November 1, 1974 when Mr Walton bought his car. I

Recent UK cases

now return to that car. It had not been fitted with the recommended washers before sale.

Mr Walton is a meticulous owner: he was, up to the purchase of the Allegro in question, a loyal customer of Leyland products. That he is no longer need occasion no surprise. He had owned a succession of Austin and other Leyland models. Apart from the dealer services, his cars have been serviced over the past 30 years, to his complete satisfaction, by the third defendants—Blue House—and still are. The driver's handbook was in the car at all material times. The Allegro he bought was a thoroughly bad car; it was in and out of Duttons throughout 1975 for various defects to be remedied and parts replaced under warranty: by way of example only, the clutch had to be replaced on no less than four occasions. Mr Walton was so dissatisfied with it that he tried in effect to get the year's warranty extended beyond 1975; Leyland authorised an examination by Duttons who reported only minor defects on November 24, 1975. The first trouble connected with the ultimate disaster occurred in January 1975 when Mr Walton noticed a noise in the *rear offside wheel* and took the car to Duttons. I am asked to infer and Duttons admit that on that occasion they fitted the larger washer when they replaced the bearing on the rear offside wheel only. The case against them proceeds on that basis. The mileage was 1,614.

The 6,000 mile service was carried out by Blue House on June 6, 1975 at a mileage of 5,014, and the 12,000 mile service on March 9, 1976 at a mileage of 11,906. At that service the brakes were attended to, the bearings adjusted on each side, and the wheels replaced. When the accident occurred without any warning on April 22, 1976 the mileage was 13,335, so that a distance of some 1,400 miles had been covered since the service; this includes five runs of about 150 miles each. I pass over for the moment the condition of the rear assembly when it was examined after the accident, in order to complete the sorry history of this car. It was repaired at a Bedford garage of a Leyland agent on a special Allegro jig and was collected by Mr Walton in July 1976 and driven back to Washington, a distance of about 200 miles. The next day he heard a grinding noise in the *rear offside wheel.* He was taking no chances and sent for a low loader from Blue House. On examination, the outer bearing was found to have collapsed but the larger washer was there and the wheel had not come off.

The car was examined by an experienced police vehicle examiner about an hour after the accident. The outer bearing had collapsed and the inner cone had been welded by excessive heat onto the stub axle. His view was that the basic cause of the bearing collapse was overtightening of the retaining nut exacerbated by lack of grease, although the destruction was such that there was nothing to point one way or another to overtightening or lack of grease by looking at the parts themselves. He agreed with other experts that there are other, though less likely, explanations of bearing collapse. He found nothing to indicate that the rear offside wheel, which was undamaged, had been overtightened.

The case against Duttons now is that they should have fitted the larger diameter washer to both hubs when the car was brought to them in January 1975 to attend to Mr Walton's complaint about the noise in the rear offside wheel. It was, it is said, common sense to have done so at a time when they had been alerted by Leyland to the risks of bearing collapse and the steps recommended to minimise the result of such failures. The allegation in the pleadings that Duttons should have fitted the new washer about October 1975 is not pursued, and that which claims that they should have done so before selling the car to Mr Walton seems to me quite unarguable since, apart from anything else, the washers were not available to dealers until November 4. It is common ground that the information available to Duttons when they worked on the wheel on January 15, 1975, was limited to that set out in the product bulletin of September 25, 1974 and the letter of October 24, to which I have already referred.

These documents were circulated by Leyland at a time when they were only too well aware of the 'wheel adrift' problem and its potential consequences in any given case. There is, in my view, no suggestion of the real gravity of the problem in either document. The letter of October 24 seems to me at the best ambiguous and at the worst misleading. How could any recipient realise the urgency of the problem when it was related, not to 100 cases of 'wheel adrift', but to a single case disclosed in a television programme?

I am impressed by the evidence that the product bulletin, with its reference to warranty claims for one and two sides replacement, would indicate to a dealer that one side could be dealt with alone if that, in a given case such as Mr Walton's, was all that was complained of. It is possible to construe the words in the letter, 'We recommend that you should fit this washer to each hub when attention is being given to the rear hub or rear brake servicing' as a recommendation to do both hubs at the same time as any work was required to either. But these are not legal documents and if in truth that was what Leyland intended by that passage in the letter, and I am far from satisfied it was, it would have been simplicity itself to say so in clear and unambiguous terms. I am satisfied that, in view of the information at their disposal on January 15, Duttons were fully entitled to limit the fitting of a new washer to the rear offside wheel, and I am glad to record that that was the view of Leyland's fairminded witness, Mr de Lassalle, who felt unable to criticise Duttons in any way for not attending to the nearside wheel. It follows in my judgment, that Duttons were blameless in this matter.

The remaining question is to what extent, if at all, responsibility for the accident should be shared between Leyland and Blue House.

Before I come to consider the position of Blue House

Walton v British Leyland

and the allegation that a mechanic at their garage negligently overtightened the retaining nut on the nearside, I set out part of the factual background which seems to me to be established:

(a) The wheel came off without warning because there was a bearing collapse and the original small diameter washer had not been changed.

(b) If the recommended larger washer had been fitted it is in the highest degree unlikely that the wheel would have come off.

(c) If the larger washer had been fitted the probability is that Mr Walton would have been able to control the car sufficiently so as to avoid the accident.

(d) The grease applied at the factory was considered to be good for 24,000 miles; checking the grease at the 12,000 service was a precaution, no more, and I think the evidence entirely fails to justify a conclusion that there was any failure to check the sufficiency of the grease at the 12,000 mile service.

(e) Possible causes of bearing collapse in addition to overtightening on adjustment and lack of lubrication are component failure, corrosion, hand brake left on.

(f) Generally the destruction in a case of bearing collapse is so extensive that it is impossible to establish its cause. This was so in the present case. Although all the experts, apart from Mr Matheson for the third party, favoured overtightening as the cause of the collapse in this case, none were prepared to exclude the possibility of another cause, such as component failure in a broad sense.

(g) The larger diameter washer was fitted by Duttons.

(h) There was no overtightening of the rear offside assembly at the time of the accident.

(i) Of 17 cases of bearing failure investigated by Leyland, seven occurred before the 12,000 mile service when there was no record of the hub having been touched. *Prima facie,* that points to a cause other than overtightening in those seven cases.

(j) No garage, apart from those of authorised dealers, received any information from Leyland as to the problem or the means of mitigating its potentially lethal results. In particular, no one at Blue House had any knowledge of the modification as to the larger washer or the importance of end float apart from the instructions in the handbook and workshop manual.

(k) The new method of adjustment to secure end float was a simple day to day job which presented no difficulty to a competent mechanic.

(l) No expert was able to advance any explanation of why it was that of all makes fitted with roller bearings, including in particular the Marina, only the Allegro appeared to have been subjected to overtightening by incompetent mechanics, assuming the theory accepted by Leyland to have been correct.

(m) Since the education programme and the standard fitting of the larger washer, it is said that there has been a fall in the incidence of 'wheel adrift' but no details were produced.

Mr Lawton accepts that Leyland had a 'deadly serious' problem on their hands, but he submits that, as a manufacturer, they were justified in concluding that there was no defect in the assembly and that they did all and more than could legally be required of them by introducing the modified washer, alerting their dealers in the way they did and conducting an education campaign in their dealers' garages. If Duttons are not to bear any share in the blame, he says, it is to be laid entirely at the door of Blue House, whose mechanic in all probability overtightened the nearside bearing when servicing the brakes on the 12,000 mile service. That would fit neatly with Leyland's theory, but I do not agree.

I have heard the evidence of Mr Ransome, the mechanic in question. He has been with Blue House for 14 years, having served his apprenticeship with the firm until he was 21, and was one of five mechanics of this standard at the time. I am sure he is a thoroughly competent mechanic. In a garage which deals with 20-30 vehicles a day, it cannot be expected that he has any detailed recollection, apart from referring to time sheets, as to what work he actually did to Mr Walton's car. He did not recall a larger washer being on one wheel and a smaller on the other; he thought he would have noticed the disparity and if he had, he thought it would have put him on his guard and he would have spoken to his foreman; the foreman might then have spoken to a dealer for an explanation. He was completely familiar with the difference between torque and end float and of the importance of achieving end float and carrying out the elementary final test to ensure it had been achieved. He knew nothing—nor did anyone else at Blue House— of the larger washer modification and its importance. Even if he did fail to notice the larger washer on one side it seems to me to put the duty of care far too high in the circumstances of this case to hold that had he done so, he should have appreciated that a difference in the size of washer on the two wheels signalled a warning which he ignored at the risk of the wheel coming off. I do not think he could possibly have foreseen such a risk. Although he, of course, conceded that he could have made a mistake with regard to end float, I find that it is highly improbable that he did; such evidence as there is from PC Warne, the vehicle examiner, indicates that the offside wheel which was dealt with at the same time was not overtightened. If Mr Ransome had seriously over-tightened the bearing in question by mistake by applying torque tightening, it seems to me that Mr Walton would have noticed the burning smell of over-heating before completing 1,400 miles, and that in any event the bearing would have probably failed before that mileage had been completed. These (*inter alia*) are matters, I think, which are contra-indicators that overtightening occurred at the Blue House Garage. There is, in my view, no compelling evidence that it was overtightening that caused the bearing collapse in the present case. It is no more than speculation in favour of one theory where other possibilities cannot be excluded, and I decline to hold that it was overtightening which caused the bearing to collapse.

Recent UK cases

What then of Leyland's responsibility in the matter? In my judgment, it is total. It is not being wise after the event to state that had the larger washer been fitted to Mr Walton's car the accident would, in all probability, not have happened. Over a period of about a year, until October 1974, Leyland were faced with mounting and horrifying evidence of Allegro wheels coming adrift. Any of the cases reported to them could have had fatal results for the occupants of the cars concerned and other road users. They assumed rightly or wrongly, that apart from isolated cases of corrosion, human error on the part of mechanics was the cause of the bearing failures. The deputy chairman was gravely disturbed; the view of the chief engineer by September 16, 1974 was that the design, not being 'idiot proof', would continuously involve risk, a risk which he thought would have been tolerable had the larger washer been fitted from the start.

From that date, therefore, if not before, the engineering section considered the risk to those who were driving Allegros which had not been fitted with the larger washers on both rear hub assemblies of their wheels coming adrift to be 'intolerable'. What, in such circumstances, is the standard of care towards users of their products to be expected of a manufacturer in the position of Leyland? They were entirely satisfied that the large washer provided a safety factor which could confidently be expected, following stringent tests, to prevent a wheel coming adrift if the bearing failed. All cars manufactured after September 16, 1974 were fitted with the approved safety device. Some steps, in my view totally inadequate, were taken to give instructions on the lines of what Dutton Forshaw were recommended to do but only to dealers. Outside this limited safety net were left, in ignorance of the risk to which Leyland knew they were subject, a very large number of Allegro owners, including Mr Walton and his passengers. In my view, the duty of care owed by Leyland to the public was to make a clean breast of the problem and recall all cars which they could, in order that the safety washers could be fitted. I accept, of course, that manufacturers have to steer a course between alarming the public unnecessarily and so damaging the reputation of their products, and observing their duty of care towards those whom they are in a position to protect from dangers of which they and they alone are aware. The duty seems to me to be the higher when they can palliate the worst effects of a failure which, if Leyland's view is right, they could never decisively guard against. They knew the full facts; they saw to it that no one else did. They seriously considered recall and made an estimate of the cost at a figure which seems to me to have been in no way out of proportion to the risks involved. It was decided not to follow this course for commercial reasons. I think this involved a failure to observe their duty to care for the safety of the many who were bound to remain at risk, irrespective of the recommendations made to Leyland dealers and to them alone.

. . . . .

It was, in my view, their duty to ensure that all cars still in stock and unsold by the time the washer palliative was proven were fitted with this safety feature before sale. It is sufficient for Mr Walton's purposes that the duty is put no higher than that. This would have saved Mr Walton and his passengers and, in my judgment, Leyland were negligent in having failed to do so.

Shirley Wallin, the widow of John David Wallin, brought an action against the manufacturers, Tretol Ltd, only. There was no other party to that action.

The issues joined between Tretol Ltd and their insurers in the Portsmouth action apply equally to the other two actions. The Wallin action has therefore been tried, and in that trial I directed that the issues between Tretol Ltd and the insurers should be tried in the Wallin action. I should add that any issues between Tretol Ltd and JD Wallin Ltd, for whom Mr Beldam appeared, were compromised during the course of the present trial and Mr Beldam disappeared. The judgment then in this, the Wallin, action—now the Matthews action because she has remarried—will determine the liability as between JD Wallin Ltd and Tretol Ltd in all three actions. It will also determine the liability as between Tretol Ltd and their insurers.

With that introduction I come to commence the judgment in the Wallin action against Tretol Ltd. As I said earlier, Mrs Wallin has, since action brought, married a gentleman called Matthews, so the present title of the action is now *Matthews v Tretol.*

There are many matters of fact which are common ground and I begin with a recital of these agreed or undisputed facts. Tretoplast was manufactured by Tretol and sold to JD Wallin Ltd. It is plastic paint. It is intended to be applied to walls by spraying the paint under great pressure by means of an airless gun or gun spray. By this method only the actual substance is sprayed. Tretoplast consisted of about 63% solvent and 37% plastic. The plastic element eventually finds itself on the wall like paint, but it is, in fact, a film of plastic which remains on the wall after spraying. The solution of solvent and plastic ceases to be so on spraying on to the wall because the solvent vaporises, while the plastic—hitherto in solution with the solvent—sticks to the wall.

The solvent vaporised is highly toxic. This was soon recognised, once Tretoplast was first used. Masks were therefore worn during the application. Air is fed to the masks by means of an air line attached to a compressor. If the vapour is inhaled a feeling of drunkenness develops fairly rapidly, depending of course on the degree of vapour in the atmosphere. Masks were worn by those applying the Tretoplast prior to the explosion, including Mr Wallin. No point arises on the masks.

The vapour mixed with the atmosphere is extremely dangerous. If vapour reaches a certain density in the atmosphere—that is air—and a source of ignition is introduced into the mixture of air and vapour from the solvent, there will be a violent explosion and fire, as happened in this case. This explosive mixture should therefore be avoided, and in any event the greatest caution is necessary to avoid and indeed to eliminate, all possible sources of ignition. Potential sources of ignition are numerous.

. . . . .

Wisdom therefore dictates that all equipment used in the vicinity of the spraying should be flameproof, which term includes not only flame but sparks and heat. Even the clothing worn by those applying the paint should not consist of nylon, which can generate electricity. Boots should not be capable of producing any spark. If they did, they could become a source of ignition.

At no material time could Tretoplast be purchased by the public at large. The product was sold only to companies or firms who were approved by the manufacturers, Tretol Ltd. These companies or firms, of whom JD Wallin Ltd was one, were termed 'applicators'. If a customer was desirous of using Tretoplast on his premises, Tretol would submit a list of three firms to the potential customer, who would then make his choice on the prices submitted by the respective firms, who would buy the Tretoplast, if they got the contract, from Tretol. The suppliers of the Tretoplast, Tretol Ltd, had the usual commercial organisation, including a Technical Services Director, Mr Singleton, and of course sales representatives. Tretol at all material times maintained contact with the applicator firms, including visiting sites of operation, but the actual operations at the sites were controlled by the applicators themselves. The application of Tretoplast demands skill, and Tretol took it upon themselves to give courses of instruction to the applicator firms. Mr Wallin was an enthusiast as regards the use of Tretoplast and its application, and his liaison with the defendants, particularly Mr Singleton, was a close one. On the evidence it would seem, and I so find, that Mr Wallin was possibly the most able and dedicated of the applicators.

Tretoplast in its solidified and settled form on the walls of a building is smooth, as one would expect, for it becomes a film without ridges on the walls. Having no ridges, it has the quality of resisting deposits, so it is especially suitable for premises such as hospitals where the highest standards of hygiene would wish to be attained.

Before Tretoplast is sprayed on the fabric of a building, such as the recovery ward of the Colchester Hospital, a great deal of preparatory work is essential. If Tretoplast is sprayed without discrimination, areas not intended for the product would also be sprayed. The preparation includes the screening or masking of those areas not intended to be sprayed.

. . . . .

It will be obvious from what I have found earlier that Tretoplast, containing as it does 63% solvent, is an inflammable liquid. The modern term, I am told by the experts, is 'flammable', but this change in fashion and designation is of no materiality. Tretol affixed certain warnings to their Tretoplast products in the form of labels.

. . . . .

I found earlier that the solvent vapour is noxious and masks have to be worn by the applicators. The vapour has a distinct, obnoxious smell so anyone in the general

1979 *Matthews v Tretol and JD Wallin*

COMMENTARY

This case provides a clear illustration of the scope of the manufacturer's duty to warn. This decision makes it clear that the manufacturer's duty to his neighbour as defined in *Donoghue v Stevenson* extends to a duty to take into account everyone who may be affected by his product including those who sell, install or, as in this case, apply it.

Indeed, the fact that such a duty existed at common law was clearly recognised by all the parties to the action including the defendants, who were respectively the manufacturers of a plastic paint intended to be applied by spraying at pressure, and the subcontractors to whom the product was supplied for application. It was also conceded for the defendants, that if the product was dangerous, they had a duty to warn the applicators of the product. The plaintiffs were the personal representatives of three men killed by an explosion and fire which occurred while the paint spraying process was being used. The case turned on whether this common law duty of care had in fact been discharged by the defendants.

The evidence was that the manufacturers took significant steps to train applicators in the use of their product. Courses were run, when various hazards in the application of the paint were discussed. However, it was clear from the evidence brought forward, as the trial judge found, that the precise danger which caused the disastrous explosion was never explained to the applicators, nor was this particular hazard identified in the warning labels which the defendants applied to the paint.

Presumably, had the warnings given by the defendants been sufficient, the case might have failed either on the basis of *Crow v Barford* (the defect in the product being apparent to the plaintiff), or damages might have been reduced by contributory negligence of the applicator. As it was, the court was able to decide the case fell fairly and squarely within the parameters of *Donoghue*, and awarded damages against the defendants accordingly.

It is at this point that a further feature of interest arose in this case concerning insurance. The manufacturers, Tretol, had public and product liability insurance cover, and in third party proceedings the defendants had brought in their insurers, Guardian Royal Exchange. The public liability section of the policy excluded injuries arising from goods which had ceased to be in the insured's custody or under his control. The paint which had caused the action had been sold to the subcontractors at the time of the action, and this exclusion from the policy was therefore held to be applicable. Further, the first defendants were not indemnified by their product liability policy either, as this excluded injury arising from 'the design plan formula or specification of the goods (*ie*

Tretoplast) instruction advice characteristics use storage or a

The decision thus underline importance of manufacturers e fully discharged their duty to war ......gerous aspects of their products, but alsc ...e need to consider carefully the terms of their relevant insurance policies.

JUDGMENT

Queen's Bench Division
June 28, 1979

*Matthews
versus
Tretol Limited and JD Wallin Limited*

Before Mr Justice Caulfield

Mr Justice Caulfield. On June 21, 1973 three men were engaged in spraying a product called Tretoplast, a plastic paint, to part of the Military Hospital at Colchester called the recovery ward. During the activity needed for the spraying, a fierce explosion and fire occurred, killing all three men. The three men were John David Wallin, David Hannen and Peter Portsmouth. Hannen and Portsmouth were employed by JD Wallin Ltd, which company had the contract to spray with Tretoplast the recovery ward. Tretoplast was produced by a company called Tretol Ltd, which company sold the Tretoplast to JD Wallin Ltd for the particular contract at the hospital. John David Wallin, although engaged in spraying, was not an employee of JD Wallin Ltd; he was the virtual proprietor of that company and was in effect his own master. Three separate actions were commenced under the Fatal Accidents Act on behalf of the respective dependants of the three men killed.

In the case of David Hannen, his personal representatives sued JD Wallin Ltd, the employers of Hannen, and Tretol Ltd, the manufacturers of Tretoplast. The two defendants to this action, recognising that the plaintiffs must succeed against one or other or both the defendants, have agreed that the liability to meet the Hannen claim will be determined in the action I hereafter mention.

The Portsmouth action was against JD Wallin Ltd and Tretol Ltd and that action has been compromised, but JD Wallin's responsibility to meet that claim will be determined in the action I said I would mention later. In the Portsmouth action Tretol Ltd, the second defendants, served a third party notice on their insurers as regards certain risks said to be covered by a policy of insurance. These insurers are the Guardian Royal Exchange. Tretol Ltd claim over against their insurers in the event of their being held liable to the plaintiff, the widow Mrs Portsmouth.

Matthews v Tretol

vicinity can be affected. This feature was well-known to the defendants and, of course, to Mr Wallin.

. . . . .

Ventilation as such was of importance for the reasons I have given, and it is argued for the defendants that, on the evidence, ventilation was stressed by the defendants to their applicators. The question arises as to the reasons advanced by the defendants for their alleged stressing of the need for ventilation. Did the defendants explain all the reasons for good ventilation, including the risks of an explosive atmosphere being created?

. . . . .

Evidence has come from the defendants through Mr Singleton that Mr Wallin was well aware of the need for good ventilation and had borrowed a Lamb air mover for a contract carried out by Mr Wallin at the Hammersmith Hospital. I accept Mr Singleton's evidence that such an air mover was borrowed by Mr Wallin, but the inference from the evidence that the reason for good ventilation was also known to Mr Wallin I shall cover later in my judgment.

There is no doubt, and I so find, that the defendants went to some trouble to teach or train their applicators and I am coming now to the main issues in the case, one of which is: assuming there is a duty at common law on the defendants to warn the applicators of any dangers of the product Tretoplast, has it been shown that there has been a breach by the defendants of that duty? I shall deal first with the question of duty.

I have no doubt on the evidence that the applicators and the defendants were the closest of neighbours, using that word in the sense in which Lord Atkin used it, though in the singular, in *Donoghue v Stevenson.* The relationship was indeed as close as one can get commercially. The defendants very properly wanted their product used and used successfully. The defendants looked to their applicators for success in the use of their product. The defendants wanted skilled applicators and were anxious to ensure that their applicators were successful. From this relationship I find there was a duty at common law on the defendants to use reasonable care towards the applicators in the use by the applicators of the product. Mr Thomas (*counsel*) virtually conceded this, including in his argument the submission that there was a duty on the manufacturers, if their product was dangerous, to warn the applicators. Mr Thomas' submission was more concerned with showing that no breach of duty had been established. I proceed on the basis not in the exact terms as Mr Thomas. I find that there was a duty on the manufacturers to take reasonable care towards the applicators, including Mr Wallin. That is the quality of the duty. Whether that duty towards Mr Wallin has been breached depends on the particular facts of this case. Expressing the duty as a duty to warn of dangers is, I take it, just another way of saying that the duty of care on the defendants included the duty to warn Mr Wallin of any danger in the use and storage of the product of which he would be ignorant.

This case is mainly concerned with the question; has the plaintiff established a breach by the defendants of the duty to take reasonable care towards Mr Wallin?

I spoke earlier of the close relationship between the applicators in general and Mr Wallin in particular. Mr Wallin and the defendants had a common interest. Wallin's success was shared by the defendants. I find, though it is not disputed, that the defendants did go to some lengths to give instructions and guidance to Mr Wallin and other applicators, and the real question in this case is whether the plaintiff has proved that the instructions and guidance given by the defendants did not reach that standard demanded by the duty to take reasonable care. I come now to review, though not in detail, the evidence on this main issue.

The defendants' organisation includes the provision of a course for applicators and the dissemination of information by either distributing information sheets or the imparting of information contained in those sheets, when those sheets have not been distributed. A course was organised for applicators, including Mr Wallin, from Monday, May 13 to Thursday, May 16, 1968. Witnesses have been called who attended that course, and Mr Singleton, the Technical Services Director who organised the training, gave evidence for the defendants. Certain other witnesses for the defendants relative to the course were Mr Austin, now a Sales Director, and Mr Geldard, now the defendants' Sales Manager. The witnesses called by the plaintiff on this point of instruction all said that, though ventilation was an item for discussion on the course and was discussed, such discussion as there was was in relation to the breathing difficulties being experienced and there was no warning of the risk of an explosive fire. All said that they were unaware that even a spark could cause an explosive fire of the vapour spray.

. . . . .

For the defence, through Mr Singleton, Mr Geldard and Mr Austin, a different version is given. Mr Singleton is, I have no doubt, an expert in airless pumps of the type used by Mr Wallin. He has great respect for Mr Wallin as a man and as a worker. Indeed, he describes Mr Wallin as 'most expert'. 'The information sheets then in existence', Mr Singleton said, 'were distributed on the course, and subsequent sheets were dispatched to the applicator firms. If the information sheets were not distributed, then the information in them was given to those attending. Ventilation was a subject discussed time and time again. The applicators' problems on ventilation, for every site was different, were discussed. Breathing apparatus was discussed, but not a lot of time was spent on masking. The problem of ventilation really came with the use of the airless spray.'

. . . . .

Then he was interrupted in his evidence because of the pattern in which the case developed and a day or so later he resumed his evidence in these terms: 'I knew that under certain circumstances fire risks and an explosive

Recent UK cases

risk due to bad ventilation and a source of ignition existed. I advised in general terms that ventilation was required. I knew of the quality of the product as soon as I joined the company, though I am not concerned with the formula of the particular product; my problem was concerned with the application of this product. We knew that the highly flammable solvents were the dangerous part in the materials and we did not need to know the exact proportions.' That was his evidence. Later, towards the end of his evidence, he expressed real horror and surprise at what had happened in Colchester. He went on to assert that he had explained the meaning of flameproof equipment and all sources of ignition.

Mr Austin and Mr Geldard both said that the safety aspect of ventilation was explained in the courses, as were other matters like clothing and flameproof equipment. This evidence, which the defendants contend should be accepted, points to knowledge of the dangers in the use of the product on the part of Mr Wallin and that therefore there has been no breach of duty shown, and in particular the danger in the use of halogen lamps was expressly raised. I make my findings later.

The balance of the evidence in the case includes evidence from two distinguished fire experts: Dr Napier for the plaintiff and Mr Taylor for the defendants. There is really only one point of importance upon which these experts differ. Dr Napier does not accept that the problem of ventilation at Colchester is relatively simple; Mr Taylor thinks it was, explaining that a Beck air remover of a certain dimension, possibly two or three inches, could have been positioned easily, with of course suitable openings made in the masking to enable that system of ventilation to be used.

. . . . .

Both experts are agreed that the conditions at Colchester, given a source of ignition, were ideal for disastrous explosive fire. Mr Taylor thinks the first fire took place in the vestibule and not in the room which was being sprayed. He thought from the photographs that there did not appear to have been an explosive effect in the recovery ward because the windows in photograph eight, which shows the windows in the recovery ward, were not cracked or broken.

The rest of the evidence can be briefly highlighted. Mr Shand, of the Department of the Environment, said there was no arrangement to close down that part of the hospital of which the recovery ward was part. The screen, erected by direct labour, he thought, was erected to stop fumes penetrating into the operating theatre. The job was small and JD Wallin Ltd were nominated as sub-contractors.

Detective Constable Walton, who took the photographs and gave his evidence solely on recollection, thought he found the halogen lamps in the sluice area close to the door of the recovery ward and he found an electric kettle in the sluice room.

Mr Langley, a superintendent chemical inspector,

explained the applicability of the regulations which applied, so it happened, only from the day of this disaster, and he gave an opinion that unless Mr Wallin was a newcomer he would be aware—that is Mr Wallin would be aware—of the risks involved in the use of Tretoplast.

Mr Richardson, an assistant divisional fire officer, who was called with his men to the fire, found Mr Portsmouth, who was one of the men working there, in the position shown on the plan. When he found him, Mr Portsmouth was not wearing a mask. The refrigerator shown in the plan was operating, and he saw the electric kettle on the other side of the partition just before the recovery ward. I have not in that review of evidence obviously included every word of evidence but highlighted certain of the main features of the evidence.

I come now to my findings—

(1) I accept from the evidence of Mr Taylor that the explosive fire originated in the room marked 'vestibule'. Mr Taylor's reasoning appears sound. This finding is not a fundamental one in view of my later findings.

(2) At the time of the explosive fire in the vestibule, which rapidly engulfed the recovery ward, there had built up an explosive fire atmosphere in the vestibule and the recovery ward, because of the vaporisation of the solvent mixed with such amount of air that the introduction of a source of ignition caused the explosive fire.

(3) I cannot find that the evidence points to one particular source of ignition. The halogen lamps are the favourite, but the electric kettle and indeed the refrigerator are other candidates. There were many other sources of ignition, as Mr Taylor asserted, and this evidence from him I accept. The source could have been one of many.

(4) The product could be most dangerous when sprayed in a room virtually unventilated. The danger is now obvious. When the right mixture of vapour and air exists and a source of ignition is introduced an explosive fire will definitely occur. The liquid had other dangers which had to be guarded against, for example in storage. The labels affixed to the product suggest some. The defendants were well aware of all these properties of the product.

(5) This product was used invariably on the inside of premises. The defendants fully understood this.

(6) Masking of windows was an essential part of the preparation of a room before spraying. The defendants knew this; indeed they included masking on their course.

(7) JD Wallin Ltd, as applicators, were frequently subcontractors as regards spraying contracts and generally speaking did not have exclusive occupation of their sites of operations. The defendants knew this. I accept from the plaintiff's witnesses that the defendants' representatives frequently called at the sites and saw the conditions under which Mr Wallin worked.

Matthews v Tretol

(8) I accept the evidence of those who attended the course—White, Wastell, Yeadon and Murphy—as to what dangers were explained. It follows that the precise danger which caused this disaster was not explained to them. Indeed, if it had been, I am sure they would never have forgotten it and their enthusiasm would have been dampened, if not wholly extinguished. They were good ordinary working men and, though all were intelligent, I am perfectly satisfied they were wholly ignorant of the danger of explosive fire and wholly ignorant, apart from a naked flame, of the dangers of sources of ignition.

(9) My last finding does not specifically refer to Mr Wallin, but, while I am satisfied Mr Wallin was an expert sprayer and an enthusiast for Tretoplast, he too was not warned by the defendants of the precise danger which existed when Tretoplast was being applied and his own natural knowledge would not cater for this omission.

(10) The labels affixed by the defendants to their products did not warn the applicators of the dangers of an explosive fire. They warned of some dangers but did not give warning, in my judgment, of the precise danger to which the applicators were exposed at Colchester.

(11) I do not accept the evidence of Mr Singleton that he warned Mr Wallin about the precise danger involved in using halogen lamps. The danger in using halogen lamps was that the surface area of those lamps, which could reach a very high temperature, as I said earlier, could be a source of ignition in a solvent charged atmosphere. I do not accept that a warning in these terms was given. From all I have heard of Mr Wallin 'of his enthusiasm and his caution' I am satisfied that if he had been given a warning not to use halogen lamps in the context of safety he would not have done so.

(12) My previous findings I find fortified by the caution shown by the defendants after the Colchester disaster. The defendants' documents and the terms of those documents show how very easy it would have been to spell out the dangers of using Tretoplast and the dangers of sources of ignition and heavily charged atmospheres with vapour.

(13) All three men were killed, I am satisfied, working in a dangerously charged atmosphere which they did not know was so dangerously charged and, further, that they did not, apart from a naked flame, appreciate the possible sources of ignition.

(14) I do not accept Mr Taylor's evidence that the question of ventilation was really a simple operation. Obviously I accept from him, and there is no dispute about it, the evidence about the efficacy of the air movers, one of which he very kindly brought to court—a very small object which could virtually fit in the pocket. Mr Taylor's version regarding ventilation is based of course upon certain openings in the masks of the windows and, as I have found earlier that masking was a necessary part of the operation, Mr Wallin was doing something which was part of a system which was approved by the defendants and Mr Taylor's idea of ventilation would not have corresponded with the method of work in the recovery ward.

The final question is to determine whether the duty of reasonable care which I find was owed by the defendants to Mr Wallin was breached. This last question occasions me no difficulty. In my judgment the duty of reasonable care demanded that the defendants should have explained, in simple terms, to Mr Wallin that not only was the vapour heavy and flammable, but that certain concentrations of the vapour in a room could produce an atmosphere which was such that, if a source of ignition was introduced, an explosive fire would occur with the most serious consequence, possibly of death. Further, possible sources of ignition should have been not only identified, but their significance explained. Mr Wallin was not, in the language of Dr Napier, a combustion specialist.

For these reasons I find Mr Wallin was ignorant of the precise dangers that occurred at Colchester. Mr Wallin knew the liquid had a low flashpoint, that it was flammable, that the vapour was heavy; but he did not know that in a given situation with virtually no ventilation an explosive fire could occur from certain sources of ignition.

I therefore find the defendants negligent and on my findings I cannot see that there is room, though this was argued, for a finding that Mr Wallin was himself negligent. As I see it, Mr Wallin should only be found guilty of negligence if, knowing the danger, he ran the risk of exposing himself to that danger. On my findings Mr Wallin did not, because he was left ignorant of the precise danger. Accordingly the plaintiff is entitled to succeed, and succeed wholly, against the defendants.

On the question of damages, the widow has remarried, but remarriage does not affect the damages. The child of Mr and Mrs Wallin has been adopted by Mrs Matthews, the former Mrs Wallin, and her husband Mr Matthews. I must therefore, in my assessment of damages, allow for the fact of this adoption in accordance with the principle explained in *Thompson v Price* [1973] 1 QB 838. This allowance must date from the date of remarriage, which was June 26, 1976 so that the dependency of the child of Mr and Mrs Wallin is between the date of death, June 21, 1973 and June 23, 1976, approximately three years. The deceased at his death was 38. His wife was 27; she is now 33. The deceased's earnings in 1971 were £1,570. Virtually no tax would be payable. In 1972 his earnings had risen to £1,750, while in 1973 he reached his highest income of £5,110, upon which he would pay approximately £1,138 tax. The average is about £2,776, but I do not think in this case it would be right to conclude that the dependency should be based on the average for the three years. By the time of his death the deceased was clearly on the upgrade, assuming Tretoplast continued to be in demand and there was no recession. Sooner or later I am satisfied that the Tretoplast boom, as regards

Recent UK cases

Mr Wallin's operations, would not have continued. Sooner or later some disaster such as this which occurred at Colchester would have occurred, which would have halted, though possibly temporarily, Mr Wallin's prosperity. There has of course been a change in the composition of Tretoplast. In fairness to the defendants, this was only discovered well after the disaster. It is now a product which does not have the dangers which I have explained in this judgment.

Further, there was, which is notorious, a recession in all the building trades from 1973 and the deceased's company, which had no great assets, would have found it difficult to survive, though from all the compliments paid to Mr Wallin I am satisfied his company would have survived, though without any growth during the lean years. The company was essentially Mr Wallin himself and, although he was a man of enthusiasm and ability, his income, I am satisfied, was basically limited to his own efforts, great though they were.

Mrs Wallin, now Mrs Matthews, is earning £40 per week from a company partially owned by her husband. She has sold the former matrimonial home to assist her husband's present operations.

I must take into account inflation since 1973. Taking into account the husband's age at death, his future prospects, the difficulties of recession, his dependence on the uncertain Tretoplast, the limitations in growth of his company, and of course taking into account the evidence of Mrs Matthews who explained to me how she was provided for by her husband, I find the dependency between the date of death and today to be £21,000. The dependency as from today I assess at a total of £45,000, so the total dependency I assess at £66,000. In fairness to the submissions which have been made both by Mr Pratt and Mr Thomas, I have not made any deduction and therefore have not taken into account the proceeds of sale of the matrimonial home.
. . . . .

There will of course be judgment accordingly, but I would ask all learned counsel to show a little patience, and I proceed to judgment in the third party proceedings, at the end of which I will invite submissions on the orders to be made.

I now turn to the judgment in the third party proceedings between Tretol and Guardian Royal Exchange. I repeat my finding, and I state simply and shortly that I have found in the main action that the plaintiff is entitled to succeed against Tretol because Tretol were in breach of the duty to take reasonable care. Reasonable care, I held, demanded that Tretol should have warned Mr Wallin and others of the dangers inherent in the application of Tretoplast.

I make another finding of fact, that the product Tretoplast behaved in a way in which it was known it would behave. When I say 'known', known by the manufacturers, given certain conditions. Because of the percentage of solvent purposely and purposefully put into the composition and because of the intentional and purposeful evaporation of the solvent in application of the fluid Tretoplast a concentration of vapour with air could and did develop from which, when a source of ignition was introduced to it, an explosive fire would occur. This was no surprise to Tretol and Tretoplast did not show a vice which was unintended or unknown. The product behaved as it was expected it would behave, given certain conditions. This finding, although undisputed, is taken from the evidence of the experts, from that of Mr Singleton and the factory inspector.

By a policy of insurance covering the period July 1, 1972 to June 30, 1973 the insurers, the Guardian Royal Exchange, agreed in respect of public liability as follows: 'The Company'—that is the insurers—'will subject to the terms of and endorsements to this Section and the conditions of this Policy indemnify the Insured against all sums which the Insured becomes legally liable to pay as damages in respect of bodily injury (including death . . .) to any person . . . happening within the Geographical Limits during the Period of Insurance in connection with the Business'. There were exceptions to this broad indemnity, in particular exception 1(d)(ii) in section A, which read as follows: 'The Company will not indemnify the Insured against liability arising from bodily injury . . . or damage . . . arising from any goods whether or not described in the Schedule (after they have ceased to be in the custody or under the control of the Insured) sold supplied repaired altered treated or installed other than food or drink for consumption on the Insured's premises'.

My first finding I do not find difficult, for it is one of construction. Plainly on the facts here the 'goods' means Tretoplast. These goods had ceased to be in the custody of or under the control of the defendants, Tretol, and the goods had been sold to Mr Wallin. Accordingly, I find the exception to which I have referred applied and the insured are not entitled to any indemnity in respect of the public liability section of this policy, even though the legal liability of the defendants, which I have found existed, happened in connection with the insured's business. The legal liability in the terms of the exception arose from goods which had ceased to be in the custody of or under the control of the defendants. Such goods have been sold and are no longer under the power of the defendants.

The same policy afforded an indemnity to the defendants under the heading 'Products Liability'. The terms of the policy, so far as they are material under this heading, read as follows: 'The Company will subject to the terms of and endorsements to this Section and the conditions of this Policy indemnify the Insured against all sums which the Insured becomes legally liable to pay as damages in respect of bodily injury (including death . . .) to any person . . . happening anywhere in the world during the Period of Insurance and caused by the Goods sold supplied repaired altered treated or installed from or in Great Britain Northern Ireland the Channel Islands and the Isle of Man in connection with the Business'.

Matthews v Tretol

I find that the damages that the defendants have been found legally liable to pay fall within the general terms of this indemnity. The liability was caused by the goods sold in connection with the business. There were, however, exceptions written into the policy. The relevant exceptions appear at page five of the policy, that is under section B and the relevant passages are identified by 1(e)(iii) and (iv) and, extracting what is relevant, it reads as follows: 'The Company will not indemnify the Insured against liability arising from . . . bodily injury . . . arising directly or indirectly from . . . the design plan formula or specification of the Goods instruction advice or information on the characteristics use storage or application of the Goods'.

Liability, Mr Thomas (*counsel*) argues, arises because of failure to warn and not because of the formula or specification of the goods, that is the Tretoplast. I do not accept Mr Thomas's argument. While recognising that the principles of construction of an exception mean that I should show caution once I have concluded that the general indemnity covers the legal liability—not only caution but there must be a very strict construction of the exception—I also think that the plain words are (1) that the words in 1(e)(iii) are perfectly plain and they should be given their ordinary meaning. This I have done and I think on the ordinary meaning of the exception it is to the effect that these goods, namely the Tretoplast, have a particular formula of 63% solvent—the balance of course was plastic—and the bodily injury which did occur arose directly from the particular formula.

Another part of the exception which I have already included in the judgment, but I repeat, is: 'The Company will not indemnify the insured against liability arising from . . . bodily injury . . . arising directly or indirectly from . . . instruction or advice or information on the characteristics use storage or application of the Goods'.

The main argument on construction addressed to me by Mr Thomas is that lack of instruction or failure to instruct are not included in the exception, and it is perfecty true that the word 'failure' does not appear in this exception. He argues that for this exception to apply legal liability must have arisen from positive instruction as distinct from a failure to instruct, or positive advice as distinct from a failure to advise, or positive information on the characteristics, use or application of the goods.

This main submission I do not accept. My finding in the main action is that the defendants failed to give such a warning regarding the characteristics and use of Tretoplast. I agree my finding is based on a failure to warn or instruct or advise. I find, as regards this exception, that the death of Mr Wallin was caused by the goods, but his death arose directly from the instruction, advice or information on the characteristics and use of the product. On a fair construction of this exception, if inadequate instruction is given and the bodily injury arises directly or indirectly from the inadequacy of the instruction, the exception, in my judgment, applies. If no instruction or advice is given,

when legal liability arises from total lack of instruction or advice the exception, in my judgment, would equally apply. I do not think I should include in the exception a word which is not there, such as 'positive'. Legal liability arising directly or indirectly from misleading positive instruction or advice, or total lack of instruction or advice, or inadequate instruction or advice, I would hold to be within the words of the exception. Accordingly I hold that the insurers are not liable to indemnify the defendants in respect of their legal liability to the plaintiff, Mrs Matthews.

There will be judgment both in the action and in the third party proceedings accordingly.

Recent UK cases

1980 *Castree v ER Squibb*

COMMENTARY

The decision in this case directed to the issue as to whether the English courts had jurisdiction in respect of the German manufacturer of a defective centrifuge machine which had disintegrated causing severe personal injuries to the plaintiff whilst using the machine in the course of employment in this country. The court confirmed that jurisdiction did exist here because the tort of negligence had not in fact occurred in Germany when the machine was manufactured but in this country, when it was put on the market by the manufacturer through its distributors without any warning as to its defects. In reaching this decision, the court highlighted again the fact that the wholesaler or distributor, as well as the manufacturer or retailer, also have a duty in tort to take care. Negligence in relation to a defective product does not arise only through its manufacture.

The retailer is of course in any event liable to the consumer for the quality of the products he is selling, and this liability is strict in the sense that he is now unable when selling to a consumer to exclude any of the implied terms as to quality and fitness, contained in the Sale of Goods Act 1979.[1] In *Godley v Perry* [1960] 1 WLR 9 the retailers' vulnerability in cases involving defective imported goods had been illustrated. Here a six year old boy had bought a plastic catapult from a newsagent. Three days later it broke when he was using it, and he lost an eye as a result. Under the Sale of Goods Act he was able to recover damages because the catapult was unmerchantable.

As long ago (in negligence terms) as 1937 [2], however, a court had also been prepared to find a retailer liable in negligence in a case involving a chemical labelled as manganese dioxide which was in fact another chemical, dangerous when heated. The manufacturer had warned that the chemical should be tested before use and had therefore not been negligent. However, the retailer had not carried out the test, had not passed the warning on, and was therefore himself liable in negligence. Similarly in *Fisher v Harrods Ltd,* [1966] 1 Lloyds Rep 500, the retailer had bought jewellery cleaner from a manufacturer and had failed to test or examine it. Had they done so, they would have established that the fluid was dangerous and its container unsuitable. They were therefore liable in negligence to pay damages for the injury caused when the fluid unexpectedly came out of the container and injured the consumer's eyes.

Finally it is worth noting that this liability throughout the distribution chain for the marketing of defective products is further underlined in the European proposals to amend the law on product liability. These provide that

[1] Unfair Contract Terms Act 1977.
[2] *Kinbach v Hollands* [1937] 3 All ER 907

the importer of a defective product from outside the EEC will be deemed to be the producer and thus strictly liable, as will the retailer in certain circumstances when he sells under his own brand name, or cannot identify the actual producer.

JUDGMENT

Court of Appeal, Civil Division
April 24, 1980

Castree
versus
ER Squibb & Sons Limited and another

Before Lord Justices Buckley, Ackner and Oliver

Lord Justice Ackner delivered the first judgment at the invitation of Lord Justice Buckley. This is an appeal by a third party (since that was its status under the order of Mr Justice Phillips) against a judgment of Mr Justice Phillips given on December 20, 1979, when he reversed a decision of the district registrar of November 7, 1979.

The appeal arises in these circumstances. The plaintiff, Miss Jayne Susan Castree, is suing for damages for personal injuries which she sustained in August 1976 when she was using a machine called a centrifuge for the purpose of separating liquids from solids. She was using that machine in the course of her employment with the defendants, who are the respondents to this appeal, and in the course of using that machine it disintegrated, causing her serious injuries. The machine was manufactured in Germany by the appellants, who are a private German company, and the machine was purchased in this country by the respondents. The respondents sought leave to issue and serve out of the jurisdiction under RSC Order II, a third party notice on the appellants. The basis on which they sought that leave has changed, but ultimately (I can put it as shortly as this) the position was that the respondents contended that the appellants were joint tortfeasors from whom they were entitled to claim contribution. They did not assert that she had any remedy against the appellants in contract, but they asserted that had the plaintiff sued the third party in negligence by way of a * *Donoghue v Stevenson* claim (see [1932] AC 562) they would have succeeded, and accordingly the basis of the application is that contained in RSC Order II, rule 1 (I)(*h*), namely that the action is founded on a tort committed in the jurisdiction.

The contention of counsel for the appellants, who has argued this case with characteristic skill, is quite simply that the tortious conduct, if there was any, of the appellants was all committed out of this country,

Castree v ER Squibb

namely, the defective design and manufacture of the machinery, and that all that happened in this country was that the plaintiff sustained her damage.

It is important at this stage to make this point in relation to the sale of the machinery in this country. The learned judge recites this in his judgment; it is alleged, and for the present purpose is to be taken as a fact, that the defendants purchased the equipment in this country from a firm acting as sole agents for the third party. The judge said: 'It does seem important to me that the third party has a distribution system as a result of which their goods are distributed in this country . . .' That assertion is essentially derived from the third party notice as originally served, in which it was alleged that 'The said centrifuge . . . was manufactured . . . and was purchased by the defendants in or about the month of November 1973 from (the appellants') United Kingdom agents'; and in the affidavit in support of the application to serve out of the jurisdiction 'the centrifuge was manufactured by the appellants and was purchased by the defendants from the manufacturers' United Kingdom agents in or about the month of November 1973'. That allegation was not controverted in the affidavit which was filed on behalf of the appellants in support of their application to set aside the order for service out of the jurisdiction.

In my judgment the learned judge rightly held that the relevant tort was committed partly within and partly without the jurisdiction, in that the product was distributed within, but manufactured outside, the jurisdiction. He then went on to consider an important authority, namely, *Distillers Co (Bio-Chemicals) Ltd v Thompson* [1971] AC 458. That was a case in which an English company, the manufacturers of a drug marketed under the name of Distaval, which contained the drug thalidomide, had sold the drug in Australia, as a result of which it was alleged that a woman who was pregnant suffered, as did the child to which she subsequently gave birth. She sought to sue Distillers in Australia on the basis that they committed the *Donoghue v Stevenson* form of negligence by virtue of their failure, when they sold the drug, to give a warning of its dangerous characteristic.

The learned judge cited various portions of the opinion of the Privy Council as given by Lord Pearson. He accepted that which counsel for the appellants says is the appropriate approach to this case (see [1971] AC 458 at 468): 'The right approach is, when the tort is complete, to look back over the series of events constituting it and ask the question: where in substance did this cause of action arise?'

The learned judge also relied on a number of other parts of the judgment of Lord Pearson: 'It is manifestly just and reasonable that a defendant should have to answer for his wrongdoing in the country where he did the wrong.' And in dealing with a suggested test, namely, the test where the last act of negligence occurred, he again quoted from the judgment of Lord Pearson: 'The last event might happen in a particular

case to be the determining factor on its own merits, by reason of its inherent importance, but not because it is the last event . . . But when the question is which country's courts should have jurisdiction to try the action, the approach would be different; the search is for the most appropriate court to try the action, and the degree of connection between the cause of action and the country concerned should be the determining factor.'

Counsel for the appellants relied heavily on a case in this court, the case of *George Monro Ltd v American Cyanamid and Chemical Corp* [1944] KB 432, and maintained that was authority for the proposition that where everything else had happened outside the jurisdiction with the exception of the actual suffering of the damage, then it was not a proper case for proceedings to be brought in this country. That was a case in which I think it can be properly said that the decision of the court was sufficiently founded on their view that the affidavit had not established that there had been any tort committed within the jurisdiction. That was the view of Wynn J when he considered that case in *Cordova Land Co Ltd v Victor Brothers Inc* [1966] 1 WLR 793.

But the fundamental point in *George Monro Ltd v American Cyanamid and Chemical Corp,* as it seems to me, is that not only had the negligent manufacture of the product taken place in America, but the goods which were the subject matter of the case were actually sold in America, so that the property passed in America. Thus everything which the company had done, against which complaint could be made, had occurred in America. There is however some assistance to be obtained from the judgment of du Parcq LJ, where he said ([1944] KB 432 at 440-441): ' . . . I am willing to infer that the negligence alleged is that the corporation put on the market a dangerous substance with written instructions to use it in a dangerous way. The act of commission was done in America and it is highly artificial to say that the tort was committed within the jurisdiction of the English courts. The principle of the rule is plain. Looking at the substance of the matter without regard to any technical consideration, the question is: Where was the wrongful act, from which the damage flows, in fact done?'

Returning to this case and bearing in mind that the application to sue the appellants in this country is based on the allegation that the plaintiff could successfully sue the appellants, one then asks oneself the question which was posed by du Parcq LJ, and the answer to that question seems to me to be clearly this: that which gave, or gives, the plaintiff her cause of complaint is not the mere manufacture of the defective machinery, which of course took place in Germany; the mere manufacture of the defective machinery is not in my judgment even the beginning of tort. That manufacture might have been manufacture for experimental purposes, or it might have been for the development of some part of the machinery. The substantial wrongdoing in this case alleged to have been committed by the appellants is putting on the

English market a defective machine with no warning as to its defects. That being, in my judgment, the position, and applying the test which is accepted on all sides to be the appropriate test, namely, to look back over the series of events constituting the tort and to ask the question where in substance this cause of action arose, I would conclude that it arose in this country.

Accordingly I would dismiss this appeal.

Lord Justice Oliver. I agree.

Lord Justice Buckley. I also agree and I do not think I can usefully add anything to what Lord Justice Ackner has said.

1981 *Lexmead v Lewis*

COMMENTARY

This highly complicated case, which reached the House of Lords on the issue of causation and the entitlement of an indemnity for damages awarded by a lower court, is interesting not only from the point of view of the particular points of law decided, but also as an illustration of a product liability action involving a number of different aspects.

The immediate cause of the tragic accident at the basis of this action was a trailer which slewed across the road having become detached from a Land Rover, and striking an on-coming car driven by the plaintiff's husband who was killed in the accident. The trial judge had found that the cause of the trailer becoming detached was a coupling which had failed due to a design defect. In addition, it was found that the farmer who owned the Land Rover and trailer had been negligent because he had noticed the defect but had continued to use the trailer on the road. Liability had therefore been apportioned at 75% against the manufacturer of the coupling and 25% against the farmer.

The farmer had in turn claimed against the supplier of the coupling who in turn claimed against the manufacturer. These claims had been dismissed by the trial judge, but on appeal by the farmer, the Court of Appeal allowed him an indemnity from the seller under the terms of the implied warranties in the Sale of Goods Act 1893. This aspect, and the supplier's claim against the manufacturer, formed the subject of the appeal to the House of Lords.

Lord Diplock expressed the principle involved in the farmer's appeal as follows: 'in what circumstances can a party A to a contract, who has been found liable for breach of a duty of care owed by him to a stranger X to the contract, recover from the other party B to the contract as damages for breach of warranty the amount of the damages for negligence which A himself has been ordered to pay X?' Their Lordships held that the extent of the supplier's liability in these circumstances depended on the terms of the warranty. In this case, the warranty was an implied one of fitness for the purpose under the terms of the Sale of Goods Act, which was held to be a continuing warranty up until the time a short period before the accident when the farmer should have noticed that part of the coupling was missing. At that point, the court held, he should have taken some action to have the problem dealt with. Failure to do so meant that his claim for an indemnity failed. In addition, the Lords held that his own negligence had broken the chain of causation between the seller's breach of contract and the farmer's liability in negligence to the plaintiff.

On the appeal relating to the fourth party proceedings, *ie* by the seller against the manufacturer, this did of course now fail as the Lords had said that the seller was not under a duty to indemnify the farmer for his liability,

Lexmead v Lewis

the damages arising from his negligence. However, in the earlier proceedings there had been a point of considerable interest here, as the seller had no direct contractual relationship with the manufacturer. The offending coupling had been purchased through a wholesaler and no record had been kept of the transaction.

The Court of Appeal had ruled however that the manufacturers were not liable to the seller in negligence because the loss suffered by him was purely economic and too remote. Stephenson LJ had observed that 'There comes a point where the logical extension of the boundaries of duty and damage is halted by the barrier of commercial sense and practical convenience'. In commenting on this argument, Lord Diplock remarked that 'While in the absence of argument it could not be right to express any final view, I should not wish the dismissal of the dealer's appeal to be regarded as an approval by this House of the proposition that where economic loss suffered by a distributor in the chain between the manufacturer and the ultimate consumer consists of a liability to pay damages to the ultimate consumer for physical injuries sustained by him or consists of a liability to pay damages to the ultimate consumer for damages for physical injuries, such economic loss is not recoverable under the *Donoghue v Stevenson* principle from the manufacturer'. It is interesting to speculate whether this aspect of the case might have pre-empted the *Junior Books* decision by a couple of years had the Lords been required to deliver a judgment on this point.

Another interesting aspect of the Lords judgment was that of the concept of the continuing nature of the implied warranty of fitness for purpose[1]. This seems to contradict the assumption held, amongst others by the Law Commission[2], that the implied terms of merchantability and fitness for purpose apply at the time of sale, and that there is no implication of reasonable durability. Again, this point did not affect the case under consideration, but it will be interesting to see if it is picked up and applied in future cases.

[1] See article by M J Leder, *'Lambert v Lewis—A Hitch in the Chain of Causation' Law Society Gazette,* May 27, 1981.

[2] Law Commission Report (No 95), 'Implied Terms in Contracts for the Supply of Goods'.

JUDGMENT

House of Lords
April 8, 1981

Lexmead (Basingstoke) Limited
versus
Lewis and others

Before Lord Diplock, Lord Elwyn-Jones, Lord Fraser of Tullybelton, Lord Scarman and Lord Bridge of Harwich

Lord Diplock. My Lords, this appeal arises out of a traffic accident, with tragic consequences, which took place as long ago as September 1972. A trailer carrying rubble became detached from a Land Rover belonging to the appellant ('the farmer') which was being driven by his servant along a road in Farnborough. The trailer careered across the road and hit a car coming in the opposite direction. In it were the plaintiff, her husband who was driving, and their two children. Her husband and son were killed; the plaintiff and her daughter suffered relatively minor injuries. It has never been suggested that the husband was in any way to blame for the accident.

The plaintiff, acting on behalf of herself and as next friend of her daughter, and also as administratrix of the estates of her husband and her son, brought an action for damages against the farmer and also the driver of the Land Rover. (There is no need for any further mention of the latter.) She subsequently joined as additional defendants, the appellants to this appeal ('the dealers'), who had sold the trailer coupling to the farmer and fitted it on the Land Rover, and the second respondents to this appeal ('the manufacturers') who had manufactured the coupling. The farmer brought third party proceedings against the dealers and the dealers in turn brought fourth party proceedings against the manufacturers. The appeal to your Lordships House is brought in these third and fourth party proceedings alone.

Damages had been agreed at £45,000 before the action eventually came on for trial before Mr Justice Stocker in October 1977. The only issue was as to how the liability for the agreed damages should be allocated between the various defendants. The hearing lasted ten days, much of the time being spent on expert engineering evidence about the design and manufacture of the coupling and the cause of its having become detached at the time of the accident.

The clear and careful judgment of Mr Justice Stocker, which is reported at [1978] 1 Lloyd's Rep 810 and to which reference can be made, contains a detailed description of the mechanical nature of the coupling. For the purposes of this appeal, however, I do not find it necessary either to repeat or paraphrase it here. What matters is his finding of fact which was: that the coupling was defective in design and dangerous in use

Recent UK cases

on the public highway and that these defects were readily foreseeable by an appropriately skilled engineer considering the problem. He accordingly found the manufacturers liable to the plaintiff for negligence in having supplied and put into circulation for use without intermediate examination a coupling that was 'defective in design and dangerous in use'.

The coupling was designed for use interchangeably with trailers fitted with either cup-shaped or ring-type means of attaching them to the towing vehicle. The trailer with which the farmer always used it had a cup-shaped means of attachment. The defect in design was: that all that prevented the coupling coming apart when a trailer with a cup-shaped means of attachment was being towed was a locking mechanism operated by a handle attached to a spindle, and the safety of this device depended on the integrity of the spindle which was hidden from view inside a metal casing. The handle protruded below the bottom of the coupling and was liable to be struck or jarred or even broken in the course of normal use, with the likelihood of causing the spindle to be distorted or sheared. This would have had the effect of causing the lock to fail and permitting the coupling to come apart. This was something that might happen without the driver of the vehicle being aware of it at the time that it occurred.

Upon the judge's findings, this was what had happened in the instant case. When the accident occurred, both the handle and the spindle were missing. The casing of the locking mechanism was full of dirt and it was this dirt alone that had prevented the lock itself from falling off entirely. The judge was satisfied by the expert evidence that the coupling must have been in this condition for between three and six months before the accident and that the farmer who knew that the handle operated the locking mechanism must have been aware that the handle at least which, unlike the spindle, was clearly visible, had been brokem off throughout that period. He found the farmer negligent in that . . . he continued to use this coupling over a period of months in a state in which it was plainly damaged without taking steps to have it repaired or even to ascertain whether or not it was safe to continue to use it in such condition.

As between the manufacturer and the farmer, the judge apportioned the liability as 75% to the manufacturer and 25% to the farmer. He acquitted the dealers of all negligence. They had purchased a coupling made by reputable manufacturers and the defect in design would not be apparent upon reasonable examination.

In the third party proceedings brought by the farmer against the dealers the farmer sought an indemnity for damages for which he was liable to the plaintiff. He relied upon the warranties implied under section 14 (1) and (2) of the Sale of Goods Act 1893 (which was in force in its unamended form at the relevant time), that the coupling should be reasonably fit for the purpose for which it was supplied, *viz* towing trailers with a Land Rover, and that it should be of merchantable quality. The

judge held that because of its defect in design which made it dangerous in use, there were breaches of both warranties for which the farmer would be entitled to nominal damages at least if he had claimed them; but the judge held that the damages for which he had found the farmer liable were caused by his own negligence in continuing to use a coupling which he knew was broken without taking steps to have it repaired or to ascertain whether it was safe. He held that the principle in *Mowbray v Merryweather* [1895] 2 QB 640, on which the farmer had relied, was subject to the limitation stated by Lord Justice Winn in *Hadley v Droitwich Construction Co Ltd* [1968] 1 WLR 37.

This limitation, in the view of Mr Justice Stocker, made it impossible for the farmer to rely upon either of the implied warranties of fitness or of merchantability as enabling him to recover from the dealers the damages he was liable to pay the plaintiff for his own negligence. The only negligence of which the farmer had been found guilty was: that when he knew that the coupling was damaged, because the handle had been broken off, he continued for months to use it in that damaged state without having it repaired or even ascertaining whether or not it was safe to continue to use it in that condition. The dealers had not impliedly warranted that if the coupling should be broken when in use, the farmer need take neither of these elementary and obvious precautions once he knew that it was in a damaged condition.

My Lords, I shall be reverting to these two authorities when I come to deal with the proceedings in the Court of Appeal. The judge's decision that the farmer had no claim against the dealers made moot the dealers' claim against the manufacturers in the fourth party proceedings. The judge accordingly dismissed them; but it is nevertheless convenient at this point to mention how that claim was framed. The dealers had not brought the coupling direct from the manufacturers but from one of several wholesalers with whom they dealt; owing to a defective system of store-keeping records they could not tell which. So they were unable to identify an immediate seller against whom they in their turn could rely upon the implied warranties of fitness or merchantability. They based their claim against the manufacturers in the alternative upon a collateral warranty, negligent mis-statement and thirdly, but it would seem a trifle mutedly, upon ordinary negligence of the kind dealt with in *Donoghue v Stevenson* [1932] A C 562.

The farmer appealed against the judge's finding of negligence against him. This appeal was dismissed by the Court of Appeal (Lords Justices Stephenson, Roskill and Lawton) (see [1980] 1 Lloyd's Rep 311) and no more need be said about it. The farmer also appealed against the dismissal of his claim for an indemnity against the dealers in the third party proceedings. The dealers, as a precaution in case they should be held liable to the farmer, appealed against the dismissal of their fourth party proceedings against the manufacturers.

The argument before the Court of Appeal lasted a

Lexmead v Lewis

broken period of seven days. The farmer's appeal in the third party proceedings against the dealers for an indemnity in respect of the damages for which he was liable to pay to the plaintiff was allowed; the dealers' appeal in the fourth party proceedings against the manufacturers was dismissed. On appeal to this House by the dealers against both these judgments of the Court of Appeal, counsel estimated that the hearing here would also take at least seven days, and that in the course of argument it would be necessary to cite a very large number of authorities, both English and foreign, to your Lordships.

My Lords, the respect which under the common law is paid to precedent makes it tempting to the appellate advocate to cite a plethora of authorities which do no more than illustrate the application to particular facts of a well-established principle of law that has been clearly stated in what, by consensus of bench and bar and academic writers, has come to be treated as the leading case upon the subject. In those cases that are no more than illustrative, however, there are likely to be found judicial statements of the principle that do not follow the precise language in which the principle is expressed in the leading case, but use some paraphrase of it that the judge thinks is specially apt to explain its application to the facts of the particular case. The citation of a plethora of illustrative authorities, apart from being time- and cost-consuming, presents the danger of so blinding the court with case law that it has difficulty in seeing the wood of legal principle for the trees of paraphrase. This, I cannot help thinking, is what must have happened in the instant case.

The farmer's case against the dealers, by the time it reached the Court of Appeal, was based exclusively on breach of a contractual warranty. So the question of legal principle involved is: In what circumstances can a party A to a contract who has been found liable for breach of a duty of care owed by him to a stranger X to the contract, recover from the other party B to the contract as damages for breach of warranty the amount of the damages for negligence which A himself has been ordered to pay to X? The question was said by Lord Esher, MR, to have arisen for the first time in the leading case of *Mowbray v Merryweather* [1895] 2 QB 640. Apart from the brief exegesis by Lord Justice Winn in *Hadley v Droitwich Construction Co Ltd* [1968] 1 WLR 37, this is the only authority to which I see any need to refer. In *Mowbray v Merryweather* the contractual warranty relied on by the plaintiffs was an implied one of fitness for purpose in similar terms to the implied warranty under section 14 (1) of the Sale of Goods Act 1893, *in casu* that tackle supplied by the defendants to the plaintiffs for use by the latter's employees in unloading a ship was reasonably fit for use for that purpose by those employees with safety to themselves. A chain forming part of the tackle was defective; as a result of this defect it broke and injured an employee of the plaintiffs. The defect could have been discovered by the plaintiffs upon reasonable examination. Their failure to examine it constituted the negligence for which da-

mages against them were awarded to the injured employee. The argument that the plaintiffs' allowing it to be used without examination was not the natural result of the defendants' breach of warranty of fitness for purpose, invoked from Lord Esher, MR an interlocutory observation that underlines the elementary justice of the principle of law that the Court of Appeal was about to lay down:

The question (—he said—) is whether the plaintiffs are not entitled to say that they were misled into their breach of duty towards the workman by the warranty.

In the Master of the Rolls's judgment the successful contention of the plaintiff, which he expressly approved, was stated in the following terms:

The plaintiffs say that they took the chain on the faith of the warranty and gave it to their workmen to use; while being so used it broke, because it was not in accordance with the warranty: that was the sole cause of its breaking; and the natural result was that this workman was injured; and he thereupon sued the plaintiffs in respect of his injuries, and they were compelled to pay him the amount which they now seek to recover from the defendant. It is true that he could not have recovered unless, as between himself and the plaintiffs, the plaintiffs had been guilty of want of care; but the plaintiffs say that, as between themselves and the defendant, they were not bound to examine the chain because the defendant had warranted it sound, that they had a right to rely on that warranty, and did rely on it, and the defendant cannot rely on a duty to use due care which was owed, not to him, but to the workman.

What was said by Lord Justice Winn in *Hadley v Droitwich Construction Co Ltd* but expressly disapproved by the Court of Appeal in the instant case is, in my view, correct and does no more than state a limitation that is plainly implicit in the *ratio decidendi* of *Mowbray v Merryweather*:

. . . in a case where A has been held liable to X, a stranger, for negligent failure to take a certain precaution, he may recover over from someone with whom he has a contract only if, by that contract, the other contracting party has warranted that he *need not*—there is no necessity—take the very precaution for the failure to take which he has been held liable in law to (X).

So in order to see whether the farmer's claim against the dealers falls within this principle the first enquiry to be made is: what are the terms of the warranty which it is claimed was broken? Mr Justice Stocker had found that there was no *express* warranty of the quality of the coupling or its fitness for the purpose of towing trailers, so the farmer was driven to rely upon the implied warranties under section 14 (1) and (2) of the Sale of Goods Act, 1893 (in its unamended form), both of which were clearly applicable to his contract with the dealers. It is, however, only necessary to refer to the warranty under sub-section (1), that the coupling as fitted to the Land Rover should be reasonably fit for towing trailers fitted with either cup-shaped or ring-type means of attachment. Fitness in this context plainly includes a warranty that it may be so used upon a public highway without danger to other users of the road.

The implied warranty of fitness for a particular purpose relates to the goods at the time of delivery under the contract of sale in the state in which they were delivered. I do not doubt that it is a continuing warranty that the goods will continue to be fit for that purpose for a reasonable time after delivery, so long as they remain in the same apparent state as that in which they were delivered, apart from normal wear and tear. What is a reasonable time will depend upon the nature of the goods but I would accept that in the case of the coupling the warranty was still continuing up to the date, some three to six months before the accident, when it first became known to the farmer that the handle of the locking mechanism was missing. Up to that time the farmer would have had a right to rely upon the dealers' warranty as excusing him from making his own examination of the coupling to see if it were safe; but if the accident had happened before then, the farmer would not have been held to have been guilty of any negligence to the plaintiff. After it had become apparent to the farmer that the locking mechanism of the coupling was broken, and consequently that it was no longer in the same state as when it was delivered, the only implied warranty which could justify his failure to take the precaution either to get it mended or at least to find out whether it was safe to continue to use it in that condition, would be a warranty that the coupling could continue to be safely used to tow a trailer on a public highway notwithstanding that it was in an obviously damaged state. My Lords, any implication of a warranty in these terms needs only to be stated, to be rejected. So the farmer's claim against the dealers fails in limine. In the state in which the farmer knew the coupling to be at the time of the accident, there was no longer any warranty by the dealers of its continued safety in use on which the farmer was entitled to rely.

The Court of Appeal reasoned that, since there was no break in the chain of causation between negligence of the manufacturers, which consisted in the defective design of the coupling, and the plaintiff's damage, there could be no such break between the dealers' breach of warranty, which likewise consisted in the defective design of the coupling, and the farmer's loss occasioned by his share of the liability for the plaintiff's damage. With respect, this reasoning was erroneous. The farmer's liability arose, not from the defective design of the coupling but from his own negligence in failing, when he knew that the coupling was damaged, to have it repaired or to ascertain if it was still safe to use. The issue of causation, therefore, on which the farmer's claim against the dealers depended, was whether his negligence resulted directly and naturally, in the ordinary course of events, from the dealers' breach of warranty. Manifestly it did not.

My Lords, it does not appear that consideration of whether the implied warranty of fitness of the coupling would be reasonably understood by the parties to the contract as continuing notwithstanding the obvious damage to its locking mechanism, played a conspicuous part in the argument before the Court of Appeal. It does not feature prominently in the farmer's printed case before this House. So it is understandable that the Court of Appeal did not deal with it specifically, although it may be that an argument on these lines was in their minds when, in allowing the farmer's appeal against the dealers in the third party proceedings, they felt it necessary to express their disapproval of the statement of Lord Justice Winn in Hadley v Droitwich Construction Co Ltd which I have already cited. This, in my view, correctly states the principle of law applicable to the farmer's claim against the dealers for breach of warranty and, for the reasons I have given, is fatal to its success. I would accordingly allow the dealers' appeal in the third party proceedings.

This makes it unnecessary for your Lordships to go on to deal with the dealers' appeal in the fourth party proceedings against the manufacturers. There is no liability for the dealers to pass on to the manufacturers; so on this ground the appeal must be dismissed. Your Lordships accordingly have heard no argument upon any of the three alternative grounds on which, if they had been liable to their buyer, the dealers would have sought to pass on that liability to the manufacturers with whom they were in no direct contractual relationship. The simplest ground was that which was based upon the duty which, as was first held authoritatively by this House in Donoghue v Stevenson [1932] A C 562, lies upon a manufacturer of an article sold by him in circumstances which make it unlikely that a distributor or ultimate purchaser will subject the goods to such inspection before use as would reveal a dangerous defect, and to take reasonable care that the article is free from any defect likely to cause injury to the user. The Court of Appeal rejected this ground of liability because, in their view, they were bound by authority to hold that what may conveniently be referred to as the Donoghue v Stevenson principle was restricted to damage by physical injury but did not extend to purely economic loss; and that the loss sustained by the dealers was purely economic loss. While in the absence of argument it could not be right to express any final view, I should not wish the dismissal of the dealers' appeal to be regarded as an approval by this House of the proposition that where the economic loss suffered by a distributor in the chain between the manufacturer and the ultimate consumer consists of a liability to pay damages to the ultimate consumer for physical injuries sustained by him, or consists of a liability to indemnify a distributor lower in the chain of distribution for his liability to the ultimate consumer for damages for physical injuries, such economic loss is not recoverable under the Donoghue v Stevenson principle from the manufacturer.

I should therefore allow the dealers' appeal in the third party proceedings and dismiss their appeal in the fourth party proceedings.

Lord Elwyn-Jones. My Lords, I have had the

advantage of reading in draft the speech of my noble and learned friend Lord Diplock. I fully agree with it and with the order he proposes.

Lord Fraser of Tullybelton. My Lords, I have had the advantage of reading in advance the speech prepared by my noble and learned friend Lord Diplock, and I agree with it. For the reasons given by him I would allow the dealers' appeal in the third party proceedings and dismiss their appeal in the fourth party proceedings.

Lord Scarman. My Lords, I have had the advantage of reading in draft the speech delivered by my noble and learned friend Lord Diplock. I agree with it: and for the reasons he gives I would allow the dealers' appeal in the third party proceedings and dismiss their appeal in the fourth party proceedings. I also agree with the order proposed by my noble and learned friend as to costs.

Lord Bridge of Harwich. My Lords, I have had the advantage of reading in draft the speech of my noble and learned friend Lord Diplock. I fully agree with it and with the order he proposes.

1982 *Junior Books v Veitchi*

COMMENTARY

Until this House of Lords judgment in July 1982, it was accepted that a plaintiff could not recover economic loss by a claim in tort where there was no danger to health or safety of any person nor risk of damage to other property of the plaintiff. Recovery of damages for example, for the rectification of the defective product itself could only be made through a claim in contract. The appellants in this case, Veitchi & Co, the flooring subcontractors who were responsible for the negligent laying of the floor, argued that for them to be made liable to the customer for the economic loss suffered as a result of the floor having to be repaired or replaced would be to extend the duty of care owed by manufacturers since the *Donoghue* case, far beyond the limits which had previously been applied—the so-called 'floodgates' argument.

Some commentators have indeed referred to this judgment as an 'epic decision' which 'dramatically extended' the bounds of product liability[1], and as having 'advanced manufacturers' liability by a small but very significant step'.[2] However, in their majority judgments, their Lordships seem to have been careful to stress that the judgments were reached on the particular facts of the case, in particular the quasi-contractual nature of the relationship between the customer and the appellants who were nominated sub-contractors.

Whilst rejecting the 'floodgates' argument as being a proper basis on which to make a decision of principle— in Lord Roskill's words 'although it cannot be denied that policy considerations have from time to time been allowed to play their part in the tort of negligence since it just developed as it were in its own right in the course of the last century, yet today I think its scope is best determined by consideration of principle rather than policy'.

Junior Books were able to satisfy all the tests which had been suggested in previous cases where the 'floodgates' argument had been debated, and which were summarised by Lord Wilberforce in *Anns v Merton LBC 1978 AC 728* as being two: first, whether there is a sufficient relationship of proximity between the alleged wrongdoer and the person who has suffered damage, such that a duty of care arises; and secondly whether, if the proximity test is satisfied, there are any considerations which should negative, reduce or limit the scope of that duty or the damages arising from a breach. In applying the first test to establish proximity the following factors were relevant: (a) Veitchi certainly knew, or were in a position to know, the identity of the person for

[1] Greville Janner 'Broadening the Law', *Product Liability International,* October 1982.

[2] AH Hermann 'Product Liability Extended', *Financial Times,* August 19, 1982.

Recent UK cases

whom the flooring was being laid; (b) Veitchi were nominated sub-contractors. Junior Books relied on their skill and judgment and Veitchi must have known that; (c) the injury to Junior Books was a direct and foreseeable result of negligence on the part of Veitchi. The very close relationship between Junior Books and Veitchi only just fell short of being a contractual one and therefore adequately satisfied the proximity test.

In considering the second test, Lord Roskill remarked that he could see nothing to restrict the duty of care which arose from the proximity which had been established. There was no relevant exclusion clause, and therefore this point did not have to be considered. Whether in a future case an exclusion could operate would, of course, now be subject to the provisions of the Unfair Contract Terms Act 1977, and to the application of a 'reasonableness' test to see whether or not it should be allowed to operate.

An interesting point raised in Lord Brandon's dissenting judgment related to the second of Lord Wilberforce's tests—*ie* whether there were factors limiting the duty of care which had arisen. He suggested that to find the appellants liable for economic loss would be to create difficulties regarding the standard of care owed in relation to supplying an article which was simply defective, as in this case, as opposed to dangerous. He felt that the standard applicable here was a matter which could only properly be established by reference to the contract. In commenting on this point, Lord Fraser said that whilst this could be a problem, there was no difficulty in the present case in ascertaining the standard by which the product should be judged because the terms of the contract were well known to all the parties. As Lord Fraser commented, whether this would have been so had the action been brought by a subsequent owner, is still an open issue.

Whilst this case is clearly a significant one, it remains to be seen whether the courts in future would be willing to apply its principle where the 'proximity' test may be less easy to satisfy.

JUDGMENT

House of Lords
July 15, 1982

Junior Books Limited
versus
Veitchi Company Limited

Before Lord Fraser of Tullybelton, Lord Russell of Killowen, Lord Keith of Kinkel, Lord Roskill and Lord Brandon of Oakbrook

Lord Fraser of Tullybelton. My Lords, I have had the advantage of reading in draft the speech of my noble and learned friend, Lord Roskill, and I am in full agreement with his conclusion and with the reasons on which he bases it. I also gratefully adopt his summary of the facts. It is enough for me to say that the appellants (defenders) are specialist sub-contractors who laid composition flooring in a factory that was built for the respondents (pursuers) at Grangemouth between September 1969 and May 1970. The respondents aver that the floor is defective, owing to failure by the appellants to take reasonable care in laying it, and that it will have to be replaced. There was no contractual relationship between the appellants and the respondents, and for some reason that has not been explained the respondents have not taken legal proceedings against the main contractors with whom they did have a contractual relationship. The respondents have raised this action against the appellants, claiming damages which consist mainly of the direct and indirect cost of replacing the floor, the action being founded on averments that the appellants were negligent in laying the floor. At the present stage of relevancy these averments must be taken as true. The appeal raises an important question on the law of delict or, strictly speaking, quasi delict which is not precisely covered by authority. The question is whether the appellants, having (as must at this stage be assumed) negligently laid a floor which is defective, but which has not caused danger to the health or safety of any person nor risk of damage to any other property belonging to the owner of the floor, may in the circumstances averred by the respondents be liable for the economic loss caused to them by having to replace the floor.

Lord Grieve, Lord Ordinary, and the Second Division of the Court of Session answered that question in the affirmative, and they have allowed to the respondents a proof before answer. The appellants maintain that the question should be answered in the negative and that the action should be dismissed as irrelevant. As I agree with my noble and learned friend, Lord Roskill, that the appeal fails I only add to this speech in order to deal in my own words with two important matters that arise.

The first is the concern which has been repeatedly expressed by judges in the United Kingdom and elsewhere, that the effect of relaxing strict limitations upon the area of liability for delict (tort) would be, in the words of Cardozo C J in *Ultramares Corporation v Touche* (1931) 174 NE 441, 444, to introduce 'liability in an undeterminate amount for an indeterminate time to an indeterminate class'. This is the 'floodgates' argument, if I may use the expression as a convenient description, and not in any dismissive or question-begging sense. The argument appears to me unattractive, especially if it leads, as I think it would in this case, to drawing an arbitrary and illogical line just because a line has to be drawn somewhere. But it has to be considered, because it has had a significant influence in leading judges to reject claims for economic loss which were not consequent upon physical danger to persons or other property of the pursuer/plaintiff.

Junior Books v Veitchi

The floodgates argument was much discussed by the High Court of Australia in *Caltex Oil (Australia) Pty Ltd v The Dredge Willemstad* (1976) 136 CLR 529, where the majority of the court held that there was sufficient proximity between the parties to justify a claim for economic loss because the defendant knew, in the words of the headnote, 'that a particular person, not merely as a member of an unascertained class, would be likely to suffer economic loss as a consequence of his negligence'. Whether the defenders' knowledge of the identity of the person likely to suffer from his negligence is relevant for the present purpose may with respect be doubted and it seems to be contrary to the views expressed in *Hedley Byrne & Co Ltd v Heller & Partners Ltd* [1964] A C 465 by Lord Reid, at p 482, and by Lord Morris of Borth-y-Gest, at p 494. But it is not necessary to decide the question in this appeal because the appellants certainly knew, or had the means of knowing, the identity of the respondents for whom the factory was being built. So if knowledge of the respondents' identity is a relevant test, it is one that the appellants can satisfy. They can also satisfy most, if not all, of the other tests that have been suggested as safeguards against opening the floodgates. The proximity between the parties is extremely close, falling only just short of a direct contractual relationship. The injury to the respondents was a direct and foreseeable result of negligence by the appellants. The respondents, or their architects, nominated the appellants as specialist sub-contractors and they must therefore have relied upon their skill and knowledge. It would surely be wrong to exclude from probation a claim which is so strongly based, merely because of anxiety about the possible effect of the decision upon other cases where the proximity may be less strong. If and when such other cases arise they will have to be decided by applying sound principles to their particular facts. The present case seems to me to fall well within limits already recognised in principle for this type of claim, and I would decide this appeal strictly on its own facts. I rely particularly on the very close proximity between the parties which in my view distinguishes this case from the case of producers of goods to be offered for sale to the public.

The second matter which might be thought to justify rejecting the respondents' claim as irrelevant is the difficulty of ascertaining the standard of duty owed by the appellants to the respondents. A manufacturer's duty to take care not to make a product that is dangerous sets a standard which is, in principle, easy to ascertain. The duty is owed to all who are his 'neighbours'. It is imposed upon him by the general law and is in addition to his contractual duties to other parties to the contract. It cannot be discharged or escaped by pleading that it conflicts with his contractual duty. But a duty not to produce a *defective* article sets a standard which is less easily ascertained, because it has to be judged largely by reference to the contract. As Windeyer J said in *Voli v Inglewood Shire Council* (1963) 110 CLR 74, if an architect undertakes 'to design a stage to bear only some specified weight, he would not be liable for the consequences of someone thereafter negligently permitting a greater weight to be put upon it'.

Similarly a building constructed in fulfilment of a contract for a price of £100,000 might justly be regarded as defective, although the same building constructed in fulfilment of a contract for a price of £50,000 might not. Where a building is erected under a contract with a purchaser, then provided the building, or part of it, is not dangerous to persons or to other property and subject to the law against misrepresentation, I see no reason why the builder should not be free to make with the purchaser whatever contractual arrangements about the quality of the product the purchaser wishes. However jerry-built the product, the purchaser would not be entitled to damages from the builder if it came up to the contractual standard. I do not think a subsequent owner could be in any better position, but in most cases he would not know the detail of the contractual arrangements and, without such knowledge, he might well be unable to judge whether the product was defective or not. But in this case the respondents, although not a party to the contract with the appellants, had full knowledge of the appellants' contractual duties, and this difficulty does not arise. What the position might have been if the action had been brought by a subsequent owner is a matter which does not have to be decided now.

For the reasons given by my noble and learned friend, Lord Roskill, and for the additional reasons which I have stated, I would dismiss this appeal.

Lord Russell of Killowen. My Lords, I have had the advantage of reading in draft the speeches prepared by my noble and learned friends, Lords Fraser of Tullybelton and Roskill. I agree with them and with their conclusion that this appeal fails. In my respectful opinion the view of my noble and learned friend, Lord Brandon of Oakbrook, unnecessarily confines the relevant principles of delict to exclude cases of such immediate proximity as the present.

Lord Keith of Kinkel. My Lords, the respondents own and occupy a factory in Grangemouth. This factory was constructed for them over a period in 1969 and 1970, under a contract between them and a company called Ogilvie (Builders) Ltd, which I shall call 'the main contractors'. The respondents' architects nominated the appellants as specialist sub-contractors for the purpose of laying a floor in the main production area of the factory. The appellants entered into a contract with the main contractors for the carrying out of this work.

According to the respondents' averments the appellants' workmanship was seriously defective in a number of respects, with the result that after two years the floor began to develop cracks over the whole of its surface. They say that it requires replacement in order to avoid the necessity for continual maintenance, which would be more expensive in the long run. They claim against the appellants for the cost of such replacement, together with certain consequential loss which they say they will suffer while the work of replacement is being carried out. The claim is founded in delict, the respondents pleading that they have suffered loss through the appellants' negligence and are entitled to reparation therefor.

It is a notable feature of the respondents' pleadings that they contain no averment that the defective nature of flooring has led or is likely to lead to any danger of physical injury to work people or of damage to property, moveable or immoveable, other than the floor surface itself, or even of economic loss through interruption of production processes. The only type of pecuniary consequential loss claimed for is that arising out of the need to replace the flooring. Had there been an averment of any such apprehended danger, I am of opinion that the respondents' case would have been clearly relevant. There undoubtedly existed between the appellants and the respondents such proximity of relationship, within the well known principle of *Donoghue v Stevenson* [1932] A C 562, as to give rise to duty of care owed by the former to the latter. As formulated in *Donoghue v Stevenson,* the duty extended to the avoidance of acts or omissions which might reasonably have been anticipated as likely to cause physical injury to persons or property. The scope of the duty has, however, been developed so as to cover the situation where pure economic loss is to be foreseen as likely to be suffered by one standing in the requisite degree of proximity: *Hedley Byrne & Co Ltd v Heller & Partners Ltd* [1964] AC 465. That case was concerned with a negligent statement made in response to an inquiry about the financial standing of a particular company, in reliance on the accuracy of which the plaintiffs had acted to their detriment. So the case is not in point here except in so far as it established that reasonable anticipation of physical injury to person or property is not a *sine qua non* for the existence of a duty of care. It has also been established that where a duty of care exists through the presence of such reasonable anticipation, and it is breached, then even though no such injury has actually been caused because the person to whom the duty is owed has incurred expenditure in averting the danger, that person is entitled to damages measured by the amount of that expenditure: *Anns v Merton London Borough Council* [1978] A C 728, 759, per Lord Wilberforce. That is the principle which in my view underlies *Dutton v Bognor Regis Urban District Council* [1972] 1 QB 373 and *Batty v Metropolitan Property Realisations Ltd* [1978] QB 554.

So in the present case I am of opinion that the appellants in the laying of the floor owed to the respondents a duty to take reasonable care to avoid acts or omissions which they ought to have known would be likely to cause the respondents, not only physical damage to person or property, but also pure economic loss. Economic loss would be caused to the respondents if the condition of the floor, in the course of its normal life, came to be such as to prevent the respondents from carrying out ordinary production processes on it, or,

short of that, to cause the production process to be more costly than it would otherwise have been. In that situation the respondents would have been entitled to recover from the appellants expenditure incurred in relaying the floor so as to avert or mitigate their loss. The real question in the appeal, as I see it, is whether the respondents' averments reveal such a state of affairs as, under the principles I have outlined, gives them a complete right of action. I am of opinion that they have relevantly averred a duty of care owed to them by the appellants, though I think their averments in this respect might have been more precise and better related to the true legal position.

It is the averments of loss which cause me some trouble. On the face of it, their averments might be read as meaning no more than that the respondents have got a bad floor instead of a good one and that their loss is represented by the cost of replacing the floor. But they do also aver that the cost of maintaining the floor which they have got is heavy, and that it would be cheaper to take up the floor surface and lay a new one. If the cost of maintaining the defective floor is substantially greater than it would have been in respect of a sound one, it must necessarily follow that their manufacturing operations are being carried on at a less profitable level than would otherwise have been the case, and that they are therefore suffering economic loss. That is the sort of loss which the appellants, standing in the relationship to the respondents which they did, ought reasonably to have anticipated as likely to occur if their workmanship was faulty. They must have been aware of the nature of the respondents' business, the purpose for which the floor was required, and the part it was to play in their operations. The appellants accordingly owed the respondents a duty to take reasonable care to see that their workmanship was not faulty, and are liable for the foreseeable consequences, sounding in economic loss, of their failure to do so. These consequences may properly be held to include less profitable operation due to the heavy cost of maintenance. In so far as the respondents, in order to avert or mitigate such loss, incur expenditure on relaying the floor surface, that expenditure becomes the measure of the appellants' liability. Upon that analysis of the situation, I am of opinion that the respondents have stated a proper case for inquiry into the facts, and that the Lord Ordinary and the Second Division were therefore right to allow a proof before answer. I would accordingly dismiss the appeal.

Having thus reached a conclusion in favour of the respondents upon the somewhat narrow ground which I have indicated, I do not consider this to be an appropriate case for seeking to advance the frontiers of the law of negligence upon the lines favoured by certain of your Lordships. There are a number of reasons why such an extension would, in my view, be wrong in principle. In the first place, I am unable to regard the deterioration of the flooring which is alleged in this case as being damage to the respondents' property such as to give rise to a liability falling directly within the principle of *Donoghue v Stevenson*. The flooring had an inherent

Junior Books v Veitchi

defect in it from the start. The appellants did not, in any sense consistent with the ordinary use of language or contemplated by the majority in *Donoghue v Stevenson*, damage the respondents' property. They supplied them with a defective floor. Such an act can, in accordance with the views I have expressed above, give rise to liability in negligence in certain circumstances. But it does not do so merely because the flooring is defective or valueless or useless and requires to be replaced. So to hold would raise very difficult and delicate issues of principle having a wide potential application. I think it would necessarily follow that any manufacturer of products would become liable to the ultimate purchaser if the product, owing to negligence in manufacture was, without being harmful in any way, useless or worthless or defective in quality so that the purchaser wasted the money he spent on it. One instance mentioned in argument and adverted to by Stamp LJ in *Dutton v Bognor Regis Urban District Council* [1972] 1 QB 373, was a product purchased as ginger beer which turned out to be only water, and many others may be figured.

To introduce a general liability covering such situations would be disruptive of commercial practice, under which manufacturers of products commonly provide the ultimate purchaser with limited guarantees usually undertaking only to replace parts exhibiting defective workmanship and excluding any consequential loss. There being no contractual relationship between manufacturer and ultimate consumer, no room would exist, if the suggested principle were accepted, for limiting the manufacturer's liability. The policy considerations which would be involved in introducing such a state of affairs appear to me to be such as a court of law cannot properly assess, and the question whether or not it would be in the interests of commerce and the public generally is, in my view, much better left for the legislature. The purchaser of a defective product normally can proceed for breach of contract against the seller who can bring his own supplier into the proceedings by third party procedure, so it cannot be said that the present state of the law is unsatisfactory from the point of view of available remedies. I refer to *Young & Marten Ltd v McManus Childs Ltd* [1969] 1 AC 454. In the second place, I can foresee that very considerable difficulties might arise in assessing the standards of quality by which the allegedly defective product is to be judged. This aspect is more fully developed in the speech to be delivered by my noble and learned friend Lord Brandon of Oakbrook, with whose views on the matter I respectfully agree.

My Lords, for the reasons which I have given I would concur in the dismissal of the appeal.

Lord Roskill. . . . I need only summarise the bare essentials. The appellants are specialist contractors in the laying of flooring. They were nominated sub-contractors under a main building contract concluded between the respondents and some main contractors. There was no privity of contract between the appellants

and the respondents. The appellants laid flooring in the production area of a factory which was being built for the respondents at Grangemouth as long ago as 1969 and 1970. In 1972 it is averred that the flooring showed defects allegedly due to bad workmanship or bad materials or both. At the time the pleadings were prepared no repair work had been carried out but it was averred that the cost of repairs would be some £50,000 to which were added certain figures which, as the Lord Ordinary said, might reasonably be described as items of economic or financial loss. The total sum claimed by the respondents was over £200,000.

My Lords, your Lordships are thus invited to deal with events which happened long ago. It is difficult to believe that in the intervening period some work has not been done to this flooring but no information was vouchsafed as to the course of subsequent events. The main building contract was not exhibited in the courts below. Your Lordships were not told whether that contract included as between the main contractors and the respondents any relevant exceptions clause, nor whether if there were such an exceptions clause it might be available for the benefit of the appellants. Nor were your Lordships told why the respondents had chosen to proceed in delict against the appellants rather than against the main contractors in contract, nor indeed why the main contractors had not been joined as parties to these proceedings. This economy of fact is in stark contrast to the wealth of citation of authority of which your Lordships have had the benefit. Thus the bare point of law has to be decided upon an assumption of the truth of the facts pleaded. But I cannot but suspect that the truth regarding the supposed deficiencies of this flooring at Grangemouth has long since been either established or disproved. Of those matters however your Lordships know and have been told nothing. Half a century ago your Lordships' House decided *Donoghue v Stevenson* upon a similar plea of irrelevancy. In that case however some three and three quarter years only had elapsed between the purchase of the allegedly offending bottle of ginger beer and the decision of your Lordships' House.

My Lords, there was much discussion before your Lordships' House as to the effect of the pleadings. I see no need to discuss them in detail. They seem to me clearly to contain no allegation that the flooring was in a dangerous state or that its condition was such as to cause danger to life or limb or to other property of other persons or that repairs were urgently or imminently required to avoid any such danger, or that any economic or financial loss had been, or would be, suffered save as would be consequential upon the ultimate replacement of the flooring. The essential feature of the respondents' pleading was that it advanced a claim for the cost of remedying the alleged defects in the flooring itself by replacement together with resulting or economic or financial loss consequential upon that replacement.

My Lords, it was because of that scope of the respondents' pleading and that that pleading was

Recent UK cases

limited in this way that the appellants were able to mount their main attack upon those pleadings and to contend that they were, at least in the absence of amendment, for which no leave has been sought at any stage, irrelevant since the law neither of Scotland nor of England made the appellants liable in delict or in negligence for the cost of replacing this flooring or for the economic or financial loss consequent upon that replacement. It was strenuously argued for the appellants that for your Lordships' House now to hold that in those circumstances which I have just outlined the appellants were liable to the respondents would be to extend the duty of care owed by a manufacturer and others, to whom the principles first enunciated in *Donoghue v Stevenson* have since been extended during the last half century, far beyond the limits to which the courts have hitherto extended them. The familiar 'floodgates' argument was once again brought fully into play. My Lords, although it cannot be denied that policy considerations have from time to time been allowed to play their part in the tort of negligence since it first developed as it were in its own right in the course of the last century, yet today I think its scope is best determined by considerations of principle rather than of policy. The floodgates argument is very familiar. It still may on occasion have its proper place but if principle suggests that the law should develop along a particular route and if the adoption of that particular route will accord a remedy where that remedy has hitherto been denied, I see no reason why, if it be just that the law should henceforth accord that remedy, that remedy should be denied simply because it will, in consequence of this particular development, become available to many rather than to few.

My Lords, I think there is no doubt that *Donoghue v Stevenson* by its insistence upon proximity, in the sense in which Lord Atkin used that word, as the foundation of the duty of care which was there enunciated, marked a great development in the law of delict and of negligence alike. In passing it should be noted that Lord Atkin emphasised that the laws of Scotland and of England were in that case, as is agreed in the present, identical. But that advance having been thus made in 1932, the doctrine then enunciated was at first confined by judicial decision within relatively narrow limits. The gradual development of the law will be found discussed by the editor of *Salmond & Heuston on Torts*, 18th ed (1981) p 289. Though initially there is no doubt that because of Lord Atkin's phraseology in *Donoghue v Stevenson*, 'injury to the consumer's life or property', it was thought that the duty of care did not extend beyond avoiding physical injury or physical damage to the person or the property of the person to whom the duty of care was owed, that limitation has long since ceased as Professor Heuston points out in the passage in *Salmond* to which I have just referred.

. . . . .

I look for the reasons why, it being conceded that the appellants owed a duty of care to others not to construct the flooring so that those others were in peril of suffering loss or damage to their persons or their property, that duty of care should not be equally owed to the respondents who, though not in direct contractual relationship with the appellants, were as nominated sub-contractors in almost as close a commercial relationship with the appellants as it is possible to envisage short of privity of contract, so as not to expose the respondents to a possible liability to financial loss for repairing the flooring should it prove that that flooring had been negligently constructed. It is conceded that if the flooring had been so badly constructed that to avoid imminent danger the respondents had expended money upon renewing it the respondents could have recovered the cost of so doing. It seems curious that, if the appellants' work had been so bad that to avoid imminent danger expenditure had been incurred, the respondents could recover that expenditure, but that if the work was less badly done so that remedial work could be postponed they cannot do so. Yet this is seemingly the result of the appellants' contentions.

My Lords, I have already said that there is no decided case which clearly points the way. But it is, I think, of assistance to see how far the various decisions have gone. I shall restrict my citation to the more important decisions both in this country and overseas. In *Dutton v Bognor Regis Urban District Council* [1972] 1 QB 373 which your Lordships' House expressly approved in *Anns v Merton London Borough Council* [1978] AC 728, the Court of Appeal held that the plaintiff, who bought the house in question long after it had been built and its foundations inadequately inspected by the defendants' staff, was entitled to recover from the defendants *inter alia* the estimated cost of repairing the house as well as other items of loss including diminution in value. There was in that case physical damage to the house. It was argued that the defendants were not liable for the cost of repairs or diminution in value. This argument was expressly rejected by Lord Denning MR [1972] 1 QB 373, 396, and by Sachs LJ at pp 403-404. Stamp LJ was however more sympathetic to this argument at p 414:

'It is pointed out that in the past a distinction has been drawn between constructing a dangerous article and constructing one which is defective or of inferior quality. I may be liable to one who purchases in the market a bottle of ginger beer which I have carelessly manufactured and which is dangerous and causes injury to person or property; but it is not the law that I am liable to him for the loss he suffers because what is found inside the bottle and for which he has paid money is not ginger beer but water. I do not warrant, except to an immediate purchaser, and then by the contract and not in tort, that the thing I manufacture is reasonably fit for its purpose. The submission is, I think, a formidable one and in my view raises the most difficult point for decision in this case. Nor can I see any valid distinction between the case of a builder who carelessly builds a house which, though not a source of danger to person or property, nevertheless owing to a concealed defect in its foundations, starts to settle and crack and becomes valueless, and the case of a manufacturer who carelessly manufactures an article which, though not a source of danger to a subsequent owner or to his other property, nevertheless owing to a hidden defect quickly disintegrates. To hold that either the builder or the manufacturer was liable except in contract would be to open up a new field of liability the extent of which could not, I think, be logically controlled, and since it is not in my judgment necessary to do so for the purpose of this case, I do not, more particularly because of the absence of the builder, express an opinion whether the builder has a higher or lower duty than the manufacturer. But the distinction between the case of the manufacturer of a dangerous thing which causes damage and that of a thing which turns out to be defective and valueless lies, I think, not in the nature of the injury but in the character of the duty. I have a duty not carelessly to put out a dangerous thing which may cause damage to one who may purchase it; but the duty does not extend to putting out carelessly a defective or useless or valueless thing. So again one goes back to consider what was the character of the duty, if any, owed to the plaintiff, and one finds on authority that the injury which is one of the essential elements of the tort of negligence is not confined to physical damage to personal property but may embrace economic damage which the plaintiff suffers through buying a worthless thing, as is shown by the *Hedley Byrne* case [1964] AC 465.'

Thus it was upon the character of the duty that Stamp LJ founded and was able to agree with the other members of the Court of Appeal in that case.

. . . . .

My Lords, I turn next to the three main Commonwealth decisions. They are *Rivtow Marine Ltd v Washington Iron Works* (1973) 40 DLR (3d) 530, a decision of the Supreme Court of Canada, *Caltex Oil (Australia) Pty Ltd v The Dredge Willemstad* (1976) 136 CLR 529, a decision of the High Court of Australia. and *Bowen v Paramount Builders (Hamilton) Ltd* [1977] 1 NZLR 394, a decision of the Court of Appeal of New Zealand. All three of these cases were decided before *Anns* reached your Lordships' House.

My Lords, in the first of this trilogy, *Rivtow Marine Ltd v Washington Iron Works* (1973) 40 DLR (3d) 530, the Supreme Court by a majority held that the manufacturer of a dangerously defective article is not liable in tort to an ultimate consumer or user of that article for the cost of repairing damage arising in the article itself, nor for such economic loss as would have been sustained in any event as a result of the need to effect repairs. But there was, if I may respectfully say so, a powerful dissenting judgment by Laskin J with which Hall J concurred. The learned judge posed as the first question whether the defendants' liability for negligence should 'embrace economic loss when there has been no physical harm in fact'. He gave an affirmative answer. After pointing out that the judicial limitation on liability was founded upon what I have called the 'floodgates'

argument rather than upon principle, he adopted the view that economic loss resulting from threatened physical loss from a negligently designed or manufactured product was recoverable. It was this judgment which my noble and learned friend Lord Wilberforce described in his speech in *Anns v Merton London Borough Council* [1978] A C 728 as 'of strong persuasive force'.

In *Caltex Oil (Australia) Pty Ltd v The Dredge Willemstad* (1976) 136 CLR 529, the High Court of Australia elaborately reviewed all the relevant English authorities and indeed others as well. My Lords, I hope I shall not be thought lacking in respect for those elaborate judgments or failing to acknowledge the help which I have derived from them if I do not cite from them, for to some extent certain of the difficulties there discussed have been subsequently resolved by the decision of this House in *Anns*.

In *Bowen v Paramount Builders (Hamilton) Ltd* [1975] 2 NZLR 546, to which Lord Wilberforce also referred in *Anns* as having afforded him much assistance, the Court of Appeal in New Zealand [1977] 1 NZLR 394 followed the Court of Appeal decision in *Dutton*. Cooke J took the view that it was enough for the purpose of the case in question to say that the damage was basically physical. But as the passage at p 423 of the report shows, he would have been prepared in agreement with the judgments of Lord Denning MR and of Sachs LJ in *Dutton* to go further.

My Lords, to my mind in the instant case there is no physical damage to the flooring in the sense in which that phrase was used in *Dutton, Batty* and *Bowen* and some of the other cases. As my noble and learned friend, Lord Russell of Killowen, said during the argument, the question which your Lordships' House now has to decide is whether the relevant Scots and English law today extends the duty of care beyond a duty to prevent harm being done by faulty work to a duty to avoid such faults being present in the work itself. It was powerfully urged on behalf of the appellants that were your Lordships so to extend the law, a pursuer in the position of the pursuer in *Donoghue v Stevenson* could, in addition to recovering for any personal injury suffered, have also recovered for the diminished value of the offending bottle of ginger beer. Any remedy of that kind, it was argued, must lie in contract and not in delict or tort. My Lords, I seem to detect in that able argument reflections of the previous judicial approach to comparable problems before *Donoghue v Stevenson* was decided. That approach usually resulted in the conclusion that in principle the proper remedy lay in contract and not outside it. But that approach and its concomitant philosophy ended in 1932 and for my part I should be reluctant to countenance its re-emergence some 50 years later in the instant case. I think today the proper control lies not in asking whether the proper remedy should lie in contract or instead in delict or tort, not in somewhat capricious judicial determination whether a particular case falls on one side of the line or the other, not in somewhat artificial distinctions between physical and economic or financial loss when the two sometimes go together and sometimes do not—it is sometimes overlooked that virtually all damage including physical damage is in one sense financial or economic for it is compensated by an award of damages—but in the first instance in establishing the relevant principles and then in deciding whether the particular case falls within or without those principles. To state this is to do no more than to restate what Lord Reid said in *Dorset Yacht Co Ltd v Home Office* [1970] AC 1004 and Lord Wilberforce in *Anns v Merton London Borough Council, supra*. Lord Wilberforce enunciated the two tests which have to be satisfied. The first is 'sufficient relationship of proximity' the second any considerations negativing, reducing or limiting the scope of the duty or the class of person to whom it is owed or the damages to which a breach of the duty may give rise. My Lords, it is I think in the application of those two principles that the ability to control the extent of liability in delict or in negligence lies. The history of the development of the law in the last 50 years shows that fears aroused by the floodgates argument have been unfounded. Cooke J in *Bowen v Paramount Builders (Hamilton) Ltd* [1977] 1 NZLR 394, 422 described the floodgates argument as 'specious' and the argument against allowing a cause of action such as was allowed in *Dutton v Bognor Regis Urban District Council* [1972] 1 QB 373. *Anns v Merton London Borough Council, supra* and *Bowen v Paramount Builders (Hamilton) Ltd, supra* as 'in terrorem or doctrinaire'.

Turning back to the present appeal I therefore ask first whether there was the requisite degree of proximity so as to give rise to the relevant duty of care relied on by the respondents. I regard the following facts as of crucial importance in requiring an affirmative answer to that question. (1) The appellants were nominated sub-contractors. (2) The appellants were specialists in flooring. (3) The appellants knew what products were required by the respondents and their main contractors and specialised in the production of those products. (4) The appellants alone were responsible for the composition and construction of the flooring. (5) The respondents relied upon the appellants' skill and experience. (6) The appellants as nominated sub-contractors must have known that the respondents relied upon their skill and experience. (7) The relationship between the parties was as close as it could be short of actual privity of contract. (8) The appellants must be taken to have known that if they did the work negligently (as it must be assumed that they did) the resulting defects would at some time require remedying by the respondents expending money upon the remedial measures as a consequence of which the respondents would suffer financial or economic loss.

My Lords, reverting to Lord Devlin's speech in *Hedley Byrne & Co Ltd v Heller & Partners Ltd* it seems to me that all the conditions existed which give rise to the relevant duty of care owed by the appellants to the respondents.

I then turn to Lord Wilberforce's second proposition. On the facts I have just stated, I see nothing whatsoever to restrict the duty of care arising from the proximity of which I have spoken. During the argument it was asked what the position would be in a case where there was a relevant exclusion clause in the main contract. My Lords, that question does not arise for decision in the instant appeal, but in principle I would venture the view that such a clause according to the manner in which it was worded might in some circumstances limit the duty of care just as in the *Hedley Byrne* case the plaintiffs were ultimately defeated by the defendants' disclaimer of responsibility. But in the present case the only suggested reason for limiting the damage recoverable for the breach of the duty of care just enunciated is that hitherto the law has not allowed such recovery and therefore ought not in the future to do so. My Lords, with all respect to those who find this a sufficient answer, I do not. I think this is the next logical step forward in the development of this branch of the law. I see no reason why what was called during the argument 'damage to the pocket' should be disallowed when 'damage to the pocket' coupled with physical damage has hitherto always been allowed. I do not think that this development, if development it be, will lead to untoward consequences. The concept of proximity must always involve, at least in most cases, some degree of reliance—I have already mentioned the words 'skill' and 'judgment' in the speech of Lord Morris of Borth-y-Gest in *Hedley Byrne*. These words seem to me to be an echo, be it conscious or unconscious, of the language of section 14 (1) of the Sale of Goods Act 1893. My Lords, though the analogy is not exact, I do not find it unhelpful for I think the concept of proximity of which I have spoken and the reasoning of Lord Devlin in the *Hedley Byrne* case involve factual considerations not unlike those involved in a claim under section 14 (1); and as between an ultimate purchaser and a manufacturer would not easily be found to exist in the ordinary everyday transaction of purchasing chattels when it is obvious that in truth the real reliance was upon the immediate vendor and not upon the manufacturer.

My Lords, I have not thought it necessary to review all the cases cited in argument. If my conclusion be correct, certain of them can no longer be regarded as good law and others may have to be considered afresh hereafter, for example whether the decision of the majority of the Court of Appeal in *Spartan Steel & Alloys Ltd v Martin & Co (Contractors) Ltd* [1973] QB 27 is correct or whether the reasoning of Edmund-Davies LJ in his dissenting judgment is to be preferred, and whether the decision of the First Division in *Dynamco Ltd v Holland & Hannen & Cubitts (Scotland) Ltd* 1971 SC 257, a decision given after *Dorset Yacht Co Ltd v Home Office* [1970] A C 1004 but before *Anns v Merton London Borough Council* [1978] A C 728, but seemingly without reference to the *Dorset Yacht* case is correct.

My Lords, for all these reasons I would dismiss this appeal and allow this action to proceed to proof before answer.

Junior Books v Veitchi

Lord Brandon of Oakbrook. My Lords, it appears to me clear beyond doubt that, there being no contractual relationship between the respondents and the appellants in the present case, the foundation, and the only foundation, for the existence of a duty of care owed by the defenders to the pursuers, is the principle laid down in the decision of your Lordships' House in *Donoghue v Stevenson*. The actual decision in that case related only to the duty owed by a manufacturer of goods to their ultimate user or consumer, and can be summarised in this way: a person who manufactures goods which he intends to be used or consumed by others, is under a duty to exercise such reasonable care in their manufacture as to ensure that they can be used or consumed in the manner intended without causing physical damage to persons or their property.

While that was the actual decision in *Donoghue v Stevenson*, it was based on a much wider principle embodied in passages in the speech of Lord Atkin, which have been quoted so often that I do not find it necessary to quote them again here. Put shortly, that wider principle is that, when a person can or ought to appreciate that a careless act or omission on his part may result in physical injury to other persons or their property, he owes a duty to all such persons to exercise reasonable care to avoid such careless act or omission.

It is, however, of fundamental importance to observe that the duty of care laid down in *Donoghue v Stevenson* was based on the existence of a danger of physical injury to persons or their property. That this is so, is clear from the observations made by Lord Atkin at pp 581-582 with regard to the statements of law of Brett MR in *Heaven v Pender* (1883) 11 QBD 503, 509. It has further, until the present case, never been doubted, so far as I know, that the relevant property for the purpose of the wider principle on which the decision in *Donoghue v Stevenson* was based, was property other than the very property which gave rise to the danger of physical damage concerned.

My Lords, I have already indicated my opinion that the wider principle on which the decision in *Donoghue v Stevenson* was based applies to the present case. The effect of its application is that the appellants owed a duty to the respondents to exercise reasonable care so to mix and lay the flooring to ensure that it did not, when completed and put to its contemplated use, constitute a danger of physical damage to persons or their property, other than the flooring itself.

. . . . .

My Lords, a good deal of the argument presented to your Lordships during the hearing of the appeal was directed to the question whether a person can recover, in an action founded on delict alone, purely pecuniary loss which is independent of any physical damage to persons or their property. If that were the question to be decided in the present case, I should have no hesitation in holding that, in principle and depending on the facts

of a particular case, purely pecuniary loss may be recoverable in an action founded on delict alone.

. . . . .

I do not, however, consider that the question of law for decision in this case is whether a person can, in an action founded in delict alone, recover for purely pecuniary loss. On the contrary, I adhere to the nature of the question of law to be decided which I formulated earlier, namely, what is the scope of the duty of care owed by the appellants to the respondents on the assumed facts of the present case.

My Lords, in support of their contentions the respondents placed reliance on the broad statements relating to liability in negligence contained in the speech of Lord Wilberforce in *Anns v Merton London Borough Council* [1978] A C 728, 751:
'Through the trilogy of cases in this House—*Donoghue v Stevenson, Hedley Byrne & Co Ltd v Heller & Partners Ltd,* and *Dorset Yacht Co Ltd v Home Office* the position has now been reached that in order to establish that a duty of care arises in a particular situation, it is not necessary to bring the facts of that situation within those of previous situations in which a duty of care has been held to exist. Rather the question has to be approached in two stages. First one has to ask whether, as between the alleged wrongdoer and the person who has suffered damage there is a sufficient relationship of proximity or neighbourhood such that, in the reasonable contemplation of the former, carelessness on his part may be likely to cause damage to the latter—in which case a *prima facie* duty of care arises. Secondly, if the first question is answered affirmatively, it is necessary to consider whether there are any considerations which ought to negative, or to reduce or limit the scope of the duty or the class of person to whom it is owed or the damages to which a breach of it may give rise: . . .'

Applying that general statement of principle to the present case, it is, as I indicated earlier, common ground that the first question which Lord Wilberforce said one should ask oneself, namely, whether there is sufficient proximity between the parties to give rise to the existence of a duty of care owed by the one to the other, falls to be answered in the affirmative. Indeed, it is difficult to imagine a greater degree of proximity, in the absence of a direct contractual relationship, than that which, under the modern type of building contract, exists between a building owner and a sub-contractor nominated by him or his architect.

That first question having been answered in the affirmative, however, it is necessary, according to the views expressed by Lord Wilberforce in the passage from his opinion in *Anns v Merton London Borough Council* quoted above, to ask oneself a second question, namely, whether there are any considerations which ought, *inter alia,* to limit the scope of the duty which exists.

Recent UK cases

To that second question I would answer that there are two important considerations which ought to limit the scope of the duty of care which it is common ground was owed by the appellants to the respondents on the assumed facts of the present case.

The first consideration is that, in *Donoghue v Stevenson* itself and in all the numerous cases in which the principle of that decision has been applied to different but analogous factual situations, it has always been either stated expressly, or taken for granted, that an essential ingredient in the cause of action relied on was the existence of danger, or the threat of danger, of physical damage to persons or their property, excluding for this purpose the very piece of property from the defective condition of which such danger, or threat of danger, arises. To dispense with that essential ingredient in a cause of action of the kind concerned in the present case would, in my view, involve a radical departure from long-established authority.

The second consideration is that there is no sound policy reason for substituting the wider scope of the duty of care put forward for the respondents for the more restricted scope of such duty put forward by the appellants. The effect of accepting the respondents' contention with regard to the scope of the duty of care involved would be, in substance, to create, as between two persons who are not in any contractual relationship with each other, obligations of one of those two persons to the other which are only really appropriate as between persons who do have such a relationship between them.

In the case of a manufacturer or distributor of goods, the position would be that he warranted to the ultimate user or consumer of such goods that they were as well designed, as merchantable and as fit for their contemplated purpose as the exercise of reasonable care could make them. In the case of sub-contractors such as those concerned in the present case, the position would be that they warranted to the building owner that the flooring, when laid, would be as well designed, as free from defects of any kind and as fit for its contemplated purpose as the exercise of reasonable care could make it. In my view, the imposition of warranties of this kind on one person in favour of another, when there is no contractual relationship between them, is contrary to any sound policy requirement.

It is, I think, just worth while to consider the difficulties which would arise if the wider scope of the duty of care put forward by the respondents were accepted. In any case where complaint was made by an ultimate consumer that a product made by some persons with whom he himself had no contract was defective, by what standard or standards of quality would the question of defectiveness fall to be decided? In the case of goods bought from a retailer, it could hardly be the standard prescribed by the contract between the retailer and the wholesaler, or between the wholesaler and the distributor, or between the distributor and the manufac-

turer, for the terms of such contracts would not even be known to the ultimate buyer. In the case of sub-contractors such as the appellants in the present case, it could hardly be the standard prescribed by the contract between the sub-contractors and the main contractors, for, although the building owner would probably be aware of those terms, he could not, since he was not a party to such contract, rely on any standard or standards prescribed in it. It follows that the question by what standard or standards alleged defects in a product complained of by its ultimate user or consumer are to be judged remains entirely at large and cannot be given any just or satisfactory answer.

If, contrary to the views expressed above, the relevant contract or contracts can be regarded in order to establish the standard or standards of quality by which the question of defectiveness falls to be judged, and if such contract or contracts happen to include provisions excluding or limiting liability for defective products or defective work, or for negligence generally, it seems that the party sued in delict should in justice be entitled to rely on such provisions. This illustrates with especial force the inherent difficulty of seeking to impose what are really contractual obligations by unprecedented and, as I think, wholly undesirable extensions of the existing law of delict. By contrast, if the scope of the duty of care contended for by the appellants is accepted, the standard of defectiveness presents no problem at all. The sole question is whether the product is so defective that, when used or consumed in the way in which it was intended to be, it gives rise to a danger of physical damage to persons or their property, other than the product concerned itself.

My Lords, for the reasons which I have given, I would decide the question of relevancy in favour of the appellants and allow the appeal accordingly.

Appeal dismissed.

1982 *Berliner v Sun Alliance*

COMMENTARY

This case links three of the most commonly recurring topics which come up whenever product liability is discussed—the motor industry, insurance and the USA. In fact this case could perhaps equally appropriately have been included in the section dealing with US product liability cases, as it deals in part with the interpretation of US legislation and case law. Nevertheless, it is in fact an English case heard in the Commercial Court before Mr Justice Bingham in November 1982.

Its interest lies, not in the fact that it developed UK law in relation to product liability any further, but because in general it illustrates the sorts of problems which can arise for foreign manufacturers wishing to export their goods to the United States and it is of particular importance for motor manufacturers in its interpretation of section 1399(e) of the National Traffic and Motor Vehicle Safety Act 1966. This legislation requires that every manufacturer importing motor vehicles into the USA must designate an agent for service of 'all administrative and judicial process'.

The case concerns the export to the USA of certain motor cycles manufactured by Norton Villiers Ltd and sold in the United States to one William McConnell who had an accident whilst riding the cycle which he blamed on a defect. The proceedings in England arose from an action brought by the American retailers and distributors as plaintiffs—who had been the defendants in an action brought by McConnell in the USA—for an indemnity against the manufacturers Norton Villiers Ltd (NVL). NVL had gone into liquidation, and so the plaintiffs were pursuing their claim against NVL's insurers. Their claim was resisted on two grounds by Sun Alliance. First that NVL had failed to notify them as insurers of 'any event which may give rise to a claim' as provided by the terms and conditions of the policy. In the final event, the case was lost on this point, as it was found that NVL had failed to comply with this condition of their policy and were not therefore covered. However, the second argument and the more interesting one was that their liability under the policy was excluded by virtue of wording in the policy which provided that 'The Company shall not be liable in respect of ... (6) any action for damage arising in connection with products supplied brought against (NVL) in any territory outside Great Britain ... in which (NVL) is represented by a branch or by any person domiciled in such territory'.

The object of this exclusion was, of course, to remove from the scope of the cover offered by the policy actions in countries where proceedings could be served against the insured.

This is where the provisions of the National Traffic and Motor Vehicle Safety Act are relevant. As we have seen, this required the designation of an agent for service of 'all administrative and judicial processes'. Such a designation had been made by NVL but not revealed to the insurers, and the question was, did the designation and service provisions of the Act apply only for the purposes of the Act or extend to civil actions also. In a 1970 case, *Bollard v Volkswagenwerke AG*, it had been held that the service provision did also relate to civil processes arising out of alleged vehicle defects, although this conclusion had been criticised in a series of rulings in other courts in the US.

Mr Justice Bingham decided that it was likely in view of these later dissenting judgments that *Bollard* had been wrongly decided, and that for civil purposes NVL had accordingly not been 'represented' in the USA at the relevant time, and were therefore entitled to be indemnified under the terms of their policy. However, as we have seen, NVL had failed to notify their insurers of the incident under the terms of the policy and the case failed on that point.

JUDGMENT

Queen's Bench Division (Commercial Court)
November 18, 1982

Berliner Motor Corporation and Steiers Lawn & Sports Inc
versus
Sun Alliance and London Insurance Limited

Before Mr Justice Bingham

Mr Justice Bingham. On October 30, 1971, William McConnell was riding his Norton Villiers motor cycle in Cook County, Illinois, when he had an accident which he attributed to a defect in the motor cycle. He accordingly brought proceedings in the Circuit Court of Cook County. The defendants whom he sued included the first plaintiffs in this action, a New Jersey corporation which acted as distributors of Norton Villiers motor cycles in the eastern United States; the second plaintiffs in this action, an Illinois corporation which retailed motor cycles, and Norton Villiers Corporation (NVC), a wholly owned Californian subsidiary of the English company, Norton Villiers Ltd (NVL), which acted as NVL's distributor in the western half of the United States. In due course, NVL, as manufacturers of the defective motor cycle, were joined as defendants by McConnell and as third party by these plaintiffs. NVC were dismissed from the action, but on March 12, 1976, McConnell recovered judgment against these plaintiffs and NVL and three days later, on March 15, 1976, these plaintiffs recovered judgment against NVL. These plaintiffs then sued on their judgment here and on July 10, 1980, this court adjudged that NVL pay to the first plaintiffs $165,524.65 plus interest and to the second plaintiffs $82,793.13 plus interest. NVL had in 1975

Recent UK cases

gone into liquidation, and the plaintiffs now seek to enforce their judgment against the defendants, Sun Alliance and London Insurance Ltd as NVL's insurers ('the insurers') under the Third Parties (Rights against Insurers) Act, 1930. The issue which arises in this action is whether NVL were entitled to be indemnified by the insurers under the policy to which I shall refer in a moment. Nothing turns on the title of the plaintiffs to sue.

On July 9, 1970, NVL completed proposals for products liability and public liability insurance in respect of their motor cycles. I read the forms together because only one policy resulted. NVL stated in their proposal that they were exporters, and then came these two questions:

(a) Has the Proposer any branch or other address(es) overseas?

(b) Is Proposer represented overseas by a resident employee or an agent holding a Power of Attorney?

If so, give details.

I have no doubt that these questions were designed to elicit whether the proposer had any business presence abroad which would permit the local service of foreign proceedings. To the first question (reading the forms together) NVL answered: 'Yes ... Norton Villiers Corpn, Calif, USA'. To the second they replied 'Independent Agents'.

Following the proposals the insurers granted NVL cover on the terms of a policy number 003T 034631. It provided that the proposal should be incorporated in and be the basis of the contract and that the truth of the proposal and observance of the terms of the policy relating to anything to be done or complied with by a beneficiary should be conditions precedent to any liability of the insurers. NVL were defined as a beneficiary. The indemnity granted was against liability at law for damages and claimant's costs and expenses in respect of accidental injury to any person anywhere in the world arising from products supplied from the United Kingdom. This indemnity was subject to a number of exceptions, of which number six lies at the heart of this case. It read as follows:

The Company shall not be liable in respect of . . .

6. any action for damages arising in connection with products supplied brought against any Beneficiary in any territory outside Great Britain Northern Ireland the Channel Islands or the Isle of Man in which the Beneficiary is represented by a branch or by any person domiciled in such territory . . .

The policy also contained this condition:
2. Upon the happening of any Event which may give rise to a claim (regardless of any Excess) the Insured shall forthwith give written notice to the Company with full particulars. Every letter claim writ summons and process shall be forwarded to the Company on receipt. Written

notice shall also be given by the Insured to the Company immediately any Beneficiary shall have knowledge of any prosecution or inquest in connection with any circumstances which may give rise to liability under this Policy. No admission offer promise payment or indemnity shall be made or given by or on behalf of any Beneficiary without the written consent of the Company which shall be entitled to take over and conduct in the name of the Beneficiary the defence or settlement of any claim or to prosecute any claim in the name of the Beneficiary for its own benefit and shall have full discretion in the conduct of any claim. The Beneficiary shall give all such assistance as the Company may require.

The policy was renewed on the same terms at the end of the first year and was in force at the time of McConnell's accident. NVL's insurance brokers, Rea Brothers (Insurance) Ltd, in their cover and debit notes to NVL relating to the policy described it as subject to 'UK Courts' jurisdiction'.

I must at this point digress to deal with a matter which becomes very material as the story unfolds. In about 1966 there came into force in the United States the National Traffic and Motor Vehicle Safety Act of that year. Its object was to impose federal control over vehicle design and manufacture in the interests of safety. It is somewhat analogous to our own Construction and Use Regulations. Its importance for present purposes lies in section 1399 (e), which provides:

It shall be the duty of every manufacturer offering a motor vehicle or item of motor vehicle equipment for importation into the United States to designate in writing an agent upon whom service of all administrative and judicial processes, notices, orders, decisions and requirements may be made for and on behalf of said manufacturer, and to file such designation with the Secretary, which designation may from time to time be changed by like writing, similarly filed. Service of all administrative and judicial processes, notices, orders, decisions and requirements may be made upon said manufacturer by service upon such designated agent at his office or usual place of residence with like effect as if made personally upon said manufacturer, and in default of such designation of such agent, service of process, notice, order, requirement or decision in any proceeding before the Secretary or in any judicial proceeding for enforcement of this title or any standards prescribed pursuant to this title may be made by posting such process, notice, order, requirement or decision in the Office of the Secretary.

In accordance with this requirement NVL in 1969 designated NVC as its agent, a fact not disclosed to the insurers and not (I think) present to the mind of NVL in 1970-71. In *Bollard v Volkswagenwerke AG,* 313 Fed Supp 126 (1970) it was held in the United States District Court for the Western District of Missouri that the service provision I have quoted related not only to process associated with the regulatory objects of the

Berliner v Sun Alliance

Act but also to inter-party civil process arising out of alleged vehicle defects. The decision was in any event understood to have that effect.

On April 27, 1972, NVL were informed that a claim had been made by one Rondenet against the first plaintiffs in Illinois. The insurers were advised on June 2. The insurers requested on June 28 that they should be kept closely informed of developments.

On July 17 NVL learned of a claim intimated by one Drake in Michigan. The insurers were told of it on July 25.

Notification of these claims clearly led to discussions between the insurers, the brokers and NVL. On about September 18, 1972 the insurers wrote to the brokers an undated letter in these terms, which I must quote in full.

'We refer to our discussions regarding the effect of the Traffic and Motor Vehicle Safety Act so far as concerns the Insured's operations in the United States and the degree of cover afforded by the above policy. Under the Policy at present we provide cover anywhere in the World in respect of products supplied from Great Britain, Northern Ireland, the Channel Islands or the Isle of Man, but by virtue of Exception six we exclude actions for damages brought in those countries outside Great Britain in which the Insured has representation through a branch or by any person domiciled in such territory or by a company firm or individual holding the Insured's Power of Attorney. Thus whilst not so limited as a UK jurisdiction clause, we do exclude actions in countries where service of a Writ is possible. So far as the Insured's operations in the USA is concerned this presented no problem in the past for the Insured had no representation, their interest being looked after by their Dealers—Norton Villiers Corporation and Berliner. They would have Insurance protecting their interest as Suppliers not engaged in manufacture, no doubt receiving a discounted rate in the knowledge that rights of recovery would exist against the UK manufacturer claims being brought back in this country.'

'The Traffic and Motor Vehicle Safety Act changes this position for under the Act it is 'the duty of every manufacturer to designate in writing an Agent upon whom service of all administrative and judicial processes may be made for and on behalf of the said manufacturer'. Thus our exception to which we have earlier made reference will then become operative and claims arising from actions brought in the USA through the designated Agent will not be covered. The Sun Alliance Group is not licensed to write insurance in the USA, our interest in that country being looked after by Underwriting Agents, Chubb & Sons who write insurance on behalf of a consortium of which we are a member. We thus have no control over their underwriting and are not in a position to direct or control business in their account. The only solution, as we see it, is for Norton Villiers Ltd to comply with the Act and designate an Agent, such Agent should then arrange for his insurance to be extended to provide for claims brought

upon him as a result of the Act. To avoid duplication in the payment of premiums it would be advisable for such agent to be treated as a 'Manufacturer' having no rights of recourse against the UK manufacturer. We would then under our policy have to remove the USA turnover amounting to the not inconsiderable sum of £3,000,000 for no risk would be left from this portion of the Insured's exports, and whilst regretting the loss of premium and may be disturbing your control of the Insurance, we can see no alternative for the Insured must comply with the terms of the Act.'

'As we mentioned on the telephone this was how we treated another large connection in which we participated under a collective policy. We trust you will find our letter helpful and can assure you that all steps were considered with a view to maintaining control under our policy and therefore through your account, but it appears this is not possible and the separate arrangements we have outlined above will need to be affected in order to comply with the requirements of the Act.'

'We now await your further instructions.'

Several points are worth noting about this letter. First, the insurers have become alive to the 1966 Act but are plainly ignorant of the designation made by NVL in 1969. Secondly, the insurers express the belief that past United States claims fall within the policy and are not excluded by the exception. Thirdly, the insurers believe that the exception will operate to exclude United States claims in future. Fourthly, the insurers do not repudiate or express unwillingness to meet any claim and give no indication that the policy conditions need not be complied with. The brokers passed on the substance of this claim to NVL, as was no doubt to be expected. It is plain that the brokers also envisaged the designation of an agent as something which would occur in the future.

McConnell started his proceedings against the plaintiffs and NVC in March 1972, but NVC were not served until December 4. The claim came to the notice of NVL not later than December 11. By the end of that month the first plaintiffs had made their third party claim against NVL, and McConnell joined NVL as a defendant on February 20. By then NVC had instructed its Chicago lawyers to act for NVL. McConnell's summons was served on NVC as agents of NVL, and NVC passed it on to their lawyers with a covering letter which read:

'Since I last spoke with you I have determined that a formal filing under the US National Traffic and Motor Vehicle Safety Act of 1966 naming Norton Villiers Corporation as agent in the USA for Norton Villiers Limited, upon whom service of all summons may be made, was made by Norton Villiers Limited in 1969. I therefore must assume that this service must be considered valid. Will you please, therefore, answer the summons on behalf of Norton Villiers Limited within the prescribed period of time.'

This letter was copied to NVL in England, who raised no protest and sought no advice. Appearance was duly

Recent UK cases

entered for NVL, and over the months following NVL through their American lawyers litigated vigorously. NVL were informed of developments as they occurred.

Four things then happened. First, steps were taken in July 1973, to vary NVL's insurance cover so as to provide that the insurers should not be liable in respect of claims arisng out of products supplied to the United States and sold through NVL's designated agents. NVC's or the distributors' insurers were to cover such risks. This variation was effective from January 1, 1973 (NVC) and October 1972 (distributors). Secondly, NVL took legal advice, as did the insurers. Thirdly, a meeting took place between NVL brokers and insurers on October 22, 1973. Mr Hillier, a director of NVL, attended on their behalf, and by this time at the latest he became aware of the designation made by NVL under the 1966 Act. Whether he appreciated the situation earlier is a question I consider below. The insurers expressed the view that no claims in the USA would be the subject of indemnity under the policy. NVL did not accept that view. Fourthly, on October 25, 1973, NVL gave the insurers notice (through their solicitors) of the McConnell claim. Up to then the insurers had received no notification whatever of this claim.

The first question argued before me was whether the McConnell claim, *prima facie* within the cover afforded by the policy, was excluded by exception 6. I do not propose to summarize the parties' contentions (those of the plaintiffs were helpfully supplied to me in typewritten form) but instead to express my conclusions upon them:

(1) The expression 'territory' is a vague term deliberately chosen to embrace both sovereign states and dependent territories. It was suggested that each state of the Union was a separate territory so that even if NVL had an agent in California they had none in Illinois. This I reject. The last thing this clause could be held to contemplate is an enquiry into the constitutional standing of the American states (or, for that matter, the regions or departments of France or the provinces of Argentina). For present purposes 'any territory outside Great Britain' includes any part of the United States.

(2) The expression 'represented' is not, I think, very precisely used, but in context its intent seems to me to be plain enough: an insured is represented in the foreign territory if it has a presence there either by one of its own branches or through a locally domiciled agent.

(3) The actions which are excluded are actions (a) for damages (b) arising in connection with products supplied (c) brought against NVL in any territory where the insured is so represented. There was argument whether the relevant action here is the Cook County action or the action against NVL in London. The plaintiffs seek to rely on their English judgment, and it seems to me that they are entitled to do so. It is of course clear that the policy does not cover the insured at all, and the exception is irrelevant, unless the insured has a liability at law for damages and claimant's costs and

expenses in respect of accidental injury to any person, but the insurers have not sought to argue that that requirement is not met in respect of either the Illinois or the English judgment.

I have already indicated my view that the United States, or Illinois, is a territory outside Great Britain for purposes of this exception. Under the construction put upon section 1399 (e) of the National Traffic and Motor Vehicle Safety Act, 1966 in *Bollard's* case, NVL were, by virtue of its designation of NVC as its agent, represented by a person domiciled in the United States (although not by a branch). The action brought against NVL in Cook County was accordingly an action for damages in connection with products supplied brought against NVL in an excluded territory. But this provisional conclusion fails to take account of two things:

(1) The first is that in a series of rulings of different courts in the United States the decision in *Bollard's* case was not followed and it was held that the designation and service provision of section 1399 (e) of the Act were for purposes of the Act only: *Rubino v Celeste Motors Inc,* DC NDNY (1974); *Volkswagenwerke AG v McCurdy,* 340 So 2d 544 (1976); *Fields v Peyer,* 250 NW 2d 311 (1977); *Sipes v American Honda Motor Co Inc,* 608 SW 2d 125 (1980); *Pasquale v Genovese,* 428 A2d 1126 (1981); *Porsche v The Superior Court of Sacramento County,* 177 Cal Reptr 155 (1981); *Low v Bayerische Motoren Werke* AG 449 NYS 2d 733 (1982). These decisions had not been given when NVC gave instructions that an appearance be entered for NVL. At that time *Bollard* was still, evidently, accepted as good law. But the question still arises whether at the date of McConnell's accident or claim NVL were 'represented' by NVC as a person domiciled in the United States. The evidence I have heard makes it clear that NVC dealt with NVL as principals, buying the motor cycles from NVL and reselling on their own account. NVC had no agency role save for the compulsory purposes of the 1966 Act. If, as seems the better view, *Bollard* was wrongly decided and the later cases express the correct rule, it seems to me to follow that NVL were not represented in the United States at the relevant time and I do not think it affects this conclusion that NVC chose to accept service and enter an appearance for NVL (although that may be important for a different reason).

(2) The second point is that the action which the plaintiffs rely on for purposes of their claim against the insurers was brought not in Illinois but in this court. Had there been no submission by NVL to the jurisdiction in Illinois NVL might have been able to resist the claim here on the ground that the Illinois court had no jurisdiction, and thus it might have been said that NVL had no liability in law in respect of which they were entitled to indemnity. But as it was the Illinois court undoubtedly did have jurisdiction and judgment against NVL was duly entered here. I need not consider the effect of an Illinois judgment based on an assumption of jurisdiction which would not be recognized here. These considerations lead me to conclude that the plaintiffs' claim

Berliner v Sun Alliance

against NVL did fall within the policy cover and not within the exception and thus NVL were *prima facie* entitled to indemnity.

If, contrary to their main contention, the plaintiffs' claim does not fall within exception 6, the insurers rely on NVL's breach of condition 2 of the policy in failing to give notification of McConnell's and the plaintiffs' claims and failing to forward the relevant documents. There very plainly was a gross breach of this condition and as a result of the breach the insurers lost any opportunity to consider what line NVL should adopt in the proceedings and to act as *dominus litis*. The plaintiffs accept that due notice was not given but rely on the letter written on about September 18, 1972 (which I have quoted above in full) as giving rise to a waiver and estoppel. It is said that in that letter the insurers denied that they were liable to NVL in respect of claims arising from actions brought in the USA against NVL and that NVL's failure to given notice was induced by the letter. I cannot accept these contentions as correct. In the first place, the insurers' letter did not deny liability to NVL in respect of actions brought in the USA: as already noted, it said (albeit on a basis soon to be proved mistaken) that the insurers had been liable in the past but would not be in the future, once an agent had been designated. The insurers did not in the letter repudiate any liability and certainly did not waive compliance with any policy condition. Nor do I think, secondly, that NVL acted in reliance on any such understanding of what the insurers had said. This is a more difficult question, and I must review the evidence in a little detail. Mr Hillier said in evidence in chief that notice of the McConnell claim was not given to the insurers because he had been convinced by the brokers that there was a defect in the Sun Alliance cover. He was referring to the conversations in September 1972, which (he said) made clear to him that the existence of NVC and the position under the 1966 Act had a fundamental effect on the cover. When cross-examined, he said that he thought he was aware of the designation at the time of those conversations; it was, however, plain from the letter which the brokers wrote to him, following receipt of the letter from the insurers in September 1972, which I have quoted, that the brokers did not know of the designation, and that caused Mr Hillier very fairly to acknowledge that it could be that he did not then know of the designation. Not surprisingly, Mr Hillier had an imperfect recollection of these events ten years ago. On his evidence alone, I would have been very doubtful if the insurers' letter had caused NVL not to give notice of the McConnell claim, but the documentary evidence suggests to me very strongly that it did not. The points which seem to me significant are these:

(1) As already mentioned, the brokers did not know in September 1972, that an agent had been designated under the 1966 Act. There was no reason to think the cover was ineffective until an appointment was made. There is no indication that NVL corrected the broker's misunderstanding. I suspect NVL shared it.

(2) When the McConnell claim was notified to NVL, a Mr Colquhoun wrote a memo to Mr Hillier saying 'Can I please assume that you will lodge this with our insurers if you judge it to be necessary'. Mr Hillier's answer contained no suggestion that the insurers had said notification was unnecessary or futile.

(3) On July 23, 1973, the brokers thought that the United States Act had been enacted in 1972. That would mean that accidents occurring before that date would not be excluded. Had NVL understood the true position I cannot think that the brokers would have been so much in the dark.

(4) On November 5, 1973, NVL wrote to their solicitors, with reference to the McConnell claim—You will see that we are in default in the same way as the Drake case and for the same reason *ie* that we have proceeded to defend the case to the best of our ability.

There is no suggestion here, or in a further letter to their solicitors on November 14, that NVL had omitted to bring the claim to the notice of the insurers because the insurers had led them to believe they need not do so.

(5) When NVL were given clear notice by the insurers' solicitors that the insurers were refusing to accept responsibiity for the McConnell claim because NVL were in breach of condition 2 of the policy in entering an appearance in Illinois and failing to give prompt notice of the claim to the insurers, NVL did not lay the blame for their omission on any representation by insurers.

The truth is, in my view, that although NVL knew after September 1972, that there was a problem over the American cover, the failure to give notice of the McConnell claim was the result of misunderstanding or miscalculation and not of inducement by the insurers. Taken at its strongest, the insurers' letter of September 1972, could only have deterred NVL from notifying claims which they knew to have arisen after the designation, and I feel sure that NVL did not have the fact or the date of the designation in mind at the relevant time.

The insurers further plead, in paragraphs 8 and 9 of their re-amended points of defence, a plea of misrepresentation arising out of the answers given by NVL to the questions I have quoted in the proposal form. The insurers put it as follows:

8. By their foregoing answers, which were warranted to be true and complete, Norton Villiers Limited represented as follows: (a) That Norton Villiers Corporation were a branch of Norton Villiers Limited. (b) That, save as aforesaid, Norton Villiers Limited had no presence in the United States of America, being represented there by independent agents.

9. The foregoing representations were inaccurate and/or incomplete in that by virtue of the foregoing Act and/or by virtue of the presence of Norton Villiers Corporation, being the designated agent thereunder,

Norton Villiers Limited had a presence throughout the United States of America and were amenable to the jurisdiction of every state.

Save that NVC may have been either a branch or an overseas address, representation (a) was made. I do not, however, think that representation (b) was made, or that NVL's answers could reasonably be understood as meaning that NVL had no representation outside California. The real representation made by NVL was that they *were* represented in the United States and if (as I have held) they were not, that was a misrepresentation. The insurers have not, however, pleaded or relied on that misrepresentation and since it is plain from their letter of September 1972, that they did not understand NVL to have made such a representation this is understandable. This defence is not in my judgment a good one.

The insurers raised two further estoppels by re-amendment. The first, pleaded in paragraph 15, was put in this way:

The Plaintiffs are estopped from contending that on the true construction of section 1399 of the National Traffic and Motor Vehicle Safety Act, 1966 a person designated under the Act was the Agent of the manufacturer only for the purposes of process under that Act since they used the said Act for the purpose of securing process of their counter-claim in the McConnell action.

The short answer to that is in my opinion that the plaintiffs are for the purposes of these proceedings standing in the shoes of NVL and there is no estoppel binding on NVL. The second estoppel, pleaded in paragraph 16, read as follows: Further NVL in any proceedings against Sun Alliance for indemnity in respect of the said judgment would have been estopped from denying that there had been valid service on themselves by virtue of section 1399 by reason of service on their designated Agent NVL.

I agree that NVL could not in the circumstances deny that there had been good service upon them in Illinois, but if my previous conclusions are correct they could deny the only proposition of importance, namely, that they were represented by a person domiciled in the United States. So I do not think either of these estoppels helps the insurers, but since I have found in their favour on the breach of condition two they do not need them and the question is somewhat academic.

My conclusion accordingly is that this action must be dismissed.

1983 *Mitchell v Finney Lock Seeds*

COMMENTARY

Most of the cases being considered in this study affect the development of the law of negligence. This case represents a particularly important development in the realm of liability for defective products arising not in negligence but under a contract of sale. For many years, the use of contractual clauses which seek to exclude or limit the contractual liability of one party to the other have come under increasingly close judicial scrutiny. In particular, the use of exclusion clauses in consumer contracts, where the consumer is likely to be in a relatively weak bargaining position and therefore has had to accept the contract conditions imposed on him by the seller, had been particularly criticised. This culminated in the passing of the Supply of Goods (Implied Terms) Act in 1973 (the provisions of which are now contained in the Unfair Contract Terms Act 1977) which states that such clauses may no longer be used in relation to the Sale of Goods Act implied terms as to quality and fitness when the goods are being sold to a consumer; their use is restricted in contracts made between businesses. However up to this time, the control of exclusion clauses depended on the judiciary, and through a series of cases starting with *Suisse Atlantique Société d'Armement Maritime SA v NV Rotterdamsche Kolen Centrale* [1967] 1 AC 36, the doctrine of fundamental breach of contract was developed to deal with cases where one party attempted to extricate himself from a really serious breach of contract going to the very root of what had been agreed, by attempting to rely on an exclusion clause. For example, where an unroadworthy car had been supplied instead of a roadworthy one. The court said that the exclusion clause had to be examined closely to see whether it was intended to apply to a case where a breach of contract had occurred which went to the very root of the contract. In such a case the seller would not be able to rely on an exclusion clause unless it covered fundamental breach.

This approach, whilst being of assistance to consumers in some cases, had also caused inequities *eg* as in *Harbutts Plasticine Ltd v Wayne Tank and Pump Co Ltd* [1970] 1 QB 447, where a contractor built faulty pipes into a factory which caused a fire, and the limited liability clause in his contract was held not to apply to fundamental breach; that he was in fundamental breach and therefore liable for the whole cost of the damage. This had been followed by *Photo Production Ltd v Securicor Transport Ltd* [1980] AC 877, where the House of Lords had expressly overruled the decision in *Harbutt* and in doing so cast great doubt on the doctrine of fundamental breach. By the time the *Securicor* case had been heard, the Unfair Contract Terms Act had of course reached the statute book, and while the events of the case were pre-1977 and therefore the reasonableness test did not apply, the need for the doctrine of fundamental breach had obviously been much reduced.

Mitchell v Finney Lock Seeds

The importance of this case in 1983 is that it gave the House of Lords an opportunity to confirm and interpret their judgment in the *Securicor* case, and also to state that their earlier decision had 'forcibly evicted' the doctrine of fundamental breach from our legal system and given it 'final quietus'. It also gave an opportunity for the Lords to consider the application of the reasonableness test in relation to exclusion clauses. The Lords made it clear that the limitation of liability clause in the seed merchant's conditions of business would have protected him had the case been decided on the common law issue alone, but that the clause should be judged only on the reasonableness test contained in the Supply of Goods (Implied Terms) Act 1973. On this basis, the clause failed as being unreasonable within the parameters laid down in the legislation; particular factors taken into account included the fact that the evidence was that the seed merchants customarily did negotiate greater settlements than just the price of the seeds in cases of this type; the type of seeds supplied was due to negligence; and finally the seed merchant could have insured against the risk of crop failure caused by supplying the wrong type of seeds without materially affecting the price.

A final interesting point is that the court also referred to the decision in what has been called *Securicor 2— Ailsa Craig Fishing Co Ltd v Malvern Fishing Co Ltd* [1983] 1 Lloyd's Rep 183 which drew an important distinction between clauses which exclude and those which limit liability, on the basis that with a limitation of liability clause it is more likely that the parties contemplate there should be a relationship between the risk undertaken by one party, and the remuneration which he is to receive. In this case, the clause in question related to limitation of liability and yet this consideration does not seem to have been applied, the only criteria for the judgment being the reasonableness test. It still seems to leave open the extent to which a draftsman can prepare a limitation of liability clause and hope that it will prove effective.

JUDGMENT

House of Lords
June 30, 1983

*George Mitchell (Chesterhall) Limited
versus
Finney Lock Seeds Limited*

Before Lord Diplock, Lord Scarman, Lord Roskill, Lord Bridge of Harwich and Lord Brightman

Lord Diplock. My Lords, this is a case about an exemption clause contained in a contract for the sale of goods (not being a consumer sale) to which the Supply of Goods (Implied Terms) Act 1973, applied. In reliance on the exemption clause the sellers sought to limit their liability to the buyers to a sum which represented only one third of 1% of the damage that the buyers had sustained as a result of an undisputed breach of contract by the sellers. The sellers failed before the trial judge, Mr Justice Parker, who, by placing upon the language of the exemption clause a strained and artificial meaning, found himself able to hold that the breach of contract in respect of which the buyers sued fell outside the clause (see [1981] 1 Lloyd's Rep 476). In the Court of Appeal both Lord Justice Oliver and Lord Justice Kerr, by similar processes of strained interpretation, held that the breach was not covered by the exemption clause; but they also held that if the breach had been covered, it would in all the circumstances of the case not have been fair or reasonable to allow reliance on the clause, and that accordingly the clause would have been unenforceable under the Act. Lord Denning, MR, was alone in holding that the language of the exemption clause was plain and unambiguous; that it would be apparent to anyone who read it that it covered the breach in respect of which the buyers' action was brought; and that the passing of the Supply of Goods (Implied Terms) Act 1973, and its successor, the Unfair Contract Terms Act 1977, had removed from judges the temptation to resort to the device of ascribing to words appearing in exemption clauses a tortured meaning so as to avoid giving effect to an exclusion or limitation of liability when the judge thought that in the circumstances to do so would be unfair. Lord Denning, MR, agreed with the other members of the court that the appeal should be dismissed but solely on the statutory ground under the 1973 Act that it would not be fair and reasonable to allow reliance upon the clause (see [1983] 1 Lloyd's Rep 169).

My Lords, I have had the advantage of reading in advance the speech to be delivered by my noble and learned friend, Lord Bridge of Harwich, in favour of dismissing this appeal upon grounds which reflect the reasoning although not the inimitable style of Lord Denning's judgment in the Court of Appeal.

I agree entirely with Lord Bridge's speech and there is nothing that I could usefully add to it; but I cannot refrain from noting with regret, which is, I am sure, shared by all members of the Appellate Committee of this House, that Lord Denning's judgment in the instant case, which was delivered on September 29, 1982, is probably the last in which your Lordships will have the opportunity of enjoying his eminently readable style of exposition and his stimulating and percipient approach to the continuing development of the common law to which he has himself in his judicial lifetime made so outstanding a contribution.

Lord Scarman. My Lords, I have had the advantage of reading in draft the speech to be delivered by my noble and learned friend, Lord Bridge of Harwich. I agree with it, and for the reasons which he gives would dismiss the appeal.

Recent UK cases

Lord Roskill. My Lords, I have had the advantage of reading in draft the speech to be delivered by my noble and learned friend, Lord Bridge of Harwich. I agree with it, and for the reasons which he gives I would dismiss the appeal.

Lord Bridge of Harwich. My Lords, the appellants are seed merchants. The respondents are farmers in East Lothian. In December 1973, the respondents ordered from the appellants 30lb of Dutch winter white cabbage seeds. The seeds supplied were invoiced as 'Finney's Late Dutch Special'. The price was £201.60. 'Finney's Late Dutch Special' was the variety required by the respondents. It is a Dutch winter white cabbage which grows particularly well in the area of East Lothian where the respondents farm, and can be harvested and sold at a favourable price in the spring. The respondents planted some 63 acres of their land with seedlings grown from the seeds supplied by the appellants to produce their cabbage crop for the spring of 1975. In the event, the crop proved to be worthless and had to be ploughed in. This was for two reasons. First, the seeds supplied were not 'Finney's Late Dutch Special' or any other variety of Dutch winter white cabbage, but a variety of autumn cabbage. Secondly, even as autumn cabbage the seeds were of very inferior quality.

The issues in the appeal arise from three sentences in the conditions of sale endorsed on the appellants' invoice and admittedly embodied in the terms on which the appellants contracted. For ease of reference it will be convenient to number the sentences. Omitting immaterial words they read as follows:

1. In the event of any seeds or plants sold or agreed to be sold by us not complying with the express terms of the contract of sale . . . or any seeds or plants proving defective in varietal purity we will, at our option, replace the defective seeds or plants, free of charge to the buyer or will refund all payments made to us by the buyer in respect of the defective seeds or plants and this shall be the limit of our obligation.

2. We hereby exclude all liability for any loss or damage arising from the use of any seeds or plants supplied by us and for any consequential loss or damage arising out of such use or any failure in the performance of or any defect in any seeds or plants supplied by us or for any other loss or damage whatsoever save for, at our option, liability for any such replacement or refund as aforesaid.

3. In accordance with the established custom of the seed trade any express or implied condition, statement or warranty, statutory or otherwise, not stated in these conditions is hereby excluded.

I will refer to the whole as 'the relevant condition' and to the parts as 'clause 1, 2, and 3' of the relevant condition.

The first issue is whether the relevant condition, on its true construction in the context of the contract as a whole, is effective to limit the appellants' liability to a refund of £201.60, the price of the seeds ('the common law issue'). The second issue is whether, if the common law issue is decided in the appellants' favour, they should nevertheless be precluded from reliance on this limitation of liability pursuant to the provisions of the modified section 55 of the Sale of Goods Act 1979, which is set out in paragraph 11 of Schedule 1 to the Act and which applies to contracts made between May 18, 1973 and February 1, 1978 ('the statutory issue').

The learned trial judge, Mr Justice Parker, on the basis of evidence that the seeds supplied were incapable of producing a commercially saleable crop, decided the common law issue against the appellants on the ground that—

. . . what was supplied . . . was in no commercial sense vegetable seed at all (but was) the delivery of something wholly different in kind from that which was ordered and which the defendants had agreed to supply.

He accordingly found it unnecessary to decide the statutory issue, but helpfully made some important findings of fact, which are very relevant if that issue fails to be decided. He gave judgment in favour of the respondents for £61,513.78 damages and £30,756 interest. Nothing now turns on these figures, but it is perhaps significant to point out that the damages awarded do not represent merely 'loss of anticipated profit', as was erroneously suggested in the appellants' printed case. The figure includes, as Mr Waller very properly accepted, all the costs incurred by the respondents in the cultivation of the worthless crop as well as the profit they would have expected to make from a successful crop if the proper seeds had been supplied.

In the Court of Appeal, the common law issue was decided in favour of the appellants by Lord Denning, MR, who said: ' . . . On the natural interpretation, I think the condition is sufficient to limit the seed merchants to a refund of the price paid or replacement of the seeds.'

Lord Justice Oliver decided the common law issue against the appellants primarily on a ground akin to that of Mr Justice Parker, albeit somewhat differently expressed. Fastening on the words 'agreed to be sold' in clause 1 of the relevant condition, he held that the clause could not be construed to mean 'in the event of the seeds sold or agreed to be sold by us not being the seeds agreed to be sold by us'.

Clause 2 of the relevant condition he held to be 'merely a supplement' to clause 1. He thus arrived at the conclusion that the appellants had only succeeded in limiting their liability arising from the supply of seeds which were correctly described as 'Finney's Late Dutch Special' but were defective in quality. As the seeds supplied were not 'Finney's Late Dutch Special', the relevant condition gave them no protection. Lord Justice Kerr, in whose reasoning Lord Justice Oliver also concurred, decoded the common law issue against the appellants on the ground that the relevant condition was ineffective to limit the appellants' liability for a

Mitchell v Finney Lock Seeds

breach of contract which could not have occurred without negligence on the appellants' part, and that the supply of the wrong variety of seeds was such a breach.

The Court of Appeal, however, were unanimous in deciding the statutory issue against the appellants.

In his judgment, Lord Denning, MR, traces, in his uniquely colourful and graphic style, the history of the courts' approach to contractual clauses excluding or limiting liability, culminating in the intervention of the legislature, first by the Supply of Goods (Implied Terms) Act 1973, secondly, by the Unfair Contract Terms Act 1977. My Lords, in considering the common law issue, I will resist the temptation to follow that fascinating trail, but will content myself with references to the two recent decisions of your Lordships' House commonly called the two Securicor cases: Photo Production Ltd v Securicor Transport Ltd [1980] 1 Lloyd's Rep 545; [1980] A C 827 ('Securicor 1') and Ailsa Craig Fishing Co Ltd v Malvern Fishing Co Ltd [1983] 1 Lloyd's Rep 183; [1983] 1 All ER 101 ('Securicor 2').

Securicor 1 gave the final quietus to the doctrine that a 'fundamental breach' of contract deprived the party in breach of the benefit of clauses in the contract excluding or limiting his liability. Securicor 2 drew an important distinction between exclusion and limitation clauses.

. . . . .

My Lords, it seems to me, with all due deference, that the judgments of the learned trial judge and of Lord Justice Oliver on the common law issue come dangerously near to re-introducing by the back door the doctrine of 'fundamental breach' which this House in Securicor 1 had so forcibly evicted by the front. The learned judge discussed what I may call the 'peas and beans' or 'chalk and cheese' cases, those in which it has been held that exemption clauses do not apply where there has been a contract to sell one thing, eg a motor car, and the seller has supplied quite another thing, eg a bicycle. I hasten to add that the judge can in no way be criticised for adopting this approach since counsel appearing for the appellants at trial had conceded 'that if what had been delivered had been beetroot seed or carrot seed, he would not be able to rely upon the clause'. Different counsel appeared for the appellants in the Court of Appeal, where that concession was withdrawn.

In my opinion, this is not a 'peas and beans' case at all. The relevant condition applies to 'seeds'. Clause 1 refers to seeds 'sold' and 'seeds agreed to be sold'. Clause 2 refers to 'seeds supplied'. As I have pointed out, Lord Justice Oliver concentrates his attention on the phrase 'seeds agreed to be sold'. I can see no justification, with respect, for allowing this phrase alone to dictate the interpretation of the relevant condition, still less for treating clause 2 as 'merely a supplement' to clause 1. Clause 2 is perfectly clear and unambiguous. The reference to 'seeds agreed to be sold' as well as to 'seeds

sold' in clause 1 reflects the same dichotomy as the definition of 'sale' in the Sale of Goods Act 1979, as including a bargain and sale as well as a sale and delivery. The defective seeds in this case were seeds sold and delivered, just as clearly as they were seeds supplied, by the appellants to the respondents. The relevant condition, read as a whole, unambiguously limits the appellants' liability to replacement of the seeds or refund of the price. It is only possible to read an ambiguity into it by the process of strained construction which was deprecated by Lord Diplock in Securicor 1 and by Lord Wilberforce in Securicor 2.

In holding that the relevant condition was ineffective to limit the appellants' liability for a breach of contract caused by their negligence, Lord Justice Kerr applied the principles stated by Lord Morton of Henryton giving the judgment of the Privy Council in Canada Steamship Lines Ltd v The King [1952] 1 Lloyd's Rep 1; [1952] A C 192. The learned Lord Justice stated correctly that this case was also referred to by Lord Fraser of Tullybelton in Securicor 2. He omitted, however, to notice that, as appears from the passage from Lord Fraser's speech which I have already cited, the whole point of Lord Fraser's reference was to express his opinion that the very strict principles laid down in the Canada Steamship Lines case as applicable to exclusion and indemnity clauses cannot be applied in their full rigour to limitation clauses. Lord Wilberforce's speech contains a passage to the like effect, and Lords Elwyn-Jones, Salmon and Lowry agreed with both speeches. Having once reached a conclusion in the instant case that the relevant condition unambiguously limited the appellants' liability, I know of no principle of construction which can properly be applied to confine the effect of the limitation to breaches of contract arising without negligence on the part of the appellants. In agreement with Lord Denning, MR, I would decide the common law issue in the appellants' favour.

The statutory issue turns, as already indicated, on the application of the provisions of the modified section 55 of the Sale of Goods Act 1979, as set out in paragraph 11 of Schedule I to the Act. The 1979 Act is a pure consolidation. The purpose of the modified section 55 is to preserve the law as it stood from May 18, 1973 to February 1, 1978, in relation to contracts made between those two dates. The significance of the dates is that the first was the date when the Supply of Goods (Implied Terms) Act 1973, came into force containing the provision now re-enacted by the modified section 55, the second was the date when the Unfair Contract Terms Act 1977, came into force and superseded the relevant provisions of the 1973 Act by more radical and far-reaching provisions in relation to contracts made thereafter.

. . . . .

The contract between the appellants and the respondents was not a 'consumer sale', as defined for the purpose of these provisions. The effect of clause 3 of the

Recent UK cases

relevant condition is to exclude, *inter alia,* the terms implied by sections 13 and 14 of the Act that the seeds sold by description should correspond to the description and be of merchantable qualty and to substitute therefore the express but limited obligations undertaken by the appellants under clauses 1 and 2. The statutory issue, therefore, turns on the words in sub-section (4) 'to the extent that it is shown that it would not be fair or reasonable to allow reliance on' this restriction of the appellants' liabilities, having regard to the matters referred to in sub-section (5).

This is the first time your Lordships' House has had to consider a modern statutory provision giving the court power to override contractual terms excluding or restricting liability which depends on the court's view of what is 'fair and reasonable'. The particular provision of the modified section 55 of the 1979 Act which applies in the instant case is of limited and diminishing importance. But the several provisions of the Unfair Contract Terms Act 1977, which depend on 'the requirement of reasonableness', defined in section 11 by reference to what is 'fair and reasonable', albeit in a different context, are likely to come before the courts with increasing frequency. It may, therefore, be appropriate to consider how an original decision as to what is 'fair and reasonable' made in the application of any of these provisions should be approached by an appellate court. It would not be accurate to describe such a decision as an exercise of discretion. But a decision under any of the provisions referred to will have this in common with the exercise of a discretion, that, in having regard to the various matters to which the modified section 55 (5) of the Act of 1979, or section 11 of the 1977 Act direct attention, the court must entertain a whole range of considerations, put them in the scales on one side or the other, and decide at the end of the day on which side the balance comes down. There will sometimes be room for a legitimate difference of judicial opinion as to what the answer should be, where it will be impossible to say that one view is demonstrably wrong and the other demonstrably right. It must follow, in my view, that, when asked to review such a decision on appeal, the appellate court should treat the original decision with the utmost respect and refrain from interference with it unless satisfied that it proceeded upon some erroneous principle or was plainly and obviously wrong.

Turning back to the modified section 55 of the 1979 Act, it is common ground that the onus was on the respondents to show that it would not be fair or reasonable to allow the appellants to rely on the relevant condition as limiting their liability. It was argued for the appellants that the court must have regard to the circumstances as at the date of the contract, not after the breach. The basis of the argument was that this was the effect of section 11 of the 1977 Act and that it would be wrong to construe the modified section 55 of the Act as having a different effect. Assuming the premise is correct, the conclusion does not follow. The provisions of the 1977 Act cannot be considered in construing the prior enactment now embodied in the modified section 55, of the 1979 Act. But, in any event, the language of sub-sections (4) and (5) of that section is clear and unambiguous. The question whether it is fair or reasonable to allow reliance on a term excluding or limiting liability for a breach of contract can only arise after the breach. The nature of the breach and the circumstances in which it occurred cannot possibly be excluded from 'all the circumstances of the case' to which regard must be had.

The only other question of construction debated in the course of the argument was the meaning to be attached to the words 'to the extent that' in sub-section (4) and, in particular, whether they permit the court to hold that it would be fair and reasonable to allow partial reliance on a limitation clause and, for example, to decide in the instant case that the respondents should recover, say, half their consequential damage. I incline to the view that, in their context, the words are equivalent to 'in so far as' or 'in circumstances in which' and do not permit the kind of judgment of Solomon illustrated by the example.

But for the purpose of deciding this appeal I find it unnecessary to express a concluded view on this question.

My Lords, at long last I turn to the application of the statutory language to the circumstances of the case. Of the particular matters to which attention is directed by paragraphs (*a*) to (*e*) of section 55 (5), only those in (*a*) to (*c*) are relevant. As to paragraph (*c*), the respondents admittedly knew of the relevant condition (they had dealt with the appellants for many years) and, if they had read it, particularly clause 2, they would, I think, as laymen rather than lawyers, have had no difficulty in understanding what it said. This and the magnitude of the damages claimed in proportion to the price of the seed sold are factors which weigh the scales in the appellants' favour.

The question of relative bargaining strength under paragraph (*a*) and of the opportunity to buy seeds without a limitation of the seedsman's liability under paragraph (*b*) were inter-related. The evidence was that a similar limitation of liability was universally embodied in the terms of trade between seedsmen and farmers and had been so for very many years. The limitation had never been negotiated between representative bodies but, on the other hand, had not been the subject of any protest by the National Farmers' Union. These factors, if considered in isolation, might have been equivocal. The decisive factor, however, appears from the evidence of four witnesses called for the appellants, two independent seedsmen, the chairman of the appellant company, and a director of a sister company (both being wholly-owned subsidiaries of the same parent). They said that it had always been their practice, unsuccessfully attempted in the instant case, to negotiate settlements of farmers' claims for damages in excess of the price of the seeds, if they thought that the claims were 'genuine' and 'justified'. This evidence indicated a clear recognition by

Mitchell v Finney Lock Seeds

seedsmen in general, and the appellants in particular, that reliance on the limitation of liability imposed by the relevant condition would not be fair or reasonable.

Two further factors, if more were needed, weight the scales in favour of the respondents. The supply of autumn, instead of winter, cabbage seeds was due to the negligence of the appellants' sister company. Irrespective of its quality, the autumn variety supplied could not, according to the appellants' own evidence, be grown commercially in East Lothian. Finally, as the trial judge found, seedsmen could insure against the risk of crop failure caused by supplying the wrong variety of seeds without materially increasing the price of seeds.

My Lords, even if I felt doubts about the statutory issue, I should not, for the reasons explained earlier, think it right to interfere with the unanimous original decision of that issue by the Court of Appeal. As it is, I feel no such doubts. If I were making the original decision, I should conclude without hesitation that it would not be fair or reasonable to allow the appellants to rely on the contractual limitation of their liability.

I would dismiss the appeal.

Lord Brightman. My Lords, I would dismiss this appeal for the reasons given by my noble and learned friend, Lord Bridge of Harwich.